T0291387

Economics, Game Theory and International Environmental Agreements

The Ca' Foscari Lectures

World Scientific Lecture Notes in Economics and Policy

ISSN: 2630-4872

Series Editor: Ariel Dinar *(University of California, Riverside, USA)*

The World Scientific Lecture Notes in Economics and Policy series is aimed to produce lecture note texts for a wide range of economics disciplines, both theoretical and applied at the undergraduate and graduate levels. Contributors to the series are highly ranked and experienced professors of economics who see in publication of their lectures a mission to disseminate the teaching of economics in an affordable manner to students and other readers interested in enriching their knowledge of economic topics. The series was formerly titled World Scientific Lecture Notes in Economics.

Published:

Vol. 7: *Economics, Game Theory and International Environmental Agreements: The Ca' Foscari Lectures*
by Henry Tulkens

Vol. 6: *Modeling Strategic Behavior: A Graduate Introduction to Game Theory and Mechanism Design*
by George J. Mailath

Vol. 5: *Lecture Notes in Public Budgeting and Financial Management*
by William Duncombe

Vol. 4: *Lecture Notes in Urban Economics and Urban Policy*
by John Yinger

Vol. 3: *Econometric Models for Industrial Organization*
by Matthew Shum

Vol. 2: *Economics of the Middle East: Development Challenges*
by Julia C. Devlin

Vol. 1: *Financial Derivatives: Futures, Forwards, Swaps, Options, Corporate Securities, and Credit Default Swaps*
by George M. Constantinides

Forthcoming:

Lectures in Neuroeconomics
edited by Paul Glimcher and Hilke Plassmann

World Scientific Lecture Notes in Economics and Policy – Vol. 7

Economics, Game Theory and International Environmental Agreements
The Ca' Foscari Lectures

Henry Tulkens
Center for Operations Research and Econometrics (CORE),
Université catholique de Louvain, Belgium

Visiting Professor,
Università Ca' Foscari Venezia

W‌P World Scientific

NEW JERSEY · LONDON · SINGAPORE · BEIJING · SHANGHAI · HONG KONG · TAIPEI · CHENNAI · TOKYO

Published by

World Scientific Publishing Co. Pte. Ltd.

5 Toh Tuck Link, Singapore 596224

USA office: 27 Warren Street, Suite 401-402, Hackensack, NJ 07601

UK office: 57 Shelton Street, Covent Garden, London WC2H 9HE

Library of Congress Cataloging-in-Publication Data

Names: Tulkens, Henry.

Title: Economics, game theory and international environmental agreements :
  the Ca' Foscari lectures / Henry Tulkens (Université catholique de Louvain, Belgium).

Description: New Jersey : World Scientific, [2019] | Series: World scientific
  lecture notes in economics and policy ; Volume 7

Identifiers: LCCN 2018044017| ISBN 9789813141223 (hc : alk. paper) |
  ISBN 9789813143012 (pbk : alk. paper)

Subjects: LCSH: Environmental economics. | Environmental policy. | Game theory.

Classification: LCC HC79.E5 .T86 2019 | DDC 333.701/5193--dc23

LC record available at https://lccn.loc.gov/2018044017

British Library Cataloguing-in-Publication Data

A catalogue record for this book is available from the British Library.

For any available supplementary material, please visit
https://www.worldscientific.com/worldscibooks/10.1142/10066#t=suppl

Desk Editors: Herbert Moses/Shreya Gopi

Typeset by Stallion Press
Email: enquiries@stallionpress.com

Printed in Singapore by Mainland Press Pte Ltd.

Foreword

Ten years ago, I launched the PhD Program in Science and Management of Climate Change at the Ca' Foscari University of Venice. The location was wonderful: the San Giorgio Island in front of St. Mark Square in Venice, an old Benedictine abbey that for centuries was devoted to study, research and pray. It is the ideal place to study climate change, its impacts and all economic implications of both mitigation and adaptation policies since it is located at the center of one of the most fragile and culturally rich ecosystems threatened by climate change.

The program was attended by a good group of students: most of them are now professors in various universities or researchers in national and international organizations. Without any doubt, the success of the PhD Program is strongly related to the quality of the teachers that were (and some are still) involved in the teaching and supervising activities. Among them, Henry Tulkens was one of the most inspiring and dedicated professors. His lectures were fascinating and his work with the students, before and after each lecture, gave them an invaluable support for their education when students and for a successful career after the completion of their PhD. I still remember the days in which Henry Tulkens was talking with the students in the long and beautiful corridors of the San Giorgio abbey, discussing with them his main ideas and results.

I am therefore very glad to see that after a few years of carefully editing, revisions and careful experimentation, those lectures are now becominga book. I am glad because Henry Tulkens' lectures will be available to all students worldwide and not only to a few lucky ones. I am glad because the book solidifies years of attentive and dedicated work. I am glad because this is one of the best textbooks on the economic analysis of international environmental agreements.

The book is of course an extended and carefully rewritten version of the Venicelectures. It covers a wide spectrum of topics in environmental economics. The first part provides the foundations. It offers elements of economics and ecological science, useful for the construction of the "economic–ecological" reference model that constitutes an integrated synthesis of the environmental problem to be analyzed. Then,the book describes the economic and game-theoretic conceptual instruments that will be used in the subsequent environmental applications.

The second part is the core of the book and of the lectures. It focuses on the interpretation of international environmental agreements through various game-theoretic and economic concepts. The book discusses how to design a treaty by combiningeconomics and game theory, assuming that international negotiators pursuethe objectives of environmental effectiveness, economic efficiency and strategic stability. Stability is the cornerstone of the analysis of international environmental agreements and readers are exposed to alternative coalitional stability concepts (some of them developed by Henry Tulkens and his co-authors). These different concepts are carefully analyzed and compared, thus providing a deep understanding of their features and usefulness.

Another important feature of the book is the combination of both theory and application. To analyze environmental agreements in practice, and in particular climate agreements, students are introduced to computableintegrated assessment models of climate change. This is probably not sufficient to give them the tools to become operational with computable general equilibrium models. For this reason, in a companion book, Henry Tulkens provides numerical presentations of many examples of the models used in this book, including the codes for treating them.

The last chapter illustrates the lengthy negotiations on a climate agreement that took place in the last 24 Conference of the Parties (COPs) and provides an economic and game-theoretic interpretation of these negotiations. Climate change is taken as the main field of application of the theoretical concepts presented in the book, but several more are conceivable (e.g. sea and ocean pollution, ozone layer depletion, acid rain, fisheries management and biodiversity).

In many cases, indeed, environmental protection is a public good, often a global common. When the dimension of the environmental problem is global, as in the case of global commons (climate, ozone layer, biodiversity, etc.), there is no supra-national authority which can enforce the provision of the environmental good. In this case, sovereign countries must decide voluntarily whether to provide the public good and hence the level of emission abatement. In practice, countries negotiate on an international agreement, which defines emission targets for each signatory and often the way to achieve these targets.

Early contributions characterized the interaction among countries as a prisoners' dilemma, inevitably leading to the so-called "tragedy" of the global common property goods. However, in the real world, at the same time, a large number of international environmental agreements on global commons was signed, often involving subgroups of negotiating countries and sometimes involving transfers and other links with other policies (trade, technological cooperation, etc.).

How can we explain that some countries decide to sign an international environmental agreement even when they could enjoy the same environmental benefit by letting other countries to abate? In other words, when the environment is a public good, a country that does not abate achieves — without paying any cost — the same environmental benefit of signatories who decide to abate. Is this enough to conclude that there is no incentive for countries to sign an international environmental agreement, i.e. that the outcome of the negotiation process will be a situation without any environmental cooperation?

This book, consistently with the most advanced literature on international environmental agreements, provides a negative answer to this last question. Indeed, by applying the appropriate concepts of coalitional stability, it shows that cooperation can emerge even when the environment is a public good and when each country decides independently, voluntarily and without any forms of commitment and/or repeated interaction.

However, cooperation may not emerge as a strategy adopted by all negotiating countries. Equilibria may be characterized by sub-coalitions and partial cooperation, as in the case of many real environmental negotiations. To go further into the analysis of real-world environmental agreements, a dynamic model of the world economy disaggregated into regions/countries becomes necessary. By using this model, it is possible to identify the size of the equilibrium coalition, and the identity of the countries signing the agreement. It is also possible to analyze how the signatory group changes when some of the economic conditions and/or the size of the impacts of climate change are modified.

This is why the book gives importance not only to the theoretical tools necessary to analyze environmental agreements, but also to the empirical models and to their dynamic features. This is a very relevant research area, confirmed by the Nobel Prize awarded in 2108 to Bill Nordhaus, the first scholar to develop, jointly with Zili Yang, a dynamic model of the world economy designed to analyze climate change policies. The model presented in this book is an evolution of Nordhaus' model, enriched and more reliable. In addition, students are offered the possibility to use Tulkens' model, which is freely available.

Let me conclude by thanking Henry Tulkens not only for his excellent lectures in Venice, but also and most importantly for his careful and attentive writing of this book, his ability to present and connect a large number of theoretical and empirical contributions, his effort to make game-theoretic tools easily understandable and useful for actual policymaking.

This book is a great contribution for the scientific community, for both economists and scientists. I do hope it will help students and young scholars to further contribute to the development of the theory and applications of international environmental agreements.

Carlo Carraro
President, European Association of Environmental
and Resource Economists Director,
PhD Program in Science and Management of Climate Change
President Emeritus and Professor of Environmental Economics,
Ca' Foscari University of Venice

Preface

Motivation

For a social scientist, attempting to understand international environmental agreements implies facing two main challenges: one is to explain the fact that the actors, sovereign countries, manage to reach agreement, in spite of their diversity and of the diversity within their own populations; the other is that the object of the agreements, the environment, be effectively reached in spite of its often elusive nature. This renders action difficult. To meet the first challenge, recourse to decision sciences is unavoidable, and to meet the second one, some exposition is necessary to natural sciences to describe and possibly master the environmental problem(s) at stake in each agreement.

This book reports on a personal enquiry of several decades on this theme, initially inspired by the part of social science called "public economics". One can find there a rich source of thought on decision processes within and among countries, as well as a framework to conduct reasoning on resource allocation, physical, environmental or immaterial, in both the private and the public sectors of our societies.

This background explains the table of contents of the present lectures, on which I now briefly comment.

Overview

The first two lectures are devoted to laying down a basic framework within which the rest of the book is developed. Only elements of economics and ecological science are involved at this stage, leading to the construction of an "economic-ecological" reference model that should provide an integrated understanding of the realities involved.

The economic and game theoretic conceptual instruments needed are then presented in Lectures 3 and 4, mostly in general terms but also in a selective way, motivated by the environmental application.

Lectures 3 and 5–7 are the heart of the series. They show how the content of a treaty can be conceived of by combining economics and game theory, when international negotiators pursue the objectives of environmental effectiveness, economic efficiency and strategic stability. As it is the author's belief that the analytical method can be used for designing policy, the exposition is made in terms that seek to inspire decision making.

In the same spirit, Lecture 8 introduces the reader to computable integrated assessment models of climate change, while Lecture 9 deals with alternative coalitional stability concepts.

The final Lecture 10 offers an interpretation in economic and game theoretic terms of the long-lasting process of worldwide diplomatic discussions taking place under the United Nations Framework Convention on Climate Change.

The book is thus not a research monograph.[1] Instead, its aim is to be an introductory synthesis on the subject matter of international environmental externalities. A synthesis because of the many disciplines involved, introductory because it is deliberately not comprehensive. Climate change is taken as the main field of application but several more are conceivable. I claim that this synthesis offers a framework within which topics such as sea and

---

[1]Another such project entitled *A Theory of Environmental Games* has been under way for a while with my colleague Parkash Chander, synthesizing and expanding on our several joint publications since the 1990s, but eventually abandoned. Notwithstanding the shift of emphasis and purpose, the present text is earmarked by this temporary joint venture.

ocean pollution, ozone layer depletion, acid rain (that is briefly alluded to in Lecture 1), fisheries management and biodiversity could be handled in a fruitful way. Each application requires to construct first the appropriate economic-ecological model relevant for this application, as in Lectures 1 and 2. Secondly, an economics Lecture 3 should show the form taken in this model by objectives such as effectiveness, efficiency, cooperation and conceivably other ones. It should be followed by introducing the relevant decision theoretic tools such as those proposed in Lectures 5–7. Next comes the identification of conditions proved to serve the retained objectives. Finally, the rest is implementation, numerical and institutional.

Target Audience

My target audience are readers who seek to learn about a body of existing and established basic knowledge rather than seeking new stuff. Among them, there are of course graduate students in economics, engineering, operations research, natural sciences, even political science or diplomatic affairs, who have a side interest in environmental issues and are eager to learn how to approach them in a scientific way. Parallel to these, I much hope to be read by students in so-called "environmental sciences" graduate programs that have flourished in the recent decades, as at Ca' Foscari.

As to prerequisites, some knowledge of basic economics (micro, macro and public economics) is a most direct route to this text. Yet, with or without such a background, familiarity with mathematical modeling of phenomena and ability to conduct reasoning in terms of models are the capacities that I rely on to present ideas and results. Along the way, readers might well learn some essentials of the disciplines that they are not "natives" of.

I see two sources of interest in modeling: one is in the universality of the mathematical language, the other is in the "cathartic" virtue that modeling has on scientific ideas. Note that I distinguish modeling from mathematics: while the former is essentially a tool to describe reality — a virtue from which environmental economics has benefited a lot — the latter is to establish conceptual relations between the components of reality. In this spirit, when mathematics are needed in this text I present them as smoothly as possible, with proofs stated explicitly when I find them important for a proper understanding of the economic-ecological reality, and I explain this importance. Mathematical developments are not made for themselves.

Credits and Acknowledgments

To institutions

The lectures are the contents of a graduate course given from 2011 to 2015 as part of the interdisciplinary doctoral program ≪Science and Management of Climate Change≫ established at *Università Ca' Foscari di Venezia* in Venice, Italy. They constitute the final and much expanded version of a series of lectures that had been invited previously at successive stages of their elaboration. The initiative came from my colleagues Carlo Carraro and Domenico Siniscalco for a presentation at *Fondazione ENI Enrico Mattei* (*FEEM*), Milan in 1991. It was then followed by presentations at *Centre for Economic Studies* (*CES-Ifo*), Munich in 1993, at *Universität Mannheim* in 1995, at *Scuola Universitaria Superiore Sant'Anna Pisa,* Italy in 1997, at *Université Paris I Panthéon-Sorbonne* in 2001, at *Umeå Universitet,* Sweden in 2003, as well as at *Académie Royale de Belgique,* Brussels in 2013. I am grateful for the cheerful hospitality I received in each of these distinguished academic institutions.

The research work on which this course is based has been developed in the framework of four successive interuniversity programs called "CLIMNEG" and "CLIMBEL" carried out at CORE-UCL, which grouped climate and economics scientists from Université catholique de Louvain, Katholieke Universiteit Leuven and the Belgian Federal Planning Office from 1994 to 2010. They were organized and financed by the Belgian Ministère de la Politique Scientifique (BELSPO). This research also benefited from the intellectual environment created at CORE-UCL by the Chaire Lhoist Berghmans "Entreprise, Économie, Environnement" during the period 2001–2015.

The Center for Operations Research and Econometrics (CORE) at Université catholique de Louvain, my permanent affiliation, has provided the unique framework without which the whole project would simply never have existed. The Department of Economics at the National University of Singapore very kindly hosted me during several visits at the time of my collaboration with Parkash Chander. I am grateful to the Department for that, as well as to the Transferable Utility Games laboratory at the University of Vigo, Spain whose website offers expert computational assistance.

Finally, for the last stage of preparation of this text I have benefited from the congenial hospitality of the members of FEEM in the beautiful premises of Isola San Giorgio Maggiore — an unforgettably inspiring location.

To colleagues

I am extremely grateful to all those who have accompanied me at various stages of this project. Jacques Drèze's fundamental 1971 contribution to public goods theory in terms of decision making, suggesting its applicability, is at the origin of all what I have done in this field. It provided a solid and rich basis for conceiving and carrying out the research projects evoked above, and eventually the long lasting work done since 1990 with Parkash Chander, Johan Eyckmans, Aart de Zeeuw and more recently Maurice Queyranne. Scientifically I owe a lot to these five colleagues in science and wish to express my high appreciation and deep gratitude for all what I have learned from them.

Next, in chronological order of our first meeting, I wish to thank, in Louvain la Neuve, Jean-Pascal van Ypersele, who introduced me to climate science and convinced me early on of the importance the problems in the field, Philippe Tulkens and Philippe Marbaix, who made me benefit more than once from their doctoral competence in the field, Etienne Loute, Marc Germain and Philippe Chevalier for their mathematical and computational support, Vincent van Steenberghe, for a stimulating and deep understanding of the economics I was trying to build and Thierry Bréchet who effectively took over the CLIMNEG programs at CORE together with many other programs that he launched. Outside of Louvain, I thank Roger Guesnerie, Claude Henry, Henry Jacoby, Denny Ellerman, Ariel Dinar, Silvia Faggian and Khiem Nguyen Tho for the substantial and occasionally quite active interest they took in the work here reviewed.

Last, but not least, I owe to Carlo Carraro the warmest grateful words. After the so many invitations in which I could present my gradual achievements, his accepting to write a foreword for this book is a renewed expression of his appreciation of my work in this field of common interest. This is for me, beyond friendship, quite an honor.

To supporters of all kinds

For their administrative assistance and secretarial help I wish to thank Monica Eberle at FEEM, Venice, Frederica Varosis at Ca' Foscari, and Fabienne Henry, Mariette Huysentruyt, Jacqueline Lenoir, Catherine Germain at the CORE secretariat.

Finally, my debt is largest, affectionate even more than material, to my patient and understanding spouse Jacqueline. It is large also to Thérèse, for her generous hospitality in most important times, and to Karen, Vicky, Hélène, Odile, Bernard, Valérie, Christine, Lennart, Jacques and Ilona with whom sharing classical chamber music occasionally, at leisure time, was an inspiration at all times.

Thanks to all.

About the Author

 **Prof. Henry Tulkens** has been teaching Political Economy, Public Economics, and Economic Dynamics at Université Catholique de Louvain, Louvain-la-Neuve, Belgium. His research is conducted at CORE (the Center for Operations Research and Econometrics), an interdisciplinary research institution within the university. He received his higher education successively at the University of Leuven, where he studied law, and at the University of Louvain, where he obtained his doctorate in Economics and was appointed in 1968. He has held visiting positions at various universities, including Paris I, Princeton, Stanford, and Laval, and was a consultant to the IMF, the EU, and various national governmental agencies. He is a Fellow of the European Economic Association, of which he was the Secretary from 1997 to 2002.

His research interests and publications bear mostly on three themes: international aspects of environmental economics, as a field of application of game theory to public goods and externalities; fiscal competition and the foundations of federalism; and efficiency analysis as a way to evaluate productive activities in both the private and the public sectors.

Several of his publications have been assembled together in *Public Goods, Environmental Externalities and Fiscal Competition: 22 Selected Papers in Public Economics by Henry Tulkens*, edited and introduced by some of his co-authors: Parkash Chander (India), Jacques Drèze (Belgium), C. Knox Lovell (US and Australia), and Jack Mintz (Canada), published by Springer, Boston in 2006. In 2009, along with Roger Guesnerie (Collège de France) he edited *The Design of Climate Policy*, CESifo Seminar Series, MIT Press, Cambridge, MA. His interest in the teaching of economics is illustrated by the third edition (De Boeck, Brussels, 2001) of the textbook *Fondements d'Économie Politique* that he initially published in 1970 with Alexis Jacquemin (EU Commission) and Paul Mercier (European Central Bank).

Contents

Foreword   v

Preface   ix

About the Author   xv

Lecture 1   Two Introductory Notions   1

The purpose and the message   2
1.1   The environment: An economic good?   3
      Environment and social sciences   3
      Environment and pollution   4
      Environment and externalities   5
      Externalities as two-dimensional commodities   6
      Directional *vs.* diffuse externalities 7
      Unilateral *vs.* reciprocal and multilateral externalities 8
      Local, transboundary and global externalities   8
      Externalities and time: Stock and intergenerational externalities . .   9
1.2   Ecological transfer functions   10
      Transfer functions 10
      Directional *vs.* diffuse externalities resulting from alternative
          transfer functions 12
      Flow *vs.* stock models 13
      A directional flow pollutant model: RAINS   14
      A diffuse stock pollutant model: The climate module
          of the RICE model   16
1.3   Conclusion   20

Lecture 2   The Economic-Ecological Reference
                Model   21

The purpose and the message   22
2.1   Components of the reference model (flow version) . . .   23
      Countries and commodities   23

Preferences 24
Production and emissions 27
The externality and the transfer function 28
2.2   States of the system 31
Feasible states 31
Institutions 32
2.3   A compact form of the reference model 33
2.4   Adaptation and protection 35
2.5   Two apologetic warnings 39
On uncertainty 39
On ecological economics 40
2.6   Conclusion 41

Lecture 3   **Economic Theory Concepts**   **43**

The purpose and the message 44
3.1   Equilibria 45
Alternative individual country behaviors 45
"Business as usual" (BAU) behavior 46
Individual environmentally nationalistic behavior 47
Standard economic properties of an individual environmentally
    nationalistic equilibrium 48
Other general properties of an individual environmentally
    nationalistic equilibrium 50
International equilibria 52
The "Business as usual" international equilibrium 52
The international environmentally nationalistic equilibrium . . . 53
Standard economic properties of an international environmentally
    nationalistic equilibrium 53
Other general properties of an environmentally nationalistic
    international equilibrium 54
Equilibria and the right to pollute 56
3.2   Efficiency 57
International efficiency 57
Economic properties of an efficient state 59
Other general properties of an efficient state 61
Multiple efficient states 63
Efficiency and the right to pollute 66
The issue of equity 67
3.3   The rationale for cooperation 68
Inefficiency and environmental abuse of equilibria
    with externalities 68

The ecological surplus to be shared 72

3.4 Modalities of cooperation 77
Who owns the right to pollute internationally? 77
The assignment of rights issue 77
Rights are wealth 81
Rights *vs.* responsibility 82
Treaties as contracts 84
The likely outcome 84
The process 85

3.5 Obstacles to cooperation 87
The informational problems 87
The value of "environmental" goods 87
The extreme difficulty of measurement 88
Willingness to pay 89
WTP for what? 91
Informational free riding 92
Non-participatory free riding 94

3.6 Concluding summary and problems left open 95
Annex: Analytical formulation of the one polluter (r)–one
polluttee (e) reference model 97

Lecture 4 Game Theory Concepts   99

The purpose and the message 100
4.1 Strategic games in general 101
4.2 Equilibrium concepts in strategic games 105
Nash equilibrium 105
Dominant strategy equilibrium 107
Coalitions and transferable utility 108
Coalitions 108
Transferable *vs.* non-transferable utility 110
Partially cooperative Nash equilibrium relative to a coalition 111
4.3 Coalitional functions and the cooperative game form . . 113
Coalitional functions in general 113
The γ-coalitional function 115
4.4 Cores and other solution concepts for cooperative games
with externalities 115
Imputations 116
The γ-core solution 117
Alternative coalitional functions and cores 122
Alternative solution concepts 124

4.5   Virtues of the core solution   125
       On cores of games without externalities   125
       On γ-cores for games with externalities   126

Lecture 5   The Global Externality Game I:
             Its γ-core   **129**

       The purpose and the message   130
5.1   Introducing the global externality game   131
       Associating games with economic models   131
       Formulation of the global externality game (GEG)   132
       Antecedents: Select literature on games with environmental
       externalities prior to 2001   135
5.2   Equilibrium concepts in the GEG   141
       Non-cooperative Nash equilibrium (NCNE)   141
          Behavioral economic and environmental
              characteristics   142
          Mathematical properties and their significance   143
              (a) Existence   143
              (b) Uniqueness   144
       Dominant strategy equilibrium   145
       Coalitions and Utilities   145
          Coalitions   145
          Transferable *vs.* non-transferable utility   147
       Partially cooperative Nash equilibria (PCNE)   147
          Mathematical properties   148
              (a) Existence   148
              (b) Uniqueness   149
          Environmental properties: Characteristics of the emissions   149
5.3   The efficient outcomes of the GEG   153
       The γ-coalitional function   153
       The Pareto efficient outcome   154
       The imputations set and alternative cooperative outcomes   154
5.4   The γ-core of the GEG: Definition and existence
       in a qualitative sense   155
       Helm's balancedness result   156
       Non-uniqueness and extensions   164
Annexes to Lecture 5   166
       Annex 1: The "lake game" of Shapley and Shubik as a
          "global externality game"   166
       Annex 2: The "prisoners' dilemma" game and
          international environmental externalities   177

Annex 3: The γ-coalitional function of the GEG is not
superadditive: An example 181
Annex 4: A crucial step in Helm's balancedness proof . 183

Lecture 6   The Global Externality Game II: Its CT Solution   187

The purpose and the message 188
6.1   The CT solution: A computable strategy and imputation
in the γ-core of the GEG 189
The linear case 189
A nonlinear case. 195
Identical players 201
6.2   Environmental and general economic characteristics . . 203
The γ-core and the optimal level of pollution 203
The γ-core and economic theory 204
Externalities *vs.* public goods 204
Which optimum among the many? 205
An amendment to the Coase theorem in the case
of international externalities 206
6.3   Specific properties of the CT solution 208
Exhibiting the transfers implicit in the solution 208
The CT transfers formula 208
The economic significance 209
How is the ecological surplus being shared at the CT solution? . . . 212
The respective positions of polluters *vs.* pollutees
at the CT solution: Graphical illustration 213
The game with 1 polluter and 2 pollutees 213
The game with 2 polluters and 1 pollutee 215
Do polluters pay at the CT solution? 215
The CT solution and the benefit principle of public finance 217
On free riding and γ-core stability 218
(a) Free riding *vs.* blocking 218
(b) The γ-assumption and coalition formation 219
(c) Preference revelation free riding and the CT solution 220
6.4   Whither the γ-core solution for the GEG? 221
On the nature of the game: A negociation on a diffuse externality . 221
The γ-partition 222
The γ-strategies of the non-members 223
The PCNE and the γ-coalitional function 223
The γ-core is self-enforcing 224

Lecture 7   The Dynamic Global Externality Game   227

	The purpose and the message	228
7.1	The dynamic economic-ecological reference model	229
	Components of the system	229
	Time and commodities	229
	Production	230
	Utilities and discounting	230
	Disutility of a stock or of a flow?	232
	Feasible paths	232
	Steady states	233
	Intertemporal equilibria	233
	Individual behavior of a country over time	233
	First-order conditions	235
	Standard economic properties of an individual equilibrium over time	236
	Other general properties of an individual equilibrium over time	237
	Time profile of the emissions along individual equilibrium path	238
	International equilibrium over time	239
	Standard economic properties of the international equilibrium over time	239
	Other general properties of the international equilibrium over time	240
	Time profile of the stock along the international equilibrium path	240
	Intertemporal international efficiency	241
	First-order conditions	243
	Standard economic properties of an efficient path	244
	Other general properties of an efficient state	246
	Multiple efficient outcomes	246
	Time profiles of the emissions and the stock along the efficient path	248
	The rationale for cooperation in the dynamic setting	249
7.2	The associated dynamic global externality game	251
	Formulation of the dynamic global externality game (DGEG)	251
	Antecedents and alternative categories of dynamic games	252
7.3	Equilibrium concepts in the DGEG	254
	Non-cooperative Nash equilibrium paths	254
	Existence and uniqueness	255
	Other properties of the non-cooperative Nash equilibrium path	257
	Linear damage functions: Equilibrium in dominant strategies	258
	Coalitions and utilities	259
	Coalitions	259

Transferability of utilities 259
Paths of partially cooperative Nash equilibria 259
Existence and uniqueness 260
Behavioral economic and environmental characteristics 261

7.4 Coalitional functions, efficient and alternative
cooperative paths 261
The γ-coalitional function, the efficient path, and the
imputations set 261
Alternative cooperative paths 263

7.5 The γ-core stable path of the DGEG: Optimal control
formulation 264
The optimal control approach 264
Critical evaluation 265
Economic considerations 265
Game theoretic considerations 266

7.6 The γ-core stable path as a sequence of
negotiations: Dynamic programming formulation . . . 267
The GTTZ alternative approach 267
The issue of cooperation *vs.* non-cooperation in an intertemporal
context 267
State variables and value functions: dynamic programming in lieu
of optimal control 268
The fallback position and the the Houba-de Zeeuw assumption on
expectations 271
Rational expectations games: introducing
the concept 272
The argument in general terms and existence 274
The cooperative solution of the dynamic global environmental game 275
Definition and existence 275
Computing the solution by backward induction — Linear damage
functions 276
The infinite horizon case 280

7.7 Concluding considerations 285

**Lecture 8 The Dynamic Global Externality Game
in Numbers: The CWS Model 289**

The purpose and the message 290
8.1 The ClimNeg World Simulation (CWS) model 291
Informal description of purpose, vocabulary and origin 291
Components of the model 293
The CWS game 297

Reducing the economic-ecological model to its decision
variables   298
Specifying the dynamic game   299
The "scenarios"   301
Description of the BAUE, NCNE, PCNE's, PESP and
CS scenarios   302
The optimization problems and their solutions   304

8.2   Key numerical results   306
8.3   Cooperation beyond efficiency in the CWS model   309
Efficient utility levels at the time horizon and the ecological
surplus   309
Individual and coalitional blockings of the Pareto efficient
scenario   310
Transfers inducing cooperation   311
Individual rationality   314
Coalitional rationality   315
Transfers in the CWS game *vs.* in the DGEG   316
A provisional stocktake   319
On the ecological surplus   319
The overall picture   319
Pre-transfer surplus sharing   320
Cooperation-enhancing surplus sharing   321
CT transfers in CWS and time: The feasibility issue   321
On distributional equity and responsibility in the CT solution . .   323
The CT solution and the ability to pay principle
of public finance   324
The computational nature of the CT solution   324

8.4   An example of policy use of CWS and its
associated game   325
8.5   Concluding consideration   327

**Lecture 9   Internal Coalitional Stability
and the Global Externality Game   329**

The purpose and the message   330
9.1   An alternative theory of coalitional stability   331
9.2   The "internal and external" stability concepts: An
informal presentation   332
9.3   Internal coalitional stability in the GEG   333
Coalitional externality and coalitional free riding   333
The equilibrium size of the coalitional externality   335

"Outside option payoff" and possible outcomes
of negotiations 339
Properties of an equilibrium with one free riding player 340
Equilibria with multiple free riding players: Problems 342
An existence issue 342
A chain of contradictory expectations 345
Analytical exploration of more general cases 346
Numerical experiments with CWS 351

9.4 Concluding considerations 352
On the scope of the internal coalitional stability concept 352
On achieving cooperation: By surplus grabbing
vs. surplus sharing? 353
On internal *vs.* γ-core stability and efficiency 353

Lecture 10   The UNFCCC Process: An Economic and Game Theoretic Interpretation   355

The purpose and the message 356

Introduction 357
From science to policy and diplomacy 357

10.1 The United Nations framework convention on climate
change, Rio 1992 358

10.2 The Kyoto Protocol, 1997 360
Main features of the Protocol 361
Economic and game theoretic ideas supporting the Protocol 362
The cap and trade scheme in the reference model 362
Efficiency and coalitional stability: A reminder on the role
of transfers 363
Competitive emissions trading in lieu of transfers 365
Agreeing on reference emissions 369
Showing the efficiency and coalitional stability
of the trading equilibrium 370
Desirability of free trade in emissions 372
JI and CDM as alternative forms of emissions trading 374

10.3 Appraising the first commitment period: 2005–2012 . . 375
Game theoretic interpretation of the post-ratification situation . . . 375
The appropriate solution concept 376
On efficiency and coalitional stability of the prevailing situation . 377
On caps and trades 379
Reflections in the wake of Kyoto, as of 2012 379
The sequence of time intervals 380
The players 380
The nature of strategies 381

Emissions abatement *vs.* temperature change 382
A fragmented *vs.* global world climate regime? 383
The participation of developing countries 384
Concluding consideration on the Kyoto Protocol 387

10.4 **The Durban ADP, the Doha amendment and the second commitment period: 2013–2020** 388

10.5 **The Paris agreement of December 2015 (COP 21)** . . . 389
The grand coalition in sight? 390
On strategies 391
Stretching the nature of strategies? 391
Changing the source of strategies 393
Implementing strategies: Stocktake, naming and shaming 394
On outcomes 395
Equilibrium with subscription 395
PCNEs, climate clubs and little creeks 397
On dynamics 399
On mitigation, adaptation, loss and damage, and transfers 401
On carbon pricing as an instrument relegated to "voluntary cooperation" 402
Concluding consideration on the Paris Agreement 404

A conclusion for the course 404

References   407

Author Index   421

Subject Index   425

Lecture 1

TWO INTRODUCTORY NOTIONS

The purpose and the message

Economics and ecological science provide appropriate descriptions of the environmental phenomena that are of concern in these lectures, among which is climate change. In this and the next lecture, a basic framework is laid down within which the argument of the following ones is developed and serves as a reference throughout. Here, just two elementary but essential notions of economics and ecological science are covered which, together with the reader's general knowledge, are sufficient for proceeding in the next lecture to the construction of an "economic-ecological" model, admittedly simple but rich enough to provide an integrated understanding of the realities involved.

Plan

Can the environment be treated as an economic good?

Ecological transfer functions

Conclusion

Lecture 1

Two Introductory Notions

1.1 The environment: An economic good?

The connection between environment and economics is not an obvious one. While this is, to some extent, due to misconceptions of what economics is about, it is also due to the state of economic science itself. Only a fairly recent adaptation of the discipline, which started from 1950 onwards, has allowed its contribution to become significant for the environmental problems dealt with in these lectures. In today's terms, the connection can be made fruitfully, as I suggest below, by first clarifying the meaning of some of the keywords involved — such as environment, pollution, externalities, and even economic commodities — and putting them in an appropriate perspective. The perspective I choose is the one offered by the economic theory called "general equilibrium", the corner stone of the entire discipline.

Environment and social sciences

If the "environment" were composed only of static elements, it would probably not be a subject matter of interest for social sciences in general; only physical sciences would be called for to describe and explain it the way it is. By contrast, it is environmental *change* that makes the environment a relevant domain of enquiry for sciences concerned with human behavior, and this from two points of view: on the one hand, mankind *adapts* to such change when it occurs, and on the other hand, mankind engages and often succeeds in *influencing* or even *inducing* environmental change.

These are also the two dimensions along which a meaningful environmental economics can develop. Indeed, (re)allocation of resources is involved in an essential way, possibly in considerable amounts, in either dimension: as environmental changes most often entail costs and/or benefits to humans, on the one hand, adapting to them either requires resources or may provide new ones. On the other hand, influencing or correcting environmental change always entails costs, as the actions involved also require resources to achieve them.

The body of environmental economics thus rests on two legs: one is the economics of whether and how society reacts to environmental change, and the other is the economics of whether and how society generates environmental change. Much of its interest is in the proper understanding of how these two aspects are interrelated.

Environment and pollution

As a preliminary question, one might ask whether there is a need for a concept such as an "environmental good", that would be specific to the field. I do not think there is such a need, and I shall devote the rest of this subsection to argue that the existing apparatus of current economics is quite adequate for both handling the reality under consideration and bringing this reality within the realm of resource allocation reasoning.[1]

Current environmental concerns bear mostly on pollution phenomena, pollution being typically the result of human actions whereby the environment is changed — degraded in most cases. In reverse, there are also actions that improve the environment, which either compensate for previous degradation or just increase some of its original qualities.

While pollution situations do not exhaust the environmental domain, they nevertheless constitute an important part of it. This finds its justification in the fact that environmental degradations have motivated to a large extent the ecological opinion movements since the early sixties as well as the actions of political groups such as green parties, through which societal concerns for the environment are expressed. In most of the subsequent developments, I shall

---

[1]This view and several of the arguments in this section have been developed earlier in Tulkens (1995).

use the vocabulary whereby pollution phenomena are described as well as their effects on the physical environment to illustrate the economic construct. In brief, I shall deal with "environmental pollution".

Environment and externalities

Environmental pollution phenomena have been recognized in the economics literature for a long time. Most often they were ranked under the general heading of "externalities", a concept originally of broader scope than what I wish to cover here with environmental pollution.[2] Yet, the currently accepted textbook notion of externalities[3] serves fairly well my purpose. I propose the following:

Definition 1.1.   *Externalities* are interactions among economic agents, bearing on each other's consumption sets, preferences and/or production sets, that do not result from exchanges.

Indeed, for environmental pollution to be dealt with in the context of general equilibrium theory, as I have announced above, this definition of externalities allows one to account for them in terms that are compatible with the language and concepts of this theory.[4] Among those, the notion of "commodity"[5] and the specification of a

---

[2]I deliberately limit myself to those forms of externalities which are relevant for the purpose of these lectures. Notice that the definition about to be given excludes the phenomenon known as "pecuniary" externalities.

[3]See, for instance, Mas-Colell, Whinston and Green (1995). Much earlier, Baumol and Oates (1975) proposed almost the same definition. Before that, lengthy debates and controversies took place for decades around the expressions of "external economies and diseconomies", which started with Sidgwick in 1883 and extended throughout the 20th century with Marshall, Pigou, Meade, Buchanan and finally Coase (1960). Laffont (1977) presents an extremely general view of the concept, while Cornes and Sandler (1996) eventually restrict the debate to what is said in the above definition.

[4]Consumption and production sets are the sets on which are defined, respectively, the utility and production functions to be introduced in Lecture 2.

[5]I shall use indifferently the terms "commodity" and "economic good", with a preference for the former because by being more neutral, it avoids the reference to what makes a good "economic" (a conceptually important point that requires introducing the notion of scarcity; see Lecture 2).

"commodity space" are basic. Externalities were not included in this specification when it was first introduced in 1954[6] but a suggestion made by Arrow (1970) corrected for that and opened the way to letting externalities become part of general equilibrium analysis. The novelty of Arrow's suggestion was in the representation he chose to give to externalities, namely to treat them *as commodities* in the same sense as the ordinary commodities were defined in 1954, and thus to simply include externalities as additional dimensions in the commodity space.[7]

Externalities as two-dimensional commodities

Upon close scrutiny, Arrow's commodity called "externality" has a special characteristic: it is of a two-dimensional nature. One dimension refers to the generation of the externality — what is generated and by whom, while the other dimension refers to the reception of it — what is received or perceived, and by whom. In environmental pollution vocabulary, this corresponds to, respectively, *emitted pollutants* as they accompany the economic activity, and *ambient pollutants* as they are present in the environment and hence inflicted on those who are affected by them. This two-fold view may be seen as an extension of the early tools of analysis of externalities, an extension specifically due to the environmental applications that have burgeoned over the last four decades.[8]

---

[6]That is, in Arrow and Debreu (1954). Externalities are explicitly excluded in Debreu's (1959) description of the commodity space.

[7]As well explained in Cornes and Sandler (1996), the purpose of this inclusion was, in Arrow's mind, to provide a logical explanation for the absence of markets for externalities: the argument is that for such "commodities" *competitive* markets cannot operate. My purpose is fundamentally different because of the important physical role given to the "transfer functions" I introduce in the next section.

[8]Between the presence of physical, chemical, organic and other materials in the environment, and the fact that they be called "pollutants" there is an implicit notion of "impact" of these materials on humans. Conceptually I would not include such impacts in the transfer functions but well in the modeling of the effects of ambient pollutants on the populations' utilities and behaviors. See more on this point in the part of Section 2.1 devoted to damage functions.

The justification for this treatment of externalities as a two-fold economic good is not only that it has descriptive merits. More importantly, it points to two quite distinct roles of the agents involved: on the one hand, emissions are an unintentional[9] by-product (often a joint product) of specific actions taken by their generators. On the other hand, reception does not result from actions by the receiving agents: it occurs passively.[10]

To reinforce the justification of the distinction introduced here, let me mention that when I shall describe economic-ecological models in more detail below, it will appear that emissions are of the nature of what is called *private* goods in economic theory, whereas ambient magnitudes most often have characteristics of *public* goods, local or global. This in turn leads to the further distinctions that follow.

Directional vs. diffuse externalities

Elaborating on ambient pollution, distinction ought to be made according to the number of simultaneous recipients, potential or actual.[11] A pollutant may indeed affect just one,[12] or a few, or many agents simultaneously, possibly all individuals in the world or even agents that are yet to be born! Thus, externalities often have a "public good" property in the sense of "non-rivalry" (a terminology introduced by Musgrave (1968)): the fact that some agents are affected by it does not modify the amount by which other agents are affected. Actually, the term "public bad" would be more appropriately descriptive of the detrimental character of

---

[9]By contrast, notice that abatement, i.e. reducing emissions, or in more technical jargon, correcting for the externality, is most often intentional on the part of agents.

[10]I ignore momentarily the fact that recipients may decide to act so as to prevent being polluted or adapt to it. But these are actions that anticipate or follow the fact of passively receiving the externality.

[11]That is, irrespective of the size of the geographical area where the pollutants are physically received — an aspect to be considered shortly.

[12]For the case of just one recipient, Arrow (1970) speaks of "personalized" externalities.

ambient pollution. "Good" applies well, though, to abatement. In that sense, clean-up activities are equivalent to the production of a public good.

This leads one to create some additional vocabulary: when the externality is such that receiving it in some amount by an agent implies that as much less is received by the other agents, the term *directional* externality captures the phenomena well. In other words, a directional externality is exhaustive and lacks public good characteristics. Whereas in the case where receiving the externality by some agent(s) does not modify the amount received by other agents, the term *diffuse* externalities is appropriate.[13] Thus, diffuse externalities are non-exhaustive and have public good characteristics.

Unilateral vs. reciprocal and multilateral externalities

A further aspect of environmental externalities, which is highly relevant in my context, is the way in which the connection occurs between the agents. The relation between generators and recipients may be *unilateral* (as in the upstream-downstream situation), but it may also be *reciprocal*, as is the case between two neighboring agents who are at the same time polluters and pollutees. Such reciprocal relation becomes what I call *multilateral* when the number of agents that are at the same time polluters and pollutees is larger than two. This is the case of several factories each of which discharges its sewage into a lake and also needs to draw pure water from the same lake (Shapley and Shubik, 1969b). This case is revisited in Annex 1 of Lecture 5.

Local, transboundary and global externalities

The size of the geographical area where an externality is exerted is another aspect to be considered, from two points of view: physical and institutional. While physical considerations determine the size

---

[13]In Chander and Tulkens (1997) the term "environmental externalities" is used, but the above taxonomy leads now to prefer "diffuse externalities", an expression introduced in Shapley and Shubik (1969b).

of the area impacted by the ambient pollutant, institutional factors come into play when the area is structured by boundaries of, say, municipalities, provinces, regions or countries: the externality then becomes "transboundary" or "transfrontier". *Local* externalities are of the same nature as local public goods, known as "club" goods since Buchanan (1965) introduced them[14]; at the other extreme, we would call *global* externalities those pollution phenomena which are international and often categorized as problems of "global public goods"[15] or rather bads. Climate change is probably the biggest such problem.[16]

Institutional factors can also be at play in the determination of the agents who generate the externality: when several emitters are located in different jurisdictions, sovereignty considerations typically constrain public action on them by requiring agreement between the jurisdictions.

Externalities and time: Stock and intergenerational externalities

In the Arrow–Debreu commodity space, the quantities of commodities are defined per unit of time and, if the analysis ought to consider them at different moments of time, they are dated and treated as different commodities. This specification also fits the case where externalities are considered over time: emissions as well as ambient pollutants can be expressed in quantities per unit of time as well as dated and thus can be introduced in intertemporal analyses.

One additional element may have to be taken into account, however, namely the property that some ambient pollutants can accumulate, such as CO_2 for instance. Here, quantities of the ambient pollutant are linked to each other over time because of the accumulation, subject to some possible decay. Externalities where accumulation does not occur (e.g. noise) are called "flow" externalities while those where it does are dubbed "stock" externalities.

---

[14]Excellently surveyed by Scotchmer (2002).

[15]See, e.g. Kaul, Grunberg and Stern (1999).

[16]Some other examples are depletion of the ozone layer, spread of AIDS or other such contagious diseases. A more recent example is terrorism.

On the recipients' side and seen from the ambient pollution point of view, another property of stock externalities is that their duration may extend over such long periods of time that they affect several successive generations of economic agents. With such intergenerational externalities, some recipients may not be contemporaneous of the emitters. This raises social problems between them when recipients consider emitters as "responsible" for the damage they incur. This is an important issue in the climate change problem.

1.2   Ecological transfer functions

Transfer functions

In my characterization of an externality as a two-fold economic good, one point was left unspecified, which should answer the following question: what is the relation between the physical magnitudes that emissions consist of, on the one hand, and reception on the other hand? At first sight this connection may seem evident because these magnitudes are sometimes identical, as in the case of noise in a room for instance. But most often the relation is complex, and surprisingly neglected in the economics literature: in water pollution, what is measured at the stage of dumping from a pipe in a lake shore, say, is of course quite different from the what affects a swimmer in the middle of the lake, due to dilution and other possible chemical transformation of the pollutants. Most conspicuously in the climatic change problem, there is a long way to go between the emissions of greenhouse gases and the ensuing changes in the world temperature. Any serious development of environmental economics must devote a considerable attention to this connection, a subject matter that belongs to ecology, a scientific discipline of its own.

Ecology may be defined as the science of the relationship of living organisms to their environment.[17] A central concept there is that of

---

[17]This expands slightly the definition that was proposed by the German biologist Ernst Haeckel in 1866. Oddly enough in our context, the first textbook on the subject was written by the Danish botanist named Eugenius Warming!

an *ecosystem*, which describes any situation where there is inter-action between organisms and their environment. It analyzes how ecosystems are structured, operate and evolve over time according to the laws of physics, chemistry, biology and other natural sciences.

Ecological science also considers the effects of external interventions on the ecosystem, among which human interventions. When these analyses are formalized mathematically, they can be summarized in the form of what is generally called "transfer functions". The arguments of these functions are variables that measure the size of the interventions (or shocks), while the values of the dependent variables describe and measure the states in which the ecosystem finds itself as a result of the interventions. In its most general form, I shall write an ecological *transfer function* for a single pollutant as a vector valued function

$$z = F(e), \qquad (1.1)$$

where $z = (z_1, \ldots, z_n) \in R_n^+$ is an n-dimensional vector and $e = (e_1, \ldots, e_m) \in R_m^+$ an m-dimensional vector. The components of the former describe the state of the ecosystem in terms of the amount of ambient pollutant present at various places, with as many components as the number of locations the analyst has chosen. The components of the latter denote the quantities of the pollutant emitted at various m locations. The components of both z and e are expressed in physical units, each per unit of time. The m locations of the emitting stage may (but need not) be the same as the n locations retained to describe the ambient stage.

A particular case of transfer function is the linear one:

$$z = A\,e, \qquad (1.2)$$

where A is a non-negative $n \times m$ matrix whose typical element a_{ij} denotes the amount of ambient pollutant at location i that results from one unit of emitted pollutant at location j. Kolstad (2000) offers a useful discussion of cases where the linear form is justified.

The idea of a transfer function for a *single* pollutant can be generalized to many pollutants by appropriately expanding the commodity space. See Tulkens (1979) for a sea waters model with many pollutants and many locations.

Directional vs. diffuse externalities resulting from alternative transfer functions

The linear case can serve to illustrate how transfer functions relate to the taxonomy of externalities developed earlier in this lecture. Indeed, alternative structures of the transfer matrix A yield several of the externality cases I have considered.

- If the elements of the matrix A are all equal to 1, the transfer function is *additive,* specifying a public good type of externality, that I have dubbed diffuse above. In that case all components of the vector z are equal and the transfer function can be written simply as $z = \sum_{i=1}^{m} e_i$, where z now denotes a scalar.[18]
- If, instead, the elements of the matrix are not equal and the elements in each column of the matrix sum up to 1, then the externality is directional in the sense that it is received in different amounts at the various locations i, actually in proportion to the numerical value of the coefficients a_{ij}.
- If the matrix structure is, say, triangular with all elements in the triangle equal to 1 and all the others equal to zero, with the locations i corresponding to some geographical ranking, the externality is additive and of an "upstream-downstream" type. The larger the number of zeros in the row corresponding to a location, the more upstream the location.

---

[18]The additive form of the transfer function is interestingly challenged and modified by Hirshleifer (1983) into two alternative forms in a discussion of the public good concept motivated by an application quite different than the environmental one. For the context he has in mind, he coins the expression of "social composition functions" to describe alternative non-additive ways of "amalgamating individual productions into social availabilities of a public good" (p. 147 of 1987 reprinted version). The spirit of his two proposals might inspire the description of some particular environmental events.

Many other particular cases of externalities can be similarly characterized by assigning appropriate structures to the transfer matrix A.

Flow vs. stock models

Referring to the time aspect of transfer functions, an important distinction ought to be made between "stock" and "flow" of a pollutant, which is in fact at the root of the notion of stock externalities mentioned in the preceding section. The distinction is made here more precise in terms of the physical nature of what the variables z_t represent. Stock models are those in which the ambient pollutant variable represents a magnitude that accumulates: the flow of emissions that take place at some point in time determine not only the amount of ambient pollutants generated but also of the level reached by the stock of accumulated ambient pollutant at that time. The transfer function then reads

$$z_{t+1} = F_t(z_t, e_t), \quad t = 1, 2, \ldots, \tag{1.3}$$

where the subscript t attached to the functional symbol suggests that the function may vary from period to period.

By contrast, flow models describe situations in which the environmental variables z in each time period depend only upon the current level of emissions e_t with their previous quantities playing no role. The transfer function then reads

$$z_t = F(e_t), \quad t = 1, 2, \ldots, \tag{1.4}$$

where the length of each period t is such that at the end of it the environmental effects of the emissions have disappeared. Such disappearance is sometimes called the "assimilative capacity" of the environment. A particular case of the stock model is the linear form

$$z_{t+1} = (1 - \delta)z_t + \beta \sum_{i=1}^{m} e_{it}, \quad t = 1, 2, \ldots, \tag{1.5}$$

where $0 < \delta \leq 1$ is the natural rate at which the stock decays or is assimilated by nature, $0 < \beta \leq 1$ is a conversion factor of total emissions into stock and e_{it} is the amount of emissions in country i at time t. Note that if $\delta = \beta = 1$, the stock model becomes the additive flow model discussed earlier. For illustrative purposes, the next two subsections discuss two specific pollution models that I have been using in applications.

A directional flow pollutant model: RAINS

The RAINS model describes the phenomenon of how acid rains occur across various parts of a continent, as a result of sulfur dioxide emissions.[19] There exist European, North American and Asian versions. Since the purpose here is only to present it as an illustrative example, I limit myself to the highly simplified version that was used in the application here reviewed.[20]

The geographical area covered by the model (see Fig. 1.1) is a portion of Northern Europe, comprising seven regions (one of which is in fact a country, which is immaterial at this stage of discussion), namely Northern, Central and Southern regions in Finland, St. Petersburg, Karelia and Kola Peninsula regions in Russia, and Estonia. The core of the model is a $n \times n$ matrix where $n = 7$, whose rows denote the regions where SO_2 emissions take place and columns the regions where depositions occur. Each element a_{ij} is the fraction of emissions in region j that ends up as deposition in region i. These numerical values are given in Table 1.1.

The directional nature of the way in which the emitted flows of SO_2 spread across the area is revealed by these figures. Note that a major proportion of every region's emissions falls back in the same region, as indicated by the diagonal elements of the matrix, when compared with the off diagonal elements. However, some interregional flows are important: in the Kola Peninsula, for instance, flows towards Northern Finland are the largest fraction of what is

---

[19]The RAINS model was introduced in Alcamo, Shaw and Hordijk (1990).
[20]See Kaitala, Mäler and Tulkens (1995).

Fig. 1.1   Map of the Northern European area covered by the acid rains model.

Table 1.1.   Regional sulphur transportation matrix (for the year 1987) of the RAINS model.

		Emitting region (j)						
		NF	CF	SF	Ko	Ka	SP	E
Receiving region (i)		1	2	3	4	5	6	7
NF	1	0.200	0.017	0.010	0.046	0.012	0.000	0.000
CF	2	0.000	0.300	0.062	0.011	0.047	0.036	0.029
SF	3	0.000	0.017	0.227	0.003	0.000	0.027	0.038
Ko	4	0.000	0.017	0.000	0.286	0.023	0.009	0.000
Ka	5	0.000	0.033	0.031	0.017	0.318	0.045	0.019
SP	6	0.000	0.017	0.031	0.003	0.012	0.268	0.058
E	7	0.000	0.000	0.031	0.000	0.000	0.018	0.221

Notes: NF: Northern Finland, CF: Central Finland, SF: Southern Finland, Ko: Kola, Ka: Karelia, SP: St Petersburg, E: Estonia. For each column the numbers do not add up to 1 because the balance of the emissions is spreading outside the area under consideration.
Source: Kaitala, Mäler and Tulkens (1995).

emitted outside the region, due, to a large extent, to the important metal mining and processing industry in the city of Nikel, situated close to the Finnish northern border. Finally, for each column of the matrix the numbers do not add up to 1, because the balance of the emissions spreads outside the area under consideration.

A diffuse stock pollutant model: The climate module of the RICE model

Within the category of stock pollution models, climate models show how the earth temperature rises as a result of increasing concentrations of the various greenhouse gases that accumulate in the atmosphere, such increases resulting in part from the flow of anthropogenic emissions. Here, the scale of the models is worldwide.

To give an idea of what these models are, I describe one from the many that have been proposed in climate science,[21] namely the climatic part of the RICE model of Nordhaus and Yang (1996), used in Eyckmans and Tulkens (2003).[22] As just suggested there are essentially three stages: emissions of the greenhouse gases, concentrations of them in the atmosphere, and the ensuing earth temperature levels.[23] An intermediate stage between the last two is what physicists call "radiative forcings". This leads to a description of the phenomenon under study by means of a system of four equations

---

[21] For a marvelously pedagogic initiatory reading on the climate change problem in general, see Maslin (2004). Houghton's (2009) textbook offers a wonderful "complete briefing" of the field. Climate (physical) mathematical modeling, its construction, its past achievement and its possible uses in the future are remarkably presented in Goosse (2015), stopping short, though, before the (social science) integrated assessment modeling such as the RICE model and other more recent ones mentioned at the beginning of Lecture 8.

[22] The CWS model is presented in detail in Lecture 8.

[23] Sea level rise sould be added here. Since it is physically proportional to the ocean temperature change, it is modeled as a function of this variable (see Goosse, 2015). Such extension is provided in Nordhaus (2009, 2010).

of which the first one reads

$$M_{t+1} = (1 - \delta)M_t + \beta_c \sum_{i \in N} e_{it} \quad t = 0, 1, \ldots; M_o \text{ given}, \quad (1.6)$$

were e_{it} is the emissions of country i at time t (in billions of tons of carbon), M_{t+1} is the atmospheric carbon concentration (measured in ppmv, parts per million in volume) in the atmosphere at time $t+1$, that results from its level M_t in the previous time interval t (an accumulated stock) and from the flow of aggregate emissions $\sum_{i \in N} e_{it}$ occurring at time t. The decay parameter $\delta \in]0, 1[$ reflects the fact that carbon has a finite life in the atmosphere, and $\beta_c \in [0,1]$ is an absorption parameter of airborne carbon emissions, which accounts for natural absorptions by the oceans and the biosphere, as well as for possible forms of carbon sequestration.[24]

The second equation is

$$H_t = H_t^c \log(z_t/z_0) + H_t^x, \quad (1.7)$$

where H_t, the radiative forcing[25] at time t of all greenhouse gas concentrations (measured in Watt/m^2), is expressed as the sum of the respective radiative forcings of the variation of the carbon present in the atmosphere at time t relative to preindustrial time taken here as 0 (in the first term) and of the other greenhouse gases H_t^x (taken here as exogenous).

A third equation determines the value of the key variable, namely temperature change at the surface of the earth:

$$\Delta T_t^{\text{at}} = \Delta T_{t-1}^{\text{at}} + \tau_1[\lambda H_t - \Delta T_{t-1}^{\text{at}}] - \tau_2[\Delta T_{t-1}^{\text{at}} - \Delta T_{t-1}^{\text{oc}}], \quad (1.8)$$

---

[24]The above equation is the same as (1.5), with M_t and M_0 substituted for z_t and z_0. In Lecture 7, the variable z_t, still designating a stock, will nevertheless be interpreted in terms of the temperature change implied by the carbon stock at time t, an implication described in the next three equations.

[25]This term refers to extraneous forces that influence the temporal evolution of the climate. Its meaning is close to what economic modelers call "exogenous" variables.

where ΔT_t^{at} measures the atmospheric temperature increase at time t since preindustrial time (in C°). This equation assigns just *one* number per time period, namely the global average surface temperature of the globe per decade. This number is specified as equal to its value one period earlier, modified by the values of the two square bracketed terms in the equation: one accounts for how the radiative forcings H_t at time t affect the temperature of the previous period, through a commonly used parameter $\lambda > 0$ called "climate sensitivity", while the other summarizes the interchanges between ocean and atmospheric temperatures.

The variable ΔT_t^{oc}, the ocean temperature increase since preindustrial times (in C°), is in turn determined by a fourth equation of the form

$$\Delta T_t^{\text{oc}} = \Delta T_{t-1}^{\text{oc}} + \tau_3[\Delta T_{t-1}^{\text{at}} - \Delta T_{t-1}^{\text{oc}}]. \qquad (1.9)$$

In the last two equations τ_1, τ_2 and τ_3 are parameters that are determined by climate modeling. Numerical values for these parameters are provided in the source reference mentioned above as well as at the beginning of Lecture 8, where these equations appear as part of the economic-ecological model developed there.

The one-dimensional representation of the world temperature by equation (1.8) for 10 years intervals is an extreme simplification, of course bypassed in the much more complex models of today, which are multi-dimensional geographically and refined temporally. Earth surface temperature is then differentiated between the cells of a three-dimensional grid that envelops the entire planet as illustrated in Fig. 1.2. The LHS of equation (1.8) is then a vector with as many components as cells in the grid. The climate models then describe by means of differential equations the interactions occurring between neighboring cells, as they result from natural forcings and human shocks such as carbon emissions for instance.

Finally, on the "other greenhouse gases H_t^{x}" mentioned above as taken as exogenous, there are essentially five of them: methane (CH4), nitrous oxide (N2O), group of hydrofluorocarbons (HFCs), perfluorocarbons (PFCs) and sulfur hexafluoride (SF6). To convert

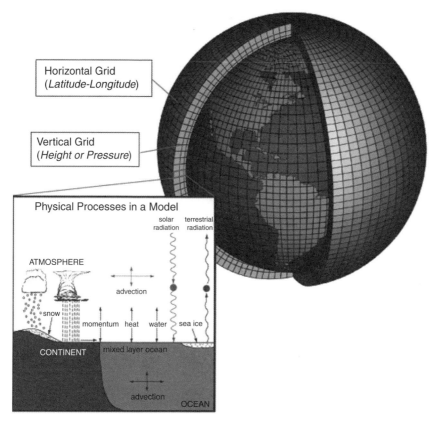

Fig. 1.2   Modeling grid around the earth.
Source: IPCC.

their amount into a single number requires conversion rates that express them in CO2 equivalent, the conversion rates being called "global warming potential (GWP)". It is interesting to observe that the determination of these parameters has an impact on the social science side of the global warming problem, to the extent that decisions based on the aggregate rather than for each gas separately, or on aggregates constituted with different GWPs, have of course different consequences. For a determination of which of the alternative methodologies produces GWPs that best takes these consequences into account, consult Edmonds, Lovell and Lovell (2017).

1.3 Conclusion

To the initial question "Can the environment be treated as an economic good?", this lecture provides a beginning of an answer, in terms that clarify the objects of the discourse: in describing the economic commodities involved on the one hand, the ecological phenomena on the other hand, and in establishing explicitly the relation between them. A fuller answer now requires that it be shown what can be achieved when the two disciplines are put to work together. This is the purpose of the next two lectures, where a major qualitative difference is introduced in the object of the enquiry, namely *behaviors*.

Lecture 2

THE ECONOMIC-ECOLOGICAL
REFERENCE MODEL

The purpose and the message

This Lecture is addressed to readers with little or possibly no familiarity with economic modeling, that is, with the tools by means of which the economic discipline represents the world that it ambitions to understand, preserve, or modify. In the spirit of the development made in Lecture 1, where it was argued that no new instrument is needed to include environmental realities in the existing tool box of economics, I deploy below the standard contents of that box, with some selected references indicating where to find more elaborate presentations if needed.

Plan

Components of the reference model (flow version)

States of the system

A compact form of the reference model

Adaptation and protection

Two apologetic warnings

Conclusion

Lecture 2

The Economic-Ecological Reference Model

2.1 Components of the reference model (flow version)

In this Lecture, I present the flow model that will be used in Lectures 3, 5 and 6. The stock model is used in Lectures 7 and 8. In both cases I make use, in their simplest forms, of an ecological transfer function representing climate change, and of an economic model compatible with general equilibrium theory.[1] I limit myself to only one pollutant.

Absent the time component, the model of Lectures 3, 5 and 6 is called "static". All its variables can be interpreted as defined per unit of time, say a year, and reproducing themselves identically year after year. In this context, capital goods are ignored in the economic part of the model, while they are introduced in the dynamic models of Lectures 7 and 8.

Countries and commodities

Consider the world economy, composed of n countries. I treat the country as the primitive economic agent and denote the countries by the index i with $N = \{i : 1, \ldots, n\}$ being the set of countries. Three categories of commodities are dealt with:

- A single composite aggregate private good[2] — think of the country's gross domestic product (GDP), whose quantities are

---

[1]See Mas-Colell, Whinston and Green (1995) for a complete technical exposition, or Malinvaud (1972) for a conceptually rich presentation.

[2]Specifying explicitly the detailed several private goods that the GDP is made of is not essential at this stage, where I only wish to present the very basic traits of an economic-ecological model. Ways to extend the model to include several private goods will be indicated when relevant.

denoted by $x_i \geq 0$ if they are consumed by country i, and by $y_i \geq 0$ if they are produced by country i. Both consumption and production are expressed and measured in identical monetary units of GDP.

- An emitted pollutant, the quantities of which are denoted by $e_i \geq 0$ when emitted in country i.
- An ambient pollutant whose quantities are denoted by $z \geq 0$.

Both of the last two are measured in their respective physical units.

Preferences

Each country's preferences — that is, the collective preferences of the country's inhabitants regarding consumption x_i of the aggregate commodity *as well as* the quality of the environment as measured by z — are represented by a utility function

$$u_i(x_i, z). \qquad (2.1)$$

This function is defined on a consumption set X_i as illustrated in Fig. 2.1, where the consumption level x_i^o is the consumers' survival threshold absent any ambient pollution. That survival threshold is assumed to be the larger the higher the amount of ambient pollutant z. Hence, the shape of the boundary of the set X_i.

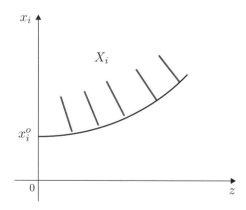

Fig. 2.1 Country i's consumption set.

Throughout the lectures, the function is assumed to be differentiable, increasing in x_i, decreasing in z, and satisfying the following assumptions:

Assumption 2.1. The utility function u_i is of the form

$$u_i(x_i, z) = x_i - d_i(z) \qquad (2.2)$$

that is, the function u_i is additively separable in its two components, and quasi-linear.

Quasi-linearity implies that utility is in fact measured in units of the composite GDP good. The second term $d_i(z)$ of the function is called the "disutility function" or the "damage function" as it represents the loss in utility from ambient pollution z due to the detrimental character of its presence in the environment. In the specification (2.2), it is expressed in the same monetary units as the consumption x_i, and the utility u_i may therefore be called the "green consumption" of country i, that is, its consumption of the goods that make up the GDP, netted out of environmental damages occurring. Being subtracted from x_i, which is what could be consumed, $d_i(z)$ is also what is called in economics terminology the "opportunity cost" for country i of the prevailing ambient pollutant z.

The measurement of damage functions is a highly complex task, both conceptually and econometrically, where impacts play an important role, as mentioned in the previous lecture.[3] I postpone the examination of this issue to Lecture 3 (see the informational problems in Section 3.5): the difficulties it raises explain that it be considered as one of the major obstacles for economics to effectively contribute to policy decisions in environmental affairs and especially climate change.

Assumption 2.2. The disutility function is strictly increasing and convex, i.e. $d_i'(z) > 0$ and $d_i''(z) \geq 0$ for all $z \geq 0$.

---

[3]An interesting inclusion of impacts in the formulation of general damage functions is achieved in Chapter 1 of Uzawa (2003) and applied in Chapter 6 on forests.

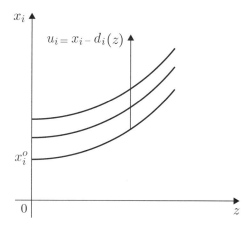

Fig. 2.2   Country i's quasi-linear utility function.

Figure 2.2 presents typical indifference curves of the utility function (2.2) in the (x_i, z) space. Their unusual upward rising shape comes from the assumption that the utility function while increasing in x_i, is decreasing in z. The quasi-linearity assumption is responsible for their congruent form (i.e. that for each given z, the partial derivative $\partial u_i(x_i, z)/\partial z \equiv d_i'(z)$ is constant at all values of x_i.

This last feature, introduced for analytical convenience, is not innocuous: it amounts to assuming that the intensity of countries' preferences for the quality of the environment is independent of their level of private good consumption. However, such an assumption is defensible when changes in private good consumption are small.

Note that Assumption 2.2 does not rule out linear damage functions. This is on purpose as one may argue that, unlike many other pollutants, damages from climate change are linear over a wide range. Linear damage functions will thus be paid special attention at several occasions throughout the book. Note also that Assumption 2.2 rules out $d_i(z) = 0$ for all $z \geq 0$, that is, that country i would consider that it is never affected by the ambient pollutant, and is thus never a "pollutee". Except for one case[4] in Lecture 3, the stronger Assumption 2.2 will be kept throughout.

Production and emissions

In each country i, production activities are represented by an aggregate production function

$$y_i = g_i(e_i), \tag{2.3}$$

where $y_i \geq 0$ is the total output produced in country i (say, its GDP) and e_i denotes the total quantity of a polluting input (e.g. fossil energy) used to produce y_i. The function constitutes the boundary of a production set Y defined in the space (e_i, y_i).

Other inputs than e_i are not explicitly mentioned in the production function and are instead subsumed in the functional symbol g_i. Although this amounts to treat them as fixed in the analysis that follows, our results will not rest in an essential way on that assumption, which is made here, again, mostly for expositional convenience.[5]

To motivate the simple modeling (2.3) of production one may invoke the fact that all production entails some pollution as a joint by-product. Thus, each amount of the "input" e_i may equivalently be interpreted as an amount of both energy use and pollutant emission, the quantities of each being possibly made equal by appropriate choice of the units. Similarly, a reduction of e_i, which implies a reduction of output, may be seen as pollutant abatement.[6]

It is assumed throughout that the production functions are defined and differentiable for all $e_i \geq 0$, and satisfy in addition:

---

[4]The case is one where the effects of alternative assignments of pollution rights either to polluters or to pollutees are better illustrated if the countries set is partitioned in two subsets: polluters only and pollutees only.

[5]An explicit treatment with one variable input was made in Tulkens (1979). The general case with many inputs and outputs of private goods is sketched out in Chander and Tulkens (1991/2002), pp. 9–10.

[6]Mitigation is another term often used for the same action, in particular in the IPCC reports.

Assumption 2.3. In every country i there exists an upper bound e_i^o to the emissions, determined by the level beyond which no gain in output can be obtained by emitting more.

Formally

$$\exists\ e_i^o > 0 \quad \text{such that } g_i'(e_i) = 0 \text{ if } e_i \geq e_i^o.$$

Assumption 2.4. Over the range $0 \leq e_i < e_i^o$ the function $g_i(e_i)$ is increasing and strictly concave, that is, $g_i'(e_i) > 0$ and $g_i''(e_i) < 0$.

The upper bounds e_i^o are introduced to express the idea that for any given level in the use of the other inputs, the amount of accompanying pollutant emissions is finite.

The first derivative $g'(e_i)$ deserves special attention, because of two possible interpretations. If taken to the right, the derivative measures the marginal gain in output (marginal product) entailed by an increase in pollutant emission, which also means, given the interpretative assumption suggested, an implied increase in the use of the accompanying energy input. When taken to the left, the derivative $g'(e_i)$ measures the marginal cost of abatement (emissions reduction), expressed in units of foregone output. The importance of this second interpretation is apparent when it is realized that a dominant fact in our heavily industrialized societies is that the level of pollution is felt to be excessive. Economic reasonings therefore most often bear on the cost of reducing emissions. The notion of marginal abatement cost then plays a central role.

Figure 2.3 presents a typical production function satisfying the assumptions just stated.

The externality and the transfer function

Most climate models assume that emitted greenhouse gases induce temperature changes irrespective of the location from which emissions take place. All greenhouse gases rise through the atmosphere and spread uniformly in the stratosphere forming a thick gaseous

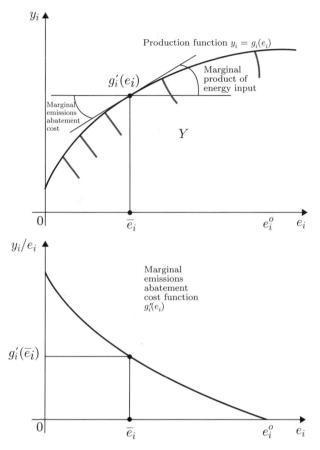

Fig. 2.3 Country i's production and marginal abatement cost functions.

sphere around the earth. This leads to global rises in temperatures and other forms of climate change on earth that cause damages. These scientific facts suggest that the transfer function in the case of greenhouse gases can be written, in first approximation, as simply

$$z = \sum_{i \in N} e_i, \tag{2.4}$$

where z stands for the resulting ambient pollution causing climate change. Since all inhabitants on earth live under the same stratosphere the quantity of ambient pollution is the same for everyone and therefore no subscript is attached to z.

The transfer function formalizes the fact that the externalities generated by the emissions of the various countries are of the multilateral type: on the one hand, they are generated by production activities within *each* country, hence denoted as emissions $e_i, i = 1, \ldots, n$; on the other hand, they are received in magnitudes z by *all* countries, which is formally accounted for by the absence of a subscript i attached to the variables z. The externalities are thus of the diffuse and transboundary type with pure public good characteristics as mentioned in Sections 1.5 and 1.7 of Lecture 1.

It will be noticed that z, the amount of ambient pollutant, does not appear as an argument in the production functions $g_i(e_i)$, although it is a common fact that firms can be affected by pollution, just as consumers. Some firms might even benefit from global warming, as agriculture, for instance, in some parts of the world. Ignoring this is again an assumption made for expositional convenience. Introducing z as a second variable in (2.3) — with appropriate specification of the derivative with respect to it — would render the model more realistic, but it would not add much to the arguments and results that are going to be developed. Yet, at times, it will be good to remember that besides consumers, producers also can be considered among those affected by the ambient pollution, irrespective of whether or not they are polluting.

To summarize this subsection, the ecological components of the model consist of the emissions vector $e = (e_1, \ldots, e_n)$, the transfer function (2.4) and the ambient pollution z, whereas the economic components of the model are the commodity vectors $x = (x_1, \ldots, x_n)$ and $y = (y_1, \ldots, y_n)$, the utility functions $u_i, i = 1, \ldots, n$, (2.2) and the production functions $g_i, i = 1, \ldots, n$, (2.3). Taken together and considered as a whole, these elements constitute what is called throughout this book the *economic-ecological system*. Sometimes, for short, I speak of the "economy" or the "world economy", but this should not make the reader forget that we are always carrying along the ecological component.

2.2 States of the system

Feasible states

For such a system, the notion of a *state* is meant to describe the simultaneous behavior of all its components at some point in time, that is, consumption, production, emissions, and the resulting values of ambient pollutant as determined by ecological relations. Accordingly, a *state* of the system is a $(3n + 1)$-dimensional vector

$$(x, y, e, z) = (x_1, \ldots, x_n, y_1, \ldots, y_n, e_1, \ldots, e_n, z).$$

When all these variables are physically compatible they constitute what is called a *feasible state*.[7] To every state of the system (x, y, e, z), whether feasible or not, there corresponds utility levels $u_i(x_i, z)$ for each $i \in N$.

Definition 2.1. A state (x, y, e, z) of the economic-ecological system is **feasible**[8] if the vector (x, y, e, z) is non-negative and such that

$$\sum_{i \in N} x_i \leq \sum_{i \in N} y_i \tag{2.5}$$

$$y_i = g_i(e_i), \quad i = 1, \ldots, n \tag{2.6}$$

and

$$z = \sum_{i \in N} e_i. \tag{2.7}$$

The feasibility condition (2.5) is economic: aggregate consumption in the economy cannot be larger than aggregate production.[9] This

---

[7]In Lecture 6, where the economic-ecological system is considered *over time*, the equivalents of states are then paths or trajectories of the variables involved.
[8]For short, we shall often call a feasible state an "allocation".

is appropriately called the "scarcity constraint" of an economy. The feasibility condition (2.6) is technological: it specifies the physical and technological limits that constrain production in each country. The feasibility condition (2.7) is ecological: the amounts and properties of ambient pollutant should be in accordance with the requirements of the laws of ecological science.

Notice that the scarcity constraint (2.5) is specified here at the world level and does not require that each country produce an amount exactly equal to what it consumes. Discrepancies (positive or negative) between local consumptions and local productions are implicitly assumed to be covered by transfers of resources between the countries. This feature will play an important role in Lectures 3 and 5–8, as well as in the policy issues of Lecture 10.

Condition (2.5) implicitly assumes no initial endowment of the private good of each country. Allowing each country i to have a positive initial endowment of the private good would not change the basic nature of the model. I thus continue to assume that the initial endowment of the private good of each country is zero. Some of our illustrative examples, however, allow the countries to have positive initial endowment of the private good.

Institutions

If institutions are introduced in this basic[10] economic-ecological model, the interactions that occur between consumers and producers as implied by equations (2.5) and (2.6) can be described in various ways, among which the following two are classical. If these

---

[9]The weak inequality in (2.5) is meant to allow for possible inefficiencies in the distribution of goods in the international sphere. However, the attention in the sequel (Lecture 3 and beyond) will concentrate on states that maximize utilities that are assumed to be strictly monotonic increasing: there will be no loss from specifying this feasibility conditions in terms of an equality, as I shall do.

[10]I call it "basic" because a full description of environmentally relevant human activities would go far beyond those we have dealt with so far, such as cleanup and recycling for instance. I leave these out because they are not essentially international.

interactions are considered in terms of free exchanges of commodities on markets and generation of externalities, one is led to formulating a *positive* theory of spontaneous equilibrium of the whole system. By contrast, if the description is inspired by some criteria or norms that the state of the system should satisfy, a *normative* theory of policies is constructed, bearing in a planning spirit on the commodities produced and consumed as well as on emissions and ambient quantities. This is the classical alternative that general equilibrium and welfare economic theories offer, respectively, to cope with worldwide problems such as, for instance, climate change. I shall follow this two-fold program in detail in these Lectures.

2.3 A compact form of the reference model

Before closing the chapter, I wish to introduce a slightly different, and possibly more intuitive, version of the reference model that has been often used in the literature on international environmental agreements. I shall not use it in these Lectures (except on a few occasions) but I present it here so as to show the reader that the two versions do in fact deal with the same reality.

Karl Göran Mäler (1989) introduced in the environmental economics literature an extremely simple economic-ecological model, which is also quite convenient because it contains all the basic ingredients necessary to make it useful for many conceivable analyses. Mäler's model is described simply by the following system of $n + 1$ functions:

$$c_i(e_i) + d_i(z), \quad i = 1, \ldots, n, \tag{2.8}$$

$$z = F(e). \tag{2.9}$$

The function $c_i(e_i)$ is called the *abatement*[11] *cost function* of country i. It denotes country i's total costs, measured in monetary

---

[11]Or mitigation cost function, in the vocabulary mentioned in Section 2.2 (Footnote 6).

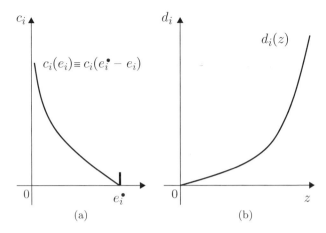

Fig. 2.4   (a) Abatement cost function. (b) Damage cost function.

units of GDP, of abating emissions by an amount $e_i^{\bullet} - e_i$ from some fixed reference level $e_i^{\bullet} > 0$. This reference level is taken as the total amount of emissions occurring absent any abatement policy in the country. The function is assumed to be decreasing and convex in its argument e_i with zero value at $e_i = e_i^{\bullet}$. The graph of the function is as shown in Fig. 2.4(a).

The function $d_i(z)$ is called, as before, the *damage function* of country i. It denotes country i's total costs, also measured in GDP monetary units, due to the damages caused by the ambient pollutant z. It is assumed to be increasing and convex. Accordingly, its graph is as shown in Fig. 2.4(b).

The function $F(e)$ in equation (2.9) is the ecological transfer function. Mäler chose the RAINS matrix as transfer function in his original model.

In this compact model, a state of the economic-ecological system is simply a $n + 1$ vector $(e, z) = (e_1, \ldots, e_n, z)$ and it is feasible if it is non-negative and satisfies (2.9). No other relations between the countries are accounted for, other than those occurring through the externality. The purpose of the compact model is to characterize emission policies, that is, values for the components of the vector e in terms of the sum total of abatement and damage costs they entail, for each country separately as in (2.8), or for all of them taken together as in

$$J = \sum_{i \in N} [c_i(e_i) + d_i(z)]. \tag{2.10}$$

The function J then represents the total cost of the world emission policy $e = (e_1, \ldots, e_n)$ leading to ambient pollution z, that is, the cost of abatement for the polluters, which is mainly a private cost, *and* the damage cost for the pollutees, which is a social cost. Thus, J represents the total cost to Society.

The compact model is quite intuitive and belongs to the class of partial equilibrium models. For that reason it is probably more accessible to non-economists. Far from being inconsistent with the preceding one, the compact model can in fact be seen as a reduced form of it. It will reappear in Lecture 5.

2.4 Adaptation and protection

A non-negligible aspect of human reactions to environmental degradation and especially to climate change is that the population may seek to adapt to, or to protect itself against the occurring changes. This behavior has two economic characteristics. On the one hand, it is only effective if it succeeds in reducing the damage caused by environmental change; otherwise it is useless that is, resource wasteful. On the other hand, it is not free: adaptation and protection require resources.

It may appear that the reference model ignores the possibility of adaptation to or protection from climate change, parallel or in contrast with emissions reduction. But it is not so. These dimensions are implicitly included in our basic model. This is seen as follows. Let $a_i \geq 0$ be an aggregate measure of the physical activity devoted in country i to adaptation and/or protection[12] and let $h_i(a_i)$ denote the amount of resources this activity requires, expressed in units of

---

[12]For example, moving populations, changing agricultural programs, or raising dikes at sea shores for protection against sea level rise.

forgone GDP. The damage reducing property of the said activity can then be accounted for by introducing the variable a_i as a second argument in the damage function d_i in (2.7), and writing the utility function as

$$u_i(x_i, z, a_i) = x_i - d_i(z, a_i), \qquad (2.11)$$

with, assuming differentiability, the following properties: $\partial d_i/\partial z > 0$, $\partial d_i/\partial a_i < 0$, $\partial^2 d_i/\partial a_i^2 > 0$, and $\partial^2 d_i/\partial z \partial a_i < 0$.

Notice that in this formulation, adaptation and protection have only domestic effects in each country i: activities a_i generate no transboundary externality.[13] Therefore, they will not play a central role in those of our arguments which focus on international externalities. But domestically, adaptation activities compete for resources with those required for abatement. The issue therefore arises as to what is the appropriate mix between the two.

Assuming, as I shall do all along this book, utility maximization by the countries, the behavior of country i with respect to both emissions and adaptation is then described by the solution of

$$\max_{(e_i, a_i)} u_i(x_i, z, a_i) = g_i(e_i) - h_i(a_i) - d_i \left(e_i + \sum_{\substack{j=1 \\ j \neq i}}^{n} e_j, a_i \right).$$

$$(2.12)$$

In this expression, the terms under the summation sign are taken as constants.

---

[13]Thus, from an international point of view they are like "private" goods. However, two qualifications are in order: (i) *Within* a country, adaptation and/or protection activities often have properties of a local public good. This is outside of my area of enquiry if by their physical definition they have no international character. Raising sea dikes in the Netherlands or rescuing the Venetian lagoon are examples of projects with only local public good properties. (ii) Some forms of adaptation and/or protection may have transboundary effects, in which case the relevant variable a_i should appear in the functions $d_i(z)$ of several (e.g. neighboring) countries. Such cases do raise interesting cooperation issues which are worth studying in the light of the theory developed in these Lectures. I leave them for another occasion.

The first-order condition with respect to a_i reads

$$h_i'(a_i) = -\frac{\partial d_i(z, a_i)}{\partial a_i}, \tag{2.13}$$

allowing one to state:

Proposition 2.1. *Country i's adaptation expenditure is optimal if made up to the point where the marginal adaptation cost becomes equal to the value of the damages avoided by this adaptation. This rule holds for every level of the ambient pollutant z.*

The derivative on the RHS of (2.13) is a function of the level of z: if the other countries modify their emissions, the condition continues to hold, with a modified optimal value of the argument a_i however.

The fact that (2.13) holds for every value of z leads one to reformulate the damage function v_i in a simpler way. Consider condition (2.13) for any z. If satisfied, it implies an amount of adaptation activities that I denote by $a_i^*(z)$. The adaptation cost is then $h_i(a_i^*(z))$ and the damage function now reads $v_i(z, a_i^*(z))$. The objective function (2.12) becomes

$$g_i(e_i) - h_i(a_i^*(z)) - d_i(z, a_i^*(z)).$$

Let me then posit

$$v_i^*(z) \equiv h_i(a_i^*(z)) + d_i(z, a_i^*(z))$$

and call it the "damage function with optimal adaptation" or a "residual damage function", residual in the sense that it accounts for damages incurred after optimal adaptation has been made. Its derivative is equal to $\partial d_i(z, a_i)/\partial z$ because

$$\frac{dd_i/z^*}{dz} = \frac{dh_i}{da_i^*}\frac{da_i^*}{dz} + \left(\frac{\partial d_i}{\partial z} + \frac{\partial d_i}{\partial a_i^*}\frac{da_i^*}{dz}\right) \tag{2.14}$$

after factoring out da_i^*/dz and using (2.13). As shown in Fig. 2.5, the function $d_i^*(z)$ is actually an envelope of a family of functions $h_i(a_i) + d_i(z, a_i)$ such that the equality (2.20) holds at every tangency point.

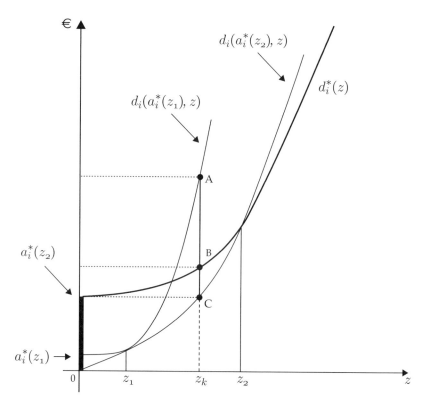

Fig. 2.5 Suffered damage cost functions with non-optimal adaptation $d_i(z, a_i)$ and with optimal adaptation $d_i^*(z)$.

Note: When the level of ambient pollutant z is z_k:

- if country i invests in adaptation an amount a_i equal to $a_i^*(z_2)$ as measured along the ordinate, it adapts **too much**, the excess cost being BC;

- if a_i is equal to $a_i^*(z_2)$ the country i adapts **too little**, excess cost being AC.

- Adaptation is **optimal** (or *balanced*) if given z, $d_i(a_i^*(z), z) = d_i^*(z)$

Equality (2.14) illustrates that when optimal adaptation holds, the marginal damage cost is *net of adjustment in adaptation cost*.[14] In the rest of the book, and unless indicated otherwise, I shall denote

---

[14]This point is of importance in the design of cost-benefit studies of investment projects in adaptation and protection. It is further developed in Tulkens and van Steenberghe (2009).

the damage function of country i with optimal adaptation simply as $v_i(z)$ dropping the superscript * to alleviate notation.

2.5 Two apologetic warnings

On uncertainty

The climate skepticism of some people, be they politicians, journalists or just part of the public opinion, is a reality that cannot be ignored in an enquiry such as this one. From a social science point of view, such attitude can be explained and interpreted as resulting from a major characteristic of the global warming problem, namely: uncertainty. Thus far, all tools of analysis I have presented are formulated in *deterministic* terms. But many natural phenomena, and even more human behaviors, are quite imperfectly accounted for in this way. Uncertainty is an inescapable component of science.

Yet, I avoid entering that dimension in these pages, with much regret. Lack of competence in that field is a first reason — I did not produce any work in it, and another reason is my care for no superficial treatment with piecemeal additions inserted here and there. The entire edifice of this book should be rethought to handle its themes properly in the context and with the tools of the economics of uncertainty. I can only leave it to another occasion or, hopefully, to followers.

In the meantime, let me single out two contributions closely connected with the contents of the rest of these lectures: Kersting (2017), who offers in his Chapter 5 entitled "Stability of global climate cooperation under uncertainty" an extension to uncertainty of my main game theoretical thesis of Lectures 5 and 6; and Bréchet, Thénié, Zeimes and Zuber (2012), who use a stochastic version of the CWS model presented in Lecture 8 and identify the impact of uncertainty on some of its results.

Finally, at a more general level, let me call the attention to the important topic of modeling the possibility of catastrophic events. Economic analyses approaching such perspectives with tools of risk analysis are offered in Keller, Bolker and Bradford (2004) and more recently in Berger, Emmerling and Tavoni (2016).

On ecological economics

Within the economics discipline, all what I do in these Lectures belongs to the subfield called today "environmental economics". It originates as such in the early sixties, a period during which interest for environmental issues arose in the western world and economic theorists started including them in their area of research. I see two strands that emerged in that new direction.

On the one hand, a microeconomic one, in which authors sought to adapt to the environmental realities the available analytical tools of externality and public goods theories, which until then were only confined to being examples of applications of theoretical welfare economics. The development of pigovian taxes and the introduction of tradable permits are early achievements in that direction. In the present lectures, I clearly follow that line, because it suits best the *decision-making* aspect of the international environmental issues I wish to deal with, and it allows to do that while remaining in the rich philosophical spirit of welfare economics.

On the other hand, a more global strand, this one in the spirit of macroeconomics and the theories of economic growth, that seeks to include environmental realities in the evolution process of our entire societies. Under the name of "ecological economics", this strand of literature developed in the eighties a stream of thought on the kind of world mankind may wish to find itself in. It focuses much on long term issues, contributing a lot to substituting *sustainability* to growth as a desirable objective for our societies. It does not exclude decision-making design and procedures, but thinks of them in a broader context than the one of the strictly individualistic philosophy of welfare economics. The two branches have expanded in parallel over the last 30 years, following paths that are often more compatible and complementary than some tend to think. The textbook by Common and Stagl (2005) introduces excellently to this branch of the field, in a conciliatory spirit.

2.6 Conclusion

It is still too early to propose an answer to the question implicitly put at the outset of Lecture 1: "can the environment be treated as an economic good?" So far, only instruments have been assembled to describe facts and *actions* in the world under scrutiny. Social sciences — economic as well as political — should now specify and explain *behaviors*, that is, connect possible actions with objectives. This is the subject matter of Lecture 3.

Lecture 3

ECONOMIC THEORY CONCEPTS

The purpose and the message

For the economic-ecological system built thus far, I consider now systematically various alternative states in which it may find itself. Two categories of states are distinguished: equilibria and optima (the popular expression for "efficient" states). Equilibria are meant to describe states that occur spontaneously between the countries, in the absence of any inter country agreement attempting to modify them. By contrast, optima refer to states of the system that meet some criterion, or norm, chosen a priori and found desirable.

The message is as follows: economic theory establishes that spontaneous equilibria of the economic-ecological system do not meet the norm of efficiency, one of the most universally recognized ones, in both its environmental and economic dimensions. Therefore, it is proposed to interpret international environmental treaties in general, and those on climate change in particular, as ways to implement environmental and economic efficiency in a world where otherwise it does not, and cannot, prevail. Obstacles to the achievement of that goal are identified, that the tools offered by classical economic theory cannot overcome. This paves the way for the introduction of game theory in the next lectures, a distinct discipline proposed to overcome some of these obstacles.

Plan

Equilibria

Efficiency

The rationale for cooperation

Modalities of cooperation

Obstacles to cooperation

Concluding summary and problems left open

Annex: Analytical formulation of the one polluter–one pollutee reference model

Lecture 3

Economic Theory Concepts

3.1 Equilibria

The expression "international equilibrium" describes the result of interactions that occur between the countries, when each of them pursues the goals it has assigned to itself. In the context of our economic-ecological model these interactions may comprise exchanges of goods, services and factors of production as well as emission and reception of externalities. A precise definition of the international equilibrium thus requires a preliminary characterization of the countries' individual behavior. This I do in the following subsection, after which two notions of international equilibrium are presented, corresponding to two different specifications of the countries' behavior.

Alternative individual country behaviors

Since I treat the countries as individual agents in the model, I apply to them the usual behavioral assumption of microeconomic theory, namely the one resulting from utility maximization[1] subject to resource constraint(s). However, when dealing with countries, there are reasons to distinguish between private and public sector behaviors. This leads to the following two alternative characterizations.

---

[1] While for individuals the utility maximization assumption seems to be a reasonable one as foundation of rationality of their behavior, on what basis can it be assumed that *countries* maximize the collective utility defined in (2.6)? The answer lies in a major theorem of the general equilibrium theory of market economies, according to which a competitive equilibrium of such economies has the property of maximizing a collective function of the kind used here. In fact, by introducing this assumption, the model I am constructing is meant to be the one of a market economy supposed to be in general equilibrium.

"Business as usual" (BAU) behavior

The term "Business as usual" (BAU) designates the situation of a country that finds its equilibrium at the highest possible GDP without caring for pollution and therefore not taking any action against it. Emissions are determined only by the necessities of production and no account is taken by anyone of their detrimental effects in terms of ambient pollution.

Definition 3.1. A country's behavior is an **individual business as usual equilibrium** if it consists in maximizing domestic consumption while ignoring damages incurred from pollutant emissions, domestic as well as foreign.

Formally this behavior is described by the solution of the following mathematical programming problem:

$$\max_{\{x_i, y_i, e_i \geq 0\}} u_i = x_i, \tag{3.1}$$

$$\text{subject to: } x_i = y_i - p_i e_i, \tag{3.2}$$

$$y_i = g_i(e_i), \tag{3.3}$$

where $p_i > 0$, a constant, is the price of energy in country i.

The disutility, i.e. damage cost, term of the utility function (2.7) is absent. For the rest, (3.2) accounts for the fact that the energy input must be acquired at some price so that the equation is a scarcity constraint at the individual level. Similarly (3.3) specifies a technology constraint at that same level.

After simplification the problem reduces to

$$\max_{\{e_i\}} u_i = g_i(e_i) - p_i e_i \tag{3.4}$$

and the solution consists of values denoted $(\bar{\bar{x}}_i, \bar{\bar{y}}_i, \bar{\bar{e}}_i)$ of the variables that satisfy (3.2) and (3.3) with $\bar{\bar{e}}_i$ such that $du_i/de_i = g'_i(\bar{\bar{e}}_i) - p_i = 0$. Let $\bar{\bar{u}}$ denote country i's utility level at this solution.

The energy usage in the country is thus characterized by the simple first-order condition

$$g_i'(\bar{\bar{e}}_i) = p_i, \qquad (3.5)$$

which means equality between the marginal productivity of the input and its price — a classical proposition in production economics. But the magnitude $\bar{\bar{e}}_i$ is also the amount of emissions prevailing at the country's individual equilibrium, according to the assimilation made in Lecture 2. Thus, the LHS of (3.5) also reveals the marginal cost of emissions abatement prevailing in country i.

As a further property of (3.5), notice in addition that a higher energy price means lower energy usage and emissions and hence lower equilibrium output, with the opposite implications of a lower energy price. Indeed, since g_i is strictly concave one has $g_i'(e_i)$ decreasing, i.e. $g_i''(e_i) < 0$, and this implies

$$dp_i \begin{Bmatrix} > 0 \\ < 0 \end{Bmatrix} \quad \text{and} \quad g_i''(\bar{\bar{e}}_i) = de_i - dp_i = 0 \Rightarrow de_i \begin{Bmatrix} < 0 \\ > 0 \end{Bmatrix}. \qquad (3.6)$$

Individual environmentally nationalistic behavior

If it is assumed instead that country i acts so as to take into account the damages caused to itself by the ambient pollution z resulting from its own emissions added up to those of the other countries, such damages being expressed by the disutility function $d_i(z)$, then the country's behavior may be characterized as follows.

Definition 3.2. A country's behavior is an **individual environmentally nationalistic equilibrium** if it consists in consumption, production, emissions and ambient pollution that maximize the domestic utility that results from consuming its domestic production minus the disutility from the ambient pollution resulting from its own emissions, taking as given the emissions of the other countries.

Formally, this behavior is described by the solution of the following mathematical programming problem

$$\max_{(x_i, y_i, e_i, z)} u_i(x_i, z) = x_i - d_i(z), \tag{3.7}$$

$$\text{subject to: } x_i = y_i, \tag{3.8}$$

$$y_i = g_i(e_i) \tag{3.9}$$

and

$$z = e_i + \sum_{j \in N \setminus i} \hat{e}_j, \tag{3.10}$$

where for all $j \in N \setminus i$, $\hat{e}_j$ are given constants.

Since country i has no control over the production and emission decisions of other countries, it must take the emissions of these other countries $j \neq i$ as given. Yet, by choosing its own economic production y_i and emission levels e_i, given the emission levels $\hat{e}_j$ of the other countries, country i in fact also chooses a level of ambient pollution z that it prefers.

After simplification the problem reduces to

$$\max_{\{e_i\}} u_i = g_i(e_i) - d_i \left(e_i + \sum_{j \in N, j \neq i} \hat{e}_j \right). \tag{3.11}$$

The solution consists of values denoted $(\hat{\hat{x}}_i, \hat{\hat{y}}_i, \hat{\hat{e}}_i, \hat{\hat{z}})$ that satisfy (3.7), (3.8), (3.9), (3.10) and the first-order conditions

$$\frac{du_i}{de_i} = g_i'(\hat{\hat{e}}_i) - d_i'(\hat{\hat{z}}) \frac{\partial z}{\partial e_i} = 0, \tag{3.12}$$

where $\hat{\hat{z}} = \hat{\hat{e}}_i + \sum_{j \in N \setminus i} \hat{e}_j$. Let $\hat{\hat{u}}$ denote country i's utility level at this solution.

Standard economic properties of an individual environmentally nationalistic equilibrium

Proposition 3.1. *The solution $\hat{\hat{e}}_i$ is unique.*

Proof. The objective function (3.11) is strictly concave, which is a sufficient condition for a unique value of the variable e_i to achieve a maximum. □

Proposition 3.2. *The individual environmentally nationalistic equilibrium* $(\bar{x}_i, \bar{y}_i, \bar{e}_i, \bar{z})$ *satisfies:*

$$g_i'(\hat{\bar{e}}_i) = d_i'(\hat{\bar{z}}). \tag{3.13}$$

Proof. At the solution of (3.11) $\hat{\bar{e}}_i$ satisfies the first-order condition (3.12) where $\partial z/\partial e_i = 1$. □

This condition (3.13) may be interpreted in two complementary ways:

(a) Considering that the derivatives present in (3.13) are derivatives to the right, the expression means that country i reaches its preferred emission policy by pushing its production and emissions up to the level where any additional gain in production obtained by allowing itself more emissions would be just equal to the additional damage it would incur, given the emissions of the other countries.

(b) Alternatively, considering that the derivatives present in (3.13) are derivatives to the left, the interpretation goes in terms of abatement as follows: country i reduces its emissions down to the level where a further reduction would entail a cost in terms of foregone output that is just equal to the damages avoided domestically by doing so, given the emissions of the other countries.

Dasgupta (1982, p. 22) calls equality (3.13) the *country i's benefit-cost rule*. This expression is best motivated if one considers a situation where it is *not* satisfied. For instance, consider that in country i

$$g_i'(\hat{\bar{e}}_i) < d_i'(\hat{\bar{z}}). \tag{3.14}$$

Then a decrease in emissions would cost to the country less in reduced output than the value of the damages thereby avoided to itself.

A decision to decrease emissions would thus increase country i's utility.

Other general properties of an individual environmentally nationalistic equilibrium

- Compared with BAU, the described behavior is most likely the result of government intervention to the extent that industry and businesses do not care about the damages d_i when choosing their emissions policy: the level $\bar{e}_i$ then results from direct, i.e. mandatory public action, or indirect by means of taxes on emissions. This is in contrast with the BAU behavior described in the previous paragraph where no such intervention occurs.

- The proviso "given the emissions of the other countries" is important: if the other countries were to change their emissions, condition (3.13) would still hold, though for different values of $\hat{\bar{e}}_i$ and $\hat{\bar{z}}$, due to a shift in the country's individual equilibrium. In fact, the higher the other countries' emissions, $\sum_{j \in N \setminus i} \hat{e}_j$, the lower are country i's emissions, $\hat{\bar{e}}_i$ — or they remain constant. This is seen as follows: Let $s \equiv \sum_{j \in N \setminus i} \hat{e}_j$. Differentiating (3.12) with respect to s and using the equality (3.9), one obtains successively

$$
\begin{aligned}
g_i''(\bar{e}_i)\frac{d\bar{e}_i}{ds} &= d_i''(\bar{z})\frac{d\bar{z}}{ds} \\
&= d_i''(\bar{z})\left(\frac{d\bar{e}_i}{ds} + \frac{ds}{ds}\right)
\end{aligned}
$$

and

$$
\frac{d\bar{e}_i}{ds}\left(1 - \frac{d_i''(\bar{z})}{g_i''(\bar{e}_i)}\right) = \frac{d_i''(\bar{z})}{g_i''(\bar{e}_i)} \leq 0 \qquad (3.15)
$$

since $g_i''(\bar{e}_i) < 0$ by strict concavity of g_i and $d_i''(\bar{z}) \geq 0$ by convexity of d_i. Thus, the equilibrium has the property that a country with strictly convex damage cost functions compensates the damage it incurs from higher emissions abroad by reducing its own. Its reaction function is thus negatively sloped. With linear damage

cost function such compensation does not occur and the slope of
the reaction function is nil.

- How do emissions under nationalistic environmental behavior,
  $\bar{e}_i$, compare with those under BAU behavior, $\bar{\bar{e}}_i$? Clearly, from
  equalities (3.5), (3.13) and strict convexity of g_i one can deduce
  that

$$\bar{e}_i \begin{Bmatrix} < \\ = \\ > \end{Bmatrix} \bar{\bar{e}}_i \Leftrightarrow d'_i(\bar{z}) \begin{Bmatrix} > \\ = \\ < \end{Bmatrix} p_i. \tag{3.16}$$

In words, the upper part of this expression shows that the
environmentally nationalistic emissions of a country are lower
than the BAU ones if the country's marginal damage cost at its
equilibrium, $d'_i(\bar{z})$, is higher than the price of energy p_i. It also
implies that the government of a country can in fact achieve
a nationalistic environmental policy by adjusting upwards the
energy prices through taxes. Alternatively the lower part of the
expression implies that by lowering the energy prices through
subsidies, the government reinforces the discrepancy between
the BAU and environmentally conscious emission levels in the
country.

- Finally if (as was mentioned in Lecture 2) the ambient pollutant
  z were also an argument in the production functions — rewriting
  them in (3.9) as $g_i(e_i, z)$ with $\partial g_i(e_i, z)/\partial z < 0$ (or > 0) — so
  as to take into account possible effects of ambient pollution on
  production, the derivative just stated would appear as an additional term in the right-hand side of equalities (3.13). This term
  would represent the marginal loss (or possibly gain) of produced
  output in country i due to impacts from ambient pollution. While
  analytically this is only a minor extension of the equilibrium
  condition (3.13) that I shall ignore to alleviate the exposition,
  its factual economic importance should not be underestimated:
  impacts of global warming on industry and agriculture are in
  fact considerable and more directly observable than those on
  consumers' utility. Actually they are given the major role in the
  numerical models dealt with in Lecture 8.

International equilibria

I now apply the above characterizations of individual behaviors to the formulation of the interactions between the n countries of the model when they are considered together. The result of these interactions is described by two international equilibrium concepts.

The "Business as usual" international equilibrium

Transposed at the international level, the expression "BAU" is encountered in the jargon of negotiations on climate change to describe the international situation in which no emissions abatement measures whatsoever are taken in any country, be it for domestic reasons only or coordinated among the countries. It thus refers to an absence of any abatement policy at the world level.

Definition 3.3. An **international business-as-usual equilibrium** is the state of the world $(\bar{\bar{x}}, \bar{\bar{y}}, \bar{\bar{e}}, \bar{\bar{z}})$ that prevails when all countries choose their individual BAU equilibrium, given the energy prices they are facing.

Formally, given a vector of prices $p = (p_1, \dots, p_n)$ the state $(\bar{\bar{x}}, \bar{\bar{y}}, \bar{\bar{e}}, \bar{\bar{z}})$ is such that for all $i \in N$, $(\bar{\bar{x}}_i, \bar{\bar{y}}_i, \bar{\bar{e}}_i)$ is the simultaneous solution of n mathematical programming of the form

$$\max_{\{x_i, y_i, e_i\}} \; u_i = x_i, \tag{3.17}$$

$$\text{subject to: } x_i = y_i - p_i e_i, \tag{3.18}$$

$$y_i = g_i(e_i) \tag{3.19}$$

where $p_i > 0$ is a constant and $\bar{\bar{z}} = \sum_{j \in N} \bar{\bar{e}}_j$.

Using the notation introduced after (3.4), this equilibrium may be referred to by the vector $\bar{\bar{u}} \underset{\text{def}}{=} (\bar{\bar{u}}_1, \dots, \bar{\bar{u}}_n)$ of utility levels reached by the n countries.

This equilibrium is characterized by the fact that equality (3.5) holds for all countries. It should actually be said "relative to energy prices $p = (p_1, \dots, p_n)$". Indeed, when these prices change, the equilibrium quantities are modified in the way implied by (3.6) in each country.

The international environmentally nationalistic equilibrium

If it is assumed instead that in every country an abatement policy is enforced by a government that implements the individual environmentally nationalistic behaviors of Definition 3.2, one is led to consider the following type of equilibrium at the world level:

Definition 3.4. An **international environmentally nationalistic equilibrium** is the state of the world $(\bar{x}, \bar{y}, \bar{e}, \bar{z})$ that prevails when all countries choose their individual environmentally nationalistic equilibrium.

Formally, the state $(\bar{x}, \bar{y}, \bar{e}, \bar{z})$ is such that for all $i \in N$, $(\bar{x}_i, \bar{y}_i, \bar{e}_i, \bar{z})$ is a simultaneous solution to n mathematical programming problems of the form

$$\max_{\{x_i, y_i, e_i, z\}} u_i = x_i - d_i(z), \tag{3.20}$$

$$\text{subject to: } x_i = y_i, \tag{3.21}$$

$$y_i = g_i(e_i), \tag{3.22}$$

$$z = e_i + \sum_{j \in N, j \neq i} \bar{e}_j. \tag{3.23}$$

I shall denote $\bar{u} \underset{\text{def}}{=} (\bar{u}_1, \ldots, \bar{u}_n)$ the vector of utility levels reached by the countries at this equilibrium.

Standard economic properties of an international environmentally nationalistic equilibrium

Since the international equilibrium presented here consists of a family of simultaneous individual equilibria of the type described in the previous section, one has from (3.13):

Proposition 3.3. *The state $(\bar{x}, \bar{y}, \bar{e}, \bar{z})$ is characterized by the system of equalities*

$$g_i'(\bar{e}_i) = d_i'(\bar{z}), \quad i = 1, \ldots, n, \tag{3.24}$$

$$\bar{z} = \sum_{i \in N} \bar{e}_i. \tag{3.25}$$

All comments made above concerning a single country's equilibrium now apply to all of them. However, the issues of existence and uniqueness of this equilibrium between countries are of a different nature than existence and uniqueness of the single country equilibrium. The reasons for that are explained below under "compatibility" and the issues themselves are further pursued in Lecture 5 at the point where I need them.

Note that at such equilibrium, there is no reason that the emissions of the various countries be identical. Their marginal abatement costs need not be equal either.

Other general properties of an environmentally nationalistic international equilibrium

In the rest of these lectures this state of the economic-ecological system is considered as the one prevailing between countries that are environmentally conscious albeit individually only, and absent any kind of agreement or coordination among[2] them. Let me point out three characteristics of it.

- *Laissez faire* and *non-cooperation.* The equilibrium consists of a family of domestic actions freely chosen by the countries, expressing behaviors that are essentially individualistic. Economically, the model specifies that each country consumes exactly what it produces. Environmentally, each country chooses its emissions to the best of its interests without taking into consideration its effects on other countries, in spite of their known damaging consequences. Paying attention to this last feature could justify that countries consider voluntarily reducing their emissions further than what (3.13) specifies, perhaps in a spirit of altruism. But that kind of motivation is not present in the individual behaviors modeled in

---

[2]This is why in Tulkens and Schoumaker (1975) the same concept was called "disagreement" equilibrium. The expression of "environmentally nationalistic equilibrium" was proposed in the more general model of Tulkens (1979) to better convey the idea of individualistic behaviors. It was adopted by Dasgupta (1982, p. 22 and ff. throughout the book).

Definitions 3.1 and 3.2: the utility of other countries is simply ignored. That behavior being assumed to be the general one, the resulting state of the system can only be one characterized by equalities (3.13) holding for all countries. The international nationalistic equilibrium of Definition 3.4 is therefore also called "non-cooperative". In Lecture 5, it will be shown to correspond to the Nash equilibrium of a game (not yet formulated) associated with the present economic-ecological model. This will prolong the non-cooperation characterization pointed out here, as well as bring about some additional properties of the concept.

- *Compatibility.* If one remembers that according to Definition 3.2, at its *individual* nationalistic equilibrium every country i chooses the level of ambient pollution z that it prefers, the question arises whether, at the *international* nationalistic equilibrium, the chosen levels are the same. In other words, are the assumed country behaviors *compatible* with one another? If not, the concept of international nationalistic equilibrium rests on an unfeasible basis, physically and logically: this equilibrium may not exist. If so, the validity of what is built on it in the rest of these lectures is seriously endangered. I postpone until Lecture 5 (Section 5.2) providing an answer to this question of compatibility between individual economic behaviors because its handling in game theoretic terms reveals that it belongs to issues requiring the use of advanced mathematical tools which here would distract the interest. Uniqueness of the equilibrium is examined by the same token and conditions are shown for uniqueness to hold.

- *Autarky.* Finally, as far as the rest of the economic-ecological system is concerned, there are no exchange of goods occurring. This extreme autarky[3] has of course nothing to do with absence of cooperation: it simply results from the fact that the model comprises only one private good. With several private goods, the concept of environmentally nationalistic international equilibrium could naturally accommodate world trade, and thereby describe

---

[3]The BAU equilibrium is similarly autarkic as to the private good. Environmentally it is trivially not nationalistic given its lack of concern.

more fully the state of the system. As mentioned before, I refrain from entering this extension in order to remain focused on the environmental issue.

At the environmentally nationalistic equilibrium the state of the economic-ecological system is such that the total amount of the ambient pollutant worldwide, $\bar{z}$, as determined by (3.25), does satisfy the ecological condition (2.7). There is no particular comment to make on this absolute amount $\bar{z}$, except that it is a well-defined[4] finite magnitude, resulting from the prevailing national emission policies, which are also well defined and finite.

Equilibria and the right to pollute

By definition, both types of equilibria imply that the countries find themselves in a situation where each of them emits at the level implied by the first-order conditions (3.5) or (3.13) depending on whether or not domestic policies of emissions reduction are in force. In either case, however, each country emits as if it had attributed to itself the right to act in this way, letting the other countries undergo the damaging effects of its emissions without asking for their consent. In fact, each country arrogates to itself the right to emit pollutants without any concern for other countries.

This situation is due to the absence of an international authority that would be empowered to grant or deny this right. Thus, both types of equilibria are, in fact, the result of anarchy in the literal sense of the word. Lecture 5 will develop implications of this situation for conceiving of negotiations on climate change and possibly agreements, if such arrangements are felt necessary.

---

[4]If a more complex ecological model were used for what I called "transfer function" in Lecture 1, the validity might be endangered of Propositions 3.1 and 3.2 (as well as 3.4 and 3.5) because the linearity of (3.10) and (3.23) plays a role in their respective arguments. Extending these propositions in nonlinear directions possibly required by realistic ecological modeling is definitely an open and desirable topic of further research.

3.2 Efficiency

International efficiency

Contrasting with the above international equilibria, supposed to describe spontaneous situations of the world, this section considers the determination of states of the economic-ecological system that are deemed to be desirable according to the criterion of efficiency. This second approach is typical of social sciences as opposed to natural sciences — among them ecology — in which there is little room for normative considerations. Here, the notion of "optimum" and the norms that inspire it play a central role. They make the present enquiry an essentially anthropocentric one.

Efficiency in the following pages has both an economic and an environmental dimension. The former concerns the activities of consumption, production and exchange of commodities and services, the latter bears on the activities that involve the specific kind of commodities that I have introduced as externalities in Lecture 1. The two dimensions are present in the following concept.

Definition 3.5. A **Pareto efficient state**[5] of the economic-ecological system is a feasible state that cannot be improved to the benefit of one country without reducing the benefit of at least one other country.

Formally, a state is efficient and denoted (x^*, y^*, e^*, z^*) if it is feasible and such that there exists no other feasible state (x', y', e', z') in which $u_i(x'_i, z') \geq u_i(x^*_i, z^*)$ for all $i \in N$ with strict inequality for at least one i.

---

[5]The complete expression is the one of an "efficient state in the sense of Pareto". "Pareto optimum" is also a frequent usage. Arrow and Hahn (1971, p. 91) recommend the use of "efficiency" rather than "optimum" to avoid letting believe that such a state is unique in the economic reality, where multiple "optima" is definitely the rule. In the model being constructed here, uniqueness does prevail (see Proposition 3.4) as a consequence of the quasi-linearity assumption made in Lecture 2 on utility functions. The justification of uniqueness is thus the same as the one given for the form of these functions.

Making use of an important proposition of welfare economics,[6] one can say alternatively that a state (x^*, y^*, e^*, z^*) of the economic-ecological system is efficient if it is a solution of the following mathematical programming problem

$$\max_{\{(x_i, y_i, e_i)_{i \in N}, z\}} \widehat{u} \underset{\text{def}}{=} \sum_{i \in N} u_i = \sum_{i \in N} [x_i - d_i(z)], \qquad (3.26)$$

$$\text{subject to: } \sum_{i \in N} x_i = \sum_{i \in N} y_i, \qquad (3.27)$$

$$y_i = g_i(e_i), \quad i \in N, \qquad (3.28)$$

$$z = \sum_{i \in N} e_i. \qquad (3.29)$$

The maximand $\widehat{u}$, that one may call the world welfare, is simply the sum of the utilities of all countries.[7] The constraints are the equations that determine a feasible state as defined in Lecture 2. After simplification[8] the problem reduces to the unconstrained form

$$\max_{\{(e_i)\}_{i \in N}} \widehat{u} \underset{\text{def}}{=} \sum_{i \in N} u_i = \sum_{i \in N} \left[g_i(e_i) - d_i \left(\sum_{j \in N} e_j \right) \right], \qquad (3.30)$$

whose solution $(e_1^*, \ldots, e_n^*)$ induces the values x_i^*, y_i^* and z^* of the other variables through (3.28), (3.27) and finally (3.29). Thus, the efficient level of the world welfare reads:

$$\widehat{u}^* = \sum_{i \in N} u_i(x_i^*, z^*)$$

$$= \sum_{i \in N} \left(g_i(e_i^*) - d_i \left(\sum_{j \in N} e_j^* \right) \right). \qquad (3.31)$$

---

[6]Based on Negishi (1960).

[7]A notational convention: a curved hat above a scalar variable, such as $\widehat{u}$, is used to denote the sum of the values of functions such as, for instance u_i, $i = 1, \ldots, n$.

[8]By substituting (3.28) in (3.27), then (3.27) in (3.26), and then (3.29) in (3.26).

The first-order conditions are[9]

$$\frac{\partial \widehat{u}}{\partial e_i} = g_i'(e_i^*) - \sum_{j \in N} (d_j'(z^*))\frac{\partial z}{\partial e_i} = 0, \quad i = 1, \ldots, n. \qquad (3.32)$$

Economic properties of an efficient state

An efficient state has various properties from which I select those that will play an important role in the sequel, either in permitting analytical developments or for the proper understanding of the social significance of the model's results.

Proposition 3.4. *At an efficient state of the economic-ecological model the emissions vector e^* solving (3.30) is unique.*

Proof. Suppose not and let $\hat{e} \neq e^*$ be two solutions of (3.30). On the one hand, if $\sum_{i=1}^{n} \hat{e}_i = \hat{z} = \sum_{i=1}^{n} e_i^* = z^*$ then one has at these solutions that $\sum_{j \in N} d_j'(\hat{z}) = \sum_{j \in N} d_j'(z^*)$ and thus, by (3.32), that $g_i'(\hat{e}_i) = g_i'(e_i^*)$ for all $i \in N$. Since the functions g_i are all strictly concave, this is possible only if $\hat{e}_i = e_i^*$ for all $i \in N$. If on the other hand, $\hat{z} \neq z^*$, say $\hat{z} < z^*$ without loss of generality, one similarly has that $\sum_{j \in N} d_j'(\hat{z}) \leq \sum_{j \in N} d_j'(z^*)$ and the concavity of the functions d_i now implies by (3.32) that $g_i'(\hat{e}_i) \leq g_i'(e_i^*)$ for all $i \in N$. This in turn implies $\hat{e}_i \geq e_i^*$ for all $i \in N$ by strict concavity of the functions g_i. However, this contradicts that $\hat{z} < z^*$. $\square$

Proposition 3.5. *The efficient state (x^*, y^*, e^*, z^*) satisfies*

$$g_i'(e_i^*) = \sum_{j \in N} d_j'(z^*), \quad \text{for all } i = 1, \ldots, n. \qquad (3.33)$$

Proof. The equality derives directly from the first-order conditions (3.32), in view of (3.29). $\square$

---

[9]Even more importantly than in the equilibrium context of Footnote 5, ecological models more complex that (3.29) might endanger the sufficiency of conditions such as (3.32) for a global maximum, due to possible non-concavities introduced from (3.29) in (3.26). Yet, numerical experiments presented in Lecture 8 have not revealed problems in this respect.

These conditions say that for efficiency to hold, no country i should push usage of its polluting input beyond the point where any marginal gain in output obtained by the country from increasing this usage becomes equal to the sum of the damage costs this increased usage entails all over the world. Alternatively (taking derivatives to the left), abatement should be pursued by every country i up to the point where any further emission reduction would reduce world damage costs by an amount less than the cost to the country of that abatement in terms of forgone output.

The summation on the right-hand side of (3.33) is due to the public good characteristic[10] of the ambient pollutant z, i.e. the "diffuse" nature of the externality that I discussed in Lecture 1: as the effects of a marginal change in emissions is felt by all countries, and efficiency is meant to maximize utility worldwide, damage costs of all countries are logically taken into account in the determination of an efficient solution.

Dasgupta (1982, p. 23) calls equality (3.33) the *international benefit-cost rule*. As above for country i's rule, the expression is best motivated if one considers a state of the system in which it is *not* satisfied. For instance, consider a state (x, y, e, z), feasible, but such that

$$\sum_{j \in N} d'_j(z) > g'_i(e_i), \quad \text{for some } i \in N. \tag{3.34}$$

In this case a decrease in emissions of *this* country i would generate a "benefit" (in world damages saved) larger that the "cost" (in reduced output) it entails. The decision of such a decrease implements the international benefit-cost rule. In the same spirit, the commentary following (3.33) suggests in its first sentence that the decision to

---

[10]The conditions (3.35) are indeed the form taken in the present model by the well known "Samuelson efficiency conditions" for public goods first enounced by him in 1954. The difference lies in the fact that the present model distinguishes between several producers of the "public good", hence the n equalities (3.33), whereas Samuelson considers only one. This apparently minor difference in model specification has in fact far going implications for the game theoretic treatment of the present subject matter.

decrease emissions would improve the aggregate world utility and not only country i's.[11]

In Lecture 10, Section 10.2, however, it is argued that the rule cannot be implemented as is. The game theoretic analysis developed in the meantime reveals problems that arise in an international context by the simultaneous implementation of the Dasgupta rule in several countries. Specific instruments are to be designed for overcoming them.

Proposition 3.6. *An efficient state* (x^*, y^*, e^*, z^*) *satisfies*

$$g_i'(e_i^*) = g_j'(e_j^*) \quad \text{for all } i, j \in N. \tag{3.35}$$

Proof. The property derives from the first-order conditions (3.33), where the RHS is identical for all i's. □

In words, the proposition asserts that world efficiency requires equalization of the marginal abatement costs across all countries[12] — a property that is in contrast with the individual environmental behaviors that prevail at the environmentally nationalistic international equilibrium.

Note that there are no similar equalities holding between the countries' marginal adaptation costs of Section 2.4 in the previous lecture: the conditions (2.13) established there hold for each country i separately. And since the level of adaptation activities a_i also differs across countries, there is no reason either that their total adaptation costs $h_i(a_i)$ be equal.

Other general properties of an efficient state

- *Cooperation and the nature of decisions.* In contrast with the *laissez faire* international equilibrium of Definition 3.4 the concept

---

[11]Symmetrically, a decision to *increase* emissions would equally implement the rule if the state under consideration were such that the inequality (3.34) is reversed.

[12]The realization of this condition was one of the main requests expressed by several groups of economists throughout the world during the preparatory negotiations of the COP 21 meeting on climate change in Paris. It was not retained in the texts signed there.

of efficient state of Definition 3.5 is not meant to describe a spontaneous behavior of the economic agents. Instead it specifies what the values of the variables of the economic-ecological model *should* be for them to implement the criterion of Pareto efficiency. That this criterion implies the idea of cooperation may be seen from its formulation as a state that (i) *maximizes* global utility and (ii) involves *all* the economic agents involved. Achievement of the former requires satisfying the latter, and this explains that a Pareto efficient outcome be sometimes called "cooperative".[13]

Now, as there is no assumption made on individual behaviors of countries striving towards that end, the outcome of an analysis of Pareto efficiency in the economic-ecological model is not spontaneous decisions. It can only be in the nature of prescribed actions, and result from computation. While this leaves open the question of who is the presriptor and does the computation,[14] it is clear that in the context of international negotiations the prescriptor can only be the countries themselves.

- *Compatibility.* No problem of compatibility of individual actions or decisions can arise in this case, given the assumed nature of decisions just described.
- *Openness thanks to transfers.* In spite of the uniqueness of the solution vector $e^* = (e_1^*, \ldots, e_n^*)$ as well as of the variables

---

[13]The study of cooperative games in the following lectures does suggest avoiding the frequent confusion between efficiency and cooperation. While I argue here that the former requires the latter, it does not imply it, the second term being conceptually much more demanding than Pareto efficiency. The concluding section of Lecture 9 elaborates on this point, which involves more than just confusion in the vocabulary.

[14]In a planned economy in general, this is precisely the role of the planner. For the climate change problem the solution brought about in Lecture 6 is of that nature. By the way, the achievement of an efficient state by computation has a long history throughout the 20th century, originally motivated by early efforts to construct a politically neutral economic theory of socialism (Barone, 1908) but eventually culminating in an economic theory of planning (Malinvaud, 1972a). In Lecture 10, I return to the parallel to be made between planning and efficiency oriented voluntary negotiations.

z^* and y_i^* through (3.29) and (3.28), respectively, the scarcity constraint (3.27) leaves a degree of freedom as far as the variables x_i^* are concerned. This results from the worldwide formulation of consumptions and productions in the economy, which implies the possibility of commodity transfers occurring between the countries. This is in contrast with the individualized "autarkic" consumptions and productions of (3.8) implied by Definition 3.4 of the international equilibrium. The concept of world efficiency thus implies by construction unhindered intercountry movements of commodities. The next section shows the very important role of this property as regards flexibility of the Pareto efficiency concept.

Multiple efficient states

Recall from Lecture 2 that feasible states of the system, when satisfying the scarcity constraint (2.5), reproduced here in equality form as (3.27), do imply for each country the triple alternative possibilities for the domestic consumption x_i of a country to be equal, larger, or smaller than its domestic production $y_i = g_i(e_i)$ — the difference, if any, being implicitly covered by transfers of the consumption good. To make this explicit, let $T = (T_1, \ldots, T_n) \in R^n$ be a vector of transfers, with $T_i > 0$ if received and $T_i < 0$ if paid out by i. The single scarcity constraint (3.27) may then be replaced by the following $2n + 1$ feasibility constraints

$$x_i^* = y_i^* + T_i \quad i = 1, \ldots, n, \tag{3.36}$$

where

$$T_i \geq -g_i(e_i^*), \quad i = 1, \ldots, n \tag{3.37}$$

and

$$\sum_{i \in N} T_i = 0. \tag{3.38}$$

This feature has the economic consequences that at an efficient state one has for each $i \in N$

$$T_i \left\{ {> \atop <} \right\} 0 \Rightarrow \hat{u}_i^* \underset{\text{def}}{=} g_i(e_i^*) + T_i - d_i(z^*) \left\{ {> \atop <} \right\} u_i^* = g_i(e_i^*) - d_i(z^*),$$

(3.39)

but also, due to (3.38),

$$\sum_{i \in N} \hat{u}_i^* = \sum_{i \in N} u_i^*.$$

(3.40)

In words, (3.39) and (3.40), respectively, say that the transfers increase or decrease the individual utilities of the countries depending upon their sign, and that while they do redistribute utilities, aggregate utility remains constant. Further, (3.39) says that the transfers do not affect the level of the environmental variables e_i^* and z^* which remain unique. This is summarized as:

Proposition 3.7. *Given an efficient state* (x^*, y^*, e^*, z^*), *any alternative state* $(\hat{x}^*, y^*, e^*, z^*)$ *where* $\forall i \in N$ $\hat{x}_i^* = g_i(e_i^*) + T_i$ *for some vector of transfers* $(T_1, \ldots, T_n) \in \mathbb{R}^n$ *satisfying* (3.37)–(3.38) *is also efficient.*

A major implication of Proposition 3.7 is the multiplicity of possible efficient states in the economic-ecological model. Given the uniqueness of the emission variables at their efficient level, the source of this multiplicity comes entirely from the possibility of transfers. This is conveniently illustrated by means of a graphical tool which is classical in welfare economics, namely the "utility possibility set".

Consider in Fig. 3.1 the case where the economic-ecological model would comprise just two countries a and b. The respective utility levels are measured[15] along the two axes, whose origins are conventionally set at the survival levels of activity and consumption in either country. The efficient state that solves the problem (3.26)–(3.29) has the utility coordinates u_a^* and u_b^* of some point E^*.

---

[15]Utilities are expressed in "green" collective consumption units, as specified in Section 2.1 of Lecture 2.

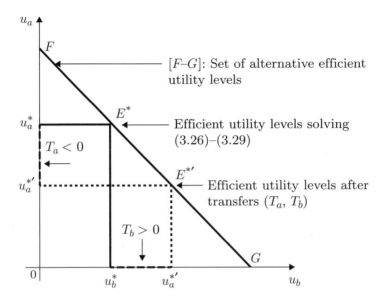

Fig. 3.1 Multiplicity of efficient states resulting from transfers.

The transfers $(T_a, T_b) \in R^2$ of the consumption good satisfying (3.36)–(3.38) induce alternative utility coordinates that, in view of Proposition 3.7, are those of a similarly efficient point $E^{*\prime}$. Repeating this exercise for any such pair of transfers induces the entire line FG made of points that are all efficient. This line is the boundary of the utility possibility set. That its slope is equal to -1, as can be derived from (3.39), is due to the quasi-linearity of the countries' utility functions.[16] With $n > 2$ countries, the multiplicity of efficient states obtained by transfers generate a (hyper) surface in the relevant n-dimensional utility space, playing the same role as the boundary line FG. The $n = 3$ case will be used extensively in Lectures 5, 6, 8 and 9.

---

[16]With strictly concave utility functions, the boundary would be a concave curve.

Efficiency and the right to pollute

Before I tackle in the next section the issues of whether and how world efficiency can be effectively achieved in the international economic-ecological system, I devote the remainder of the present section to some properties of the concept, in relation with other notions that often inspire designers of an international order. In common parlance, efficiency has often an all-encompassing connotation that sometimes makes people believe that it will "solve all problems". And indeed, who is ever against it? Yet, the concept is surely not a panacea, and it is in fact pretty neutral.[17]

Let us observe first that the concept of efficiency is totally independent of the rights notion. Indeed, the notion of rights, and consequently the term, do not appear in any way in Definition 3.3. Similarly, there is in that definition no reference to the property of anything, that individuals might own: it is thus independent of the institutions that protect property. Therefore in environmental matters, achievement of efficiency is independent of the question of who "owns" the environment and how much of it is available, individually or in total. An important implication of that independence is encountered when one considers, following Ronald Coase (1960), the *achievability* of efficiency under alternative regimes of ownership of environmental rights. Essentially, the well-known "Coase theorem" simply asserts that the achievement of efficiency by means of agreements between emitters and recipients of externalities cannot logically be prevented by whether ownership of the environment is assigned either to emitters or to the recipients. The independence just pointed out is one of the reasons for this assertion.

Efficiency is also a concept that does not rest on behavioral assumptions made on individual economic agents — in our case, the countries. It is just a well-defined state of the system for the realization of which nothing is presupposed.

---

[17]Efficiency is sometimes confused, erroneously, with "effectiveness" (especially in some French literature), a quite distinct notion indeed.

These two features are in contrast with the equilibrium concepts introduced in Section 3.1. There, an essential component, always present in the definitions, was a reference to explicit behavioral and/or ownership assumptions.

The issue of equity

Equity, or justice, or fairness (I take them as synonyms for the time being) are other concepts that serve to characterize states of society, which in the present enquiry is the economic-ecological system. Here also, as it was the case with rights, all these three terms are absent from the Definition 3.3 of efficiency. At first sight, the concept may thus seem to be neutral *vis-à-vis* equity.

However, the above formulation of efficiency in terms of the world's welfare maximization problem (3.26)–(3.29) does lend itself to introduce some equity considerations. Indeed, one form taken by the economic theory of justice[18] consists of expressing judgments on the relative utility levels of the economic agents in alternative economic states, according to some criterion such as, e.g. strict equality, or some "acceptable" degree of inequality, or still maximization of the utility of the least well off.

At the solution of the problem (3.26)–(3.29), the relative utility levels are unambiguously determined if among the several values of x_i^* that satisfy (3.27) one has $x_i^* = y_i^* = g_i(e_i^*)$ for all $i \in N$. But other values such as $x_i^* + T_i$ defined in Proposition 3.7 do modify these relative levels and thus may represent alternative views as to what a just distribution of utilities is. The efficiency criterion implemented in the economic-ecological model thus allows for including feasible redistributive decisions inspired by equity, without destroying efficiency. Actually, an infinity of possible redistributive transfers is possible. This confirms the neutrality mentioned earlier of the efficiency concept *vis-à-vis* equity, as well as its compatibility with it at the implementation stage. Thus, the economic-ecological model does not prescribe, by itself, any environmentally

---

[18]A good example of which being Boadway and Bruce (1984).

motivated redistribution, but it leaves to another conceptual source the criterion for choosing among the many redistributive schemes it allows for.

This view of equity, formalized by the simple aggregation of the agents utilities, is called utilitarianism. Other forms of aggregation exist in the literature, but I shall refrain from reviewing them because in each case, the separability Assumption 2.1 of the countries' utility functions will step in to make us realize that environmental variables are the same in all efficient states, with the consequence that equity considerations are concentrated on the consumption levels x_i and thus conceptually separated from the issue of efficiency in curbing the externality.[19] While not ignoring the importance of a wider way of dealing with equity by disposing of Assumption 2.1, I prefer at this stage to remain focused on the environmental issues.

3.3   The rationale for cooperation

Inefficiency and environmental abuse of equilibria with externalities

Let me now contrast the two categories of states of the system as identified so far by means of the economic-ecological model, namely equilibria and efficient states. This can be done from two points of view: societal and environmental.

Proposition 3.8. *Neither the BAU international equilibrium nor the environmentally nationalistic international equilibrium are efficient states.*

Proof. Each of the states involved has been characterized in terms of necessary conditions that they satisfy: (3.5) and (3.13) for the two types of equilibria, respectively, and (3.33) for efficiency. As neither of the former two satisfy the latter, the claim follows.   □

---

[19]This separation between efficiency and equity has been the theme of a long lasting controversy between Samuelson and Musgrave, evoked at the Biarritz public economics conference of 1966 and reported in Margolis and Guitton (1969).

Proposition 3.9. *At a Pareto efficient state the global amount z^* of ambient pollutant is lower than $\bar{z}$, the global amount at the international environmentally nationalistic equilibrium.*

Proof. Given the transfer function that determines z^* and $\bar{z}$ consider the vectors $e^* = (e_1^*, \ldots, e_n^*)$ and $\bar{e} = (\bar{e}_1, \ldots, \bar{e}_n)$ which, respectively, solve the systems of equalities (3.24) and (3.33). If z^* were equal to $\bar{z}$ this equality would imply

$$\sum_{j \in N} d_j'(z^*) = g_i'(e_i^*) = d_i'(\bar{z}) = g_i'(\bar{e}_i) \ \forall i.$$

This is impossible because $d_i'(z) > 0 \ \forall i \in N$ according to Assumption 2.2, which implies

$$\sum_{j \in N} d_j'(z) > d_i'(z) \ \forall z.$$

Therefore, the above equalities must be such that

$$g_i'(e_i^*) = \sum_{j \in N} d_j'(z^*) > d_i'(\bar{z}) = g_i'(\bar{e}_i) \ \forall i.$$

Given the strict concavity of the functions $g_i(e_i) - d_i(z)$ and thus $g_i'(e_i)$ decreasing (recall Fig. 2.3), this implies[20]

$$z^* = \sum_{i \in N} e_i^* < \sum_{i \in N} \bar{e}_i = \bar{z}. \tag{3.41}$$

□

Recalling $\widehat{u}^*$ defined in (3.31) and letting $\widehat{\bar{u}} = \sum_{i \in N} \bar{u}_i$ from the vector $\bar{u}$ stated after Definition 3.4, the concrete significance of the previous propositions is further enhanced by stating:

Proposition 3.10. *The world welfare at a Pareto efficient state of the economic-ecological model is higher than at the international environmentally nationalistic equilibrium.*

---

[20]Note that (3.41) does not imply $e_i^* < \bar{e}_i \ \forall i \in N$.

Formally:

$$\widehat{u}^* = \sum_{i \in N} \left(g_i(e_i^*) - d_i \left(\sum_{j \in N} e_j^* \right) \right)$$

$$> \sum_{i \in N} \left(g_i(\bar{e}_i) - d_i \left(\sum_{j \in N} \bar{e}_j \right) \right) = \widehat{\bar{u}}$$

Proof. Suppose the inequality is reversed. Then the LHS, defined by the solution of the problem (3.26)–(3.29), would not be a maximum. An equality cannot hold either because the two sides cannot simultaneously satisfy the necessary conditions (3.24) and (3.33) which are incompatible. □

The failure of equilibria to achieve Pareto efficiency is a "societal" one in the sense that it results from organizational inabilities of our societies to avoid welfare waste. That the accompanying environmental degradation be called an "abuse" finds its justification in the same spirit: according to the pure economic theoretic reasoning of Proposition 3.9, a more efficient world would imply less pollution. Environmental and economic concerns thus point in the same direction.

The fact reported by Proposition 3.8 is typical of economies with externalities. Their spontaneous equilibria, which I take in this book to be market equilibria, are inefficient when externalities are present. In other words, externalities generate market failures and these are taken as a justification for governmental intervention. In this perspective the BAU international equilibrium is a case of *double* market failure entailed by the environmental externality: first at the domestic level, with the ignorance of domestic damages, and second at the international level, with the ignorance of spillover effects on other countries. The BAU equilibrium is thus a sheer "ignorance" equilibrium, about which one may talk not only of inefficiency, but also of anarchy.

In the case of the environmentally nationalistic international equilibrium, there are in this case two causes of inefficiency: the first one relates to the level of z, which is too high (violation of (3.41), source of Proposition 3.9), and the second one is the non-equality of marginal abatement costs across countries (violation of (3.35)). Therefore, when such equilibrium prevails, removing the second kind of inefficiency at the world level could be achieved even without changing the level of z, by just reallocating the national emission levels between the countries so as to equate their marginal abatement costs.[21]

Since I interpret the non-cooperative equilibria as spontaneous outcomes of the ecological interactions that occur between countries even when they are environmentally conscious, the contents of Propositions 3.8 and 3.9 may be taken as a *raison d'être* for international negotiations that would strive at achieving efficiency at the world level and provide a better environmental quality. Such a statement prompts two questions however: why negotiations? and why efficiency?

The first question is of institutional nature. If another state of the world is considered to be more desirable than the one that prevails spontaneously, how can it be achieved? Compulsion is not an option, if the context is the one of several independent and peaceful countries: their sovereignty precludes any coercion being exerted on them from the outside. A common planner could conceivably compute the solution of the optimization problem, but empowering him with the authority to implement the efficient plan he thus constructs would amount for the countries involved to renounce their sovereignty in this field. Therefore, voluntary negotiations bearing on alternative emissions schemes are the only realistic alternative, from an institutional point of view, to bring countries to states of the system other than the environmentally nationalistic equilibrium. Procedures based on benefit-cost calculations and describing how such negotiations might occur to the benefit of all parties, have been proposed in the literature: first in the form of *tâtonnement*-like

---

[21]Helm (2003) exploits this property in his analysis of initial allowances of tradable emissions permits.

models[22] written in terms of differential equations systems proposed by Tulkens (1979), Chander and Tulkens (1992a, 1992b), Kaitala, Mäler and Tulkens (1995),[23] and also in more operational discrete time processes by Germain, Toint and Tulkens (1996a, 1996b).

Answering the second question is less straightforward. Indeed, is it a generally evident fact, worldwide, that efficiency is an objective of negotiations?[24] Can efficiency be considered as a natural or logical outcome, consciously or unconsciously? Momentarily, I shall take this as an assumption, leaving a discussion of its foundations for later developments, in the light of what game theory has to offer. In the meantime, the notion of ecological surplus that follows provides an argument in that direction.

The ecological surplus to be shared

Within the model of the economic-ecological system I am working with, the externalities are the only source of the inefficiencies just highlighted. Were it not for them — that is, if I ignored the ecological part of the model altogether, as if there were no emissions and no concern for environmental quality, the states of what remains of the system would be general equilibria of the markets that the world economy consists of. Economic theory establishes conditions under which such equilibria *are* efficient states, in the sense of the general Definition 3.3. Throughout these lectures I shall assume that these conditions are satisfied, so that our scrutiny of the efficiency issues arising at the economic-ecological interface is not blurred by inefficiencies stemming from other sources.

---

[22]Inspired by Drèze and de la Vallée Poussin (1969).

[23]Drèze (1995, p. 120) recognizes this numerical application as a first instance of putting in practical use the process of searching for an economic optimum. Markowska and Zylicz (1999) present a further numerical application of the same model.

[24]Under the heading of "broad but shallow" agreements, Barrett (2003) argues that in effective agreements it is often the case that less efficiency is traded off against a wider participation. The concept of partially cooperative Nash equilibrium, to be introduced in Lectures 4 and 5, may be considered to offer a theoretical foundation for this quite plausible idea.

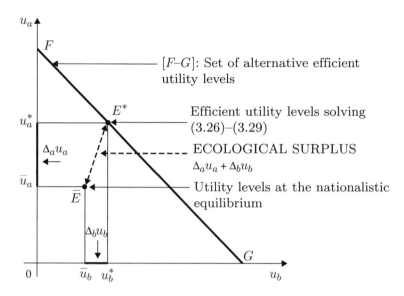

Fig. 3.2   The ecological surplus.

This methodological[25] assumption allows one to characterize by means of the convenient expression of "ecological surplus" the discrepancy between inefficient equilibria and efficient states just uncovered. The discrepancy is not only in the ecological variables of lower emissions and better environmental quality; it also materializes in differences in the quantities of the economic goods available. Together, these two components induce differences in the utility levels of the countries and both are captured in the notion of ecological surplus.

Let me present the idea by turning again, in Fig. 3.2, to the case of two countries a and b introduced above. Here, the coordinates $\bar{u}_a$ and $\bar{u}_b$ of point $\bar{E}$ are the utility levels implied by Definition 3.2 of the environmentally nationalistic equilibrium. Point E^* is again the efficient state that solves the problem (3.15)–(3.18). What matters now are the relative positions of the points $\bar{E}$ and E^* *vis-à-vis* one

---

[25]This by no means implies that I believe the assumption to be fulfilled in reality. As in many other analyses, it is used here as a benchmark.

another, as determined by the theory that was just explained: being inefficient, the equilibrium $\bar{E}$ *must* be at a distance from E^*, but also of all the points of the line FG since these are all efficient. Thus, $\bar{E}$ must lie somewhere to the left and below the line of efficient states. The distance between $\bar{E}$ and this line represents, in utility terms, what is meant by the ecological surplus.

In the general terms of the reference economic-ecological model, one has:

Definition 3.6. The **ecological surplus** is the magnitude which represents the aggregate collective gain that world societies can secure themselves by moving from the non-cooperative international environmentally nationalistic equilibrium to a worldwide environmentally efficient state of the world.

Formally, in the economic-ecological model, the ecological surplus consists of the difference

$$
\widehat{u}^* - \widehat{\bar{u}} \underset{\text{def}}{=} \sum_{i \in N} \left(g_i(e_i^*) - d_i \left(\sum_{j \in N} e_j^* \right) \right)
$$

$$
- \sum_{i \in N} \left(g_i(\bar{e}_i) - d_i \left(\sum_{j \in N} \bar{e}_j \right) \right). \tag{3.42}
$$

To illustrate with the two countries case and measure the distance just mentioned, let Δu denote the surplus, which from the above description can be written as

$$
\Delta u = (u_a^* + u_b^*) - (\bar{u}_a + \bar{u}_b) > 0.
$$

Using an obvious notation, it can be rewritten as

$$
\Delta u = \Delta_a u_a + \Delta_b u_b
$$
$$
\underset{\text{def}}{=} [u_a(e_a^*, z^*) - u_a(\bar{e}_a, \bar{z})] + [u_b(e_b^*, z^*) - u_b(\bar{e}_b, \bar{z})],
$$

$$
\tag{3.43}
$$

where explicit use is made of the variables of the economic-ecological model. This form shows that the surplus comprises two components, one for each country. Recall now that the location of point E^*, its coordinates (u_1^*, u_2^*) and the emissions $(e_1^*, \ldots, e_n^*)$ correspond to the solution of problems (3.26)–(3.29) where the scarcity constraints are such that $x_i^* = y_i^* = g_i(e_i^*) \ \forall i$, that is, the efficient solution with no transfers. This solution thus contains a particular way of sharing the surplus, which the RHS of (3.43) makes explicit. Figure 3.2 illustrates.

However, as was argued in Proposition 3.4 and illustrated in Fig. 3.1, transfers of the private good between the countries that accompany the efficient state E^* can generate other efficient states of the system. Here, one may further argue that such transfers can serve as alternative ways to share the surplus of moving from $\bar{E}$ and E^*. Indeed if after that move some transfers (T_a, T_b) are implemented, the final outcome is another Pareto efficient state, $E^{*\prime}$, which in fact corresponds to another way of sharing the surplus. Thus, once an efficient solution is determined in terms of emissions, transfers appear to be a complementary tool for choosing how to share the collective gain generated by that move from Nash to Pareto. Several alternative cases can be envisaged, among the infinity that are available. Consider the following successively in Fig. 3.3:

- Transfers accompanying the gain from Nash to Pareto which concentrate all of the surplus on country a, leaving none of it to country b. The final outcome in utility terms is point N.
- Similarly, if transfers are such that all the gain is concentrated on country b and none of it accrues to country a, the final outcome is point M, the total amount of the ecological surplus being attributed to b.

Any other point on the line NM implies sharing the surplus in different proportions between a and b than was the case at E^*. More extreme than the two polar cases of N and M are conceivable, such as those represented by a point such as R. Not only is the entire gain from the environmental cooperation reaped by one party only (party a in this case), but this party is also securing itself an additional gain conceded by the other party.

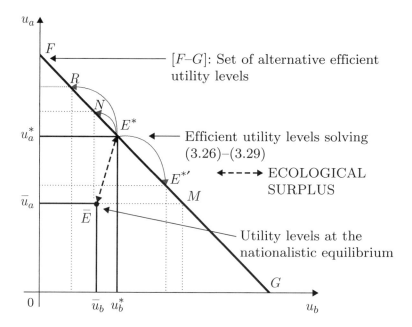

Fig. 3.3   **Alternative transfers to reallocate the ecological surplus.**

In all these cases the surplus remains defined by the distance between $\bar{E}$ and E^* and is always measured by this distance; the sharing of it through the transfers has no effect on its magnitude.

At a more general level, alternative ways of sharing the ecological surplus appear as alternative choices of the efficient state of the system — a choice that can result only from negotiations between the countries, since there is no authority to impose it to the parties. This reveals vividly how searching for efficiency in that context does in fact imply large possibilities of rivalry between the parties, each trying to secure for itself a larger part of the surplus. Analyzing the nature of this struggle, conceiving solutions of it, and finding compelling reasons for a particular outcome are precisely the theme on which game theory offers results. This is the task ahead in Lectures 5 and ff.

To summarize the point made and illustrated in this subsection, the world can secure itself an ecological surplus by moving from anarchy to efficiency in issues of transboundary pollution. However, there is an infinity of ways for the countries to share the global surplus that the gain in efficiency can generate. Are there concepts to resolve the uncertainty that this infinity generates?

3.4 Modalities of cooperation

Who owns the right to pollute internationally?

The assignment of rights issue

Accepting equilibria as the starting point of negotiations implies that the parties find themselves in the situation described above, where the generators of the externality have arrogated to themselves the right to emit pollutants. It was also mentioned that the reason for this situation is the absence of an international authority empowered to grant this right. Instead, the countries must *generate by themselves* the right they wish both to exert and to see respected. How can this occur?

Let me remark first that the issue is not exclusively one of international nature: within each country, how does the state assign pollution rights to economic agents such as households, firms, or local public bodies like municipalities or governmental agencies? How does it make the selection? More fundamentally and independently of the agents' institutional status, the issue is whether rights are (or should be) assigned to polluters or to pollutees.

This last question has been clarified in the literature for some time. It was first raised by Coase (1960), whose main thesis was to show that, whatever the initial allocation of rights either to the polluters or to the pollutees, an efficient outcome can occur spontaneously by letting the parties engage in mutually advantageous spontaneous bargaining. This has come to be known as the

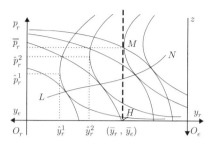

Fig. 3.4 A one polluter (r)–one pollutee (e) economy with classical (non-quasi-linear) utilities.

Coase theorem. It is well illustrated by means of the Edgeworth box-like diagram[26] of Fig. 3.4, which can be constructed by using a special case of a two agents version of our reference economic-ecological model where the countries are "specialized" in the following sense: only one of them, the "polluter", is an emitter of the externality, and ignores any damage caused to himself or to anyone else, while the other country, the "pollutee", is affected by the emissions of the polluting country while not emitting himself.

Formally, in the notation of the present reference model, let the polluter be denoted as country "r", with utility function (2.2) reduced to $u_r(x_r, z) = x_r$ since not being polluted implies $d_r(z) = 0$ for all values of z. Let its production function (2.3), whereby emissions are generated, be $g_r(e_r)$ with $g_r(0) = 0$, and let $\omega_r > 0$ be an assumed given amount of its initial resources. The country chooses its levels of consumption x_r and emissions e_r so as to satisfy the scarcity and technical constraints lumped together as $x_r + g_r(e_r) = \omega_r$. In the (x_r, e_r) space defined by the left orthant of Fig. 3.5, the set of points that satisfy this equation constitutes an indifference curve passing through ω_r and yielding the utility level $u_r(\omega_r)$. The convexity of this curve results from the assumed concavity of the

---

[26]Varian (1990, pp. 539, 542) illustrates a model less general than the one which appeared and was used as the main tool of analysis in Tulkens and Schoumaker (1975, p. 247 and ff). In this original version, reproduced in Fig. 3.4, utilities are indeed not assumed to be quasi-linear. One implication is that efficient emission levels are not the same in all Pareto efficient states.

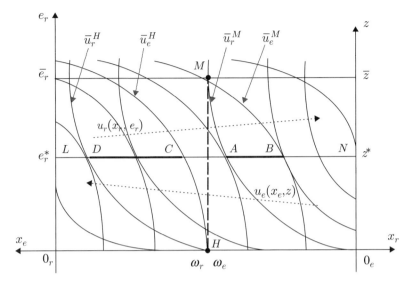

Fig. 3.5 A one polluter (r)–one pollutee (e) version of the reference model.

production function. Letting ω_r vary, an indifference map made of a family of congruent such indifference curves is generated, to the left of point H for lower values of ω_r and to the right for higher values.

Furthermore, letting the pollutee be denoted as country "e", its utility function is as in (2.2), that is, $u_e(x_e, z) = x_e - d_e(z)$ with $d_e(0) = 0$. No production function is associated with it by definition, and $\omega_e > 0$ denotes the amount of its initial resources. While the country chooses its consumption x_e so as to satisfy the resource constraint $x_e = \omega_e$, it is also a recipient in amount z of the externality generated by the polluter's emissions. In the (x_e, z) space defined by the orthant on the right of Fig. 3.5, the set of points whose coordinates satisfy the equation $\omega_e = x_e - d_e(z)$ constitutes an indifference curve passing through ω_e and yielding the utility level $u_e(\omega_e - d_e(0))$. The convexity of this curve results from the assumed convexity of the disutility function d_e. Letting ω_e vary, an indifference map made of a family of congruent such indifference curves is generated, to the left of point H for higher values of ω_e and to the right for lower values.

Finally, assuming the transfer function to be $z = e_r$, all feasible states of the economy are conveniently represented by the points in the open top box obtained by drawing the two indifference maps side by side with ω_r coinciding with ω_e as done in Fig. 3.5.

Figure 3.5 illustrates as follows Coase's reasoning about rights assignment and efficiency in externality problems. On the one hand, if the right to exert the externality is assigned to the polluter, namely country r, the joint individual behaviors of the polluter and the pollutee (country e) imply a nationalistic equilibrium allocation represented by point M, where both parties consume all of their respective resources ω_r and, ω_e. The polluter makes full use of his right by emitting $\bar{e}_r$, and this implies imposing $\bar{z}$ on the pollutee. Clearly in this situation an ecological surplus can be obtained if the two parties negotiate a mutually beneficial move to any of the allocations represented by points of the segment AB on the line LN of efficient allocations, a segment enclosed between the indifference curves passing through point M.

On the other hand, if the right is assigned to the pollutee, country e, the nationalistic equilibrium consists in the polluter, country r, being denied the right to exert the externality and the two parties just consuming all of their respective resources, a situation represented by point H. Here too an ecological surplus can be obtained by negotiating a move to any point on the line segment CD that belongs to LN and is enclosed between the indifference curves passing through ω_r and ω_e, that is, point H. In this case also, existence of an ecological surplus is identified (not the same, though, as the previous one[27]), and efficiency[28] can be reached.

Since efficiency is obtained in either case, Coase concludes that when efficiency is the sole objective, it does not matter to whom

---

[27]Transposed in the space of utilities of Fig. 3.2, the two possible regimes of rights assignment described in Fig. 3.5 appear as in Fig. 3.6, where the same labels M and H are attached to points representing the alternative regimes of the system. This illustration will be of further use in Lecture 5.

[28]With the strictly concave utilities assumed by Tulkens and Schoumaker (1975) the *property* of efficiency can still be obtained, but the efficient *level* of the externality differs with the assignment of rights between the polluter and the pollutee. Indeed Fig. 3.4 suggests that the level of efficient emissions is lower when the right is assigned to the pollutee rather than to the polluter.

is assigned the right to emit the externality. Therefore, no state intervention is necessary. Mutually advantageous private bargaining among the parties is sufficient to achieve the objective.

Rights are wealth

Another major aspect of Coase's theorem, vividly illustrated by the role of points M and H in the diagram, is that the question of to whom to allocate the rights is essentially a distributional one. Indeed, these points play exactly the same role as alternative initial endowments in the standard Edgeworth box illustration of exchange in general equilibrium theory. And similarly, rights on the environment, whether given to polluters, pollutees, or anyone else, are like property rights on commodities: they provide benefits to their owners, either when these exert these rights, or when they sell them.

Auctioning is a conceivable method for allocating these rights, which can be compared to auctioning land[29] or other common property resources. Notice that auctioning allows for both the polluters and the pollutees to acquire the rights and the alternative thus seems to disappear when one wonders to which one of these two categories to attribute the rights. But this is in fact an illusion: since the rights in question are essentially permissions to use the environment, that is, to emit polluting substances, the very notion of permits contains the fact that those who do not hold them may not emit: permits are thus an expression of rights belonging to those actors who do *not* exert the externality, i.e. the pollutees. Those who do want to exert it must acquire the right to do so, be it directly from the prospective pollutees by means of a contract, or from some public authority whose role as an intermediary is in fact to protect the pollutees' rights and properly organize the way they are exerted.

By contrast, the often mentioned and practiced technique of giving away rights to pollute under the name of "grandfathering" is clearly an allocation of rights to polluters.

---

[29] As suggested in a note by Ellerman (2005).

Coming back to the more general question of how pollution rights are assigned in general, and of how they could be in the international context of our enquiry, let us observe at this point that Coase took for granted the existence of a public authority that assigns and enforces such rights. He did not envisage a transnational problem like climate change where there is no such authority. For our purposes his theorem is in fact of little use because, as I wrote before, in an international context, the countries must generate by themselves the allocation of rights that is going to prevail worldwide, and this allocation is a quintessential part of the agreement, no less than its efficiency to which Coase's analysis is limited. But the problems raised by this allocation are of strategic nature, to be tackled by means of other conceptual tools than those used thus far, namely those of game theory. Lectures 4 and 5 will introduce them followed by developments showing the progress they hopefully allow one to make.

Rights vs. responsibility

In the case of a negative externality, the fact of being allocated a right to exert it amounts for its beneficiary to be allowed to hurt someone else, be it immediately or after some time. Now, in all civilized worlds, hurting implies responsibility accompanied by the requirement of compensation for the damage created to victims. This is the most common form of the "polluters pay" principle[30]: polluters should not only compensate for the discomfort and the damage they cause, they should also cover the cost of the clean up.

The requirement of compensation is obviously an implication of the rights being attributed to pollutees. When taken into account, it entails larger and different amounts than those of the coasean argument, a point illustrated on Fig. 3.5 as follows. When exerting

---

[30]Several other forms, actually eight of them, including taxation, are analyzed in detail in Tulkens and Schoumaker (1975).

his externality freely, the polluter brings the system from point H to point M. This causes the pollutee a damage which is measured in utility terms by the distance between the pollutees' two indifference curves passing through points M and ω_e, respectively. If initiated at M, the coasean bargaining leads to some point — call it the bargaining point — on the AB line segment, which implies a payment by the pollutee to the polluter of some amount (equal to ω_e, minus the abscissa of the bargaining point). But the compensation for the externality to be exerted at all should be measured by the distance between the bargaining point and point C, that is, the point that leaves the pollutee indifferent to H at the utility level prior to the occurrence of the externality. Eventually, point C implies a payment from the polluter to the pollutee. Thus, coasean bargaining ignores compensation.

In the dynamic stock pollutant setting, the notion of responsibility and its ensuing compensation finds an application over time: indeed it then takes the form of requiring compensation today for the damages created by *past* emissions. The time element results from the fact that stock pollutants are like "durable" goods. It extends the aspect "responsibility of the emitters — compensation of the victims" of the pollution problem by giving it an intergenerational dimension. This is the spirit of a well-known Brazilian proposal[31] in matters of climate change, a theme to be taken up again in Lecture 10.

Let us observe, finally, that when a natural phenomenon is at the origin of the damage, the *victim pays principle* is usually accepted, albeit often amended by solidarity from others on a voluntary basis or intervention by the state. By contrast, when humans are at the origin of damages, it is expected that the authors of these damages should pay a compensation. The reason for this difference lies in the fairly universal notion of responsibility which applies in the latter case while not in the former.

---

[31] A good exposition of this proposal can be found on the UNFCCC website.

Treaties as contracts

The likely outcome

The multiplicity of efficient states as illustrated with Figs. 3.2 and 3.5 leaves a considerable degree of indeterminacy as to which one is likely to occur as an outcome of an international environmental agreement. However, a simple look at the pictures immediately suggests that not all optima are equally acceptable: for instance, extreme points such as L and N in Fig. 3.5 are clearly not, because it hurts common sense that the entire benefit of economic and ecological activity be concentrated into one or just a few hands.

Beyond this simple argument, let us observe that because the agreement must be voluntary (the absence of a supranational authority prevents that any solution be imposed), another criterion is to play a role in this respect, namely the one of individual rationality: it consists in requiring that the agreement induces for any country a utility level not lower than the one prevailing at the no agreement equilibrium.

Recall, however, that Figs. 3.4–3.5 suggest two conceivable environmentally nationalistic equilibria, M and H, depending upon how rights are assigned between polluters and pollutees. But in our international context rights are not assigned because they are not enforceable and as a result, the polluters arrogate to themselves the right to emit, as mentioned before. Thus, only the nationalistic equilibrium of type M is a relevant reference for determining the individual rationality of a proposed agreement.

Combined with the efficiency requirement, this argument leads one to conclude that only states represented by points of the segment AB of Fig. 3.5 are likely outcomes. All other states can be excluded.

A stronger version of the same idea is the one of coalitional rationality[32]: for no group of countries can states of the world be accepted that would induce for them welfare levels lower than the ones they could secure themselves as a group, outside of the

---

[32]This property, also called "coalitional stability", may be seen as one form of self enforcement, as discussed in the last section of Lecture 6.

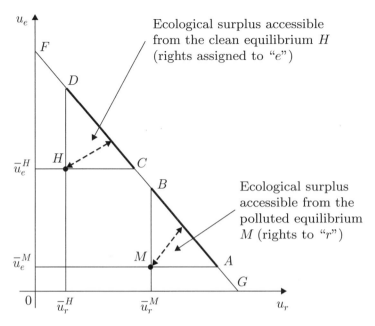

Fig. 3.6 **The conceivable surplus under alternative regimes of rights assignment.**

agreement, even if efficient. This extension finds a strong justification in the inevitable necessity of group-wise action when a diffuse, i.e. public good type, externality is at stake as it is the case with many transfrontier pollution problems. This puts a further restriction on the set of efficient sates as likely outcomes of negotiations. It cannot be illustrated with Fig. 3.6, but it will be with the extension of it presented in some figures of Lecture 6. Will this restriction eventually lead to locate a single point on the line AB as a likely outcome? The answer is in Lecture 6.

The process

The arguments just presented bear on the acceptability of the outcome. Their justification rests on the fact that international agreements are necessarily voluntary. Another aspect of them, also linked with their voluntary character, appears if one considers the process through which the outcome is obtained. In this perspective, and viewing this process not in its temporal dimension but rather in its logical structure: international agreements, or treaties, can be seen as contracts,[33] bilateral or multilateral. An essential component of a contract is that there be a *quid pro quo*, in other words an exchange between the parties.

There are indeed common traits between the social interactions that occur in bargaining about externalities and those occurring in the exchange of commodities. They are clear only, however, after the rights to exert the externality have been specified. Turning back again to Fig. 3.5, there are at least two possibilities in this respect: with the rights assigned to the polluter, the bargaining is between him reducing his emissions and the pollutee offering some economic good in exchange; if rights are to the pollutee, the bargaining is between him allowing the polluter to act and the polluter offering some economic good in exchange for that permission. Note that in physical terms, with rights assigned to the pollutee, only the polluter does something: in the joint move from point H to some point on the CD locus of efficient agreements, he emits *and* he pays; the pollutee is entirely passive. By contrast, when rights are to the polluter, things are more symmetric: in the joint move away from M to the locus AB, the polluter abates while the pollutee pays. This difference cannot exist with commodity exchanges, where the two parties are always in the symmetric position of both giving away some material good and receiving a counterpart.

Another important difference with exchanges of ordinary economic goods is that a problem of *free riding* typically arises in international pollution bargaining, which does not arise with commodity exchanges. The diffuse character of the very nature of the environmental contract entails that one party — the recipients of the externality — comprises by definition several individuals, some of which may abstain to participate in the agreement and yet benefit from it. By contrast, commodity exchanges take place through essentially bilateral transactions. While tempting, the analogy with

---

[33]See Reuter (1995).

contracts is thus at best an approximate one. The important issue of free riding is taken up again and more completely in many parts of these lectures, first towards the end of the present one, and then again in Lectures 6 and 9.

3.5 Obstacles to cooperation

The informational problems

In addition to the issues covered so far, the achievement of an efficient outcome is also predicated by the nature and extent of the information available to the parties — information that they generate themselves or that they somehow obtain. One may see two aspects to the problems that arise in this respect. A first one is the valuation of the "environmental"[34] goods *per se*, irrespective of the uses made of this valuation. The second aspect is the revelation of that value in decision and negotiations processes.

The value of "environmental" goods

Here the question is: why is it justified to attach value to the environment and if so, why attempting to measure that value? It is customary in environmental economics to distinguish between three possible forms of environmental values, respectively, called (i) usage value, (ii) option value and (iii) existence value. Let me briefly review them before examining their relevance for climate change.

Usage value is the one attributed to an environmental resource by those who effectively use it. In market economies, it is considered to be reflected in the market price that the resource commands, provided the market is sufficiently competitive. Option value is meant

---

[34]Quotation marks are used here to excuse myself from using occasionally this vocabulary that was criticized as unnecessary in Lecture 1. Please understand it as a shortcut for "commodities that constitute the environment."

to capture the value attached to the mere possibility of using the resource by people who currently make no use of it. It is of major importance in problems that involve irreversible actions. Existence value, finally, corresponds to the value attached to the existence of the resource, compared to its loss, by people who do not use it and never intend to.

What relevance has these three forms of environmental value in the face of the climate change phenomenon? The impacts of climatic change that have the characteristics of global public goods that nobody can avoid — typically temperature changes — imply that there is a usage value for everyone since the entire population is concerned. This value corresponds to the damages incurred presently and in the future. For more local unavoidable impacts, such as those of sea level rise, for instance, the corresponding local damages also determine the environmental usage value, limited to the potentially affected population.

As far as option values are concerned, they are most importantly involved in timing decisions, both of emission abatement and of choice of adaptation activities.

As to the existence value, I wish to argue first, at a general level, that it lies beyond the one of economic value, that is, beyond the value notion attached to economic goods. Indeed, economic goods are defined by scarcity, and scarcity only exists in relation to needs. How can there be scarcity of goods that no one will ever need? In other words, why does one need the existence of such goods? Strictly speaking, the notion of existence value is an elusive one, to the extent that one cannot have economic value without scarcity. Its justification must be found in other notions and sources of value than those on which the economic discipline is built. In most of these lectures, I assume that all these values are subsumed in the disutility functions $d_i(z)$.

The extreme difficulty of measurement

In addition to the conceptual complexities just evoked (and the few more mentioned hereafter), a considerable informational obstacle to cooperation is the one of measurement of both abatement and damage costs. For the worldwide climate change modeling of the kind I am presenting here the difficulties are particularly acute because of the huge geographical dimension of the problem and the extreme variety of the sectors where damages may occur. Moreover, the phenomenon to be apprehended consists in an extremely complex chain that Edmonds, Lovell and Lovell (2017) remind one to be with links as follows: "emissions → atmospheric concentrations → radiative forcing → climate change → climate impacts → economic damages and costs." On abatements costs, Tulkens and Tulkens (2006) report on overestimation.

On damage costs, Chapter 4 of Nordhaus and Boyer (2000) describe in a compact, yet quite authoritative way the methodologies in use and the results obtained at the time. Roson and Sartori (2016) present similar methodologies and results as obtained from a major data source. The case of disasters, dealt with in Wahlstrom and Guha-Sapir (2015), is an example of the work involved in a particular but most extreme damage area.

More recently Nordhaus and Moffat (2017) show that the present state of research, and hence knowledge, on *global* economic impacts and damage of climate change is astonishingly poor, first in itself and then by comparison with other disciplines related to climate. I can only relay these authors' warning (p. 3) of urgency of the matter and recommendation for the development of "a damage module that meets the overall criteria for scientific basis (National Research Council 2017)."'

Willingness to pay

The second aspect of the informational problem is the one that arises with the revelation of preferences for the environmental goods, in view of decision making. The essence of the issue is the elicitation of the values just discussed. How can these values be expressed?

For decades now, economic modeling postulates that preferences for any commodity can be expressed in terms of an alternative, that is, an amount of some other economic commodity used as *numéraire* — be it money, or income, or even possibly labor, and considered in exchange. This postulate is also applied to the goods that are present in our environment — for short, the "environmental goods". Technically, the value of one unit of an environmental good is thus defined as the minimum amount of *numéraire* commodity that can be substituted for that unit of the environmental good while leaving the consumer indifferent.

This reference to substitutability, implying an assumption that substitution is always feasible, may be seen as a strongly limiting one, because it is often felt that the values at stake involve quite other elements than physical commodities. This view of values is in effect quite materialistic. At the same time it is inescapable because the essence of economic reasoning is precisely about substitution: if there exist at all alternative ways of allocating resources, it is because they may be substituted for one another, to varying extents. Since the decisions involved in environmental policy affairs bear on resource allocation, consistency requires that the values involved refer precisely to these alternatives. Willy-nilly, environmental values have to be expressed in material terms if they have to be included in economic reasoning.

Preference — or value — revelation thus reduces to revealing numbers, which are conveniently designated by the expression "willingness-to-pay" (WTP). In the context of my reference economic-ecological model, the *numéraire* consists in quantities of the single private good. The need for these numbers in the process of decision making appears, for instance, in the fact that efficiency conditions are expressed in terms of WTP's, as it was seen in the equalities (3.4): checking for optimality involves evaluating with numbers the two sides of these equalities. When the numbers reveal that these equalities are not met, as in (3.2) characterizing non-cooperative equilibrium, they may serve as very useful indicators as to the direction in which efficiency improving decisions can be taken. More generally, benefit-cost analyzes of projects involving public goods rest, in the same spirit, on numerical evaluations of WTPs for these goods.[35]

WTP for what?

Climatic change is not a public *good* that results from production: it is rather to be avoided! Therefore, the expression of "WTP" is to be understood in the particular sense of WTP *to avoid the change to occur.* This is illustrated in Fig. 3.7 where, for a given country's utility function and a prevailing state s, the maximum WTP to avoid a change in ambient concentration such as LM is represented by the amount BA of private good. An alternative notion to be found in the benefit-cost literature is the one of "minimum willingness to accept" (WTA), in our case: *to accept a detrimental change to occur.* This is illustrated by the amount CB for a climatic change LM.

The notion WTA is appropriate for evaluating the benefits of adaptation decisions (i.e. the minimum acceptable compensation to be obtained to cover the future damages entailed by LM), whereas

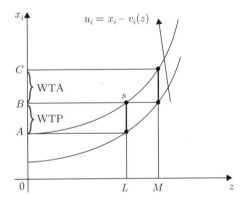

Fig. 3.7 Country i's willingness to pay *vs.* willingness to accept.

---

[35]Recall Dasgupta's rules which apply Propositions 3.2 and 3.5 using these numbers.

the WTP to avoid the change is rather relevant for mitigation actions (that is, emissions abatement), since this is exactly what these actions will entail. A common wisdom concerning this distinction is that the former is generally larger that the latter.[36]

In the reference model used throughout these lectures, the two notions coincide because of the quasi-linearity of the utility functions, as shown by the congruence of the indifference curves.

Informational free riding

When Samuelson 1954 identified the necessary conditions for efficiency to prevail in situations involving public goods — that he expressed in terms of WTPs and marginal costs,[37] he immediately pointed out the logical difficulty of obtaining this information correctly, due to a behavioral phenomenon that he was the first to call "free riding". Briefly stated, free riding as he conceived it consists in any typical economic agent revealing incorrectly his WTP for a public good when being asked for it, because of two alternative possible situations. Either the questioned person knows (or believes) that the amount he reveals will serve as a basis for a payment he will have to make when the public good is provided, or the person knows (or believes) that no such payment will be requested from him after provision has occurred.

In the first case, the person will understate his willingness to pay, hoping to pay less for a good that will be provided anyhow on the basis of the other people's answers. Thus, the information basis on how much of the good to produce is biased downwards. In the second case, the person will overstate his preference since no matter how large the answer is, he will get the good anyway independently of any payment. Here, the information basis on how much of the good to produce is biased upwards.

---

[36] See Kolstad and Guzman (1999) for an interesting discussion of the justification of the two theses, followed by the authors' own justification.

[37] Actually, he formulated them in the equivalent terms of marginal rates of substitution (in consumption) and marginal rates of transformation (in production) between the public good and a *numéraire* private good.

In this description, there is implicitly a benevolent planning authority[38] in charge of providing the good on the basis of the information just discussed and securing its financing one way or another. Planning and mechanism design approaches, such as, respectively, the "MDP processes" of Malinvaud 1970–1971 and Drèze and de la Vallée Poussin (1971) in their public goods versions,[39] as well as the "mechanisms" of Clark (1971), d'Aspremont and Gérard-Varet (1975, 1976), and Groves and Ledyard (1977), show that it is possible to empower such an authority with ways to get around the issue of misrepresentation.[40] But, as mentioned repeatedly above, there is no such authority in our context of international externalities where little use can be made of these otherwise remarkable results.

However, parallel to that literature, the MDP process received, in the Tulkens (1979) paper cited above, an alternative institutional interpretation in terms of environmental *negotiations* aiming at the achievement of world efficiency between independent countries. Beyond the differential equations formalism, this interpretation was actually inspired by Buchanan's (1968) theory of public goods. This interpretation also inspired the further development of the MDP process[41] in terms of "local" games, taking place at each step *along* the process towards an efficient state.[42] Working under the rough assumption of perfect information and thus leaving aside the informational problem of preference revelation (PR), the authors of this approach pursued the study of local games as precursors of the "global" games, which were to become the appropriate to fully exploit

---

[38]The producer being necessarily the State because of the impossibility of selling the good against a price that would remunerate a private producer.

[39]These approaches were developed by Roberts (1979), Henry (1979), and Schoumaker (1979). See also Yen (1987). Champsaur and Laroque (1981) is the most elaborate stage of this strand of literature.

[40]I am a bit anticipating on Lectures 4 and ff., as all these approaches use game theoretic tools. I return to them in concluding Lecture 6.

[41]Again, in Chander and Tulkens (1992, 1991, 2002), as well as in Kaitala, Mäler and Tulkens (1995).

[42]Local games are defined and treated in detail in Tulkens and Zamir (1979), in the non-environmental context of pure exchange economies, before their application to the GEG in Chander and Tulkens (1992, 1991/2002).

the potentials of game theory for the environmental externalities problems. This is what I am about to report on in Lectures 5 and 6 hereafter.

Non-participatory free riding

Another notion of free riding in the presence of public goods emerged in the early eighties when environmentally minded theoretical economists introduced a slight modification of the production side of the Samuelson model of public goods, so as to allow for multiple producers of it.[43] In an international context this extension was obviously necessary but the sovereign character of the countries made it equally necessary to recognize the voluntary character of the provision of the public good, i.e. in this case abatement of the environmental externality.

In this setting, a special form of interaction between economic agents has been identified, namely the one consisting in "letting the job be done by others": with multiple producers of an externality, a given level of the total can be achieved by different levels of contributions by the participants. Free riders in this sense are those who do not do much themselves, counting on the effort made by others. This is free riding in the production of the good, distinct from free riding in expressing the demand for it, that is, in revealing willingness to pay for the good.

Here, the necessarily voluntary character of the provision of the public good, that is, abatement of the environmental externality, together with the fact that the externality is multilateral, shifted the attention from the issue of individual consumers revealing preferences to the problem of having several States participate or not in international environmental agreements. The expression of

---

[43]Together with this modification, the phenomenon of transboundary pollution is now better designated as the emission of *an externality with public good characteristics* — i.e. "diffuse" as proposed in Lecture 1.

free riding reappeared here not as a PR problem but instead as a way to behave in the face of such agreements.

Thus, two forms of free riding were proposed[44] to be called respectively, "PR free riding" *vs.* "non-participatory (NP) free riding" — one could also say "allocational free riding". Notice that the two forms are not mutually exclusive, but I am not aware of any work that treats them simultaneously. The game theoretic developments that follow do privilege the latter, mainly in Section 6.3 of Lecture 6, because it is the form in which results have been the richest and contribute most to avoiding that free riding be an obstacle to efficiency. There will be occasional allusions to the former, however.[45]

Finally a third (and I surmise new) notion of free riding is identified in Lecture 9 under the name of "coalitional free riding". Being linked in an essential way with the notion of coalition in cooperative games with externalities, it cannot be presented at this stage, but it turns out in Lecture 9 that it plays a major role in the theory of stability of international environmental agreements.

3.6 Concluding summary and problems left open

In this lecture, economic theory concepts have been called upon in order to characterize the states in which the world may find itself, according to the representation of it given by the economic-ecological model constructed in Lecture 2. This characterization had two

---

[44]In Chander and Tulkens (2009, pp. 178–179).

[45]Another notion of free riding has been put forward by Finus (2001, pp. 183 and ff.), to designate the behavior that consists in signing an agreement and then not complying with it. I am not sure that "free riding" is an appropriate wording in this case. Non-compliance is breaching an agreement that was adhered to. The two senses described above are different in that free riding is described as either not signing the agreement, or being part of it under abusively favorable conditions because of an information bias. By contrast, given an existing agreement, compliance or non-compliance are decisions which, to anticipate the vocabulary of the next lectures, are strategies of another game.

aspects: descriptive and evaluative. The descriptive characterization consisted in proposing to interpret observed states of the system through the lens of a concept of international equilibrium — an equilibrium that results from the countries' assumed search for their self interest in environmental affairs. The concept was the international environmentally nationalistic equilibrium. The normative characterization, instead, proposed judgments on conceivable states of the system: judgments on states that are implications of *a priori* defined concepts or values, or judgments on observable states such as those described as equilibria. Criteria inspiring these judgments were essentially environmental and allocational efficiency, as well as equity. The motivation for presenting this intellectual construction was to provide a rationale for the existence of international environmental agreements in general, as well as a possible source of inspiration for the negotiations whereby such agreements are being prepared, like currently on climate change for instance.

Such being the objective, and given what has been presented up to here, which problems should one consider to be left open and to be tackled at this stage? Let me point out the following seven:

- Can an agreement be designed that satisfies everybody? Every individual country as well as every possible group of countries?
- In such agreement, what is the role for the sharing of the ecological surplus between the countries?
- In such agreement, what is the respective status of the polluters and of the pollutees?
- In such agreement, how about free riding?
- Is the agreement to be a fixed one over time or revisable?
- How can the agreement be implemented in practice?
- Finally, what is the answer to the initial question: can the environment be treated as an economic good?

Many of these questions are of "practical" nature. Yet, rather than taking refuge in casual empiricism, with common sense answers, or in just calling on experience of professionals, I shall search for answers in an extension of the theoretical basis presented thus far. The extension consists in borrowing concepts and techniques from game theory, with the intention of making them contribute to the answers sought for. This is the objective of the rest of these lectures.

Annex: Analytical formulation of the one polluter (r)–one pollutee (e) reference model

Refer to Fig. 3.5, p. 79.

The economic-ecological system:

For a polluter only, indexed $i = r$, the utility and production functions combined are

$$u_r \equiv x_r + g_r(e_r), \text{ with } g_r'(e_r) = 0 \text{ for some } e^\circ,$$
$$(d_r(z) = 0 \text{ for all } z \geq 0)$$

and $\omega_r > 0$ is an initial endowment of the consumption good.

For a pollutee only, indexed $i = e$, the utility function (no production function) is

$$u_e \equiv x_e - d_e(z), \text{ with } d_e'(z) > 0 \text{ for all } z \geq 0$$
(index e not to be confused with the variable e_r)

and $\omega_e > 0$ is an initial endowment of the consumption good.

The externality *emitted* is e_r, the externality *received* is z.

The ecological constraint is $e_r = z$.

Outcomes:

Efficiency: $L-N$ is the set of efficient states

Equilibria:

- *If the polluter has the right to pollute,*
  M: Non-cooperative equilibrium $(\bar{x}_r^M, \bar{x}_e^M, \bar{e}_r^M, \bar{z}^M)$, with utilities

$$\bar{u}_r^M = \underset{\{x_r, e_r\}}{\text{Max}} \ x_r + g_r(e_r) \text{ subject to } x_r \leq \omega_r,$$

$$= \bar{x}_r^M + g_r(\bar{e}_r^M) \text{ where } \bar{x}^M r = \omega_r \text{ and}$$

$$\bar{e}_r^M \text{ is such that } g_r'(\bar{e}_r^M) = 0,$$

$$\bar{u}_e^M = \underset{\{x_e\}}{\text{Max}} \ x_e - v_e(z) \text{ subject to } x_e \leq \omega_e, \ z = e_r,$$

$$= \bar{x}_e^M - v_e(\bar{z}^M) \text{ where } \bar{x}_e^M = \omega_e, \ \bar{z}^M = \bar{e}_r^M$$

and sets:

$\{x_r \geq 0, e_r \geq 0 | x_r + g_r(e_r) = \bar{u}_r^M\}$, the polluter's indifference curve passing through M,

$\{x_e \geq 0, z \geq 0 | x_e - d_e(z) = \bar{u}_e^M\}$, the pollutee's indifference curve passing through M.

- *If the pollutee has the right not to be polluted,*
  H: Non-cooperative equilibrium $(\bar{x}_r^H, \bar{x}_e^H, \bar{e}_r^H, \bar{z}^H)$, with utilities

$$\bar{u}_r^H = \underset{\{x_r, e_r\}}{\text{Max}} \ x_r + g_r(e_r) \text{ subject to } x_r \leq \omega_r, \ e_r = 0,$$

$$= \bar{x}_r^H + g_r(\bar{e}_r^H) \text{ where } \bar{x}_r^H = \omega_r \text{ and } \bar{e}_r^H = 0,$$

$$\bar{u}_e^H = \underset{\{x_e\}}{\text{Max}} \ x_e - d_e(z) \text{ subject to } x_e \leq \omega_e, \ z = e_r,$$

$$= \bar{x}_e^H - d_e(\bar{z}^H) \text{ where } \bar{x}_e^H = \omega_e \ \text{ and } \ \bar{z}^H = 0$$

and sets:

$\{x_r \geq 0, e_r \geq 0 | x_r + g_r(e_r) = \bar{u}_r^H\}$ the polluter's indifference curve passing through H,

$\{x_e \geq 0, z \geq 0 | x_e - d_e(z) = \bar{u}_e^H\}$ the pollutee's indifference curve passing through H.

Lecture 4

GAME THEORY CONCEPTS

The purpose and the message

Today, game theory constitutes a vast body of knowledge. Therefore, no comprehensive coverage of it can be envisaged here. Instead, I introduce the reader to it in two steps: in this lecture, a selection is made of forms of games and concepts that are of direct relevance for dealing with the unresolved issues raised at the end of Lecture 3. They are simply described with minimal mathematical treatment. In Lectures 5–7, these same concepts are put to use in the framework of the economic-ecological model, this time with full and detailed mathematical treatment.

Before tackling this specific objective, the message I hope to convey with this lecture is that game theory, thanks to its abstract formulation, is in fact a quite encompassing tool, susceptible of widening substantially the discourse on the functioning of Societies — much beyond the sole environmental issues and their economic dimension.

Plan

Strategic games in general

Equilibrium concepts in strategic games

Coalitional functions and the cooperative game form

Cores of games and other solution concepts
in cooperative games

Virtues of the core solution

Lecture 4

Game Theory Concepts

Per se, game theory has nothing to say on pollution in general and on climate change in particular. Indeed, it essentially consists of an intellectual framework designed to understand what occurs when decision-makers interact in relation to phenomena that are of concern to them.[1] The description of what these phenomena are, as well as the objects of the decisions, must come from other sciences.

The phenomena and the decision problems I am concerned with in these lectures having been expounded in the preceding lectures, I now enter into a toolbox that should allow one at later stages to come to grips seriously with these problems. The presentation is made at a certain level of abstraction, because the instrument is of that nature, given its intended generality. Therefore, no reference whatsoever to environmental facts, nor to economic concepts in this lecture. I strictly stick to the language of the theory.

4.1 Strategic games in general[2]

In the sense used in these lectures, a game is a mathematical object. Among its many possible forms, the one being presented in this section, called the strategic form, is the most directly applicable to

---

[1] The discipline of game theory would therefore be better named "Interactive decision theory" as suggested by Aumann (1987). Among the major applications of game theory that are reviewed in this paper Aumann does not list environmental problems, presumably because such applications were very scarce at that time, as reported in the subsection "Antecedents" at the beginning of Lecture 5.

[2] Throughout these lectures, the presentation of game theoretical concepts as well as the choice of terminology are inspired by the lectures of Aumann (1989) and the classical textbooks of Osborne and Rubinstein (1994) and Maschler, Solan and Zamir (2011), as well as by the widely used economics textbook of

our project. Other forms, like the extensive form, or the coalitional function form, will be introduced or alluded to later when useful for the same purpose.

Definition 4.1. A **game in strategic form** (or a *strategic game*) is a triplet (N, Σ, v) where:

- $N = \{i : i = 1, 2, \ldots, n\}$ denotes a set of individuals (actors), called **players**,
- $\Sigma = \Sigma_1 \times \cdots \times \Sigma_n$ denotes a set joint actions, called **strategies**, where for each $i = 1, 2, \ldots, n, \Sigma_i$ is the set of strategies $\sigma_i \in \Sigma_i$ that player i has access to and can choose from,
- $v = (v_1, \ldots, v_n)$ is a vector of **payoffs** of the players, where for each $i, v_i \in R$ is the payoff of player i.

The words "player", "strategy" and "payoff" in this definition deserve some explanatory comment. The first one is a remnant of the origin of the theory: in its full-fletched current developments the "players" under consideration are, as suggested earlier, individuals considered to be able to act freely on anything. Much more than just participants in a parlor game. "Strategies" are plain actions that the players have access to, with no necessary tactical or military connotation whatsoever: only the material feasibility of these actions for each individual player is at stake. The word "payoff", finally, designates the way in which a player evaluates for himself what occurs in the interaction process under study, be it in monetary units or in more qualitative or abstract terms. Thus, the "mathematical object" designated as a "game" is a quite general way to describe who does what and why in well-defined interactive situations between a given set of individuals who act according to a well-defined objective.

Two more components of a game are needed to develop the announced analyses:

Mas-Colell, Whinston and Green (1995), which presents game theory in a way that best connects it with economic theory. In French, for a presentation akin to the present lectures, Dequiedt, Durieu and Solal (2011) as well as Dehez (2017) are recommended.

Definition 4.2. For a game (N, Σ, v) a **strategy profile** is a specification of a strategy for each player. With $\sigma_i \in R$ denoting the strategy of player i, a strategy profile is just a list of strategies, denoted by the vector $\sigma = (\sigma_1, \ldots, \sigma_n) \in R^n$.

Definition 4.3. For any individual player i in a strategic game (N, Σ, v), a **payoff function**[3] denoted $v_i(\sigma)$ formalizes the dependency of his payoff v_i upon the strategy profile σ.

If the image of the function is a real number, this number is called the value of $i's$ payoff.

Notice that since the argument is the vector $\sigma = (\sigma_1, \ldots, \sigma_n)$, $v_i(\sigma)$ means that the payoff of each player i depends not only on his own strategy choice σ_i but also on the strategies of the other players $\sigma_j, j \in N, j \neq i$. A game with payoff functions so specified allows one to handle externalities between the players. In particular, the formulation includes the possibility for a player to react to the choices of the other players in choosing his own strategy. There is thus a qualitative distinction to be made between the components of the vector σ in the function $v_i(\sigma)$: the component σ_i of σ is a decision variable for player i, whereas all the other components $\sigma_j, j \neq i$ are not; they are decided by other players. But they affect player i's payoff, in a passive way for him.

Being thus equipped with the apparatus of the players' strategies and payoffs, what does the game theorist pretend to accomplish? The answer lies in the word "outcome", more precisely in the ability of making statements about the outcome of the interactions between the players, as it may result from among their possibly infinite conceivable actions. The expression of "making statements" may be understood as predicting, but prediction is not the main objective of game theory. Rather, the aim is to identify, as outcomes of a game, actions of the players that are "interesting" in the sense of

---

[3] There is a logical connection between the payoff function v in a game and the utility function u in economics as introduced in Lecture 2 and used throughout Lecture 3. The necessary clarification of the relation between payoffs and utilities is given below, in the subsection devoted to transferable and non-transferable utility.

having remarkable properties given the characteristics of the game's components. When an outcome has such properties it is called a **solution**, and the arguments that support the claimed interest is a **solution concept**. The game theorist thus essentially conceives of solution concepts, on the one hand, and on the other hand he enquires about and shows which solution concepts are appropriate for which specific games.

Having that perspective in mind, I shall in this lecture deal with at least four solution concepts, namely the Nash equilibrium, the partially cooperative Nash equilibrium, the core, and the internally stable solution. The reason for this choice is that in Lecture 5 these concepts will be shown to have interesting properties when applied to one particular category of games called "global externality games".

In the above definition of a game, said "in strategic form", there is no mention of who moves when and in what order while the game is being played. In common parlance, this refers to what the rules of the game are. When these are included in the definition, the game is said to be "in extensive form". This form will not be dealt with in these lectures, for the simple reason that, to my knowledge, hardly any work has ever been done on an extensive form of the global externality game on which I wish to concentrate from Lecture 5 on. Of course, such an extension would be of considerable interest[4] since it could bear on the ways in which the process of the negotiations develops before an outcome is reached and not only on the outcome itself, as I shall do in these lectures.

Finally, as a transition to and a preparation for the analytical developments to come, I introduce now two apparently formal assumptions, bearing on the nature and properties of the components of the games that will be handled:

Assumption 4.1. Each strategy set Σ_i is a non-empty, convex, compact subset of some Euclidian metric space.

---

[4]For directions, consult Osborne and Rubinstein (1994), parts II and III, Mas-Colell, Whinston Green and (1995, pp. 221–228) and Maschler, Solan and Zamir (2013. Chapter 3, pp. 39–70).

Assumption 4.2. Each payoff function $v_i(\sigma)$ is continuous in σ and quasi-concave in σ_i over the space specified in Assumption 4.1.

I qualified as "apparently" formal these two mathematical assumptions because their justification is more than that: they are needed for representing with sufficient realism *within the game* the phenomena involved with environmental externalities, both in their physics as well as in their economics. This point will be illustrated in Lecture 5 with a counter-example involving the famous "Prisoner's dilemma" game in the *Antecedents* subsection of Section 5.2.

4.2 Equilibrium concepts in strategic games

Nash equilibrium

As a first category of conceivable outcomes of any game, "equilibria" are solutions whose interest lies in the fact that they rest on behavioral characteristics of the players considered only as independent individuals, in contrast with groups or coalitions where ties are assumed between the players. One of such outcomes, the Nash equilibrium, is indeed a concept built on the following two behavioral assumptions:

Assumption 4.3. Each player is "rational" i.e. chooses a strategy in a way that maximizes his payoff.

Assumption 4.4. Players act simultaneously, but independently: they do not act in concert.

Definition 4.4. **A non-cooperative Nash equilibrium** (NCNE) — a Nash equilibrium for short — of the strategic game (N, Σ, v) is a strategy profile $\bar{\sigma} \in \Sigma$ such that for all $i \in N$, $\bar{\sigma}_i = \arg\max_{\sigma_i \in \Sigma_i} v_i(\bar{\sigma}_1, \ldots, \bar{\sigma}_{i-1}, \sigma_i, \bar{\sigma}_{i+1}, \ldots, \bar{\sigma}_n)$.

The gist of this concept lies in an issue of *compatibility* between the individual behaviors. Indeed, compatibility is problematic whenever the adoption by any player i of the strategy σ_i that maximizes his payoff u_i is rendered difficult, if not impossible, by the simultaneous strategy choices made by the other players. Obviously, the difficulty is coming from the fact of the externality through which the respective choices made by the players influence one another. Compatibility does obtain when each player finds his best strategy, given the ones chosen by the others, these being felt also best, in turn, by the latter. The complexity of this multilateral compatibility issue is considerable. It can be disentangled by means of the mathematical tool of the fixed point of a mapping from a set into itself, as shown in Nash (1951).

The mapping at stake is from the set of strategies of all players, Σ, into itself. A fixed point of that mapping is indeed a n-dimensional strategy profile each component of which is a maximum for the payoff function of the corresponding player, given the $n-1$ strategies chosen by the other players. That the properties assumed above on the strategy sets Σ_i and on the payoff functions $v_i(\sigma)$ are sufficient conditions for the existence of such a fixed point of the mapping is established by a theorem which is of common use in mathematical economics. A detailed presentation of it can be found e.g. in Mas-Colell, Whinston and Green (1995, Proposition 8.D.3, p. 253).

For the audiences these lectures are addressed to, what is essential is to realize the importance of the existence concept from a social science point of view. Combining the notion of compatibility between interdependent behaviors, on the one hand, with the extreme individualism of that characterizes these behaviors, on the other hand, is by no means an evident or simple thing. There are in fact situations where such combination cannot prevail, *for logical reasons.* This is precisely what is revealed and demonstrated by the non-existence of a Nash equilibrium in such cases. When the formulation of the game realistically describes the facts, the message of non-existence of an equilibrium is one of conceptual inconsistency in the modeling of the situation. This is why the economic-ecological modeling of Lectures 2 and 3 will be submitted to that consistency test in Lectures 5 and 6, after being converted into the mold of strategic games dubbed GEG and DGEG, respectively.[5]

---

[5]Specifically, the environmentally nationalistic international equilibrium of the economic-ecological model will be put to that existence test.

There are many other arguments than the one of compatibility between individualistic behaviors presented here, that are put forward as justifications of the Nash equilibrium concept in general, as can be seen from the game theory authors that I have referred to thus far.[6] The reason for the justification I have selected is that it seems to me to be the most relevant one for the international environmental application pursued in this work.

One may further ask oneself whether the mapping can have more than one fixed point. This may be the case, again, depending upon properties of the game associated with the underlying economic-ecological model. In this lecture, I shall simply assume uniqueness, letting the possible multiplicity feature being taken up — as it will in Lecture 5 — in the light of the reality to be apprehended by the model.

Dominant strategy equilibrium

Definition 4.5. A strategy of a player is a **dominant strategy** if it is as good or better for him than any other strategy he has access to, no matter what strategies might be selected by other players.

When the game is such that there exists such a strategy for some or all player(s), these do not need neither to know the strategies of the other players nor even to assume rationality on their part.

Definition 4.6. A **dominant strategy equilibrium** of the strategic game (N, Σ, v) is a strategy profile $\bar{\sigma} \in \Sigma$ such that for each $i \in N$, $\bar{\sigma}_i$ is a dominant strategy.

Obviously, a dominant strategy equilibrium is also a Nash equilibrium. In general, games do not have any dominant strategy equilibrium, but one or several such strategies may occur in particular cases. An example involving the global externality game is the one presented in Section 5.2. The equilibrium in such case has properties that may not hold in general.

---

[6]See, e.g. Mas-Colell, Whinston and Green (1995, pp. 248–249), or Maschler, Solan and Zamir (2013, Section 4.9, pp. 100–102).

Coalitions and transferable utility

Coalitions

I now relax the assumption that each player chooses his strategy independently and allow that some players choose their strategies in concert. Such players are then said to form a **coalition**. A coalition, denoted S, is any subset of N, the all players set. For any S, let $\Sigma_S = \prod_{i \in S} \Sigma_i$ be the set of all strategies accessible to the members of S as a coalition, and let $\sigma_S \underset{\text{def}}{=} (\sigma_i)_{i \in S}$ denote[7] a vector of strategies chosen by the members of S, within Σ_S. Note that σ_S is not a strategy profile of the game, since it is only a s-dimensional vector, not a n-vector. But letting[8] $\sigma_{-S} \underset{\text{def}}{=} (\sigma_j)_{j \in N, j \notin S}$ be any vector of strategies chosen by the players not in S, one has $\sigma = (\sigma_S, \sigma_{-S})$ to designate the strategy profile prevailing when coalition S forms.

To characterize the behaviors *as a group* of the members of a coalition as well as the outcome of these joint behaviors, i.e. in order to relate the former — the strategies, to the latter — the payoffs, one may posit:

Assumption 4.5. Within any coalition S, the members choose their strategies so as to maximize the sum of their individual payoffs resulting from their joint actions.

Formally, the assumption consists in associating with any S the number

$$w(S; .) = \max_{\{\sigma_S \in \Sigma_S\}} \sum_{i \in S} v_i(\sigma_S; .). \tag{4.1}$$

The number $w(S; .)$ represents the highest aggregate payoffs that the coalition members can reach by choosing jointly their strategies. It will be called below the *worth* of the coalition.

---

[7] The expression $(\sigma_i)_{i \in S}$ is the s-dimensional vector ($s = |S|$) whose components are the strategies of the players members of coalition S.

[8] I do not use the notation $\sigma_{-S} = (\sigma_j)_{j \in N \setminus S}$ to avoid confusion by reading that $N \setminus S$ is a coalition, which will not be the case in the theory here under construction.

But the assumption and its formalization (4.1) require that four quite important remarks be made first:

(i) Referring to the sum of the payoffs of the coalition members implicitly contains the necessity that the units in which they are expressed be comparable. This puts a restriction on applications of the theory: what the values of the payoff functions represent must allow for such comparability. This point is elaborated upon in the next subsection.

(ii) To assume that only the sum is being maximized also implies that the members agree to divide among them in any way they please the total amount of the payoffs they achieve as a group. Thus, under Assumption 4.5, the behavior of a coalition is considered independently of what sharing arrangement of the total payoff among the members might prevail.

(iii) In order that the coalition's behavior be effectively treated as the one of the group, it is considered that the members operate under what is called "binding agreements" and act as a block. By definition, the analysis with coalitions excludes that some members might leave the group they are in for any reason.

(iv) Finally, and most importantly for our purposes in the rest of these lectures, the second part of the argument in the expression (4.1) has been left open, due to the fact that the behavior of the players not in S is unspecified. A specification is of course necessary for the payoffs u_i to be well defined in terms of a strategy profile $\sigma = (\sigma_S, \sigma_{-S})$ and not σ_S alone. The missing components are to be obtained from complementary assumptions made on the behavior of the players not in S. Several options can be considered, one of which will be presented in terms of individual behaviors stated in Definition 4.7, and then included in the way expression (4.1) appears in Definition 4.11. Some other options[9] are considered at the end of Section 4.4.

---

[9]Maschler, Solan and Zamir (2011, p. 661) explicitly exclude externalities *between coalitions* in their exposition of cooperative games, although they do not do so when dealing with individual players.

Transferable vs. non-transferable utility

The strategic games in which a behavioral assumption is made such as Assumption 4.5 in its additive form (4.1) are called *games with transferable utility*[10] (TU games, for short). This expression implies the comparability property of the individual payoffs mentioned in remark (i) above. Readers trained in welfare economics may have recognized in (4.1) a utilitarian additive social welfare function defined on the payoffs of the coalition members and their strategies.

If instead of summing up the payoffs into a scalar-valued expression as done in (4.1), only the s-dimensional vector of payoffs achieved by the members of S is taken into consideration, then the result of a coalition's behavior is expressed in a way that does not imply comparability of the individual payoffs. In this case Assumption 4.5 is to be reformulated in terms of vector maximization, in the sense of Kuhn and Tucker (1951). The games in which the worth of coalitions is so expressed in terms of vectors rather than scalars are called *games with non-transferable utility* (NTU games). With this formulation the comparability restriction of remark (i) is obviated.

Then, remarks (ii) and (iii) do not apply either, since alternative sharing arrangements on the outcome of the game are now reflected in the respective levels of the individual payoffs, thus in the vectors that characterize each S. By contrast, remark (iv) remains fully applicable, and to be dealt with shortly below as announced.[11]

The mathematical treatment of coalitions in the NTU form is understandably more complex than in the TU case, because of the multidimensional representation of each coalition's objective. For that reason, many more results are available in the literature on TU games, both in terms of the variety of solution concepts available as well as of knowledge of their properties.[12]

---

[10]Transferable *payoffs* would be more consistent with the idea at stake, but the terminology is of so general use that it is better to stick to it.

[11]In Lecture 9, I deal with some aspects of coalition *formation*, in the sense of why individual members might leave or stay in a coalition, that is, abandon or comply with their binding agreements — thus answering partly remark (iii).

[12]To my knowledge, the fullest treatment of NTU games is to be found in Peleg and Sudhölter (2007).

Apart from this mathematical interest, the distinction between TU and NTU has more or less importance depending upon which part of reality the game is supposed to handle, in other words, depending upon what the strategies and the payoffs are intended to represent in the real world. This brings in issues of conceptual nature that are genuine to the branch(es) of science that deal with that part of reality. In the case of the present lectures, these branches are social science and economics in particular. This is material for Lecture 5, where the needed economic concepts will be explicitly called upon.[13] In the present lecture, where the discourse is purely game theoretical, I do stick to "payoffs" (actually TU ones) and ignore the term "utility".[14]

Partially cooperative Nash equilibrium relative to a coalition

A third equilibrium concept, designed and introduced in the 1990s[15] for the purpose of dealing with games with externalities, is the following:

Definition 4.7. Given a coalition $S \subset N$, a **partially cooperative Nash equilibrium relative to** S (PCNE r.t. S) of the strategic game (N, Σ, v) is a strategy profile $\tilde{\sigma}^S = (\tilde{\sigma}_1^S, \ldots, \tilde{\sigma}_n^S)$ also denoted $\tilde{\sigma}^S = (\tilde{\sigma}_S^S, \tilde{\sigma}_{-S}^S)$ such that

$$(\tilde{\sigma}_i^S)_{i \in S} = \arg\max_{(\sigma_i^S) \in \Sigma_S} \sum_{i \in S} v_i(\sigma_S^S, \tilde{\sigma}_{-S}^S) \tag{4.2}$$

---

[13]Kornek, Lessman and Tulkens (2014) provide an introduction to the issues involved.

[14]Yet, future extensions to NTU games of the theoretical results presented in these lectures are much called for, less for the sake of mathematical generality than for economic reasons, an example of which appears in the application to climate change of Lecture 8.

[15]In the two companion papers by Chander and Tulkens (1995, 1997), under the slightly different terminology of *"partial agreement* Nash equilibrium (PANE) relative to a coalition". I feel that the expression I am introducing here with Definition 4.7 is more appropriate.

and

$$\forall j \in N, j \notin S, \quad \tilde{\sigma}_j^S = \underset{\sigma_j^S \in \Sigma_j}{\arg \max} \ v_j(\sigma_j^S, \tilde{\sigma}_{-j}^S). \tag{4.3}$$

The strategy profile so defined is the one that results from introducing in the strategic game (N, Σ, v) an additional behavioral assumption on coalitions, which reads:

Assumption 4.6. (called henceforth: **the γ-assumption**) — If some players form a coalition S and coordinate their actions to maximize their joint payoffs, then the other players remain acting in isolation, that is, they each choose the strategy that maximizes their individual payoff, given the strategies chosen by the coalition members and the remaining other players.

With this assumption, a behavior is specified for the non-members of S, as announced at the end of remark (iv) above. In formal terms, facing the set S, the individual players act as singletons $\{j\} \subset N \backslash S$. I now can meaningfully state:

Definition 4.8. For the strategic game (N, Σ, v) the **worth of a coalition** S is the number

$$w_S = \max_{\{\sigma_S \in \Sigma_S\}} \sum_{i \in S} v_i(\sigma_S; \tilde{\sigma}_{-S}^S), \tag{4.4}$$

where $\tilde{\sigma}_{-S}^S$ is defined as in (4.3) above.

If one considers singletons as coalitions of a single player, the PCNE r.t. S is nothing else, formally, than the Nash equilibrium of a game whose players are S and the family of singletons $\{\{j\} \subset N \backslash S\}$, thus in number equal to $1 + |N \backslash S|$. In a coalition formation perspective, starting from, say, a Nash equilibrium as an initial situation — which results from a partition of the all players set in n singletons —, one may see any PCNE r.t. some S as resulting from another partition, consisting of the collection of sets $[S \subset N, \{\{j\} \subset N \backslash S\}]$.

Can the concept of PCNE relative to a coalition S be considered as a "solution" of the game strategic game (N, Σ, v)? Yes, to the extent that it can serve to describe what happens when a coalition forms, both inside and outside of it. To make that description convincing, however, one should offer an argument such as e.g. stability of the coalition, to explain why coalition S stays formed, and why the other players stay isolated at their individual equilibrium.

Arguments asserting that coalitional stability of a PCNE can hold for any $S \subset N$ in the general strategic game (N, Σ, v) — call it "subcoalition stability" — cannot be found in the literature, to my knowledge. In the particular case of the global externality game of Lectures 5 and 6 the notion of subcoalition stability will be reexamined.

Finally, as it was the case with the Nash equilibrium of Definition 4.4, conditions of existence of a PCNE relative to a coalition S in the strategic game (N, Σ, v) have to be established. Given the analogy with the Nash equilibrium, this is done by using the same fixed point argument as mentioned above, after having noticed that the expression (4.1) of the worth of a coalition has, with respect to σ, the same continuity and concavity properties as the individual payoff function $v_i(\sigma)$. And as before, uniqueness of the PCNE relative to any S can be obtained from some stronger assumptions than Assumptions 4.1 and 4.2. Presenting the proofs of these properties will be of more interest when their effects will be seen in the applied GEG model of Lecture 5.

4.3 Coalitional functions and the cooperative game form

Coalitional functions in general

I now proceed to introduce a notion that may be seen as a natural complement for coalitions S to the individual payoff functions $v_i(\sigma)$. I do it in three stages. Consider first the following general mathematical object:

Definition 4.9. Given a finite set N, a **coalitional function** is a scalar valued function, denoted $w(.)$ that associates with every subset

$S \subseteq N$ a real number,

$$w(S) \in R, \tag{4.5}$$

with the convention that $w(\emptyset) = 0$.

As stated, $w(S)$ is a mapping from coalitions to values: the argument of the function is S, that is, a set (not a number as usual), the domain of the function is the set of subsets of N and the value is just a number.[16]

Next, consider momentarily a strategic game where there would be no externalities in the sense of Definition 4.1. For each set S of that game let the payoff be simply the mathematical object $w(S)$. One speaks of a *coalitional game* — also of a *cooperative game* — when its description only specifies such a coalitional function, without explicit reference to underlying strategies that would determine $w(S)$ for each S. In that setting, an alternative designation of a game is:

Definition 4.10. The **coalitional function form**, or **cooperative form**, of a game is the pair (N, w) where N is the set of players and w is a coalitional function.

Strategy profiles are not visible in the pair (N, w). Yet, when this pair is used with the purpose of dealing with properties of a strategic game (N, Σ, v), a connection must be made for each S, between the strategy set Σ_S and the coalitional function $w(S)$.[17] Turning now back to games with externalities, such a connection can be established with the expression (4.1) where the strategies of the players are made explicit, provided however that the strategy profile σ be fully specified. The gap in (4.1) can be filed up by referring to the profile $\tilde{\sigma}^S$ specified in Definition 4.7: there, the strategies of the non-members of S based on the γ-assumption are well defined

---

[16]Prior to 1987, a coalitional function was called a "characteristic function" in the main game theory literature.

[17]Without connection with some strategic form, game theoretic developments on the sole coalitional function run the risk to be reduced to sheer mathematical exercises on the properties of the function, without throwing any light on the actions involved. This plagues some of the literature on coalitional stability of the global externality game that I shall cover in Lecture 9.

by (4.3), — namely $(\tilde{\sigma}_j^S)_{j\in N, j\notin S}$. This leads one now to specify the coalitional function that follows.

The γ-coalitional function

Definition 4.11. The γ-**coalitional function** derived from the strategic game (N, Σ, v) is the function $w^\gamma(S)$ that associates with every coalition $S \subseteq N$ the real number

$$w^\gamma(S) = \sum_{i\in S} v_i(\tilde{\sigma}^S) \quad \text{if } S \subset N, \tag{4.6}$$

$$= \sum_{i\in N} v_i(\sigma^*) \quad \text{if } S = N, \tag{4.7}$$

where if $S \subset N$, $\tilde{\sigma}^S \in \Sigma$ is the PCNE r.t. S of $(4.2) - (4.3)$

and if $S = N, \sigma^* = \arg\max_{\sigma\in\Sigma} \sum_{i\in N} v_i(\sigma)$.

The superscript "γ" is attached to the functional symbol w to remind one that the function rests on the "γ-assumption" 4.6 stated above. Notice that the uniqueness (assumed above) of the PCNE r.t. S ensures that this function is well defined.

4.4 Cores and other solution concepts for cooperative games with externalities

The Nash equilibrium and its variant covered up to now are solution concepts that rest on the assumption of exclusively individual behaviors. Therefore, one speaks of a "non-cooperative" form for the games that use these concepts. By contrast when the assumption is added that coalitions can form and are part of the analysis, one deals with a "cooperative" form of the game. In this case, coalitions become an additional component of the "mathematical object", and their presence triggers imaginations so that other solution concepts emerge, of which the PCNE r.t. S is one example. The concept of "core of a game" is another one, probably the most famous. It will occupy a central place in what follows. After its presentation I briefly evoke a few other ones. Prior to that, the following notion is needed, to serve as a framework for the developments to come.

Imputations

In a sense, a core solution of a game is the extreme opposite of the Nash equilibrium solution. While the latter is individualistic, the former is an expression of cooperation between the players. What it does is to identify, for the highest possible level of aggregate payoffs, a sharing scheme of that aggregate among *all* the players of the game, which has interesting properties in terms of cohesion of the cooperating players. If the game is in strategic form, the core solution also identifies the strategy profile that provides the highest aggregate payoffs.

This is formalized by the following notion:

Definition 4.12. For games in coalitional function form (N, w^{γ}) as well as for strategic games (N, Σ, v) in their coalitional function form, an **imputation** specifies for each player $i \in N$ his part in the total maximal payoff that they can achieve by acting together as a single coalition.

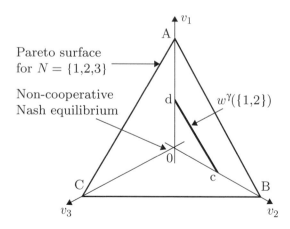

Fig. 4.1 The imputations set and a coalition's worth.

Formally, an imputation[18] is a vector of payoffs $v^* = (v_1^*, \ldots, v_n^*) \in R_+^n$ such that $\sum_{i \in N} v_i^* = w^\gamma(N)$ as defined in (4.7).

There are of course many ways to share the total payoff $w^\gamma(N)$. The set of imputations is thus in some sense the menu from which to choose an outcome of the game among the many efficient ones, when an additional property is sought for. This is well described in Fig. 4.1 where the axes are those of the payoffs of a three players game. The origin is conventionally set at the payoff levels of the payers at the NCNE. Within the positive orthant of that space, the coordinates of every point belonging to the triangular surface ABC, are a vector that satisfies the definition of an imputation. This surface, the set of imputations of the game also called the Pareto surface, is precisely the "menu" from which to select for the game some solution that might have "interesting" properties.

Various criteria are offered by game theory to select within that menu. For instance, taking a coalition formation point of view, of particular interest would be those imputations that ensure cohesion *within* N, in other words, stability of the grand coalition of this 3 players game. I focus on that criterion hereafter and in most of the rest of these lectures, but evoke nevertheless a few alternatives below.

The γ-core solution

To make precise the idea of "coalitional stability" of an imputation, take some imputation $v^* = (v_1^*, \ldots, v_n^*)$ and consider some coalition $S \subseteq N$ and its worth $w^\gamma(S)$. In the three players game of Fig. 4.1, just as the imputations surface ABC represents the worth $w^\gamma(N)$ of coalition $N = \{1, 2, 3\}$, the worth $w^\gamma(S)$ of coalition $S = \{1, 2\}$ is represented by the payoff possibility line labeled dc.

---

[18] For readers of Myerson (1991), let me save them time by mentioning that what I call here an imputation, using the classical terminology of Aumann, is the same as what he calls an "allocation" (meaning implicitly an allocation of the jointly achieved payoff among the members of the grand coalition).

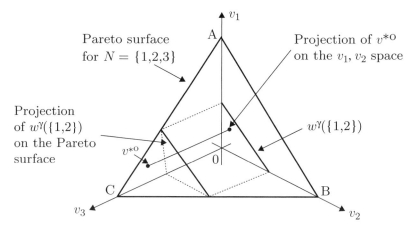

Fig. 4.2   An imputation unacceptable for (or blocked or dominated by) the members of coalition {1,2}.

Suppose now that some imputation vector, say v^{*o}, is so specified that the payoffs of the members of S at v^{*o}, that is, $(v_i^{*o})_{i \in S}$, are such that the inequality $\sum_{i \in S} (v_i^{*o}) < w^\gamma(S)$ holds. Then v^{*o} assigns to the members of S payoffs that add up to *less* than what these players can obtain by themselves as revealed by the worth $w^\gamma(S)$. This is visualized in Fig. 4.2 where the point v^{*o} on the Pareto surface, an imputation, is projected on the (v_1, v_2) space, and the projection appears to lie *below* the payoff possibility line of coalition $S = \{1, 2\}$ which represents the value of $w^\gamma(S)$. For the members of S, the imputation v^{*o} is then unacceptable,[19] as well as the strategy profile whereby it has been generated implicitly or explicitly. As a result, for these players it is not coalitionally rational to accept v^{*o}

---

[19]The terminology in the field has evolved considerably over the years to designate this situation. Unacceptability as mentioned here was originally, i.e. in the early core theoretic literature, said to induce a "blocking" behavior against an imputation such as v^{*o}. Shapley (1973) rightly suggested to substitute the expression that v^{*o} "[can be] improved upon". More, recently Maschler, Solan and Zamir (2011, p. 687) propose to say that v^{*o} is "coalitionally (ir-)rational". Aumann's argument on "domination", mentioned in the concluding section, convinces me that this term is the best suited to the specific context where I intend to use the core concept. The unacceptability I am referring to here thus means "being dominated".

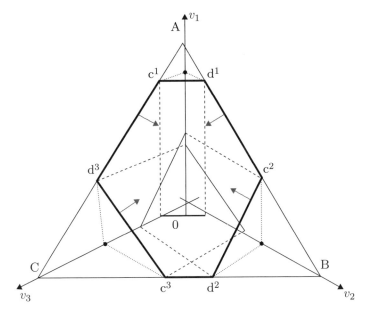

Fig. 4.3   The γ-core (area $c^1d^1c^2d^2c^3d^3$): the "anchored" case.

as an outcome of the game. And the all players coalition N to which the proposal is addressed, cannot be maintained. But can another imputation be found that does not trigger such a reaction from $\{1,2\}$?

The gist of a core solution is precisely the identification of imputations by now denoted v^{**}, that are immune of such reaction on the part of *any* coalition S. This is expressed as follows.

Definition 4.13.   The γ-**core of the coalitional game** (N, w^γ) is the set of imputations of the game which, for all coalitions $S \subset N$, assign to their members aggregate payoffs that dominate the worth of those coalitions.

Formally, the γ-core of the game is the set of imputations $v^{**} = (v_1^{**}, \ldots, v_n^{**}) \in R_+^n$ such that

$$\forall \, S \subset N, \quad \sum_{i \in S} v_i^{**} > w^\gamma(S). \tag{4.8}$$

In Fig. 4.3, the γ-core of the game (N, w^γ) appears as the set of points making up the area $c^1d^1c^2d^2c^3d^3$: all of them dominate whatever the three possible coalitions $\{1,2\},\{1,3\}$, or $\{2,3\}$ can achieve by themselves. Small arrows point to the area of undominated imputations. In other terms, the introduction of the coalitional rationality criterion amounts to chop off from the set of imputations the outcomes Ac^1d^1, Bc^2d^2 and Cc^3d^3 in spite of them being efficient.

In the above terms, the γ-core concept is formulated for a game in coalitional function form, the solution being presented as a vector in the payoffs space. However, as already mentioned, if the game is specified in the strategic form (N,Σ,v), to any imputation v^{**} having the γ-core property stated in Definition 4.13 there necessarily corresponds some profile σ_N in the space of joint strategies of all players. When use is made of the γ-core concept as a solution of any game in strategic form, that correspondence is the necessary vehicle through which game theoretic results can percolate in the reality for which game theory is called upon. This is precisely what I am heading to in Lectures 5 and 6.

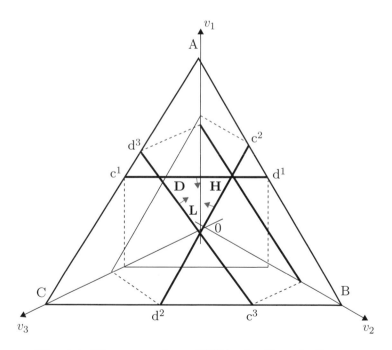

Fig. 4.4   The γ-core (area DHL): the "interior" case.

Figure 4.3 is just an example, however. Indeed the γ-core may have other shapes, such as the area DHL in Fig. 4.3, for instance, due to alternative characteristics of the coalitional function $w^\gamma(S)$: here, stronger coalitional powers are at play,[20] the strength of each coalition being visualized by the distance from the origin of the coalition's line that measures its worth.

With coalitional powers still stronger than those in Figs. 4.3 and 4.4 as measured by $w^\gamma(S)$ for each S, the intersection between the areas delimited by the three thick payoff possibility lines Ad^3c^3B, Ac^2d^2C, d^3ABc^3 may be empty, as in Fig. 4.5. In this case the game has no γ-core. Thus, as was the case for the Nash equilibrium, a γ-core solution may not exist in many games.

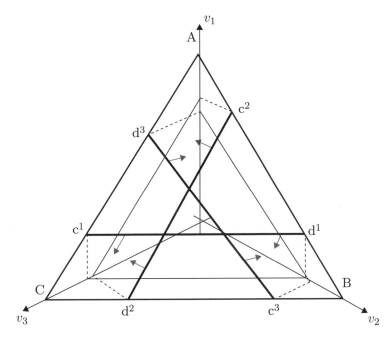

Fig. 4.5 A coalitional game for which the γ-core is empty.

---

[20]With the terminology of "anchored" and "interior" cores used in Fig. 4.4, I am following Gilles (2010).

However, for coalitional games *without externalities* it has been discovered in the 1960s that a property called balancedness of the game — actually, a property of the coalitional function and of the strategy sets, if any — is a necessary and sufficient condition for the core to be non-empty. The result holds for both TU and NTU games. Whether that property can play the same role in the environmental application of Lecture 5, *in spite of the externalities*, and thereby make the γ-core concept useful for dealing with the issues raised at the end of Lecture 3, is the main topic of Lecture 5.

As to uniqueness of the γ-core solution, there is no such property to be expected under Assumptions 4.1 and 4.2: at that level of generality, the core is rarely a one point solution concept.[21]

Alternative coalitional functions and cores

Other behavioral assumptions than the γ Assumption 4.6 have been proposed on which to build alternative coalitional functions in games with externalities. I present here the following two, if only because of their illustrious origin. They were indeed proposed by Von Neumann and Morgenstern (1944) and elaborated upon in the terms discussed by Aumann (1961, Sections 8–9).

On the one hand, there is the α-**coalitional function**, based on the assumption that the players outside the coalition S adopt the strategies that are least favorable to the coalition. In that case, S moves first and chooses the best strategy for itself, knowing what are the strategies accessible to the complement of S in N and assuming that this complement would choose the strategy which is worst for S. Formally, the function reads

$$w^{\alpha}(S) = \max_{\{\sigma_S \in \Sigma_S\}} \min_{\{\sigma_{N \setminus S} \in \Sigma_{N \setminus S}\}} \sum_{i \in S} v_i(\sigma_S, \sigma_{N \setminus S}). \quad (4.9)$$

The value $w^{\alpha}(S)$ thus represents the highest payoff that coalition S can guarantee itself no matter what strategies are adopted by the players outside the coalition.

---

[21] In Lecture 6, I refer to some cases of interest, one of which is a voting game on environmental policies.

On the other hand, the β-**coalitional function** is based on the assumption that to every strategy chosen by the players outside the coalition S, the players in S can react and choose their best strategy, given the one chosen by $N\backslash S$. Thus, if $N\backslash S$ moves first (as a coalition) and chooses the worst for S, and then S chooses the best for itself. In this way coalition S guarantees itself the highest payoff that it can be held down to by $N\backslash S$. Formally, this leads one to specify the function as

$$w^\beta(S) = \min_{\{\sigma_{N\backslash S}\in\Sigma_{N\backslash S}\}} \max_{\{\sigma_S\in\Sigma_S\}} \sum_{i\in S} v_i(\sigma_S, \sigma_{N\backslash S}). \qquad (4.10)$$

Thus, parallel to the γ-coalitional function from which the γ-core was derived, the α-coalitional function and the β-coalitional function allow one to derive, respectively, the α-core and the β-core of the coalitional games (N, w^α) and (N, w^β), respectively.

The assumed behaviors of the players who are non-members of a coalition, in each form (4.6), (4.9) or (4.10) of the coalitional function, are different forms of threat on their part *vis-à-vis* the coalition. The effectiveness of each threat materializes in its effect, when it is exerted, on the level reached by the value of the coalitional function $w(S)$. Under the α-assumption, the threat is in some sense maximal and it is less so under the β-assumption. But in both cases the assumed behavior is aggressive *vis-à-vis* S, without any obvious reason. Therefore, these two alternative concepts will not be further developed in these lectures. By contrast, the γ-assumption might be called one of "reasonable"[22] behavior in the sense of its maximal neutrality with respect to S. In the environmental game of the next lecture it does find a natural application.

Finally, a coalition $S \subset N$ considered together with the family of singletons $\{\{j\} \subset N\backslash S\}$ constitutes a partition of the set N, called a "coalition structure". Recalling that there are many other partitions conceivable of a set, the γ-assumption 4.6 amounts to assume that when S forms, the all players set fragments itself into *this* particular

---

[22]As originally formulated on p. 13 of the 1994 version of Chander and Tulkens (1997).

partition. Why this one — let me call it the γ-coalitional structure — and not another one? Beyond the justifying arguments put forward above, no general theory of coalition formation can be called upon currently to propose a more satisfactory answer. I can only refer to a very recent and remarkable step forward in research on that topic made by Bloch and van den Nouweland (2014), under the heading of "partition function games". It allows one to characterize the γ-core solution concept in a wide but abstract framework whose exploration in these pages would take us too far afield.

Alternative solution concepts

Several other solution concepts than the core are offered by the cooperative games literature. The main ones are called Shapley value, bargaining set, kernel, nucleolus, as well as Von Neumann and Morgenstern stable set. Each one of these concepts rests on alternative criteria for selecting outcomes within the imputations set, criteria that are different than the "blocking" one used above for the core. All these concepts are covered in detail in Osborne and Rubinstein (1994) as well as in Maschler, Solan and Zamir (2011). However, they have not been formulated for games with externalities: when these authors reach the cooperative game sections of their texts, including sections on the core, they all formulate games in coalitional function forms that ignore the possibility of externalities between coalitions,[23] as well as externalities between players when the strategic form is used.[24] To my knowledge, no extension similar to the one performed here above for the core of games with externalities is done for any of the five alternative solution

---

[23]See Maschler, Solan and Zamir (2011 p. 661). Yet, for individual players these authors assume payoff functions with externalities (p. 77, last lines).

[24]In Osborne and Rubinstein (1994) "markets with transferable payoffs" (pp. 263–264) and "exchange economies" (pp. 269–271) are the only economic models with which these authors associate a cooperative game in strategic form. In either case it is of course natural that externalities be excluded, and they mention that explicitly for coalitions on p. 264 and for individual players on p. 271. That restriction also applies to all the non-core solution concepts they deal with.

concepts just mentioned. Yet, two interesting steps in that direction are accomplished in that direction: first by van Steenberghe (2003 Section 4 and 2004) who uses the γ-coalitional function to define a γ-Shapley value and a γ-nucleolus for the particular environmental game of Lecture 7 — a contribution to which I shall return in that lecture. Second by Rogna (2016) who exploits the fact that the nucleolus always belongs to the core and hence proposes to use it as a selection within the γ-core motivated by Rawlsian considerations of justice.

4.5 Virtues of the core solution

"An outcome x of a game *dominates* another outcome y if there is a coalition S that can achieve x by its own efforts, each of whose members prefers x to y. The *core* of the game is the set of all undominated outcomes" (Aumann, 1985, p. 24).

On cores of games without externalities

Among the various solution concepts offered by cooperative game theory, the core occupies a prominent position. Various reasons for that are stated in that same paper of Aumann's, but for the audience these lectures are addressed to, I like to retain the following: "Intuitively, it is perhaps the clearest and most transparent concept in the theory of games" (p. 28). From my experience as an economist, exposed to game theory while not being a game theorist myself, I fully share this view and the content of these lectures obviously reflects this opinion. The first of the above quotations, although not really a definition, summarizes excellently the concept: with the term "domination" it is suggested that a core solution in some sense imposes itself over any other.[25]

---

[25] I am tempted to add the property of "self enforcement", an expression which is intuitively appealing although not received as a concept in general game theory textbooks (it never appears in their index). As it is much invoked in the game theoretically inspired literature on international agreements, I discuss that notion in Lecture 9.

More specifically, the core solution has the property of efficiency, and it specifies how to share the so achieved common gain. This sharing has the property of individual rationality[26] as well as of coalitional rationality,[27] as mentioned with Definition 4.13. Stability against deviations, be they individual or groupwise, is also sometimes invoked.

On γ-cores for games with externalities

Yet, the global externality phenomenon that motivated my recourse to game theory over the years since 1990 did meet with the stumbling block that the prevailing cooperative game theory literature of that time was ignoring externalities[28] — except for the early paper by Shapley and Shubik 1969.[29] An extension was thus necessary, and discussions with Parkash Chander in Stockholm in 1993 under the intellectual stimulus of Karl Göran Mäler,[30] led us to the formulation of the "γ-approach" for this class of games. Leaving modesty aside, we had to innovate, and that was it.

In defense of the γ-coalitional function and the γ-core derived from it, let me criticize here a misleading view of the γ-assumption. The presence of singletons in presentations of the approach is often made in terms that consider them as the result of a "disintegration" of the subset $N \backslash S$ of the remaining players in the face of a coalition S. This view is almost always inspired by thinking of the coalition aiming at *blocking an imputation*. In that perspective, the question

---

[26]This is sometimes called "profitability" or "win–win", *vis-à-vis* the *status quo*.
[27]Also called "strategic stability".
[28]In a private conversation during a visit in Jerusalem in 1975, Michael Maschler has warned me that going in that direction was one of the hardest research tracks he could think of. A prudence confirmed in the ignorance of the externality phenomenon in the Maschler, Solan and Zamir (2011) treatise.
[29]To be discussed in Section 5.1 and Annex 1 of Lecture 5.
[30]I personally was looking for a way to overcome Mäler's assertion in his 1989 paper that cooperative game theory concepts are not bringing sharper results than Pareto optimality, because of the property of extreme aggressivity of the α-coalitional function, as evoked above. By reducing the power of coalitions, the α-core may end up not being even a proper subset of the imputations set. I come back to that point in the framework of the applied GEG in Lectures 5 and 6.

is indeed fairly naturally raised of why the complement $N \backslash S$ *should* disintegrate in singletons. But such view need not be held to, because it is in fact a partial one, linked with a specific behavior in a particular circumstance, namely the one of facing an imputation.

A wider view can be suggested, in the spirit of coalition formation. More precisely, and independently of any proposed imputation, one may instead consider an initial state of the game where the players are just a collection of singletons, thus at the NCNE. Given this datum, considering the formation of any coalition S with letting the other players remain singletons is just assuming that these stay as they are. No disintegration is taking place. The γ-core theory then explores the properties of a game where this particular coalition structure emerges upon the formation of any coalition S. In this perspective, the important concept is the one of PCNE r.t. a coalition, applicable to any coalition. The possible non-emptiness of the γ-core means that with the γ-coalitional structure holding for every S, the emergence of an efficient and coalitionally rational strategy profile is likely because it is justified by the fact that it dominates all other profiles possibly emanating from so structured coalitions. *The blocking idea, absent from this argument, is simply not necessary* for a γ-core solution to make sense.

This point will be further and fully developed, including proofs of non-emptiness of the γ-core, when applied to a basic environmental game to be constructed in the following lecture.

Lecture 5

THE GLOBAL EXTERNALITY GAME I: ITS γ-CORE

The purpose and the message

With this lecture the purpose is to establish the second link of the interdisciplinary chain described at the outset, namely the link between economics and game theory. The exposition gradually wraps the economic reality of the multilateral externality problem of Lecture 3 into the mold of the game theory concepts covered in Lecture 4. These concepts will now be handled with full technical details.

The message is spread over this lecture and the next. Presently, it consists in constructing a game, dubbed GEG, associated with the economic-ecological model, in showing that the concepts of non-cooperative Nash equilibrium, partially cooperative Nash equilibrium relative to a coalition, and γ-coalitional function can meaningfully be applied to this game so as to achieve the objectives of environmental effectiveness, economic Pareto efficiency and γ-core coalitional stability. The presentation is in general terms and therefore somewhat abstract. Lecture 6 pursues with a development that allows for policy decisions implementing the objectives.

Plan

Introducing the global externality game (GEG)

Equilibrium concepts in the GEG

The efficient outcomes of the GEG

The γ-core of the GEG:
definition and existence in a qualitative sense

Annexes:

1. The "lake game" of Shapley and Shubik as a GEG
2. The "prisoners' dilemma" and international environmental externalities
3. The γ-coalitional function of the GEG is not superadditive
4. A crucial step in Helm's balancedness proof

Lecture 5

The Global Externality Game I: Its γ-core

5.1 Introducing the global externality game

The particular kind of game presented in this lecture has become a fairly standard tool in the analyses of international environmental problems. However, it is often formulated in different ways, with sometimes inappropriate vocabulary and varying notation. The presentation that follows of the "global externality game"[1] (GEG) is intended to become a standard one, similar to the standards that "market games" or "voting games" have become in other applications of game theory in social science.

Associating games with economic models

The idea of considering economies in terms of games — below, I shall say "associating games to economies" — originates in one of the last chapters (the 64th) of Von Neumann and Morgenstern (1944). After several papers by Shapley and Shubik in the 1960s where market exchanges are considered as strategies in some game in strategic form,[2] and competitive market equilibrium (an economic concept) is put in relation with the core (a game theory concept[3]), a considerable flow of intellectual production has been generated by this idea. Extensions beyond competitive equilibrium have flourished in many directions of economics, such as imperfectly competitive markets,

---

[1] "Jeu avec externalité globale" me semble être la meilleure expression en français.
[2] Called "normal" form at the time.
[3] The core concept had been introduced in game theory by Gillies in 1953 but the idea of an outcome of exchanges that no subset of traders can improve upon for its members was in fact first formulated by the economic theorist Edgeworth in 1881.

131

production economies, and economies with public goods. Sharp results have been obtained.[4] Although economies with externalities were not left behind as attested by the antecedents mentioned hereafter, the outcome in terms of model formulations and results is somewhat mixed for these economies, as my review will show. Yet, for the specific form of diffused externalities, the formulation proposed below may claim for some generality, given the results it leads to.

Formulation of the Global Externality Game (GEG)

Following the Ariadne's thread constituted by the reference economic-ecological model, I combined in Lectures 2 and 3 ecological science with economics. Here, I wish to extend the chain from economics to game theory.

This task is fairly simple. Starting from the general definition given in Lecture 4, a game becomes a GEG in the sense of these lectures by establishing precise links between the components of the game and those of the economic-ecological model. This I call "associating" a game with the model, and it is done here as follows.

Recall equations (2.7)–(2.12), whereby our model describes the economic-ecological system of the n countries of the world. It consists of, for each country $i \in N$:

- the consumer-citizens' aggregate utilities:

$$u_i = x_i - d_i(z), \qquad (5.1)$$

- the variables x_i, y_i and e_i of consumption, production and pollutant emissions, respectively, as well as z, the prevailing amount of ambient pollutant in the world.

---

[4]For example, confirmation of the Edgeworth conjecture on large markets, characterization of Nash–Cournot oligopolistic equilibrium, strategic stability properties of the Lindahl equilibrium with public goods, as well as the non-extension of the Edgeworth conjecture for economies with public goods.

These are subject to:

- the domestic feasibility constraints

$$x_i = y_i = g_i(e_i), \tag{5.2}$$

- the scarcity constraint at the world level

$$\sum_{i \in N} x_i = \sum_{i \in N} y_i, \tag{5.3}$$

- the ecological constraint of the ecosystem, called transfer function in Lecture 1:

$$z = \sum_{i \in N} e_i. \tag{5.4}$$

Substituting now (5.2) and (5.4) in (5.1) one gets for the countries' utilities the new expression

$$v_i(e) = g_i(e_i) - d_i \left(\sum_{j \in N} e_j \right). \tag{5.5}$$

This reduces the model (5.1)–(5.4) into the form (5.5) where the only independent variables are the emissions e_i, all the other variables being determined once the e_i's are specified.

Next, consider the triplet (N, E, v) where:

(i) N, the set of players, corresponds to the set of n countries of the world, indexed $i = 1, \dots, n$,

(ii) $E = \{e \in R^n_+ | e \in E_1 \times \cdots \times E_i \times \cdots \times E_n\}$, the set of joint strategies, where for each $i = 1, \dots, n$ $E_i = \{e_i : 0 \le e_i \le e^\circ\}$ is the set of country i's possible emissions e_i, within an upper bound e°, and E corresponds to the set of simultaneous such possible emission decisions by all countries i, and

(iii) $v = (v_1, \dots, v_n)$, a vector of payoff functions where for each $i = 1, \dots, n$, $v_i = v_i(e)$ is specified as in (5.5), and corresponds to the utility function (5.1) of country i.

This leads one to state:

Definition 5.1. The **GEG** in strategic form is the triplet (N, E, v) whose elements are specified by (i)–(iii) above.

Clearly, the triplet (i)–(iii) is the same object as the model specified by (5.1)–(5.4). In other words, an abstract object — the game — is thus "associated" with the description of reality aimed at by the economic-ecological model.

The game so formulated[5] is in *strategic* form. Further down below the same game is presented in *coalitional* form. An *extensive* form of the GEG would essentially require a specification of the process through which the players explore their strategy sets and each of them eventually chooses the emission strategy e_i that prevails at the solution. I do not deal with this last aspect, except for some remarks I shall have to make in Lecture 10, relating the extensive form with the formulation of the so-called NDCs in the UNFCCC process.

Because plugging (5.4) in (5.1) results in payoff functions (5.5) with $e = (e_1, \ldots, e_n)$ as argument, the game is one with externalities of the "diffuse" type according to the terminology of Lecture 1. Seen from the point of view of the decisions taken by all players in the game, the vector e is a strategy profile of the game (N, E, v) in the sense of the general Definition 4.2.

The game is also a "global" one for two reasons: on the one hand, by their physical nature, these externalities affect all countries in the world, hence all players; on the other hand, the number of players is fixed: no player can "leave game". That leaving the game is not

---

[5]A similar exercise can be performed with the c+d model of Section 2.4, where the players set is as in (i), the strategies are "abatement", i.e. emissions reduction from some exogenously given level, and the payoff of each player-country i is, instead of (iii), the total cost $J_i = c_i + d_i$ of emissions reduction c_i and endured damages d_i. This model becomes a "cost game" of the kind found in Maschler, Solan and Zamir (2011, Chapter 16, p. 661 and ff.). Many of the game theoretic analyzes and results presented here below could be transposed to this alternative partial equilibrium framework, but their economic interest (and relevance for use in integrated assessment models as in Lecture 8) would be more limited due to the restricted character of this modeling of the economy, compared with the general equilibrium spirit of the economic-ecological model handled here.

an option for the players defines the qualifier "global" that I attach now[6] to the externality game under study.

As an important note on the practice of interdisciplinary research, let me call the attention to the fact that "associating a game with an economic model" is a method that Aumann (1987) credits to Von Neumann and Morgenstern and that I follow literally.[7] Osborne and Rubinstein (1994) present a coalitional game associated with an exchange economy (p. 271) in terms quite similar — *mutatis mutandis* — to those I use above for the GEG. This view is also adopted in Maschler, Solan and Zamir (2013, pp. 704–705) albeit with a slightly different terminology: they "derive" a game from a market while here above, following Aumann's word in an oral presentation heard at Core, I "associate" the game with the economic model.

Antecedents: Select literature on games with environmental externalities prior to 2001

To my knowledge, the earliest paper introducing game theoretic arguments in an economic analysis involving externalities is Davis and Whinston (1962). The externality considered is between the activities of two firms, the solution concept is the Nash equilibrium, contrasted with the outcome of joint profit maximizing after merger. The economic model is one of a duopoly where the cost function of each agent is influenced by the output of the other. Apparently not an environmental topic, but later developments of the field have

---

[6]Thus, I now substitute "global" for the expression of "environmental" game used in Chander and Tulkens (1995, 1997). The former terminology was correctly conveying the diffuse character of the externality being dealt with, but not the possibility of a fixed number of players. The present emphasis on climate change, where the fixed number of players-countries is unavoidable, justifies the change in terminology.

[7]On p. 64, Aumann pursues with the words: "... This is to be distinguished from the more usual methodology of economics and other social sciences, where the building of a formal model and a solution concept, and the application of the solution concept to the model, are all rolled into one". An implicit advice of not doing so?

made appear close connections between formal oligopoly models and the typical environmental game.[8]

Shapley and Shubik (1969b) offered, in Section III (second part) of a very densely written paper, the first game theoretic analysis that deals exactly with the problem of central concern in these lectures. The compactness of the economics, the parsimony of the modeling, and the absence of proofs may explain that the important results of that text remained out of reach of the attention of economists, even theoretically minded, who were at that time an emerging group of "environmental economists". With the equipment of the conceptual and analytical framework described in the following pages, one can better see now that this contribution is a seminal one, whose importance justifies here a special treatment of its own. Annex 1 to this lecture is devoted to it,[9] but it will be better appreciated after mastery of the γ-core concept presented in Lectures 5 and 6.

Scarf (1971) examines the alternative concepts of α- and β-cores of a game with externalities. These are directional, and not diffuse as in the GEG. He obtains existence for the former, but not for the latter. Later however Laffont (1977, p. 100), dealing with an externality model of the diffuse type, asserts that the α- and β-cores coincide if in that game, for any coalition S there exists a strategy uniformly worst for all members of S. As this is applicable to the GEG, the distinction between α- and β-cores is not of direct use for my purpose. But as seen towards the end of Lecture 4, there is an interest in discussing the difference of assumptions made in either case on the behavior of the complement of a coalition to better understand the relevance of the γ-assumption.

---

[8]In particular in the controversy on the stability of coalitions. See more on this in Lecture 9.

[9]While I focus on the "Lake game", because it fits well the climatic problem of my concern in these lectures, the 1969b article deals with quite many other forms of externalities. The authors show that for each of them the game theoretic results vary considerably. This illustrates the point on which Lectures 1 and 2 and 5 rest: the specifics of each alternative underlying economic-ecological model determine what game theory has to say on externalities.

Connolly (1972) claims a "core" solution in an analysis of trade in international public goods. However, it is hardly more than a Pareto efficient one in a game with two players. Moreover, the focus on tradability of public goods exported by one country makes this trade model inappropriate for dealing multicountry negotiations. Here, the title promises more than what the paper delivers.

In 1979, Dasgupta and Heal devote a brief section of their book (pp. 13–17) to coalitions and to the role they might play in determining states of an economic system with externalities. They are concerned by states that "can be regarded as *viable*", that is, states "that no coalition can reject". The argument used for rejection by a coalition is one that they call "upsetting", they contrast it with "blocking" in its α-core version[10] and they derive some characterizations of a series of "viable" (or equilibrium) states implied by these notions. However, both of them eschew an essential component of externalities when coalitions are considered, namely the reaction of the non-members of a coalition: upsetting assumes there is none, while the α-coalitional function assumes the worst.[11] Between these extremes, the γ-assumption presented in Lecture 4 and further commented in Lecture 6 appears to introduce a behavioral consideration that was missing at that time.

In a further book, Dasgupta (1982) challenges (pp. 23–24) the often repeated assertion that the famous prisoners' dilemma game is a good representation of the coordination problem posed by international environmental externalities. His point is that while the essence of the game[12] is that the players have access to a *dominant* strategy, this need not be the case with the standard and basic environmental economic model, so that the game corresponds to an extreme, excessively restrictive, description of the source of

---

[10]Remember in Lecture 4 the alternative coalitional functions subsection in Section 4.4.

[11]A disputable combination of these two assumptions leads to an attractive but equally disputable diagram 2.1 of theirs, p. 16.

[12]According to the original formulation, to be found in Luce and Raiffa (1957, pp. 94–102) and is credited to the mathematician A.T. Tucker.

non-cooperative equilibrium in international environmental economic affairs. I elaborate on this point in Annex 2 to this lecture[13] and justify there my henceforth ignoring of the prisoners' dilemma in the rest of this text.

Mäler (1989) introduces the very convenient $c + d$ model that I presented at the end of Lecture 2, precisely with a game theoretical intention. In that paper, the externality is of the directional type, and the analysis bears on non-cooperative equilibrium as well as cooperative solution concepts, with essentially negative results for the latter, due to limiting the enquiry to the α-core. However, at the occasion of putting the Mäler model in a numerical setting, Kaitala, Mäler and Tulkens (1995) present an algorithm to compute an efficient solution, which the authors interpret as a negotiation process towards the optimum. Here, cooperative game considerations do appear, but only in a "local" sense, that is, in games formulated at each step of the algorithm along the path that converges to the efficient outcome. From one step to the next one, the progress of the negotiation is determined by the core of an appropriately defined "local" game. Initially, this notion of coalitional stability had been proposed in Chander and Tulkens (1991/2002, 1992a, 1992b).

Moving from "local" to "global" games, Chander and Tulkens produced in 1994 and published in 1995 and 1997 the version[14] of the GEG in which they introduced the γ-core solution concept, presented now in Lectures 4–6. Parallel to that, Barrett (1994) and Carraro and Siniscalco (1992) introduced an alternative coalitional stability concept inspired from oligopoly theory. I devote to it Lecture 9 hereafter.

Cornes and Sandler (1996), in the second edition of a revised and much enlarged first edition of a book *The theory of externalities, public goods and club goods* published in 1986, entitle their entire

---

chapter 9 "Game theory and public goods". Their presentation is rather encyclopedic, with one section (9.1) on "Cooperative provision of public goods" and the following five ones devoted to non-cooperative models.[15] The chapter contains a quite extended discussion of the prisoners' dilemma game.

Regretfully, my lectures take little inspiration from this otherwise remarkable synthesis on the subject matter of its title, for four reasons. A first one is that the notion of "environment" is totally absent from the book: it is therefore missing a major field of application of the theories of externalities and public goods. Second, the text is characterized by skepticism *vis-à-vis* cooperative game concepts in general and the core concept in particular (p. 305). I am afraid this is because it does not clearly distinguish between public goods and externalities.[16] A key factor in this fuzziness is the ignorance of the possibility of a public good being produced by *several* producers. In my opinion it is this apparently minor modification[17] to the standard theory of public goods (which always assumes a *single* producer), together with its connection with the theory of externalities, which opens the way, by means of the GEG, to all the by now presumably clear game theoretic developments offered in the following pages. Third, that same ignorance also prevents the authors from dealing with international aspects of environmental externalities, which are totally absent of the book, including the coalitional stability developments of the early 1990s mentioned above. Fourth, the phenomenon of stock externalities is unfortunately not covered and not even mentioned throughout the book, with the result of no dynamics.[18]

---

[15]Except for a part of Section 9.4 (pp. 320–321) which briefly evokes a literature on information games associated with decision processes aiming at achieving cooperative optimality with public goods.

[16]There is no parallel separate chapter on "game theory and externalities".

[17]Introduced in the model of Tulkens (1979).

[18]The related topic of intergenerational externalities is well approached, but unfortunately buried in a development of the theory of clubs, which is of little relevance for my current concern with the physically *global* externalities of climate change. On the disputable recourse by Nordhaus (2015) to a non-standard form

This critique of mine may be qualified by acknowledging a difference of purpose: Cornes and Sandler (1996) aim at surveying the whole field designated by the title of their book, essentially at the theoretical level. The applications they consider are only occasional illustrative examples. In my present work, the application to international environmental negotiations is central. This brings me to sometimes extend the existing theory of externalities and public goods on points that can be overlooked when the purpose is a more general one.

Hanley and Folmer (1998) is the first collective book devoted to the topic "game theory and the environment". Interestingly, 14 out of the 17 papers assembled deal with international environmental problems. The subfield of international issues thus appears to be *the* area of applied externality theory most in search of concepts and techniques that prevailing economic theory cannot provide. It also questions most directly game theory, static as well as dynamic, on its ability — or inability — to handle externality problems in a decision and policy making spirit. In this book, the distinction between non-cooperative and cooperative approaches dominates the way of thinking, which is perhaps not so much the case as of today. Combining the two is a major objective in the present lectures.

Finus (2001) is a first single author's book of direct relevance for the topic of my lectures. It presents a close to comprehensive[19] coverage of the state of the arts at that time with plenty of technical details. Many topics are accompanied by his judgments and evaluations, which reflect the time of writing and some would not be supported today anymore. While a few of them may be challenged in some pages below, the lectures to follow will show a total agreement of mine with a wish expressed by the author in the concluding paragraph of his book: that "theoretical concepts [be] more often applied to concrete environmental problems [and] toward policy recommendations with respect to the design of IEAs".

---

of the theory of clubs in climate mattrers, see Tulkens (2016) and Section 10.5 of Lecture 10.

[19]The qualification comes from the ignorance by the author of the Shapley and Shubik (1969b) paper, that I described above as fundamental.

Finally, and although beyond the time limit set to this section, mention should be made of the book edited by Finus and Caparrós (2015), because it is a very useful tool for acceding many of the major pieces of a literature pretty much dispersed and extending over almost three decades.

5.2 Equilibrium concepts in the GEG

For the strategic game (N, E, v) defined in the previous section and derived from the economic-ecological model of Lecture 2, one may consider now, along the lines of Lecture 4, outcomes in general, and specific solutions in particular. Once solutions are obtained, they will be translated back, so to speak, in the economic-ecological model so as to inspire at the levels of these disciplines further developments of normative, positive or empirical nature. The introduction of so-called "integrated assessment models" in Lecture 8 will illustrate these developments with numbers from worldwide econometric models.

Non-cooperative Nash equilibrium (NCNE)

I begin by noticing that the mathematical assumptions on which general strategic games with externalities are built are satisfied in the game (N, E, v) defined presently. These are Assumption 4.1 (non-emptiness, convexity and compactness of individual strategy sets E_i, subsets defined in some Euclidian metric space), and Assumption 4.2 (continuity in e and quasi-concavity in e_i of the payoff functions $v_i(e)$ over the space that E belongs to). Next, given the economic-ecological model with which the strategic game (N, E, v) is associated, it makes sense to also introduce in the GEG the behavioral Assumption 4.3 (rationality of the players, here the countries) and, at this stage at least, Assumption 4.4 (simultaneous but independent individual actions). On that basis it is meaningful to state:

Definition 5.2. A **non-cooperative Nash equilibrium** (NCNE) **of the GEG** in strategic form (N, E, v) is a strategy profile $\bar{e} \in E$ such that for all $i \in N$, $\bar{e}_i = \arg\max_{e_i \in E} v_i(\bar{e}_1, \ldots, \bar{e}_{i-1}, e_i, \bar{e}_{i+1}, \ldots, \bar{e}_n)$.

Behavioral economic and environmental characteristics

Behaviorally, my using here the Nash equilibrium as the first solution concept to deal with the issues of the global environmental problem finds its justification in the following: at this starting stage of the enquiry, one needs a game theoretic representation of the system as it stands in the absence of any negotiation, that is, a representation corresponding to what was defined in Lecture 3 as an "environmentally nationalistic equilibrium" of the economic-ecological model. This is exactly what is obtained with the Nash equilibrium of the game once one realizes that it implements Assumptions 4.3 and 4.4.

Thus, the Nash equilibrium concept is used here in the positive sense of offering a description of an existing state of the world. It is neither predictive nor prescriptive.[20]

Given this analogy between the game and the model, a Nash equilibrium of the GEG is a solution, using (5.5) and (5.4), of the system of equations:

$$g'(\bar{e}_i) = d'_i(z)_{|z=\bar{z}} \frac{\partial z}{\partial e_i}, \quad i = 1, \dots, n. \tag{5.6}$$

These first-order conditions have the same economic interpretation as in Lecture 3. In particular the RHS of (5.6) implies that the equilibrium strategy $\bar{e}_i$ of every player i, while determined by his own production and damage functions, also depends on the strategies e_j, $j = 1, \dots, n, j \neq i$ of all the other players, present in $d'_i(z)$ since $\bar{z} = \sum_{i \in N} \bar{e}_i$.

The environmentally nationalistic equilibrium of Lecture 3 was also called "non-cooperative". This was anticipating the analogy with the usual characterization of the Nash equilibrium, the main concept in the category of non-cooperative games. In the GEG, the non-cooperation element in the nationalistic equilibrium resides in

---

[20]This view is not much in line with the many interpretations of the Nash equilibrium offered in game theoretic texts (see for instance Myerson (1991), or Maschler, Solan and Zamir (2011, Section 4.8). This may be explained by the particular context of externalities I am in, where I am looking for a representation of the prevailing outcome when the externality is uncontrolled.

the fact that the individual behaviors $\bar{e}_i$ are dictated by the sole criterion of own domestic advantage (only d_i determines the strategy choices $\bar{e}_i$ in (5.6)), ignoring the damages of all j's, $j \neq i$.

Of course, even more nationalistic is the BAU equilibrium defined before, but there is nothing environmental in that nationalism since the environment is simply ignored in that concept. Not taking it as a starting point means that I do not wish to deal here with the essentially domestic issues of why and how countries move from the anarchical BAU equilibrium to the NCNE.

Mathematical properties and their significance

In the spirit of the remarks made in Section 4.2 on the intellectual importance that formal properties of mathematical concepts be well established when applied to a specific model, I present about the Nash equilibrium in the GEG two properties, with their proofs, that are used in the sequel. The arguments reproduce those of Chander and Tulkens (1997).

(a) *Existence*

Proposition 5.1. *For the strategic game* (N, E, v) *there exists a strategy profile* $\bar{e} \in E$ *which is a Nash equilibrium.*

Proof. The existence property is established by showing (i) that the Nash equilibrium $\bar{e}$ is a fixed point of some mapping constructed from the components of the game, and (ii) that this mapping does have a fixed point.

As to assertion (i) given any strategy profile $e = (e_1, \ldots, e_n)$ of the game, consider the vector $e_{-i} = (e_1, \ldots, e_{i-1}, e_{i+1}, \ldots, e_n)$ of individual strategies of all players except i's. With this vector, associate the best strategy that player i has access to and consider this best strategy as the image of a function denoted $b_i(e_{-i})$. Repeating this for all players i yields a vector of n functions $(b_1(e_{-1}), \ldots, b_i(e_{-i}), \ldots, b_n(e_{-n}))$ which constitute a mapping from R_+^{n-1} to R_+^n. Clearly, the Nash equilibrium of Definition 5.2 is a vector $\bar{e} = (\bar{e}_1, \ldots, \bar{e}_n)$ such that $\bar{e}_i = b_i(\bar{e}_{-i})$ for all $i = 1, \ldots, n$.

But a vector that satisfies this equality is also a fixed point of the mapping just constructed.

As far as assertion (ii) is concerned, it is demonstrated by having recourse to a well-known theorem of Brouwer's saying that the mapping has a fixed point if satisfies the conditions that each player's strategy set be compact and convex, and that each player's payoff function be concave with respect to his own strategy, as well as continuous and bounded. All these conditions are met in the GEG, since they satisfy Assumptions 4.1 and 4.2 as mentioned above. Therefore the mapping has a fixed point, and this fixed point is the Nash equilibrium of the GEG.   □

(b) *Uniqueness*

Proposition 5.2. *For the strategic game* (N, E, v) *the Nash equilibrium* $\bar{e} \in E$ *is unique.*

Proof. Suppose that there exists another Nash equilibrium, say $\hat{e} = (\hat{e}_1, \ldots, \hat{e}_n) \neq \bar{e} = (\bar{e}_1, \ldots, \bar{e}_n)$ Without loss of generality[21] suppose that $\sum_{i \in N} \hat{e}_i \leq \sum_{i \in N} \bar{e}_i$ entailing $\hat{z} = \sum_{i \in N} \hat{e}_i \leq \bar{z} = \sum_{i \in N} \bar{e}_i$. $\hat{z} = \sum_{i \in N} \hat{e}_i \leq \bar{z} = \sum_{i \in N} \bar{e}_i$. From the first-order conditions (5.6) one would have then $d_i(\hat{z}) \leq d_i(\bar{z})$ as well as $g_i'(\hat{e}_i) \leq g_i'(\bar{e}_i)$ for each $i \in N$. But given the concavity of the production functions and the convexity of the damage functions, this last inequality would imply $\hat{e}_i \geq \bar{e}$, for each $i \in N$, which contradicts the assumption that $\sum_{i \in N} \hat{e}_i \leq \sum_{i \in N} \bar{e}_i$.   □

The importance of these two apparently only formal properties is shown in the interpretative section above for the former, and will appear in Section 5.3 and ff. for the latter where it is shown to play an inescapable role in the development of the concept of γ-coalitional function.

More generally, the existence property of a Nash equilibrium of the GEG, together with the idea of compatibility between behaviors that it conveys, is also a key argument for supporting another kind of compatibility, namely the one between the methodologies

---

[21]That is, if the inequalities that follow are reversed.

of ecological modeling on the one hand and of economic theory on the other hand. This reinforces the claim made in Lecture 1 in that direction.

Dominant strategy equilibrium

Do players have dominant strategies in the GEG? As argued in the general terms of Lecture 4 (Section 4.2), this depends upon the form and properties of their payoff functions — thus of their utilities in the underlying economic-ecological model. The GEG does not have dominant strategies under the assumptions made up to now on the payoff functions.

However, if the damage function of a player i is linear in z, then his individual equilibrium strategy $\bar{e}_i$ is independent of the other players' strategies: indeed, the derivative $d_i'(z)$ in (5.6) is a constant in this case. Thus, $\bar{e}_i$ also satisfies Definition 4.5 of a dominant strategy for player i. Transposing this to all players in the game, one is led to state:

Proposition 5.3. *For the strategic game (N, E, v), the Nash equilibrium is a dominant strategy equilibrium if for all players i the function d_i is linear.*

Proof. Linearity of d_i for all i's implies that all players have access to a dominant strategy. Therefore, the Nash equilibrium, if it exists, is a dominant strategy equilibrium.

Existence is ensured by the fact that the conditions of Proposition 5.1 are satisfied under the linearity here assumed. Similarly, uniqueness holds with the same arguments as in the proof of Proposition 5.2. □

Coalitions and utilities

Coalitions

Let me now drop the second part of Assumption 4.4 and consider that some players in the GEG choose their strategies in concert and thereby form what is called in game theory a "coalition". Some additional notation is needed to handle this new component of the game, which can be directly transposed to the GEG (N, E, v) from the notation introduced in Section 4.2 for the general strategic game (N, Σ, v). A coalition, denoted S, is any subset of N, the all players set. For any S, let $E_S = \prod_{i \in S} E_i$ be the set of all strategies accessible to the members of S as a coalition, and let $e_S \underset{\text{def}}{=} (e_i)_{i \in S}$ denote[22] a vector whose components are the strategies chosen within E_S by the players members of S. Note that e_S is not a strategy profile of the game, since it is only a s-dimensional vector, not a n-vector. But letting $e_{-S} \underset{\text{def}}{=} (e_j)_{j \in N, j \notin S}$ be any vector of strategies chosen by the players not in S, one has that, given any S, any strategy profile $e = (e_1, \ldots, e_n)$ may be written as $e = (e_S, e_{-S})$.

Introducing the behavioral Assumption 4.5 on coalitions (members of a coalition choose their coordinated strategies so as to maximize the sum of their individual payoffs) has led me, in Lecture 4, to propose in expression (4.1) to formalize a coalition's objective by a number such as:

$$w = \max_{\{e_S \in E_S\}} \sum_{i \in S} v_i(e_S; \cdot). \qquad (5.7)$$

This prompted four remarks which, although formulated there for the general strategic game (N, Σ, v), all apply to the GEG (N, E, v). Given the specific characteristics of the latter, I further elaborate, here below, on the first remark on comparability of payoffs and transferability of utilities, as the issue is one of economic theory directly relevant to the GEG. The fourth remark, on the behavior of players when they are not members of a coalition, is taken up in the following subsection.[23]

---

[22] The expression $(e_i)_{i \in S}$ denotes the s-dimensional vector $(s = |S|)$.

[23] As a fifth remark it is worth recalling that we are not in the extensive form of the game, where coalitions possibly form in the bargaining process of concocting alternative joint strategies *vis-à-vis* the other players. Here, in the strategic form, the coalition's members are considered to already agree among themselves, as a block, on a well-defined menu of joint strategies, from which one will be implemented at the solution of the game. This is often expressed by saying that "binding agreements" hold together the coalition members.

Transferable vs. non-transferable utility

Mathematical as well as conceptual issues raised by adding up the players' payoffs in a general strategic game have been considered in Section 4.2. In the particular context of the GEG, while no further mathematical remarks are needed concerning (5.7), some further conceptual questions are still to be considered. The GEG being an "applied" game, strategies are not abstract objects as in Lecture 4. They represent well-defined actions bearing on precise quantities of physical goods, namely emissions of a pollutant. As specified in (5.5), the payoffs that are derived from these actions are expressed in the same physical units of the *green* consumption component of the country's gross domestic product (GDP). This assimilation of payoffs with utilities and eventually with units of aggregate green consumption raises the economic problem of intercountry comparability: one unit of GDP may not mean the same thing, in general, for different countries, say poor *vs.* rich ones.

Once more, my excuse for not engaging into formulations of the analysis that would take into account these differences is that I give priority to the strictly environmental issues without letting other ones interfere with the reasoning. I feel that when the latter will be completed at the basic level, the other issues will be better treated in their own dimensions, with due account of the knowledge that will have been acquired in the meantime.[24]

Partially cooperative Nash equilibria (PCNE)

The third equilibrium concept that was introduced in Lecture 4 has the following form in the GEG context.

Definition 5.3. Given a coalition $S \subset N$, a **partially cooperative Nash equilibrium relative to** S (PCNE r.t. S) of the GEG in strategic form (N, E, v), is a strategy profile $\tilde{e}^S = (\tilde{e}_1^S, \ldots, \tilde{e}_n^S)$,

---

[24]An attempt at handling NTU games in the framework of integrated assessment model is presented in the sketchy Note of Kornek, Lessman and Tulkens (2014).

also denoted $\tilde{e}^S = (\tilde{e}^S_S, \tilde{e}^S_{-S})$, such that

$$(\tilde{e}^S_i)_{i \in S} = \arg\max_{(e^S_i) \in E_S} \sum_{i \in S} v_i(e^S_S, \tilde{e}^S_{-S}) \qquad (5.8)$$

and

$$\forall j \in N, j \notin S, \quad \tilde{e}^S_j = \arg\max_{e^S_j \in E_j} v_j(e^S_j, \tilde{e}^S_{-j}). \qquad (5.9)$$

The concept was introduced to give a basis to the behavioral Assumption 4.6 according to which when a coalition S forms, the other players remain acting in isolation, each maximizing his individual payoff. As was mentioned there, it is meant to offer an answer to remark (iv) that followed the incomplete definition (4.1) of the worth of a coalition in any game with externalities. Here, in the particular framework of the GEG, there are some specific behavioral aspects of this answer, due to the factual significance of the strategies defined at a PCNE r.t. S within the economic-ecological model. These behaviors are essentially emissions and play an important role in the developments to follow. I therefore establish first the basic properties of existence and uniqueness that justify this role. Economic and environmental interpretations follow.[25]

Mathematical properties

(a) *Existence*

Proposition 5.4. *In the strategic game (N, E, v), for any coalition $S \subset N$ there exists a strategy profile $\tilde{e}^S = (\tilde{e}^S_1, \ldots, \tilde{e}^S_n)$ which is a PCNE relative to S.*

Proof. When the coalition S is assumed to form, its behavior is similar to the one of a single player. The specific strategy set and payoff function of the coalition have the same properties as those of

---

[25]In Chapter 7 of Uzawa (2003) the opposite assumption is made that the complement of N also forms as a coalition and that for any S a genuine equilibrium occurs between S and its complement. Implications are discussed in fn. 38, p. 165.

a single player. One thus has to do with a game with $n-s+1$ players, to which the existence proof of Proposition 5.1 applies. $\qquad\Box$

(b) *Uniqueness*

Proposition 5.5. *In the strategic game* (N, E, v)*, for any* $S \subset N$*, the PCNE relative to* S*,* $\tilde{e}^S$*, is unique.*

Proof. As argued in the proof of the previous proposition, one has to do with a game with $n-s+1$ players. To this game Proposition 5.2 applies. $\qquad\Box$

Environmental properties: Characteristics of the emissions

At a PCNE of the GEG relative to some coalition S, the state of the economic-ecological system is such that the total amount of the ambient pollutant is, in view of (5.4),

$$\tilde{z}^S = \sum_{i \in S} \tilde{e}_i^S + \sum_{j \in N, j \notin S} \tilde{e}_j^S.$$

Observe first that Definition 5.3 implies that the equilibrium emissions $(\tilde{e}_1^S, \ldots, \tilde{e}_n^S)$ satisfy the first-order conditions

$$\forall i \in S, \quad g_i'(\tilde{e}_i^S) = \sum_{k \in S} d_k'(\tilde{z}^S) \tag{5.10}$$

and

$$\forall j \in N, j \notin S, \quad g_j'(\tilde{e}_j^S) = d_j'(\tilde{z}^S). \tag{5.11}$$

The economic meaning of these "marginal" equalities is best seen as a combination of the similar ones (3.21) and (3.11) holding, respectively, at a Pareto efficient state of the economic-ecological model and at the NCNE. Differences are important, though, as they will play a role in the sequel. On the one hand (5.10) differs from (3.21) in the fact that it involves only the coalition members: it states that for each of them, the emissions are pushed to a point where their respective marginal abatement cost is equal to the sum (running over $k \in S$) of *just the members'* marginal damage costs. On the other hand (5.11), identical to (3.11), states that for each of the outsiders, emissions are such that their marginal abatement cost is equal to their own marginal damage cost, a condition similar to the one holding at the Nash equilibrium with no coalition. However, the amount of their emissions need not be the same as at the NCNE, because as a reaction to the reduction of emissions by the coalition the non-members adjust[26] their individual equilibrium emissions $\tilde{e}_j^S$: in (5.11), the d_j''s are indeed functions of all variables $\tilde{e}_i^S$, $i = 1, \ldots, n$, through $\tilde{z}^S$.

Next, how does the PCNE relative to a coalition S compare, in terms of absolute amounts of emissions, with the state of the system at the NCNE where no coalition forms? There are three aspects to that question: total pollution, emissions of the coalition members, emissions of the non-members. These are detailed in the following three propositions.

Proposition 5.6. *At the PCNE relative to any S, the prevailing strategy profile $\tilde{e}^S = (\tilde{e}_1^S, \ldots, \tilde{e}_n^S)$ is such that*

$$\tilde{z}^S = \sum_{i \in N} \tilde{e}_i^S \leq \sum_{i \in N} \bar{e}_i = \bar{z}. \tag{5.12}$$

i.e. *the worldwide total emissions are lower than or equal to what they are at the NCNE.*

Proof. Suppose that (5.12) does not hold and instead, that $\tilde{z}^S \geq \bar{z}$ does. If so, for every $i \in N$ one has that $d_i'(\tilde{z}^S) \geq d_i'(\bar{z})$ since d_i' is increasing. Comparing the properties (5.6) and (5.10)–(5.11) of the NCNE and the PCNE, respectively, one has

$$\forall i \in S, \quad \sum_{k \in S} d_k'(\tilde{z}^S) = g_i'(\tilde{e}_i^S) \geq g_i'(\bar{e}_i) = d_i'(\bar{z})$$

and

$$\forall j \in N, j \notin S, \quad d_j'(\tilde{z}) = g_j'(\tilde{e}_j^S) \geq g_j'(\bar{e}_j) = d_j'(\bar{z}).$$

---

[26]This adjustment is nil if the damage function is linear.

Given the strict concavity of all functions g_i these inequalities imply that $\tilde{e}_i^S \leq \bar{e}_i$ for every $i \in N$. As this contradicts the supposition, one must have $\tilde{z}^S \leq \bar{z}$. □

However, one also has:

Proposition 5.7. *At the PCNE relative to any S, the prevailing strategy profile* $\tilde{e}^S = (\tilde{e}_1^S, \ldots, \tilde{e}_n^S)$ *is such that*

$$\forall j \in N, \ j \notin S, \quad \tilde{e}_j^S \geq \bar{e}_j \tag{5.13}$$

i.e. the individual emissions of the non-members of the coalition, who act as singletons, are equal to or larger than what they are at the NCNE.

Proof. By Proposition 5.6, $\tilde{z}^S \leq \bar{z}$, which implies $v_j'(\tilde{z}^S) \leq v_j'(\bar{z})$ $\forall j \in N, j \notin S$. Equilibrium conditions (5.11) and strict concavity of the functions g_i then imply (5.13). □

This shows that given the reductions of the coalition's emissions, the non-members have an incentive to increase theirs. This outside effect is sometimes called "leakage" and also "free riding".[27] Proposition 5.7 establishes its logical possibility in any GEG, and its importance in actual environmental affairs is by now hardly a disputed empirical matter.[28] Carraro and Siniscalco (1993, p. 325) interpret leakage in terms of negative slope of the best reply function of the members of $N \backslash S$ to an emissions reduction of S. This leads them to announce instability of cooperation, at variance with the stability results that are obtained below with the further development of the PCNE concept by means of the coalitional function.

However, combining Propositions 5.6 and 5.7, it appears to be a property of the PCNE concept applied to any GEG that in

---

[27]This is the "non-participatory" kind of free riding announced in Lecture 3, that will be examined in the context of the γ-core in the concluding Section of Lecture 6 and again in Lecture 9 in the discussion of concepts of stability of coalitions.

[28]One can hardly help thinking of the US emissions that have increased since 2005 while, under the Kyoto Protocol, the rest of the world has reduced his. See more on this in Lecture 10. The interpretation that I shall give there of the Protocol is in that spirit.

spite of leakage, such equilibrium entails a lower aggregate amount of emissions: leakage does not cancel the environmentally friendly character of Proposition 5.6.

Proposition 5.8. *At the PCNE relative to any S, the prevailing strategy profile $\tilde{e}^S = (\tilde{e}_1^S, \ldots, \tilde{e}_n^S)$ is such that*

$$\sum_{i \in S} \tilde{e}_i^S \le \sum_{i \in S} \bar{e}_i. \tag{5.14}$$

i.e. *the coalition members' total emissions are lower than or equal to what they are at the NCNE.*

Proof.   The claim (5.12) of Proposition 5.6 may be written as

$$\sum_{i \in S} \tilde{e}_i^S + \sum_{j \in N, j \notin S} \tilde{e}_j^S \le \sum_{i \in S} \bar{e}_i + \sum_{j \in N, j \notin S} \bar{e}_j.$$

In this expression, one has, in view of Proposition 5.6:

$$\sum_{j \in N, j \notin S} \tilde{e}_j^S - \sum_{j \in N, j \notin S} \bar{e}_j \underset{def}{=} A \ge 0.$$

Therefore,

$$\sum_{i \in S} \tilde{e}_i^S + A \le \sum_{i \in S} \bar{e}_i.$$

implies

$$\sum_{i \in S} \tilde{e}_i^S \le \sum_{i \in S} \bar{e}_i.$$

$\square$

Intuitively, when a coalition S forms, members reduce their emissions because they do take into account the detrimental effect of their emissions on their fellow members of the coalition, in addition of the effect on themselves.

Note provisionally that it is *not* shown here that $\tilde{e}_i^S \le \bar{e}_i$ for *individual i's$\in S$*. The concavity and convexity properties of the functions involved that I used are not sufficient and an additional condition is required for that inequality to hold. It is introduced below as Proposition 6.1 when needed.

5.3 The efficient outcomes of the GEG

The γ-coalitional function

I now turn to the coalitional function w^γ of the global externality game (N, E, v), an application of the coalitional function that was proposed in Lecture 4 for the general strategic game (N, Σ, v). After the NCNE and its variants where coalitions are either not considered or just taken as given, recall that the purpose is to avail ourselves a tool that allows to define and characterize solutions of the game where a constructive role is recognized to coalitions, that is, for short, *cooperative* solutions. A main motivation is the quest for efficiency in the economic-ecological model, after having amply shown the inevitable inefficiencies of individualistic behaviors and strategies in global environmental affairs.

Let $S \subset N$ be some coalition and let $\tilde{e}^S = (\tilde{e}_1^S, \dots, \tilde{e}_n^S)$ be the PCNE r.t. S of Definition 5.4. For each $i \in N$ this strategy profile yields payoffs

$$v_i(\tilde{e}^S) = g_i(\tilde{e}_i^S) - d_i \left(\sum_{j \in N} \tilde{e}_j^S \right). \qquad (5.15)$$

Limiting oneself to the payoffs of the members of S only,[29] and considering now all coalitions including N, one may propose the following notion:

Definition 5.4. The **γ-coalitional function of the GEG** in strategic form is the function that associates with coalitions $S \subseteq N$ the values

$$w^\gamma(S) = \sum_{i \in S} \left[g_i(\tilde{e}_i^S) - d_i \left(\sum_{j \in N} \tilde{e}_j^S \right) \right] \underset{\text{def}}{=} \sum_{i \in S} \tilde{v}_i^S \quad \forall S \neq N,$$

$$(5.16)$$

---

[29]Thus, leaving out of consideration the payoffs of the non-members of S, which remain well defined nevertheless. They will reappear in the further theoretical discussion of coalition stability in Lecture 9.

$$= \sum_{i \in N} \left[g_i(e_i^*) - d_i \left(\sum_{j \in N} e_j^* \right) \right] \underset{\text{def}}{=} \sum_{i \in N} v_i^* \quad if \ S = N$$

(5.17)

where for every $i \in N$,

$$e_i^* = \underset{\{e_i\}_{i \in N} \in E}{\arg \max} \sum_{i \in N} \left[g_i(e_i) - d_i \left(\sum_{j \in N} e_j \right) \right].$$

The Pareto efficient outcome

The strategy profile $e^* = (e_1^*, \ldots, e_n^*)$ defined by (5.17) is, in economic terms, the vector of emissions at a Pareto efficient state of the economic-ecological system, or equivalently in game theoretic terms, the Pareto efficient strategy profile (PESP) of the game. It satisfies the first-order conditions (3.33).

This profile induces a vector of payoffs $(v_1^*, \ldots, v_n^*) \in R^n$ henceforth denoted as v^*.

The imputations set and alternative cooperative outcomes

The payoff vector v^* is unique, due to the uniqueness of $e^* = (e_1^*, \ldots, e_n^*)$ — recall Proposition 3.4. But the assumption of transferability of payoffs allows one to meaningfully specify any vector $\phi = (\phi_1, \ldots, \phi_n) \in R^n$ satisfying $\sum_{i \in N} \phi_i = \sum_{i \in N} v_i^*$. Such a vector ϕ defines for the GEG what in Definition 4.12 was introduced under the term of *imputation*. This prompts the following:

Definition 5.5. The **imputations set of the GEG** in strategic form is the set of vectors $\phi = (\phi_1, \ldots, \phi_n) \in R^n$ such that

$$\sum_{i \in N} \phi_i = w^\gamma(N). \tag{5.18}$$

Since all imputations are Pareto efficient, any vector ϕ different from v^* must be the result of some sharing scheme amongst all players of the gain $\sum_{i \in N} v_i^*$ achieved by them jointly using the strategy profile $e^* = (e_1^*, \ldots, e_n^*)$. This scheme is understood as being implemented by means of transfers.

As was stated in Section 4.4, the set of imputations is a menu from which to choose an efficient solution beyond efficiency, that is, with additional properties. Definition 5.5 just stated thus prompts the question: which criterion to retain for this choice in the case of the GEG? The various general solution concepts offered by cooperative game theory and listed in Lecture 4 correspond each to a specific criterion, yet they all relate to some form of cohesion of the all players group: the core, the bargaining set, the nucleolus, the Shapley value, the Von Neumann–Morgenstern stable set. The γ-coalitional function is a common instrument that can be used to explore what each solution concept can bring about when a problem is modeled as a GEG.

In the following pages, I focus on only one of these concepts, the γ-core, because I feel that the kind of cohesion it conveys is best adapted to my query of stability in international environmental negotiations. This choice does not imply a disinterest of mine in contrasting the core with the other solution concepts just evoked[30] — an exercise to which I warmly invite the reader, but preferably after having taken cognizance of all the virtues of the core.

5.4   The γ-core of the GEG: Definition and existence in a qualitative sense

In Definition 4.12, the γ-core was defined for a game in coalitional function form. The comment that followed mentioned that if a game is specified in strategic form, to any imputation having the core property there necessarily corresponds some strategy profile(s) that induce(s) such an imputation. The GEG being a game in

---

[30]I discard however the α-, and β-cores for the reasons stated at the end of Lecture 4.

strategic form, Definition 4.12 of the γ-core is now to be transposed into:

Definition 5.6. **The γ-core of the GEG in strategic form** is the set of strategy profiles inducing imputations which, for every coalition $S \subset N$, assign to the members aggregate payoffs that dominate the worth of the coalition.

Alternative equivalent formulations are: "the set of strategy profiles inducing imputations such that there exists no alternative strategy profile by means of which any coalition $S \subseteq N$ can improve the payoffs of all its members", and, in earlier terminology: the set of strategy profiles "that no coalition $S \subseteq N$ can block, using a strategy of its own".

Knowing that for many games the core is empty, calling upon this solution concept for the GEG requires that the existence issue be settled before proceeding to any other relevance consideration. This is thus the place to deal with that task,[31] for which the economic theorist has to turn to game theorists. Two approaches are available: a qualitative one, i.e. abstract, that consists in identifying a class of games for which it is known that the core is non-empty, and in showing then that the GEG belongs to that class. The other approach is constructive, in the sense of exhibiting an explicit imputation of the GEG and its underlying strategy profile for which it is shown that it satisfies the Definition 5.6. The former approach is followed hereafter and closes this Lecture, while the latter opens Lecture 6, which is devoted to exploring its many properties.

Helm's balancedness result

Among the cooperative games, those belonging to the class called "balanced games" are the ones known to have a non-empty core. I thus have essentially to show that the GEG is a balanced game, and then verify that the theorem on non-emptiness of the core applies to the GEG.

---

[31] Readers who for a reason or another wish to escape this somewhat demanding intellectual exercise may safely jump to Theorem 5.1 and the graphical arguments that follow it, and then to Lecture 6.

Independently of any game, balancedness is a property of a collection of subsets S of $N = \{i | i = 1, \ldots, n\}$, a finite set. Let C be any collection and denote C_i denote the collection of its subsets that contain i. C is called a *balanced collection of subsets* S if a vector $(\delta_S)_{S \in C}$ of positive weights can be associated with the collection, weights such that $\forall i \in N$, $\sum_{S \in C_i} \delta_S = 1$.[32] Balancedness is thus a property of the collection of subsets that signals the subsets containing i.

Transposing this terminology to the cooperative game theory context, one has N, the set of players with its subsets S called coalitions, C a collection of coalitions, and C_i the collection of coalitions that i is a member of. Then a *coalitional game* (N, w) *is balanced* if the coalitional function w is such that for every balanced collection C of coalitions S, a weighted sum of the worths[33] $w(S)$ that these coalitions can achieve is less than or equal to what the grand coalition can achieve — the weights being those whereby the balanced collection of coalitions is defined. Formally:

Definition 5.7. **The game** (N, w) **is balanced** if for every balanced collection C of coalitions S and its associated vector $(\delta_S)_{S \in C}$ the coalitional function satisfies the inequality

$$\sum_{S \in C} \delta_S w(S) \leq w(N) \tag{5.19}$$

or equivalently

$$\sum_{i \in N} \sum_{S \in C_i} \delta_S w(S) \leq w(N).$$

---

[32] A balanced collection of subsets of N is akin to, but not exactly the same as a partition of the set N. Examples are given in the original paper of Shapley (1967) and in Scarf (1967). A partition of N is a balanced collection of N's subsets with weights = 1. Aumann (1985, Section 12), as well as Osborne and Rubinstein (1994) and Maschler, Solan and Zamir (2011) give a quite illustrative interpretation of the role of the balancing weights δ_S in the balancedness concept for a game, in terms of the fraction of his time a player i might spend in a coalition.
[33] Recall that the "worth" of a coalition S is just an expression for the value, at S, of the coalitional function $w(S)$.

At this point the challenge is to find out whether the γ-coalitional function w^γ of the GEG satisfies (5.19). However, as this game is basically one in strategic form, the issue is not only to find out whether the players can achieve payoffs satisfying (5.19) but more fundamentally, that is, behaviorally, whether there exists one or several *strategy profiles* that yield payoff values satisfying this inequality. The challenge is taken up in the following constructive form:

Lemma 5.1. (Helm (2001)) *For the GEG (N, E, w^γ), for any balanced collection C of its coalitions with its associated vector of weights such that $\forall i \in N$, $\sum_{S \in C_i} \delta_S = 1$, and given the PCNEs $\tilde{e}^S = (\tilde{e}_1^S, \dots, \tilde{e}_n^S)$ relative to all of its coalitions $S \subset N$, the strategy profile $\tilde{e}^C = (\tilde{e}_1^C, \dots, \tilde{e}_n^C)$ defined by:*

$$\tilde{e}_i^C = \sum_{S \in C_i} \delta_S \tilde{e}_i^S, \quad i = 1, 2, \dots, n \tag{5.20}$$

induces coalitional payoffs that satisfy the inequality (5.19) where $w = w^\gamma$. Therefore the GEG is a balanced game.

Proof. With the strategy profiles $\tilde{e}^S = (\tilde{e}_1^S, \dots, \tilde{e}_n^S)$ relative to all S's, one has for each S, remembering Definition in (5.16)

$$w^\gamma(S) = \sum_{i \in S} \left(g_i(\tilde{e}_i^S) - d_i \left(\sum_{j \in N} \tilde{e}_j^S \right) \right).$$

Inequality (5.19) to be satisfied reads thus, more completely

$$\forall C, \sum_{S \in C} \delta_S w^\gamma(S) = \sum_{S \in C} \delta_S \left(\sum_{i \in S} \left(g_i(\tilde{e}_i^S) - d_i \left(\sum_{j \in N} \tilde{e}_j^S \right) \right) \right)$$
$$\leq w^\gamma(N). \tag{5.21}$$

In (5.20) the emissions strategy of each player i is specified, given that $\sum_{S \in C_i} \delta_S = 1$, as a convex combination of the strategies of this player in the coalitions he is a member of, at the various PCNE's relative to the coalitions S present in C_i. Thus, if the game is such that the aggregate payoff achieved by the grand coalition N is larger than what can be achieved by this "balanced weighed average" of the strategies that all coalitions, then the game is balanced.

To prove this inequality I proceed in two steps: first by showing that the strategy profile (5.20) induces for the grand coalition N an aggregate payoff at least as large as the LHS of (5.21), that is,

$$\sum_{i \in N} g_i(\tilde{e}_i^C) - \sum_{i \in N} d_i \left(\sum_{j \in N} \tilde{e}_j^C \right) \geq \sum_{S \in C} \delta_S w^\gamma(S) \qquad (5.22)$$

and next by arguing that this aggregate payoff is also less than or equal to the RHS of (5.21), that is,

$$\sum_{i \in N} g_i(\tilde{e}_i^C) - \sum_{i \in N} d_i \left(\sum_{j \in N} \tilde{e}_j^C \right) \leq w^\gamma(N). \qquad (5.23)$$

Proceeding with step one, let us distinguish, within $w^\gamma(S)$ in (5.21), the respective roles of the production activities $g_i(e_i)$ and of the damage cost incurred $d_i(\sum_{j \in N} e_j)$ of the members i of each S, that is,

$$w^\gamma(S) = \sum_{i \in S} g_i(\tilde{e}_i^C) - \sum_{i \in S} d_i \left(\sum_{j \in N} \tilde{e}_j^C \right). \qquad (5.24)$$

In the first summation term, the concavity of the production functions g_i implies that, for any $i \in N$,

$$g_i(\tilde{e}_i^C) = g_i \left(\sum_{S \in C_i} \delta_s \tilde{e}_i^S \right) \geq \sum_{S \in C_i} \delta_s g_i(\tilde{e}_i^S). \qquad (5.25)$$

In the second summation term, the convexity of the damage cost functions d_i implies that, also for any $i \in N$,

$$d_i \left(\sum_{j \in N} \tilde{e}_j^C \right) = d_i \left(\sum_{S \in C_i} \delta_s \sum_{j \in S} \tilde{e}_j^S + \sum_{S \in C \setminus C_i} \delta_s \sum_{j \in S} \tilde{e}_j^S \right)$$

$$\leq \sum_{S \in C_i} \delta_s d_i \left(\sum_{j \in N} \tilde{e}_j^S \right). \qquad (5.26)$$

This last inequality may not be seen as immediate as (5.25), however, because in the detailed argument of the function d_i on the LHS of (5.26) there appear variables that are not decisions taken by members of coalitions S containing i, as all variables are in (5.25). Is the inequality, implied by convexity, still holding? I reproduce in Annex 4 to this Lecture the rather subtle argument whereby Helm (2001, p. 144) establishes (5.26).[34]

In the meantime, by putting together the last two inequalities and summing over all players, one gets that

$$\sum_{i\in N} g_i(\tilde{e}_i^C) - \sum_{i\in N} d_i\left(\sum_{j\in N}\tilde{e}_j^C\right) \tag{5.27}$$

$$\geq \sum_{i\in N}\sum_{S\in C_i}\delta_S g_i(\tilde{e}_i^S) - \sum_{i\in N}\sum_{S\in C_i}\delta_S d_i\left(\sum_{j\in N}\tilde{e}_j^S\right)$$

$$= \sum_{S\in C}\delta_S\sum_{i\in S} g_i(\tilde{e}_i^S) - \sum_{S\in C}\delta_S\sum_{i\in S} d_i\left(\sum_{j\in N}\tilde{e}_j^S\right)$$

$$= \sum_{S\in C}\delta_S\left(\sum_{i\in S} g_i(\tilde{e}_i^S) - \sum_{i\in S} d_i\left(\sum_{j\in N}\tilde{e}_j^S\right)\right)$$

$$= \sum_{S\in C}\delta_S w^\gamma(S) \tag{5.28}$$

which completes step one, that is, (5.22) is satisfied.

As to step two, the aggregate payoff obtained in (5.27) with the constructed strategy profile $\tilde{e}^C = (\tilde{e}_1^C, \ldots, \tilde{e}_n^C)$ is less than or equal

---

[34]For those readers who will skip it, let me point out that essential points in that argument are more than just mathematical: they derive from Propositions 5.7 and 5.8 which are *economic* characterizations of what happens in the presence of externalities in the model and in the game.

to $w^\gamma(N)$, the RHS of (5.23), because by its definition in (5.17)

$$w^\gamma(N) \underset{\text{def}}{=} \sum_{i \in N} \left[g_i(e_i^*) - d_i \left(\sum_{j \in N} e_j^* \right) \right]$$

is the maximum feasible payoff in the game. Therefore, (5.23) is satisfied by the payoff induced by the strategy profile (5.20) and one obtains

$$\sum_{S \in C} \delta_S w^\gamma(S) \le w^\gamma(N), \text{ as was to be shown.}$$

$\square$

Having thus constructed from the economic-ecological model a feasible strategy profile that induces payoffs implying that the GEG is balanced, the main result concerning the γ-core is now easily obtained as:

Theorem 5.1. *The global externality game* (N, E, w^γ) *has a non-empty γ-core.*

Proof. For the class of coalitional games with transferable utility, concave payoff functions and compact strategy sets, the theorems of Bondareva (1963) and Shapley (1967) establish that balancedness of the game is a necessary and sufficient condition for the core to be non-empty.[35] Given Assumptions 4.1 and 4.2 the global externality game (N, E, w^γ) belongs to the said class, and Lemma 5.1 establishes that the game has the balancedness property. Therefore, the Bondareva–Shapley result applies and the GEG has a non-empty γ-core. $\square$

Graphically the γ-core of a GEG with three players has a structure similar to at least one of the possible ones of the general

---

[35]For a most detailed and pedagogic proof of the Bondareva–Shapley result theorem, see Maschler, Solan and Zamir (2011, Chapter 17, pp. 695–702). A more compact proof is given in Osborne and Rubinstein (1994, Chapter IV, pp. 262–263), provided attention is paid to the fact that these authors talk about "balanced weights" instead of "balancing weights" for balanced collections of coalitions — an innocuous shift in terminology that Helm also makes.

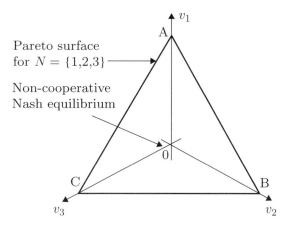

Fig. 5.1   Area ABC: the imputations set of the GEG.

case presented in Figs. 4.3–4.4 towards the end of Lecture 4, except that here the economic-ecological model is in the background: this allows for economic interpretation of these figures, and may have an impact on the possible geometric shapes of the γ-core.

In the payoff space R_+^3 of Fig. 5.1, in which the origin is again conventionally set at the Nash equilibrium, the coordinates of any point in the triangular area ABC are those of a vector of payoffs that add up to $w^\gamma(N)$ as in (5.18) above, where $N = \{1,2,3\}$. That surface is the equivalent, in a three agents economy, of the Pareto efficient line drawn for a two countries economy in Fig. 3.1 of Lecture 3. Hence the present imputations surface is also the Pareto surface of the economic-ecological model. Each of its points, being an *imputation* of the game, is a way to allocate among the three countries the efficient aggregate utility that they can secure themselves by acting environmentally together.

As mentioned earlier, the γ-core concept expresses the idea of selecting, beyond efficiency, imputation(s) that meet the additional criterion of coalitional rationality. Within the set ABC of imputations, the γ-core is thus a subset whose elements meet that criterion. Figures 5.2 and 5.3 reproduce the two examples of Lecture 4. In either case, the γ-core consists of a subset of imputations represented by points lying within the areas $c_1d_1c_2d_2c_3d_3$ and DHL, respectively. Notice that the "interior" γ-core has the property that in all

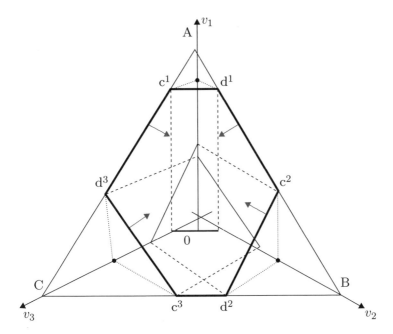

Fig. 5.2 A game with an "anchored" core (area $c^1d^1c^2d^2c^3d^3$).

imputations it consists of, all players have a higher payoff than at
the NCNE, i.e. in economic terms, all countries are strictly better off
in utility terms at the core solution than at their nationalistic non-
cooperative equilibrium. This is not the case with the "anchored"
core: points belonging to edges such as c^1d^3, for instance,[36] are
imputations for which one coordinate, v_3 in this example, is equal
to zero. This implies no gain for this player-country in the move of
the system from Nash to Pareto letting the benefit of that move go
entirely to the other countries. The possibility of γ-core solutions
with that feature will be observed in the next lecture.

   I do not reproduce Fig. 4.5 which showed that in the general case
of strategic games with externalities, the said areas may not exist,
reflecting the fact that the core is empty. Here, in the case of the
GEG, Helm's Lemma 5.1 allows one to say that Fig. 4.5 is a logical
impossibility.

---

[36]Typically, edges that can be projected entirely on a single axis.

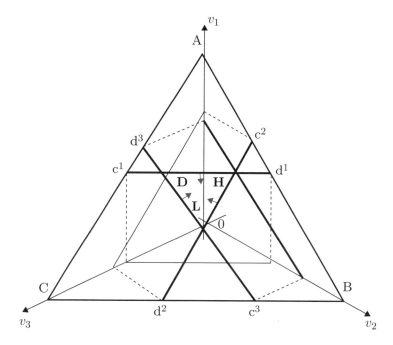

Fig. 5.3   A game with an "interior" core (area DHL).

Non-uniqueness and extensions

The preceding figures also illustrate that the γ-core of the GEG is *not* a one-point solution concept in general: several imputations of the game may have the property required by Definition 5.6. But for some parameter values, the γ-core of the GEG may reduce to one imputation only. This is the case, for instance, if all players are identical (see Section 6.1 in Lecture 6).

The possible multiplicity of γ-core solutions naturally prompts the question: are there reasons for choosing among them? This requires introducing still another selection criterion, beyond those of efficiency and coalitional stability that inspire all the preceding developments. Let me mention three such criteria, among many conceivable ones: (i) the alternative concept of "internal–external" coalitional stability, (ii) the concept of Shapley value, and (iii) the concept of Nucleolus.

Lecture 9 is devoted to showing that the alternative concept mentioned under (i) is generally not compatible with core theoretic stability. I postpone the exposition of this argument to a later stage while the other two concepts deserve immediate attention because their connection with the core concept is quite immediate. On the one hand, the Shapley value — a one point solution concept — is known to belong to the core of a game (without externalities) in general, when the game is convex.[37] Because the GEG is not superadditive, in general, as established in Annex 3, it is also not convex. Yet, Rogna (2016) produced a numerical example where the Shapley value does belong to the γ-core of the GEG. He thus produced a one point selection within the set of the γ-core solutions, which has the additional virtues conveyed by the Shapley value.

On the other hand, it is known that the nucleolus always exists in any coalitional game, and it always belongs to the core of a game, when the latter is non-empty. Being a one point solution concept, it also offers a selection in the γ-core — a selection inspired by the rawslian notion of justice and therefore called "Rawlsian core" in Rogna (2016). In an earlier contribution, van Steenberghe (2004) introduced the nucleolus in a simulation model of the γ-core that I refer to in Lecture 8.

Before entering in these attractive extensions,[38] to be kept for future occasions, there remains a lot to explore with the γ-core: in Lecture 6, one particular γ-core solution, in Lecture 7 its extension

---

[37] As established by Shapley (1971a).

[38] Rather than an extension, Chapter 7 of Uzawa (2003) presents another "core" solution to his "global warming game", based on the different assumption mentioned above (Footnote 25) on the behavior of non-members of coalitions. Using also a balancedness argument, he shows existence for the core concept so constructed, subject to a condition ((6) p. 210) "so stringent that it may be satisfied only for an extremely limited class of global warming game". Apart from this limitation, the text gives neither a motivation nor an interpretation for the assumption he retains. In the preliminary version of their paper, Chander and Tulkens (1994, p. 13) had considered the complement of S forming as a coalition, calling it the "delta" assumption, without introducing an equilibrium concept between the two coalitions however. With a "delta" characteristic function, they conjectured that the core might be empty in general because with positive

to dynamics, that is, to stock global externalities, and in Lecture 8 the confrontation with the realities of implementation with numerical economic-ecological models.

Annexes to Lecture 5

Annex 1: The "lake game" of Shapley and Shubik as a "global externality game"

The purpose of this Annex is to show the close connection between the game named "The Lake" of Shapley and Shubik (1969b) (hereafter *SSL game*[39]), and the GEG presented in Lecture 5. While the formulation of the former is one of a finite game, at variance from the continuous specification of the latter, a similar major game theoretic property is obtained, namely an explicit solution in the core — actually the γ-core. The gain from this exercise is that the more explicit economics of the latter allows one to better appreciate the fundamental importance of the two authors' early contribution, theoretically first, but also for the computational and policy developments that followed until today, as shown in Lectures 6 through 10.

The game

Using the format of Lectures 4 and 5 for stating a general strategic game, consider the game — call it *"the GEG version of the SSL game"* — that consists of the triplet (N, T, v) where

(i) N is a set of n **players** indexed $i = 1, \ldots, n$,

(ii) $T = \{t \in R_+^n \mid t \in T_1 \times \cdots \times T_i \times \cdots \times T_n\}$ is a set of joint strategies where for each $i = 1, \ldots, n$

---

externalities the formation of the complement of S as a coalition reinforces, possibly much, the worth of S. No credible interpretation of that formation was offered either.

[39] An identical presentation is in Shubik (1984, p. 542).

$T_i = \{t_i | t_i \in \{0,1\}\}$, is the set of **strategies** t_i that player i has access to, and T is the set of strategy sets that all players i have simultaneously access to, and

(iii) $v = (v_1, \ldots, v_n)$ is a vector of **payoffs**, one for each player. These payoffs v_i are identical[40] functions of the strategies chosen by all players, formally specified as

$$v_i(t) = Bt_i + C \left[(1 - t_i) + \sum_{j \in N, j \neq i} (1 - t_j) \right]$$

$$\text{where } 0 < C < B < nC. \tag{5.A1.1}$$

I shall be using the numerical values of the parameters that are proposed in an example given by Straffin (1993), so that for each $i = 1, \ldots, n$ the payoff function (5.A1.1) reads:

$$v_i(t) = 50\, t_i + 20 \left[(1 - t_i) + \sum_{j \in N, j \neq i} (1 - t_j) \right]$$

$$\text{where } B/C < n \text{ implies } n \geq 3. \tag{5.A1.2}$$

Economic interpretation: The players i are n identical factories located around a lake, in which they all discharge their waste, and from which they all also collect water to cool their equipment. Polluted waters damage this equipment at a cost C per factory. But factories can also treat their sewage before discharging it, at a cost B. The alternative strategies of the factories, $t_i = 1$ or 0, mean: factory i treats its sewage (i.e. abates), or does not, respectively. Strategies are thus defined in terms of abatements — and not of emissions as in the GEG. The vector $t = (t_1, \ldots, t_n)$, is called a strategy profile of abatement decisions by all players. Finally, the payoff function (5.A1.1) represents each factory i's total cost, which consists of, respectively, the treatment cost of its sewage (first term

---

[40]Doing away with the identical players assumption is feasible by individualizing the parameters B_i and C_i, $i = 1, \ldots, n$.

of the payoff function), and (second term) the damage cost it incurs from the degraded quality of the lake's waters, as it results from the treatments — or non-treatments — done by itself and the other factories.

Assumption 5A.1. When considered in isolation, each player chooses the individual strategy that minimizes his individual total cost.

A dominant strategy

Proposition 5A.0. *For every player i, the strategy $t_i = 0$ is a dominant strategy, that is, a strategy that minimizes player i's total cost, irrespective of the strategy choices of the other players.*

Proof. It is claimed that

$$0 = \arg\min_{t_i \in T_i} v_i(t)$$

$$= 50t_i + 20 \left[(1 - t_i) + \sum_{j \in N, j \neq i} (1 - \overset{\circ}{t_j}) \right] \ \forall \overset{\circ}{t_j}, j \neq i.$$

Indeed, the second term of the expression within brackets is a constant for player i. Therefore, switching from $t_i = 0$ to $t_i = 1$ increases $v_i(t)$ from 20 to 50. □

Nash equilibrium

Definition 5A.1. For the SSL game, a **non-cooperative Nash equilibrium** (NCNE) is a strategy profile $\bar{t} = (\bar{t}_1, \ldots, \bar{t}_n)$ such that:

$$\forall i \in N, \quad \bar{t}_i = \arg\min_{t_i \in T_i} v_i(\bar{t}) = 50t_i$$

$$+ 20 \left[(1 - t_i) + \sum_{j \in N, j \neq i} (1 - \bar{t}_j) \right] \ \forall \bar{t}_j, \ j \neq i.$$

$$(5.A1.3)$$

Proposition 5A.1. *For the SSL game, the strategy profile*

$$\bar{t} = (\bar{t}_1, \ldots, \bar{t}_n) \quad \text{where } \bar{t}_i = 0 \; \forall i \in N \tag{5.A1.4}$$

is a NCNE. It is also the only one.

In words, it is an equilibrium[41] that no clean up occurs at all.

Proof. At the strategy profile (5.A1.4) the payoff functions read:

$$\forall \; i \in N, \; v_i(\bar{t}) = 50\bar{t}_i + 20 \left[(1 - \bar{t}_i) + \sum_{j \in N, j \neq i} (1 - \bar{t}_j) \right]$$

$$= 20 \; n. \tag{5.A1.5}$$

Suppose $\bar{t}$ is not a NCNE. Then for any alternative strategy profile

$$\bar{\bar{t}} = (\bar{\bar{t}}_1, \ldots \bar{\bar{t}}_n) \text{ where for some } i, \bar{\bar{t}}_i = 1 \text{ and } \bar{\bar{t}}_j = 0 \; \forall j \neq i$$

one has for player i:

$$v_i(\bar{\bar{t}}) = 50\bar{\bar{t}}_i + 20 \left[(1 - \bar{\bar{t}}_i) + \sum_{j \in N, j \neq i} (1 - \bar{\bar{t}}_j) \right]$$

$$= 50 + 20(n - 1)$$

$$= 30 + 20n > 20n = v_i(\bar{t}). \quad \left(\begin{array}{l} \text{i.e. } = B + C(n-1) \\ \quad = B - C + Cn > Cn \end{array} \right).$$

Thus, given (5.A1.3), the profile $\bar{\bar{t}}$ does not satisfy the definition of a NCNE.

As to uniqueness, if there were two different profiles asserted to be a NCNE, one of which being the one of the proposition, uniqueness would follow from a similar reasoning on the other profile. □

Remark 5A.1. Given Proposition 1, the NCNE of the SSL game is called an "equilibrium in dominant strategies", a property which is known for all GEGs where the damage cost function is linear (see Proposition 5. 3).

---

[41] "international environmentally nationalistic", in the vocabulary of Lecture 3.

Pareto efficiency

Definition 5A.2. For the SSL game, a **Pareto efficient strategy profile** (PESP) is a strategy profile $t^* = (t_1^*, \dots, t_n^*)$ such that

$$t^* = \underset{(t_1, \dots t_n)}{\arg \min} \sum_{i \in N} v_i(t) = 50\, t_i + 20 \left[(1 - t_i) + \sum_{j \in N, j \neq i} (1 - t_j) \right].$$

Proposition 5A.2. *For the SSL game, if $n \geq 3$, then the strategy profile*

$$t^* = (t_1^*, \dots, t_n^*) \quad \text{where } t_i^* = 1 \; \forall i \in N \qquad (5.\text{A}1.6)$$

is a PESP. It is also the only one.

In words, it is environmentally efficient ("optimal") that each player cleans its own sewage.

Proof. At the strategy profile (5.A1.6) the payoff functions read, for each $i \in N$:

$$
\begin{aligned}
v_i(t^*) &= 50 t_i^* + 20 \left[(1 - t_i^*) + \sum_{j \in N, j \neq i} (1 - t_j^*) \right] \\
&= 50
\end{aligned}
$$

so that

$$\sum_{i \in N} v_i(t^*) = n50. \qquad (5.\text{A}1.7)$$

Suppose t^* is not a PESP. Then for any alternative strategy profile

$$t^{*^\circ} = (t_1^{*o}, \dots, t_n^{*o}) \text{ where for some } i, t_i^{*^\circ} = 0 \text{ and } t_j^{*^\circ} = 1 \; \forall j \neq i$$

one has

$$v_i(t^{*°}) = 50t_i^{*°} + 20 \left[(1 - t_i^{*°}) + \sum_{j \in N, j \neq i} (1 - t_j^{*°}) \right]$$

$$= 20$$

and

$$\forall j \neq i, \; v_j(t^{*°}) = 50t_j^{*°} + 20 \left[(1 - t_i^{*°}) + \sum_{j \in N, j \neq i} (1 - t_j^{*°}) \right]$$

$$= 50 + 20.$$

Hence,

$$\sum_{k \in N} v_k(t^{*°}) = 20 + (n - 1)(50 + 20)$$

$$= -50 + n(50 + 20)$$

$$> \sum_{i \in N} v_i(t^*) = n50 \text{ for } n \geq 3$$

$$\left(\begin{matrix} \text{i.e. } C + (n - 1)(B + C) \\ -B + n(B + C) \\ > nB \text{ for } B < nC \end{matrix} \right).$$

Therefore no profile such as $t^{*°} = (t_1^{*°}, \ldots, t_n^{*°})$ satisfies the definition of a PESP. As to uniqueness, if there were two different profiles asserted to be a PESP, one of which being the one of the proposition, uniqueness would follow from a similar reasoning on the other profile. □

Partially cooperative Nash equilibria

Assumption 5A.2. When a coalition $S \subset N$ forms, the coalition members cooperate and choose the joint strategy $(\tilde{t}_i^S)_{i \in S}$ that minimizes the sum of their individual total cost. This sum is called the coalitions' payoff. The other players, remaining singletons, choose their strategy as in Assumption A5.1.

Definition 5A.3. For the SSL game, given a coalition $S \subset N$, a **partially cooperative Nash equilibirum relative to** S

(*PCNE* r.t. S) is a strategy profile denoted $\tilde{t}^S = (\tilde{t}_1^S, \ldots, \tilde{t}_n^S)$ which is such that[42]

$$(\tilde{t}_i^S)_{i\in S} = \underset{(t_i^S)}{\arg\min} \sum_{i\in S} v_i(t^S)$$

$$= \sum_{i\in S}\left(50t_i^S + 20\left[(1-t_i^S) + \sum_{j\in N, j\neq i}(1-\tilde{t}_j^S)\right]\right)$$

$$= \sum_{i\in S}\left(50t_i^S + 20\left[(1-t_i^S) + \sum_{j\in S, j\neq i}(1-\tilde{t}_j^S)\right.\right.$$

$$\left.\left. + \sum_{k\in N, k\notin S}(1-\tilde{t}_k^S)\right]\right) \tag{5.A1.8}$$

and

$$\forall k \in N, k\notin S, \quad \tilde{t}_k^S = \underset{t_k^S}{\arg\min}\ v_k(t^S)$$

$$= 50t_k^S + 20\left[(1-t_k^S) + \sum_{j\in N, j\neq k}(1-\tilde{t}_j^S)\right]. \tag{5.A1.9}$$

This concept, absent from the Shapley and Shubik (1969b) paper, provides the basis for the γ-core construction that follows.

Proposition 5A.3. *For the SSL game, given a coalition $S \subset N$, the strategy profile*

$$\tilde{t}^S = (\tilde{t}_1^S, \ldots, \tilde{t}_n^S) \text{ where } \tilde{t}_i^S = 1\ \forall i \in S \text{ and } \tilde{t}_k^S = 0\ \forall k \in N, k \notin S, \tag{5.A1.10}$$

is a PCNE relative to S. It is the only one.

---

[42]The notation $(\tilde{t}_i^S)_{i\in S}$ stands for the s-dimensional vector whose components $\tilde{t}_i^S$ are components of the n-dimensional vector $\tilde{t}$ whose index $i$is the one of a player $i \in S$.

In words, if a coalition forms, all its members do treat their sewage while the non-members do not.

Proof.   Let $s = |S|$, $0 < s < n$.

At the strategy profile $\tilde{t}^S$ (5.A1.10) the payoff functions read

$$\text{for } S, \sum_{i \in S} v_i(\tilde{t}^S) = \sum_{i \in S} \left(50\tilde{t}_i^S + 20 \left[(1 - \tilde{t}_i^S) + \sum_{j \in S, j \neq i} (1 - \tilde{t}_j^S) \right. \right.$$

$$\left. \left. + \sum_{k \in N, k \notin S} (1 - \tilde{t}_k^S) \right] \right)$$

$$= s(50 + 20[(0) + (0) + (n - s)]), \qquad (5.A1.11)$$

and

$$\forall k \in N, k \notin S, \; v_k(\tilde{t}^S) = 50\tilde{t}_k^S + 20 \left[(1 - \tilde{t}_k^S) + \sum_{i \in N, i \neq k} (1 - \tilde{t}_i^S) \right]$$

$$= 20(n - s). \qquad (5.A1.12)$$

One must show that (5.A1.10)–(5.A1.12) satisfy the Definition 5A.3. To that effect, suppose $\tilde{t}^S(10)$ is not a PCNE r.t. S, and consider then the following three alternative profiles:

- $\tilde{t}^{So} = (\tilde{t}_1^{So}, \ldots, \tilde{t}_n^{So})$ where for some $i \in S$, $\tilde{t}_i^{So} = 0$ while $\forall k \in S$, $k \neq i$, $\tilde{t}_k^{So} = 1$ and $\forall j \in N, j \notin S, \tilde{t}_j^{So} = 0$
- $\tilde{t}^{Soo} = (\tilde{t}_1^{Soo}, \ldots, \tilde{t}_n^{Soo})$ where $\forall i \in S$, $\tilde{t}_i^{Soo} = 1$, while for some $k \in N, k \notin S, \tilde{t}_k^{Soo} = 1$ and $\forall j \in N, j \notin S, j \neq k, \tilde{t}_j^{Soo} = 0$
- $\tilde{t}^{Sooo} = (\tilde{t}_1^{Sooo}, \ldots, \tilde{t}_n^{Sooo})$ where for some $i \in S$, $\tilde{t}_i^{So} = 0$ while $\forall k \in S, k \neq i, \tilde{t}_k^{So} = 1$ for some $k \in N, k \notin S, \tilde{t}_k^{Soo} = 1$ and $\forall j \in N, j \notin S, j \neq k, \tilde{t}_j^{Soo} = 0$.

In neither of these three cases the profile satisfies the definition of a PCNE r.t. S. Indeed, with $\tilde{t}^{So}$ the payoff functions (5.A1.11)–(5.A1.12) become, in the coalition's part of (5.A1.11):

$$
\begin{aligned}
\sum_{i \in S} v_i(\tilde{t}^{So}) &= 20 + (s-1)(50+20) \\
&= -50 + s(50+20) \\
&> \sum_{i \in S} v_i(\tilde{t}^S) = s50 \text{ if } s \geq 3
\end{aligned}
\qquad
\begin{pmatrix}
\text{i.e.} C + (s-1)(B+C) \\
-B + s(B+C) \\
> sB \text{ if } B < sC
\end{pmatrix}.
$$

Similarly, with $\tilde{t}^{Soo}$, $\tilde{t}_k^{Soo} = 1$ for some $k \in N, k \notin S$ does not satisfy (5.A1.9) for player k. Finally, $\tilde{t}^{Sooo}$ compounds these two negative statements.

As to uniqueness, the argument used above for the uniqueness of the Nash equilibrium applies again. □

Coalitional function

Definition 5A.3 and Proposition 5A.3 allow one to specify

Definition 5A.4. For the SSL game, a **γ-coalitional function** is the function $w^\gamma(S)$ that associates

- with every $S \subset N$, the real number

$$
w^\gamma(S) \underset{\text{def}}{=} \sum_{i \in S} v_i(\tilde{t}^S) = \sum_{i \in S} \left(50\tilde{t}_i^S + 20 \left[(1 - \tilde{t}_i^S) + \sum_{j \in N, j \notin S} (1 - \tilde{t}_j^S) \right] \right)
$$

$$
= s(50 + 20(n - s)) \qquad (5.A1.13)
$$

where $\tilde{t}^S = (\tilde{t}_1^S, \ldots, \tilde{t}_n^S)$ is the PCNE relative to S of Definition 5A.3, and
- with N, the real number

$$
w^\gamma(N) \underset{\text{def}}{=} \sum_{i \in N} v_i(t^*) = 50t_i^* + 20 \left[(1 - t_i^*) + \sum_{j \in N, j \neq i} (1 - t_j^*) \right]
$$

$$
= n50 \qquad (5.A1.14)
$$

where $t^* = (t_1^*, \ldots, t_n^*)$ is the PESP of Definition 2.

Remark 5A.2. This coalitional function[43] differs from the one used by Shapley and Shubik on p. 681 (right column). The difference comes from the absence of definition of the strategies of the players, so that the argument of their function is the size of the coalition, s, rather than the coalitions' actions as I do here. What a coalition actually does is in fact implicit, the authors leaving it to the reader to guess, as in Proposition 5A.3, that the coalition members treat their own waters with no treatment made by the non-members, who are not a coalition and remain singletons.

Interestingly, this is exactly what is called the "γ-assumption" introduced by Chander and Tulkens (1997) for the GEG, and proposed for strategic games with externalities in general in the Lecture 4 of this series.

γ-core solution

Definition 5A.5. For the SSL game, a γ-**core solution** is any strategy profile $t = (t_1, \ldots, t_n)$ such that for every coalition $S \subset N$ the payoffs $(v_i(t))_{t \in S}$ of its members are collectively better (i.e. lower) than at the PCNE with strategy profile $\tilde{t}^S = (\tilde{t}_1^S, \ldots, \tilde{t}_n^S)$ that they could obtain by themselves. Formally, $t = (t_1, \ldots, t_n)$ such that $\forall S$, $\sum_{i \in S} v_i(t) < \sum_{i \in S} v_i(\tilde{t}^S)$.

Proposition 5A.4. *For the SSL game, the PESP $t^* = (t_1^*, \ldots, t_n^*)$ is a γ-core solution.*

In words, the Pareto efficient solution is also a γ-core solution.

Proof. Given that for the PESP $t^* = (t_1^*, \ldots, t_n^*)$ one has by (5.A1.7) for every S and s

$$\sum_{i \in S} v_i(t^*) = s50 \qquad (5.A1.15)$$

---

[43] This is a post-1988 terminology for the expression "characteristic function" used by the authors at the time of their paper.

and for the PCNE $\tilde{t}^S = (\tilde{t}_1^S, \ldots, \tilde{t}_n^S)$ relative to any coalition S one has by (5.A1.11):

$$\sum_{i \in S} v_i(\tilde{t}^S) = \sum_{i \in S} \left(50\tilde{t}_i^S + 20 \left[(1 - \tilde{t}_i^S) + \sum_{j \in N, j \notin S} (1 - \tilde{t}_j^S) \right] \right)$$

$$= s(50 + 20(n - s)). \tag{5.A1.16}$$

The proposition is true if (5.A1.15) $<$ (5.A1.16) for every $S \subset N$ and thus for every s, that is, if

$$\sum_{i \in S} v_i(t^*) = 50s < \sum_{i \in S} v_i(\tilde{t}^S) = s(50 + 20(n - s))$$

or $50s < s50 + s20(n - s)$

or still $0 < s20(n - s)$.

This is obviously the case since $0 < s < n$.   □

Thus the γ-core of the *GEG version of the SSL game* is non-empty, as is the core of the 1969 Lake game — which is implicitly a γ-core, in view of Remark 5A.2.

Remark 5A.3. The PESP t^* is a γ-core solution with no transfers. This is in line with Proposition 6.3 on the γ-core of the GEG with identical players stated in Lecture 6. If players were not identical, with parameters individualized as mentioned in Footnote 40, transfers would probably be necessary. In the present finite game format, their formulation may not be obvious, even if inspired by those proposed in Lecture 6 for the continuous case.

Conclusion

The essential difference between the original *S and S Lake Game* and its presently proposed *GEG version* lies in the very first lines of this Annex, namely the specification of strategies. In the former game, strategies are (implicitly) coalition participation, formally, the variables s. In the formulation of the latter game, strategies are physical actions of pollutant emission, the variables t. Professor Dinar, in private correspondence on an earlier version of this text, sees in this difference that the strategy set is "richer" in the second case and that this might affect the core outcomes. He also suggests that with the SSL game, the externality between players operates only indirectly (through the media of the lake water), whereas with the GEG strategies, the interaction is direct. Hence, the SSL game might be only a special case of the GEG.

In my view, the stated difference lies essentially in the fact that the GEG is constructed in association with the decision variables of an explicit and formal economic-ecological model (in the spirit of Aumann's considerations in this respect as reminded at the beginning of this Lecture), whereas this is not the case in the SSL game. The closer description of the real actions of the players in the specification of the game, rather than only an implication of these actions for coalition formation or non-formation, allows one to better describe the effective outcome of the game in economic terms.

Annex 2: The "prisoners' dilemma" game and international environmental externalities

The message here is that the prisoners' dilemma game is too rough a tool to describe the inefficiency claimed to be inevitable in international environmental interactions. I wish to argue here that the claim is due to the lack of economic modeling underlying the game's specification. In particular, the game restricts to an extreme and exaggerated case — because it hides it — the physical externality phenomenon which is at the source of the said inefficiency.

In environmental economics texts mention is often made of the prisoners' dilemma to illustrate the difficulty of achieving cooperation at the international level. To that effect, the game is presented in the minimal terms of a numerical example that comprises two identical players (i and j), each having access to two strategies ("pollute (P)" and "keep clean (C)"), and payoff levels represented by the numbers in the four cells of Fig. 5A.1 (in each cell, the first number is the payoff of player i, the second number the payoff of player j, each of these payoffs being induced by the strategy pair mentioned on top and to the left of the cell).

		Player j's Strategies:	
		C	P
Player i's	C	3, 3	1, 4
Strategies:	P	4, 1	2, 2

Fig. 5A.1   The prisoners' dilemma game — An example.

The main argument is that the pair of strategies (P, P) is a Nash equilibrium (with payoffs of the cell 2, 2) because for any other pair of strategies the induced payoffs have the property that for at least one of the two players another strategy yields a higher payoff. Therefore none of these other pairs of strategies can be sustained. For instance, the strategy pair (C, C) (with payoffs 3, 3) is such that, if proposed, then player i by choosing P instead of C has a higher payoff, 4, instead of 3. Thus (C, C) cannot be sustained. Admittedly, this assertion is made assuming that player j sticks to the strategy C. But suppose player j does not stick to C, and quite understandably so: after the move by player i, j's payoff is now equal to 1, but then j is better off by switching to P. Overall result: The strategy pair (P, P) is reached, and in that situation none of the players has an interest in switching to any other strategy. (P, P) can be sustained and is thus an equilibrium. Yet, the strategy pair (C, C), which is efficient, Pareto dominates (P, P) and is therefore preferable for all. There is thus incompatibility between efficiency and equilibrium. All this is well known, and it is shown in Lecture 5 that inefficient equilibrium is the case in all GEGs satisfying standard assumptions. Where is the dilemma, then?

The story goes on as follows. In the game of Fig. 5A.1 the strategy (P, P) has an additional property: for each player, the strategy P is the best one *whatever strategy is chosen by the other player*. P is therefore called a "dominant" strategy for the player who logically has only *that* strategy to play.[44] The dilemma is in the inevitability of the dominant strategy.

---

[44]And (P, P) is called an "equilibrium in dominant strategies"

The point made in Dasgupta (1982) is that in games associated with environmental externalities between countries, the structure of the underlying interactions between the players does *not* provide them with dominant strategies, *in general*. With a standard model very close to those of Lecture 2 he gives a simple example of that. If so, the economics of the environmental problem tell us that in the standard case, the best strategy of any player is not a dominant one, and *does* vary with the strategies chosen by the others, contrary to what the numbers imply in the game here above. This is also the point made in Lecture 3 in the second comment following Proposition 3.2, and the comment goes farther with equation (3.15), which specifies the sign of the slope of the reaction function.

Turning back to the game of Fig. 5A.1, one may trace the source of the dominant strategy property to the fact that for the strategy pair (P, C), player j's payoff, 1, is smaller than 2, his payoff at the equilibrium. Indeed, if instead of 1 this payoff is $2 + \varepsilon > 2$, then j does not switch to P, and (P, C) becomes a Nash equilibrium — not in dominant strategies, though, and (P, P) is not an equilibrium anymore.[45] This shows that the prisoners' dilemma quandary is due to the dominant strategy property present in the example, independently of the fact that the equilibrium is inefficient.

How can one explain the numerical value of the payoffs in the above game? By digging a bit into the behaviors behind the payoffs, the answer can be found to lie, I believe, in the special kind of externalities hidden, but present, in the numbers of Fig. 5A.1. I disentangle them as follows. Consider the Nash equilibrium payoffs cell (2,2), assumed to prevail. If, starting from there, player j decides to change his mind and play the strategy C, the resulting strategy pair is (P, C) with payoffs (4, 1). Why 4 for player i? Well, because player i benefits from the positive externality generated by j's move to C, giving him a cleaner environment. Fair enough. But why only 1

---

[45]If one sticks to the identical players assumption and applies the same reasoning to player I, having him change his mind from the initial (P, P) situation to (C, P) where I's payoff is symmetrically raised to $2 + \varepsilon > 2$, then (C, P) is a second Nash equilibrium.

			Player j's strategies	
			C_j	P_i
			Payoffs	
Player i's	C_i	Payoffs	$a_i = v_i(C_i, C_j),\ a_j = v_j(C_i, C_j)$	$b_i = v_i(C_i, P_j),\ c_j = v_j(C_i, P_j)$
strategies	P_i		$c_i = v_i(P_i, C_j),\ b_j = v_j(P_i, C_j)$	$d_i = v_i(P_i, P_j),\ d_j = v_j(P_i, P_j)$

Fig. 5A.2 The prisoners' dilemma game — A more general formulation.

for player j? Why is the move to C *so* costly to him that he ends up even worse than before his move? One can see here the combination of two facts: the cleaning cost borne by j, which is evident, *plus* a possible negative externality that results from player i's increasing his polluting emissions (a reaction called "leakage", see Proposition 5.7). There are thus two reciprocal externalities at play. But the game looses its prisoners' dilemma character if the intensity of just one of these externalities is modified, as just shown with the payoff $2 + \varepsilon$ substituted for 2.

At a more general level than just the single numerical example of above, consider the presentation of Fig. 5A.2 where the identical players assumption is dropped (which is unnecessary in the argument) and the payoff functions made explicit in terms of their arguments. Dasgupta and after him several authors of game theory textbooks have pointed out that for any game in bi-matrix form to be a prisoners' dilemma game the following couple of conditions on the payoffs structure must be satisfied:

$$c_j > a_j > d_j > b_j \quad \text{and} \quad c_j > a_j > d_j > b_j.$$

One may verify that these conditions are satisfied in the game of Fig. A5.1, while they are not when for either i or j, or both, "b" is replaced by "$d + \varepsilon > b$".

Conclusion: the structure of the numbers used in the presentation of the prisoners' dilemma game corresponds to a quite particular case of externalities.[46] The general phenomenon of reciprocal externalities

---

[46]In his quite extended presentation and discussion of the prisoners' dilemma game, Finus (2001) astonishingly does not invoke the externality concept to explain the "PD effect" here under discussion. On pp. 22 and 24, he only refers to "the cost–benefit structure [for the] Pareto inferior result", and alludes just

may take many other forms and intensities than what this compact but rigid form of the bi-matrix game can account for. Other forms of environmental externalities induce other payoffs that are well accounted for in the standard GEG with its underlying economic-ecological model. In the spirit of Aumann's words quoted above (Section 5.1) on associating games with economic models, this illustrates that only an explicit specification of the behaviors that generate the payoffs can make the game to correctly represent the reality under study.

Note finally that in the prisoners' story that accompanies the non-environmentally motivated initial presentation of the game in Luce and Raiffa 1957 (p. 97 and ff.), there is no question of an "externality" between the players, in any of the economic senses reviewed in the introductory Lecture 1.

Annex 3: The γ-coalitional function of the GEG is not superadditive: An example

(Chander, private communication).

Take a three players game, where e_i denotes pollutant emissions by player i and $z = e_1 + e_2 + e_3$ the resulting amount of ambient pollutant, with payoff functions

$$v_1 = 6e_1 - \tfrac{1}{2}e_1^2 - \tfrac{1}{2}z^2,$$
$$v_2 = 3e_2 - \tfrac{1}{2}e_2^2 - z,$$
$$v_3 = 3e_3 - \tfrac{1}{2}e_3^2 - z.$$

Notice that player 1 emits more than the other two, who are identical, and suffers less damage.

It is asserted that

$$w^\gamma(\{2\} \cup \{3\})(=-3) < w^\gamma(\{2\})(=-1) + w^\gamma(\{3\})(=-1) = -2.$$
$$(5.A3.1)$$

Let me explain.

---

in passing to free riding, which is actually a behavior of the recipient of an externality.

For this game, the NCNE is the strategy profile $(\bar{e}_1, \bar{e}_2, \bar{e}_3)$ obtained as follows:

$\partial v_2/\partial e_2 \;=\; 3 - e_2 - 1 \;=\; 0 \;\Rightarrow\; \bar{e}_2 \;=\; 2$ and similarly, $\partial v_3/\partial e_3 = 0 \Rightarrow \bar{e}_3 = 2$. Then, $\partial v_1/\partial e_1 \;=\; 6 - e_1 - (e_1 + e_2 + e_3) \;=\; 0$ where $e_2 = \bar{e}_2$ and $e_3 = \bar{e}_3 \Rightarrow \bar{e}_1 = 1$.

This profile yields payoffs $\bar{v}_1 = -7$, $\bar{v}_2 = -1$, $\bar{v}_3 = -1$.

By definition, the coalitional function w^γ is superadditive if for every pair of non-overlapping subsets S and T, both $\subset N$, $w^\gamma(S \cup T) \geq w^\gamma(S) + w^\gamma(T)$.

For the above game, consider the PCNE's relative to S, to T and to $S \cup T$, respectively, whereby the coalitional function w^γ is defined for each of these subsets (Recall Definition 5.3). Let $S = \{2\}$ and $T = \{3\}$. If the argument of w^γ is a singleton, say $\{i\}$, the value of the function $w^\gamma(\{i\})$ is equal to the payoff $\bar{v}_i$ of this player at the NCNE. From the above calculation, one thus has $w^\gamma(\{2\}) = -1$, and $w^\gamma(\{3\}) = -1$.

For other subsets of N, say K, $w^\gamma(K) = \sum_{i \in K} \tilde{v}_i^K$ where each $\tilde{v}_i^K$ is the payoff of player i at the PCNE r.t. K. Thus, the PCNE relative to $S \cup T$ is the strategy profile $(\tilde{e}_1^{S \cup T}, \tilde{e}_2^{S \cup T}, \tilde{e}_3^{S \cup T})$ obtained as follows:

$$\left.\frac{\partial(v_2 + v_3)}{\partial e_2}\right|_{\substack{e_1 = \tilde{e}_1^{S \cup T} \\ e_3 = \tilde{e}_3^{S \cup T}}} = 3 - e_2 - 1 - 1 = 0 \Rightarrow \tilde{e}_2^{S \cup T} = 1 \text{ and similarly,}$$

$$\left.\frac{\partial(v_2 + v_3)}{\partial e_3}\right|_{\substack{e_1 = \tilde{e}_1^{S \cup T} \\ e_2 = \tilde{e}_2^{S \cup T}}} = 3 - e_3 - 1 - 1 = 0 \Rightarrow \tilde{e}_3^{S \cup T} = 1, \text{ and}$$

$$\left.\frac{\partial v_1}{\partial e_1}\right|_{\substack{e_2 = \tilde{e}_2^{S \cup T} \\ e_3 = \tilde{e}_3^{S \cup T}}} = 6 - 2e_1 - 2 = 0 \Rightarrow \tilde{e}_1^{S \cup T} = 2.$$

Plugging these strategies in the functions v_2 and v_3 above, the payoff of coalition $S \cup T$ is

$$w^\gamma(S \cup T) = \tilde{v}_2^{S \cup T} + \tilde{v}_3^{S \cup T} = -3$$

whereas with the strategies $(\bar{e}_1, \bar{e}_2, \bar{e}_3)$ these functions yield the following payoffs for S and T separately:

$$w^\gamma(\{2\}) = -1 \text{ and } w^\gamma(\{3\}) = -1.$$

As they add up to -2 this confirms the assertion (5.A3.1) made above.

The reason for non-superadditivity lies in the externality: at the PCNE wrt coalition $\{2,3\}$, the outside player 1 increases his emissions e_1 compared to the NCNE, and this weakens coalition $S \cup T$. This illustrates the phenomenon of "leakage", identified by the theory in Proposition 5.7.

Annex 4: A crucial step in Helm's balancedness proof

To assert the balancedness of the GEG, it must be shown, among other points, that at the PCNE's $\tilde{e}^C = (\tilde{e}_1^C, \ldots, \tilde{e}_n^C)$ of any balanced collection C of coalitions, the damage cost function of any player i satisfies

$$d_i \left(\sum_{j \in N} \tilde{e}_j^C \right) \leq \sum_{S \in C_i} \delta_s d_i \left(\sum_{j \in N} \tilde{e}_j^S \right). \tag{5.26}$$

In words, that at any $\tilde{e}^C$ and for each player i the damage cost generated by the emissions (5.20) of all countries is lower than or equal to the weighted sum of the damage cost generated by the emissions of the coalitions of which i is a member, at their respective PCNE's. To establish that, the successive steps (following expressions

(14)–(17) of Helm 2001) are:

$$
d_i \left(\sum_{j \in N} \tilde{e}_j^C \right) = d_i \left(\sum_{j \in N} \sum_{S \in C_j} \delta_s \tilde{e}_j^S \right)
$$

$$
= d_i \left(\sum_{S \in C} \delta_s \sum_{j \in S} \tilde{e}_j^S \right)
$$

$$
= d_i \left(\sum_{S \in C_i} \delta_s \sum_{j \in S} \tilde{e}_j^S + \sum_{S \in C \setminus C_i} \delta_s \sum_{j \in S} \tilde{e}_j^S \right).
$$

(5.A4.1)

Thus, the total emissions that create damage cost for i are split between emissions made by the coalitions that contain i and emissions made by the coalitions that do not contain i.

Consider the second term of weighted sums of emissions in the argument of d_i in (5.A4.1). One may write that

$$
\sum_{S \in C \setminus C_i} \delta_s \sum_{j \in S} \tilde{e}_j^S \leq \sum_{S \in C_i} \delta_s \sum_{j \in N \setminus S} \tilde{e}_j^S
$$

(5.A4.2)

i.e. that the (weighted sum) of the emissions made by the coalitions that do not contain i is lower than or equal to the (weighted sum) of the emissions made by players external to coalitions that do contain i. This assertion (Lemma 1 in Helm) is an implication of Propositions 5.7 and 5.8 in the text of this Lecture. Indeed from Propositions 5.8 one has that at the PCNE of any S the emissions of the members are less than or equal to what they are at the NCNE:

$$
\sum_{j \in S} \tilde{e}_j^S \leq \sum_{j \in S} \bar{e}_j.
$$

As this applies also to the coalitions not in C_i, one has:

$$\sum_{S \in C \setminus C_i} \delta_s \sum_{j \in S} \tilde{e}_j^S \leq \sum_{S \in C \setminus C_i} \delta_s \sum_{j \in S} \bar{e}_j$$

$$= \sum_{S \in C} \delta_s \sum_{j \in S} \bar{e}_j - \sum_{S \in C_i} \delta_s \sum_{j \in S} \bar{e}_j$$

$$= \sum_{j \in N} \bar{e}_j - \sum_{S \in C_i} \delta_s \sum_{j \in S} \bar{e}_j$$

$$= \sum_{S \in C_i} \delta_s \left(\sum_{j \in N} \bar{e}_j - \sum_{j \in S} \bar{e}_j \right)$$

$$= \sum_{S \in C_i} \delta_s \sum_{j \in N \setminus S} \bar{e}_j.$$

Now, calling upon Proposition 5.7 saying that $\forall j \in N,\, j \notin S,\, \tilde{e}_j^S \geq \bar{e}_j$, one has for the RHS of the last expression

$$\sum_{S \in C_i} \delta_s \sum_{j \in N \setminus S} \bar{e}_j \leq \sum_{S \in C_i} \delta_s \sum_{j \in N \setminus S} \tilde{e}_j^S$$

and thus for its LHS

$$\sum_{S \in C \setminus C_i} \delta_s \sum_{j \in S} \tilde{e}_j^S \leq \sum_{S \in C_i} \delta_s \sum_{j \in N \setminus S} \tilde{e}_j^S.$$

With the inequality (5.A4.2) so established, plugging its RHS in the second term of weighted sums of emissions in the argument of d_i in (5.A4.1) leads one to rewrite it as

$$d_i \left(\sum_{j \in N} \tilde{e}_j^C \right) \leq d_i \left(\sum_{S \in C_i} \delta_s \sum_{j \in S} \tilde{e}_j^S + \sum_{S \in C_i} \delta_s \sum_{j \in N \setminus S} \tilde{e}_j^S \right)$$

$$= d_i \left(\sum_{S \in C_i} \delta_s \left(\sum_{j \in S} \tilde{e}_j^S + \sum_{j \in N \setminus S} \tilde{e}_j^S \right) \right)$$

after factoring out $\leq \delta_S$. Finally, by convexity of the function d_i,

$$d_i \left(\sum_{S \in C_i} \delta_s \left(\sum_{j \in S} \tilde{e}_j^S + \sum_{j \in N \setminus S} \tilde{e}_j^S \right) \right) \leq \sum_{S \in C_i} \delta_s d_i \left(\sum_{j \in S} \tilde{e}_j^S + \sum_{j \in N \setminus S} \tilde{e}_j^S \right).$$

Therefore,

$$d_i \left(\sum_{j \in N} \tilde{e}_j^C \right) \leq \sum_{S \in C_i} \delta_s d_i \left(\sum_{j \in N} \tilde{e}_j^S \right) \tag{5.26}$$

as was to be shown.

Lecture 6

THE GLOBAL EXTERNALITY GAME II:
ITS CT SOLUTION

The purpose and the message

Here, pursuing on the track laid down in Lecture 5, a particular solution of the GEG, called the "CT solution" is highlighted. While being explicitly grounded in the γ-core theory, it is also computable, thereby opening the way to policy decisions inspired by that theory. The actions prescribed for implementing this solution of the GEG are formulated. Among these actions, some transfers of resources between countries are shown to play an important role in stabilizing the grand coalition. These transfers are effective stabilization-wise only if they are computed according to a quite specific formula.

Detailed economic interpretations are given, supported by graphical illustrations. They show how the ecological surplus is shared among the parties at the CT solution, thereby implementing the objectives of environmental effectiveness, economic efficiency and coalitional stability announced in concluding Lecture 3.

Plan

The CT solution: a computable strategy and imputation in the γ-core of the GEG

Environmental and general economic characteristics

Specific properties of the CT solution

Whither the γ-core solution for the GEG?

The Global Externality Game II: Its CT Solution

6.1 The CT solution: A computable strategy and imputation in the γ-core of the GEG

The existence theorem of the last section is essentially a qualitative statement: it does not tell neither how to achieve, nor even how to compute a γ-core solution for the GEG. The applied nature of our enquiry in these lectures cannot be satisfied with such an abstract result. I therefore turn now to a formulation of a solution in the γ-core that can be computed. The existence result is thereby usefully complemented. This is the second approach, called constructive, that was announced above.

The problem is now one of exhibiting an imputation in the γ-core of the game (and equivalently in the core of the economy), thus of locating within the set of Pareto efficient payoffs a point having the property stated in Definition 5.6.

The linear case

For the purpose just stated, it is convenient to introduce temporarily the following:

Assumption 6.1. For all countries, thus for all players, the damage function is linear.

Formally, for all $i \in N$, $d_i(z) = \pi_i z$ with $\pi_i > 0$.

Given $(e_1^*, \ldots, e_n^*)$ the efficient strategy profile of the GEG and $z^* = \sum_{i \in N} e_i^*$ the resulting efficient ambient pollutant level, as well as $(\bar{e}_1, \ldots, \bar{e}_n)$ the NCNE strategy profile of the GEG, consider for each $i \in N$ the particular payoff

$$v_i^{**} = x_i^{**} - \pi_i z^*, \tag{6.1}$$

where

$$x_i^{**} = g_i(\bar{e}_i) - \frac{\pi_i}{\sum_{j \in N} \pi_j} \left(\sum_{j \in N} g_j(\bar{e}_j) - \sum_{j \in N} g_j(e_j^*) \right). \tag{6.2}$$

Referring to the economic-ecological model, x_i^{**} is some consumption amount of the composite GDP good in country i computed from the emissions strategies $(\bar{e}_1, \ldots, \bar{e}_n)$ and $(e_1^*, \ldots, e_n^*)$. At the world level, these consumptions are feasible for all countries as seen by summing (6.2) over all i's. The rationale of the structure of expression (6.2) will appear below after having seen its properties.

Observe now that the vector $(v_1^{**}, \ldots, v_n^{**})$ of payoffs (6.1) is an imputation of the game, induced by the strategy profile $(e_1^*, \ldots, e_n^*)$. Indeed by plugging (6.2) in (6.1) one gets:

$$\sum_{i \in N} v_i^{**} = \sum_{i \in N} [x_i^{**} - \pi_i z^*]$$

$$= \sum_{i \in N} \left[g_i(\bar{e}_i) - \frac{\pi_i}{\sum_{j \in N} \pi_j} \left(\sum_{j \in N} g_j(\bar{e}_j) - \sum_{j \in N} g_j(e_j^*) \right) - \pi_i z^* \right] \tag{6.3}$$

$$= \sum_{i \in N} g_i(\bar{e}_i) - \frac{\sum_{i \in N} \pi_i}{\sum_{j \in N} \pi_j} \left(\sum_{j \in N} g_j(\bar{e}_j) - \sum_{j \in N} g_j(e_j^*) \right) - \sum_{i \in N} \pi_i z^*$$

$$= \sum_{j \in N} g_j(e_j^*) - \sum_{i \in N} \pi_i z^*$$

$$= \sum_{i \in N} [g_i(e_i^*) - d_i(z^*)] = w^\gamma(N) \tag{6.4}$$

as defined in (5.7).

Then, the most remarkable property of this imputation is the following:

Theorem 6.1. (Chander and Tulkens, 1997): *The imputation $v^{**} = (v_1^{**}, \ldots, v_n^{**})$ defined by (6.1)–(6.2) belongs to the γ-core of the global environmental game (N, w^γ) if the linearity Assumption 6.1 is satisfied.*

Proof.[1] I proceed by contradiction. Suppose it is claimed that the imputation $v^{**} = (v_1^{**}, \ldots, v_n^{**})$ does not belong to the γ-core. By definition of the γ-core, such claim amounts to assert that there is a coalition that can block v^{**}, that is, a coalition S that can induce the strategy profile $(\tilde{e}_1^S, \ldots, \tilde{e}_n^S)$ of the PCNE relative to itself with the corresponding payoffs $(\tilde{v}_1^S, \ldots, \tilde{v}_n^S)$ whereby the members of S do improve for themselves upon the alleged γ-core payoffs $v^{**} = (v_1^{**}, \ldots, v_n^{**})$. Formally, a coalition S such that

$$\sum_{i \in S} \tilde{v}_i^S = \underbrace{\sum_{i \in S} g_i(\tilde{e}_i^S) - \sum_{i \in S} \pi_i \tilde{z}^S}_{B} > \underbrace{\sum_{i \in S} x_i^{**} - \sum_{i \in S} \pi_i z^*}_{C} = \sum_{i \in S} v_i^{**}.$$

With this strategy profile $(\tilde{e}_1^S, \ldots, \tilde{e}_n^S)$, one can construct the payoff vector $\hat{v} = (\hat{v}_1, \ldots, \hat{v}_n)$ where for each $i = 1, \ldots, n$,

$$\hat{v}_i = \underbrace{\hat{x}_i - \pi_i z^*}_{A} \tag{6.5}$$

and

$$\hat{x}_i = \underbrace{g_i(\tilde{e}_i^S) - \frac{\pi_i}{\sum_{j \in N} \pi_j} \left(\sum_{j \in N} g_j(\tilde{e}_j^S) - \sum_{j \in N} g_j(e_j^*) \right)}_{D} \tag{6.6}$$

as well as

$$z^* = \sum_{j \in N} e_j^*.$$

The vector $\hat{v}$ happens to be an alternative imputation,[2] and it is proved below that the vector $\hat{v}$ dominates the vector v^{**}. But an imputation cannot dominate another one, by definition. Then the allegedly blocking coalition leads to a logical impossibility, and therefore it cannot exist. As such impossibility prevails for any

---

[1] The argument is taken from the mentioned reference with the notation and wording adapted to the present exposition.
[2] Whose feasibility can be checked in an exercise similar to the one performed in (6.3)–(6.4).

tentatively blocking coalition S that could be envisaged, the non-existence of any such coalition proves the theorem.

Dominance of $\hat{v}$ over v^{**}, that remains to be proved, results from combining the following two steps, where it is shown, respectively:

(i) for the members of S, that $\sum_{i \in S} \hat{\nu}_i > \sum_{i \in S} \nu_i^{**}$ (i.e. that $\sum_{i \in S} A > C$)
(ii) for the players not in S, that $\hat{x}_i \geq x_i^{**} \ \forall i \in N \backslash S$ (i.e. that $D \geq E$).

As to step (i), getting $\sum_{i \in S} A > C$ is obtained via B in the following way: $\sum_{i \in S} A > B > C$. One has from (6.5)–(6.6):

$$\sum_{i \in S} \hat{v}_i = \sum_{i \in S} \hat{x}_i - \sum_{i \in S} \pi_i z^*$$

$$= \sum_{i \in S} \left[g_i(\tilde{e}_i^S) - \frac{\pi_i}{\sum\limits_{j \in N} \pi_j} \left(\sum_{j \in N} g_j(\tilde{e}_j^S) - \sum_{j \in N} g_j(e_j^*) \right) \right]$$

$$- \sum_{i \in S} \pi_i z^*$$

$$= \sum_{i \in S} g_i(\tilde{e}_i^S) - \frac{\sum\limits_{i \in S} \pi_i}{\sum\limits_{j \in N} \pi_j} \left[\sum_{i \in N} \pi_i z^* - \sum_{i \in N} \pi_i \tilde{z}^S \right.$$

$$\left. + \left(\sum_{j \in N} g_j(\tilde{e}_j^S) - \sum_{j \in N} g_j(e_j^*) \right) \right] - \sum_{i \in S} \pi_i \tilde{z}_{A'}^S. \qquad (6.7)$$

Call $A'(= \Sigma_{i \in S} A)$ the RHS of (6.7) and consider now only the expression within square brackets. It may be written

$$\sum_{j \in N} \pi_j (z^* - \tilde{z}^S) + \left(\sum_{j \in N} g_j(\tilde{e}_j^S) - \sum_{j \in N} g_j(e_j^*) \right)$$

or

$$\sum_{j \in N} \pi_j \left(\sum_{i \in N} e_i^* - \sum_{i \in N} \tilde{e}_j^S \right) + \left(\sum_{i \in N} g_i(\tilde{e}_i^S) - \sum_{i \in N} g_i(e_i^*) \right)$$

or still

$$\sum_{i \in N} \left[\sum_{j \in N} \pi_j (e_i^* - \tilde{e}_i^S) + (g_i(\tilde{e}_i^S) - g_i(e_i^*)) \right].$$

Here, one has $\forall i \in N, \sum_{j \in N} \pi_j (\tilde{e}_i^S - e_i^*) > g_i(\tilde{e}_i^S) - g_i(e_i^*)$ due to the strict concavity of the functions g_i and the fact that the first-order condition $\sum_{j \in N} \pi_j = g_i'(e_i^*)$ holds at every e_i^*. The square bracket being thus negative, the second term of (6.7) is positive. If one subtracts this second term from the RHS, (6.7) implies the inequality

$$\sum_{i \in S} \hat{v}_i > \sum_{i \in S} g_i(\tilde{e}_i^S) - \sum_{i \in S} \pi_i \tilde{z}^S, \quad \text{i.e.} \quad \sum_{i \in S} A = A' > B.$$

To go now from B to C, remember that it is claimed that S can get the RHS (B) of this inequality as an improvement upon v^{**} (i.e. C) for the members of S. If so, the imputation $\hat{v}$ is *a fortiori* such that $\sum_{i \in S} \hat{v}_i > \sum_{i \in S} v_i^{**}$, and this establishes step (i).

As to step (ii), concerning the players who are not members of S, one has to show that

$$\hat{x}_i = \underbrace{g_i(\tilde{e}_i^S) - \frac{\pi_i}{\sum_{j \in N} \pi_j} \left(\sum_{j \in N} g_j(\tilde{e}_j^S) - \sum_{j \in N} g_j(e_j^*) \right)}_{D}.$$

$$\geq \underbrace{g_i(\bar{e}_i) - \frac{\pi_i}{\sum_{j \in N} \pi_j} \left(\sum_{j \in N} g_j(\bar{e}_j) - \sum_{j \in N} g_j(e_j^*) \right)}_{E} = x_i^{**}, \ \forall i \in N \backslash S.$$

$$(6.8)$$

Given Propositions 5.6 and 5.7, when the damage functions are linear, the PCNE r.t. S, $\tilde{e}^S$, and the NCNE, $\bar{e}$, are such that $\tilde{e}_i^S = \bar{e}_i \quad \forall i \in N \backslash S$ and $\tilde{e}_i^S \leq \bar{e}_i \quad \forall i \in N$, implying that $\forall i \in N \backslash S \quad g_i(\tilde{e}_i^S) = g_i(\bar{e}_i)$ as well as $\sum_{j \in N} g_j(\tilde{e}_j^S) \leq \sum_{j \in N} g_j(\bar{e}_j)$. One thus gets in (6.8) $\hat{x}_i \geq x_i^{**} \quad \forall i \in N \backslash S$, which establishes step (ii), as required for the theorem to be proved. $\qquad \square$

From now on the imputation (6.1)–(6.2) will be called in these lectures "the CT solution" of the global externality game. As announced, the structure of expression (6.2) can now be explained as follows, together with (6.1) of which it is an essential component. The CT solution consists of, for each country i:

(a) the emissions level e_i^* and the ensuing z^*, which ensure world environmental efficiency;

(b) the aggregate consumption x_i^{**}, equal to i's production at the pre-negotiations Nash equilibrium $g_i(\bar{e}_i)$, minus a fraction $\frac{\pi_i}{\sum_{j \in N} \pi_j}$ of the difference between the total world productions at the environmentally nationalistic equilibrium $\sum_{j \in N} g_j(\bar{e}_j)$ and at the Pareto efficient state $\sum_{j \in N} g_j(e_j^*)$ — the fraction being equal to the countries' relative marginal disutilities π_i of the ambient pollutant z.

The difference between the total productions "at Nash" and "at Pareto" is to be seen as the aggregate cost, in forgone GDP, entailed by the move of the entire economic-ecological system from the pre-negotiation inefficient state where $\bar{z}$ prevails to the alternative state with $z^* < \bar{z}$, which is Pareto efficient and environmentally more friendly. The essence of the solution consists in the fact that it allocates among the countries the cost of that global move according to the fractions $\frac{\pi_i}{\sum_{j \in N} \pi_j}$. Recall that these disutilities have also been called in Lecture 2 the countries' willingnesse's to pay for a marginal reduction of the ambient pollutant, an interpretation that has some interest of its own in the transfers issue that follows.

Indeed, while computing the amounts x_i^{**} for all $i \in N$ may of course be done directly from equation (6.2), the (assumed) efficient emissions e_i^* do generate domestic productions $y_i^* = g_i(e_i^*)$ and thus possible domestic consumptions $x_i^* = y_i^*$ which may differ from the x_i^{**}'s. Considered over all i's these differences thus constitute a transfer scheme between the players, implicit in the n expressions (6.2). This is dealt with in detail in Section 6.3, where the transfers accompanying the solution are made explicit and dubbed "CT transfers". In this way, the solution lends itself to quite suggestive further economic interpretations with the help of new graphical illustrations.

A nonlinear case

A useful generalization of Theorem 6.1 is obtained by doing away with the linearity Assumption 6.1 and replacing it by:

Assumption 6.2. Within each coalition $S \subsetneq N, |S| \geq 2$, the convex aggregate damage function $\sum_{i \in S} d_i(z)$ is such that $\sum_{i \in S} d_i'(z^*) \geq d_j'(\bar{z}) \forall j \in S$ where z^* and $\bar{z}$ are the values of these variables at the efficient state and at the Nash equilibrium, respectively.

The assumption says, loosely speaking, that within each coalition the marginal damage cost of ambient pollution, which decreases anyway, should not fall "too much" between the non-cooperative Nash equilibrium and the Pareto efficient emissions. It allows one to establish the following property that characterizes the individual emissions of the coalition members at a PCNE more completely than Proposition 5.8.

Proposition 6.1. *At the PCNE relative to any S and under Assumption 6.2, the prevailing strategy profile $\tilde{e}^S = (\tilde{e}_1^S, \ldots, \tilde{e}_n^S)$ is such that*

$$\tilde{e}_i^S \leq \bar{e}_i \quad \forall i \in S, \tag{6.9}$$

i.e. *the emissions of each coalition member are lower than or equal to what they are at the non-cooperative Nash equilibrium.*

Proof. As a preliminary argument one needs to establish that

$$\tilde{z}^S = \sum_{i \in N} \tilde{e}_i^S \geq \sum_{i \in N} e_i^* = z^*. \tag{6.10}$$

Suppose not. Then, given the convexity of the functions $d_i(z)$, the first-order conditions of a PCNE and those of an efficient state imply that $d_i'(z^*) \geq d_i'(\tilde{z}^S)$ for all $i \in N$, from which it follows that $g_i'(e_i^*) \geq g_i'(\tilde{e}_i)$. All the functions $g_i(e_i)$ being strictly concave this last inequality implies that $e_i^* \leq \tilde{e}_i^S$ $\forall i \in N$. As this contradicts our supposition one must have (6.10), as well as, by convexity again,

$$\sum_{i \in S} d_i'(\tilde{z}^S) \geq \sum_{i \in S} d_i'(z^*) \; \forall S \subset N.$$

Since from Assumption 6.2 $\sum_{i \in S} d_i'(\tilde{z}^S) \geq d_j'(\tilde{z})$ $\forall j \in S$, and from the first-order conditions of any PCNE's one has $g_j'(\tilde{e}_j) \geq g_j'(\bar{e}_j)$ for all $j \in S$, (6.9) is obtained due, again, to the strict concavity of the functions $g_i(e_i)$. $\square$

Consider now for each $i \in N$ the payoff (6.1) where instead of (6.2) one has:

$$x_i^{**} = g_i(\bar{e}_i) - \frac{d_i'(z^*)}{\sum\limits_{j \in N} d_j'(z^*)} \left(\sum_{j \in N} g_j(\bar{e}_j) - \sum_{j \in N} g_j(e_j^*) \right). \quad (6.11)$$

The difference between (6.2) and (6.11) is found in the coefficients of relative marginal disutilities evaluated at the optimum z^*, whereby the aggregate cost of reducing all emissions is shared among the players-countries. Theorem 6.1 can then be modified into:

Theorem 6.2. (Chander and Tulkens, 1997): *The imputation* $(v_1^{**}, \ldots, v_n^{**})$ *defined by* (6.1) *and* (6.11) *belongs to the γ-core of the GEG (N, w^γ) if the nonlinearity Assumption 6.2 is satisfied.*

Proof.[3] As the sequence of arguments is of the same nature as in the proof of Theorem 6.1, I reproduce this sequence almost verbatim, to facilitate spotting the differences due to the convex function $d_i(z)$ replacing the linear one $\pi_i z$, as well as the implications revealed by Proposition 6.1.

Proceeding again by contradiction, suppose it is claimed that the imputation defined by (6.1) and (6.11) does not belong to the γ-core. Then there should exist a coalition S that can block v^{**} by means of the strategy profile $(\tilde{e}_1^S, \ldots, \tilde{e}_n^S)$ of the PCNE

---

[3]The argument is taken from Chander and Tulkens (1997), with the notation and wording adapted to the present exposition.

relative to itself with the corresponding payoffs $(\tilde{v}_1^S, \ldots, \tilde{v}_n^S)$, whereby the members of S do improve for themselves upon the payoffs $v^{**} = (v_1^{**}, \ldots, v_n^{**})$. Formally, a coalition S such that

$$\sum_{i \in S} \tilde{v}_i^S = \underbrace{\sum_{i \in S} g_i(\tilde{e}_i^S) - \sum_{i \in S} d_i(\tilde{z}^S)}_{\mathbf{B}} > \underbrace{\sum_{i \in S} x_i^{**} - \sum_{i \in S} d_i(z^*)}_{\mathbf{C}} = \sum_{i \in S} v_i^{**}.$$

With this strategy profile $(\tilde{e}_1^S, \ldots, \tilde{e}_n^S)$, one can construct the payoff vector $\hat{v} = (\hat{v}_1, \ldots, \hat{v}_n)$ where for each $i = 1, \ldots, n$,

$$\hat{v}_i = \underbrace{\hat{x}_i - d_i(z^*)}_{\mathbf{A}} \tag{6.12}$$

and

$$\hat{x}_i = \underbrace{g_i(\tilde{e}_i^S) - \frac{d_i'(z^*)}{\sum_{j \in N} d_j'(z^*)} \left(\sum_{j \in N} g_j(\tilde{e}_j^S) - \sum_{j \in N} g_j(e_j^*) \right)}_{\mathbf{D}}. \tag{6.13}$$

as well as

$$z^* = \sum_{j \in N} e_j^*.$$

The vector $\hat{v}$ happens to be an alternative imputation,[4] and it is proved below that the vector $\hat{v}$ dominates the vector v^{**}. Since an imputation cannot dominate another one, by definition, the allegedly blocking coalition leads to a logical impossibility and therefore it cannot exist. As with Theorem 6.1, the non-existence of any such coalition proves Theorem 6.2.

Dominance of $\hat{v}$ over v^{**} results from combining the following two steps, where it is shown, respectively:

(i) for the members of S, that $\sum_{i \in S} \hat{v}_i > \sum_{i \in S} v_i^{**}$ (i.e. that $\sum_{i \in S} \mathbf{A} > \mathbf{C}$ here above),

---

[4]Whose feasibility can be checked in an exercise similar to the one performed in (6.3)–(6.4).

(ii) for the players not in S, that $\sum_{i \in N \setminus S} \hat{x}_i \geq \sum_{i \in N \setminus S} x_i^{**}$ i.e. that $\Sigma_{i \in N \setminus S} \mathbf{D} > \Sigma_{i \in N \setminus S} \mathbf{E}$ in (6.13) and (6.11) respectively.

As to step (i), getting $\sum_{i \in S} \mathbf{A} > \mathbf{C}$ is obtained via $\mathbf{B}$ in the following way: $\sum_{i \in S} \mathbf{A} > \mathbf{B} > \mathbf{C}$. One has from (6.12)–(6.13):

$$
\sum_{i \in S} \hat{v}_i = \sum_{i \in S} \hat{x}_i - \sum_{i \in S} d_i(z^*)
$$

$$
= \sum_{i \in S} \left[g_i(\tilde{e}_i^S) - \frac{d_i'(z^*)}{\sum_{j \in N} d_j'(z^*)} \left(\sum_{j \in N} g_j(\tilde{e}_j^S) - \sum_{j \in N} g_j(e_j^*) \right) \right]
$$

$$
- \sum_{i \in S} d_i(z^*)
$$

$$
\geq \sum_{i \in S} g_i(\tilde{e}_i^S) - \frac{\sum_{i \in S} d_i'(z^*)}{\sum_{j \in N} d_j'(z^*)}
$$

$$
\times \left[\sum_{i \in N} d_i'(z^*) \left(\sum_{j \in N} \tilde{e}_j^S - \sum_{j \in N} e_j^* \right) \right] - \sum_{i \in S} d_i(z^*) \qquad (6.14)
$$

using the concavity of the functions g_i and the efficiency conditions $\sum_{i \in N} d_i'(z^*) = g_j'(e_j^*)$ for all $j \in N$. But in the RHS of this expression, one has

$$
\sum_{i \in S} g_i(\tilde{e}_i^S) - \frac{\Sigma_{i \in S} d_i'(z^*)}{\Sigma_{j \in N} d_j'(z^*)} \times \left[\sum_{i \in N} d'(z^*)(\tilde{z}^s - z^*) \right],
$$

and thus:

$$
\sum_{i \in S} \hat{v}_i = \sum_{i \in S} \hat{x}_i - \sum_{i \in S} d_i'(z^*) z^* \geq \sum_{i \in S} g_i(\tilde{e}_i^S) - \sum_{i \in S} d_i'(\tilde{z}^S) \tilde{z}^S.
$$

This implies

$$\sum_{i \in S} \hat{v}_i = \sum_{i \in S} \hat{x}_i - \sum_{i \in S} d_i(z^*)$$

$$\geq \sum_{i \in S} g_i(\tilde{e}_i^S) - \sum_{i \in S} d_i(\tilde{z}^S)$$

$$- \left[\sum_{i \in S} d_i(z^*) + \sum_{i \in S} d_i(\tilde{z}^S) - \sum_{i \in S} d'_j(z^*)(z^* - \tilde{z}^S) \right]$$

and by convexity of the functions $d_i(z)$, implying that the magnitude within square brackets is negative,

$$> \sum_{i \in S} g_i(\tilde{e}_i^S) - \sum_{i \in S} d_i(\tilde{z}^S), \quad \text{i.e.} \quad \sum_{i \in S} \mathbf{A} > \mathbf{B}.$$

To go now from $\mathbf{B}$ to $\mathbf{C}$, remember that it is claimed that S can get the RHS ($\mathbf{B}$) of this inequality as an improvement upon v^{**} (i.e. $\mathbf{C}$) for the members of S. If so, the imputation $\hat{v}$ is *a fortiori* such that $\sum_{i \in S} \hat{v}_i > \sum_{i \in S} v_i^{**}$, as is to be proved in (i).

As to step (ii), one has to show that $\Sigma_{i \in N \backslash S} \mathbf{D} > \Sigma_{i \in N \backslash S} \mathbf{E}$. This is done as follows using properties of the economic-ecological model. On the one hand, one has from (6.13) that

$$\sum_{i \in N \backslash S} \hat{x}_i = \sum_{i \in N \backslash S} g_i(\tilde{e}_i^S) - \sum_{i \in N \backslash S} \frac{d'_i(z^*)}{\sum_{j \in N} d'_j(z^*)}$$

$$\times \left(\sum_{j \in N} g_j(\tilde{e}_j^S) - \sum_{j \in N} g_j(e_j^*) \right)$$

$$= \sum_{i \in N \backslash S} g_i(\bar{e}_i) - \sum_{i \in N \backslash S} \frac{d'_i(z^*)}{\sum_{j \in N} d'_j(z^*)}$$

$$\times \left(\sum_{j \in N} g_j(\bar{e}_j) - \sum_{j \in N} g_j(e_j^*) \right)$$

$$+ \left(\sum_{i \in N \setminus S} g_i(\tilde{e}_i) - \sum_{i \in N \setminus S} g_i(\bar{e}_i) \right)$$

$$+ \sum_{i \in N \setminus S} \frac{d'_i(z^*)}{\sum_{j \in N} d'_j(z^*)} \left(\sum_{j \in N} g_j(\bar{e}_j) - \sum_{j \in N} g_j(\tilde{e}_j) \right) \qquad (6.15)$$

$$= \sum_{i \in N \setminus S} x_i^* + \left(\sum_{i \in N \setminus S} g_i(\tilde{e}_i^S) - \sum_{i \in N \setminus S} g_i(\bar{e}_i) \right)$$

$$+ \sum_{i \in N \setminus S} \frac{d'_i(z^*)}{\sum_{j \in N} d'_j(z^*)} \left(\sum_{j \in N} g_j(\bar{e}_j) - \sum_{j \in N} g_j(\tilde{e}_j) \right)$$

$$= \sum_{i \in N \setminus S} x_i^* + \left[\left(\sum_{i \in N \setminus S} g_i(\tilde{e}_i^S) - \sum_{i \in N \setminus S} g_i(\bar{e}_i) \right) \right.$$

$$\left. - \sum_{i \in N \setminus S} \frac{d'_i(z^*)}{\sum_{j \in N} d'_j(z^*)} \left(\sum_{j \in N \setminus S} g_j(\tilde{e}_j^S) - \sum_{j \in N \setminus S} g_j(\bar{e}_j) \right) \right]$$

$$- \sum_{i \in N \setminus S} \frac{d'_i(z^*)}{\sum_{j \in N} d'_j(z^*)} \left(\sum_{j \in S} g_j(\tilde{e}_j^S) - \sum_{j \in S} g_j(\bar{e}_j) \right).$$

On the other hand, by Proposition 5.7 $\tilde{e}_i^S \geq \bar{e}_i$ for all $i \in N \setminus S$ and by Proposition 6.1 $\tilde{e}_i^S \leq \bar{e}_i$ for all $i \in S$. Therefore the sum of all terms in the RHS of the last expression is strictly positive. One thus gets from (6.15) $\sum_{i \in N \setminus S} \hat{x}_i > \sum_{i \in N \setminus S} x_i^{**}$ which establishes (ii) as required for the theorem to be proved. $\square$

Compared with the linear damage function case of Theorem 6.1, the property that $\tilde{e}_i^S \leq \bar{e}_i$ for all $i \in S$ plays a key role in the last part of the above proof of the nonlinear case.

Identical players

Assumption 6.3. In the GEG and thus in the underlying economic-ecological model, all players-countries are identical.

Formally, for all $\forall i, j \in N$, the functions $d_i = d_j$ and $g_i = g_j$.

The interest of working with this assumption is essentially methodological. Economically, it is of course not realistic in the framework of a *global* externality game (recall that "global" here means all countries of the world). But it can be useful as a benchmark to characterize solutions as done at some occasions below.

Accordingly, Theorems 6.1 and 6.2 are further modified into:

Theorem 6.3. *The imputation assigning equal payoffs with zero transfers to all players belongs to the γ-core of the GEG (N, w^γ) if the identical players Assumption 6.3 is satisfied.*

Proof. [5] Let $u^* = (u_1^*, \ldots, u_n^*)$ be the efficient payoff vector and for any $S \subset N, S \neq \emptyset$, consider $\tilde{e}^S = (\tilde{e}_1^S, \ldots, \tilde{e}_n^S)$ the PCNE r.t. S as well as $\tilde{u}^S = (\tilde{u}_1^S, \ldots, \tilde{u}_n^S)$ the payoffs vector at $\tilde{e}^S$. Note that with identical players, $u_i^* = u_j^* \; \forall i, \; j \in N$, $\tilde{e}_i^S = \tilde{e}_k^S$ and $\tilde{u}_i^S = \tilde{u}_k^S \; \forall i, k \in S$ as well as $\tilde{e}_j^S = \tilde{e}_l^S$ and $\tilde{u}_j^S = \tilde{u}_l^S \; \forall j, l \notin S$. However, from the first-order conditions (5.10) and (5.11) of a PCNE one has that $\tilde{e}_i^S < \tilde{e}_j^S$ and $\tilde{u}_i^S < \tilde{u}_j^S \; \forall i \in S, \; j \notin S$. Furthermore, recall the inefficiency property of the PCNE r.t. any S, that is, $\sum_{i \in N} \tilde{u}_i^S < \sum_{i \in N} u_i^*$. This inequality may be written

$$\sum_{i \in S} \tilde{u}_i^S + \sum_{j \notin S} \tilde{u}_j^S < \sum_{i \in S} u_i^* + \sum_{j \notin S} u_j^*. \tag{6.16}$$

---

[5]The theorem is inspired from, and extends, the Corollary to Proposition 6 in Chander and Tulkens (1997, pp. 398–399), whose proof is based on showing that the assumption of identical utilities implies (6.9) and then applying the Theorem 6.2 to obtain existence. The more direct proof given here, with identical players and independent of Theorem 6.2, is an edited version of one due to Chander (private communication).

By definition of the γ-coalitional function $\sum_{i \in S} \tilde{u}_i^S = w^\gamma(S)$ and $\sum_{i \in N} u_i^* = w^\gamma(N)$, the imputation u^* dominates the worth of S if one shows that in (6.16)

$$\sum_{i \in S} u_i^* > \sum_{i \in S} \tilde{u}_i^S \qquad (6.17)$$

and this imputation belongs to the γ-core of the game if (6.17) holds for all coalitions S.

Under the identical players Assumption 6.3, the inefficiency inequality (6.16) reads

$$s\,\tilde{u}_i^S + (n-s)\,\tilde{u}_j^S < s\,u_i^* + (n-s)\,u_j^*, \quad \forall i \in S,\ \forall j \notin S$$

where $s, n = |S|, |N|$, respectively. This expression contains the domination property (6.17) of u^* over the coalition S in the form $s\,u_i^* > s\,\tilde{u}_i^S \ \forall i \in S$, because it reduces to

$$-nu_j^* + s\,\tilde{u}_i^S + n\,\tilde{u}_j^S - s\,\tilde{u}_j^S < s\,u_i^* - s\,u_j^*, \quad \forall i \in S,\ \forall j \notin S$$

or

$$-n(u_j^* - \tilde{u}_j^S) < s(u_i^* - u_j^*),$$

where the difference on the left is positive and the one on the right is zero since

$$u_i^* = u_j^* \ \forall i,\ j \in N. \qquad \square$$

Note that transfers are inexistent in this case, which is confirmed below with the formula of CT transfers given in (6.19). Theorem 6.3 reveals that it is the diversity of the players-countries which is the source of the role played by transfers in the achievement of coalitional stability, in contrast with the fact that they have no role in the achievement of efficiency.

Moreover, the non-emptiness of the γ-core with any number of identical players may usefully be compared with the non-existence results with more than three players under the other coalitional stability theory considered in Lecture 9.

6.2   Environmental and general economic characteristics

Theorem 5.1 together with its Lemma 5.1 as well as Theorems 6.1 and 6.2 are the central elements of these lectures. To get a full appreciation of their scope for social science in general, beyond the specific interest of the mathematical methodology used to construct them, one has to go back to the economic-ecological model and explore at that level the significance of the results.

The γ-core and the optimal level of pollution

Environmentally, the γ-core concept in general and its CT particular solution do not bring anything more than the efficient levels of emissions and of ambient pollutant that the plain economic reasoning of Lecture 3 had readily identified by means of classical tools of economic analysis. Strictly speaking, game theory brings nothing new, neither to the description nor to the understanding of the physical components of the pollution phenomenon at its optimal level. Yet, implementation of this optimum requires knowledge of it in numerical terms. Thus far, nothing has been said on the method whereby this knowledge could be acquired.

The members of my audience who are familiar with modeling techniques in economics and/or operations research have already realized, from Lecture 3 on, that since the efficient levels in question are the solution of mathematical programming problems, they can be obtained by means of well known algorithms that compute these solutions as soon as the parameters of the objective functions and constraints are known. This is exactly what is done in Lecture 8 with a numerical model slightly more elaborate than the reference model used thus far in these lectures.

As there is no reason neither to believe nor to assert[6] that this optimal level of pollution be ever achieved spontaneously by privately

---

[6]Sometimes, believers in the optimality virtues of market organization — which are real as far as standard economic goods are concerned — transpose them abusively to other goods for which these virtues fail to hold, as, for instance, those that generate diffuse externalities. This is not to be confused with giving a

motivated market forces, the computation just mentioned is the only way to approach world efficiency. Modeling tools of the kind to be presented in Lecture 8 are thus inescapable components of the negotiations activities here under study. Yet, the decision process *within* the negotiations, given these computation, is of the nature of voting games. This is explored in Currarini and Tulkens (2014) and would deserve a development of its own, not covered here.

The γ-core and economic theory

Externalities vs. public goods

Is the γ-core theory a contribution to the theory of externalities or to the theory of public goods? I boast to answer: to both! As to externalities, thanks to Arrow's (1971) ingenious modeling of externalities as a two-dimensional commodity, recalled in Lecture 1, one can disentangle the often confusing discourses on whether pollution is an externality or a public good (bad). As I argued, emissions of pollutant are of the nature of a private good, while reception of it is of the nature of a public good in those cases where the medium between emission and reception has the physical property of having diffuse effects. The expressions (6.1)–(6.2) of the outcome of the CT solution reflects this two-fold component.

Indeed on the one hand, the first term of (6.2) and of (6.11) specifies a production level for a private good at the non-cooperative Nash equilibrium, that generates as a by-product in each country i an amount $\bar{e}_i$ of pollutant emissions. On the other hand, the second term of (6.2) and of (6.11) contains a scheme, $\frac{\pi_i}{\sum_{j \in N} \pi_j}$, of sharing among the countries the aggregate cost of the change in the public good, that is, of the ambient diffuse pollutant from $\bar{z}$ at Nash to z^* at Pareto.[7]

---

role to markets in the *allocation* of given amounts of emission permits, which is presented in Lecture 10.

[7]Such cost sharing scheme of the public good component, namely the ratio of relative marginal willingness's to pay for the public good, is not specific to the

As to the theory of public goods, the GEG with its γ-core solution may be seen as formalizing the voluntary exchange theory of public goods that Buchanan (1968) opposed to the state planning view that was prevalent at the time. I elaborate on this view in the concluding Section 6.4.

Which optimum among the many?

In Section 3.2 of Lecture 3, it was stated that in an economic-ecological model of the kind I am working with there are an infinity of efficient states. The point was illustrated in Fig. 3.1 for the special model of a two countries economy where one country is only a polluter and the other a pollutee only. In two subsequent illustrations (Figs. 3.5 and 3.6) a distinction was introduced between two subsets of (also infinite) efficient states, each relative to a different no-negotiation point labeled H or M, respectively. To which one of these two no-negotiation points does the γ-core correspond, and, as a corollary to that question, to which one of the two efficient subsets do the negotiations lead? Furthermore, within the retained subset, which point does the CT solution select?

The answers to these questions are contained in the expressions (6.1)–(6.2) that define the γ-core strategy profile of the CT solution: the Nash equilibrium emissions mentioned in (6.2) are those of point M in Fig. 6.1 (which reproduces Fig. 3.6 with some additions). Therefore the set of efficient states accessible from M is the set of points making up the line segment BA. Furthermore, B is the point selected by the CT solution in this case. I realize that this may not be transparent at this stage for all readers, but it will after the paragraphs that follow. Let me first present the gist of the argument by sticking momentarily to the two countries illustration

---

present model. It has properties of general interest in the theory of public goods, elaborated upon in Chander (1993) and used in Kaitala, Mäler and Tulkens (1995) as well as in Chander and Tulkens (1991/2002). Chander and Tulkens (1997) also suggest that a connection can be made with so-called "Lindahl prices" for public goods, as well as with the concept of "ratio equilibrium" of Kaneko and Silvestre.

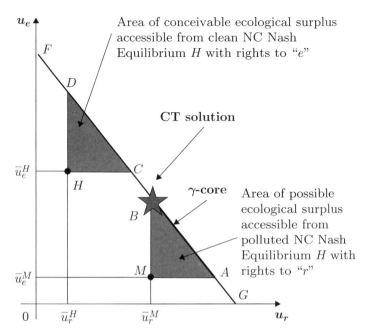

Fig. 6.1 The γ-core and the CT solution in the payoffs space of the "one polluter 'r'–one pollutee 'e'" economy.

and lift thereafter the restriction to two player-countries in the three-dimensional Figs. 6.2(a) and (b) of pp. 214–216.

An amendment to the Coase theorem in the case of international externalities

The celebrated Coase (1960) theory of externalities, evoked in Lecture 3, says essentially (i) that when the right to exert a detrimental externality is unambiguously assigned by some authority empowered to grant it — right to emit if assigned to the polluter or right to forbid emitting if assigned to the pollutee — voluntary bargaining among the parties under the established assignment can be beneficial to both and thereby result in an efficient agreement; and (ii) that to which of the two parties these rights are allocated by the said authority does not matter for the bargaining to occur and be beneficial for both parties. Thus, an efficient outcome can occur in *either* case of rights assignment (*H* or *M* in Fig. 6.1).

However in international affairs, among which climate change, no supranational authority exists empowered to assign rights to emit pollutants. As a result, polluters have the opportunity to arrogate the rights to themselves. Therefore, the message of the γ-core solution for international global negotiations consists in the following amendment:

(1) *In agreement with Coase*, bargaining among countries *can lead to mutually beneficial voluntary agreements* — and the γ-core is an illustration of that, when this bargaining occurs on the basis of rights being recognized as *de facto* owned and exerted by the polluters (point M).

(2) *In disagreement with Coase*, if rights are asserted to belong to the pollutees (point H), as implied if the de facto allocation of rights to polluters is *not* recognized, then there is no basis on which bargaining among countries can occur, the reason being that *rights so assigned cannot be enforced* due to the lack of supranational authority. And no basis for bargaining makes no voluntary agreement possible.

Thus, just the first half of the Coase theorem applies to international externalities, and this only with the quite specific assignment of rights recognized as arrogated by the polluters. The second half is irrelevant, because inapplicable.[8]

This provides the logical foundation for considering that the γ-core theory of the outcome of international environmental negotiations rests on an assumed Nash equilibrium starting point where pollution emission rights are *de facto* detained by the pollutant emitters. As announced, this is point M in Fig. 6.1 and restricts to the segment AB the set of efficient points (or "optima") reachable by negotiations. Which one among these points the CT solution selects comes shortly, after transfers are introduced in the picture.

---

[8]Using the interesting distinction introduced by Starrett (1972) between the "possession rule" and the "common use rule", in the case of international externalities only the former can prevail, the latter being unenforceable, and only on that basis he considers the core to be well defined.

6.3 Specific properties of the CT solution

Exhibiting the transfers implicit in the solution

As pointed out above in the last comment that followed the linear case, every γ-core solution of the GEG contains implicitly payoff transfers between the players, or, in the terms of the economic-ecological model, transfer payments of GDP between the countries. The precise reason is as follows: the solution contains by definition the vector of efficient emissions $e^* = (e_1^*, \ldots, e_1^*)$ which has been shown to be unique (Proposition 3.4). But there is no reason that the components x_i^{**} prescribed for the outcome in the γ-core be such that x_i^{**} equals $y_i^* = g_i(e_i^*)$. As soon as for some $i \in N$, $x_i^{**} \neq y_i^* = g_i(e_i^*)$, the scarcity constraint (3.16) of the model requires non-zero transfers to occur between at least two countries.

The CT transfers formula

More important than this arithmetic is the fact that the transfers implicit in the solution v^{**} have the special virtue of inducing the γ-core stability property of that solution. *This is due to their special structure*, to be revealed shortly. To that effect, consider the following rearrangement of the n components of the γ-core imputation vector:

$$v_i^{**} = x_i^{**} - \pi_i z^*$$

$$= g_i(\bar{e}_i) - \frac{\pi_i}{\sum_{j \in N} \pi_j} \left(\sum_{j \in N} g_j(\bar{e}_j) - \sum_{j \in N} g_j(e_j^*) \right) - \pi_i z^*$$

$$= g_i(e_i^*) - \pi_i z^*$$

$$+ \left[(g_i(\bar{e}_i) - g_i(e_i^*)) - \frac{\pi_i}{\sum_{j \in N} \pi_j} \left(\sum_{j \in N} g_j(\bar{e}_j) - \sum_{j \in N} g_j(e_j^*) \right) \right]$$

$$= g_i(e_i^*) - \pi_i z^* + T_i,$$

$$= v_i^* + T_i, \quad i = 1, \ldots, n, \tag{6.18}$$

where T_i stands for the expression within square brackets in the line preceding (6.18). One easily verifies that globally $\sum_{i \in N} T_i = 0$, so that, for every i, $T_i \in R$ is indeed a transfer of the GDP commodity between the countries, received by i if > 0 or paid if < 0, and globally the budget of these transfers is balanced.[9] The units are those of the composite commodity, exchange rates issues being ignored. Given (6.18) the "CT solution" of (6.1)–(6.2) is thus sometimes called, albeit redundantly, the "CT solution with transfers."

The economic significance

In the form (6.8), the economic significance of the CT solution appears more completely on seven counts. First, given the imputation vector $(v_1^*, \dots, v_n^*)$, the CT transfers are of course a way to reallocate the payoffs among the players so as to form a new, similarly efficient vector $(v_1^{**}, \dots, v_n^{**})$.[10]

Second, from (6.8) the CT transfer of each i appears to consist of two components:

$$T_i = \underbrace{(g_i(\bar{e}_i) - g_i(e_i^*))}_{\substack{\text{(a) compensation for the move} \\ \text{from Nash to Pareto}}} - \underbrace{\frac{\pi_i}{\sum_{j \in N} \pi_j} \left(\sum_{j \in N} g_j(\bar{e}_j) - \sum_{j \in N} g_j(e_j^*) \right)}_{\substack{\text{(b) share in the world total cost of the move} \\ \text{from Nash to Pareto}}}.$$

$$(6.19)$$

The rationale of this structure is partly economic and partly game theoretic. As indicated underneath the respective components mentioned in (6.19), the significance of each term is to be seen as follows:

- Term (a) is the amount of output change in country i between its production at the nationalistic equilibrium and at the efficient

---

[9] The transfer formula presented here is identical to the one appearing in Chander and Tulkens (1997, p. 392, ftn. 10).

[10] The argument is formulated here with the notation π_i of the linearity Assumption 5.1. It is easily checked that it holds *verbatim* with the nonlinearity Assumption 6.2.

state. This part of the transfer wipes out that difference, which is normally positive but possibly negative as the case may be, and brings i back at its output level of the nationalistic equilibrium. In other words, this term neutralizes for i the private good effect of the solution that brings him from $\bar{e}_i$ to e_i^*. It reflects the private good component of the CT solution described in Section 6.2.

• Term (b) is country i's payment (always negative) of its share $\frac{\pi_i}{\sum_{j \in N} \pi_j}$ in covering the aggregate cost of the reduction of global production allowing the move from $\bar{z}$ at Nash to z^* at Pareto. It reflects the public good component of the solution similarly highlighted earlier.

Third, if the CT transfers have the property of inducing stability in the sense of the core, this is entirely due to the specific form just commented about, grounded in public goods theory. In other analyses, the idea of transfers is often taken up by authors to make them achieve other objectives, such as distributional justice for instance. Their formulae are based on parameters such as population levels, or GDP per capita, or emissions per capita, and many others. But in so doing, the coalitional stability property is lost: Theorems 6.1 and 6.2 do not hold.[11]

Fourth, there is clearly nothing distributional in (6.18). Yet, *combining* coalitional stability with other criteria is conceivable, and has been introduced in an interesting extension of a numerical model done by van Steenberghe (2003). In a further analytical development inspired by the Rawls theory of justice, Rogna (2016) points out that the game theoretic concept of nucleolus may be used as a way to select within the γ-core an imputation motivated by distributive considerations. Indeed, the nucleolus has Rawlsian distributive properties and it always belongs to the core of a cooperative game. He

---

[11]By contrast, the multiple numerical experiments of transfer conceptual by simulations made in Lessman *et al.* (2015) suffer from the lack of theoretical background supporting them. The so called "optimal" transfers of Carraro, Eyckmans and Finus (2006) and Weikard (2009), reviewed in Nagashima (2010) are an exception in this respect. They are designed so as to implement "internal stability", a concept critically discussed in Lecture 9 below.

therefore rightly concludes that the "Rawlsian nucleolus" he proposes is the core solution with the highest redistributive properties. In other words, the Rawlsian nucleolus is the most beneficial solution among the many coalitionally stable ones, for the countries whose welfare level is lowest.

Fifth, if one thinks of the CT solution in terms of implementation in practice, formula (6.19) is to be used in the following two simple instructions addressed to each player-country $i \in N$:

(i) operate the efficient emissions strategy e_i^*, and enjoy the ensuing utility level $g_i(e_i^*) - \pi_i(z^*)$, and

(ii) receive or pay the transfer T_i.

If followed by all players-countries, the outcome of these two instructions is a state of the system in the γ-core of the GEG, according to Theorem 6.1. In that sense, the solution vector $(v_1^{**}, \ldots, v_n^{**})$ with components rewritten as in (6.18), is an implementable and constructive expression of the CT imputation.[12]

Sixth, can the CT solution be seen as a spontaneous, i.e. voluntary outcome of interactions between the parties or is a planner necessary for it to prevail? No clear-cut answer can be given to that question. But neither of these institutional responses need to be assumed. In view of all the virtues that have been described, if the solution is proposed by, say, an empire, why would it be rejected? For sure, the efficient strategy profile e^* as well as the stability enhancing transfers T must somehow be specified. But since no process has been formulated thus far from which it would be shown that these magnitudes could spontaneously emerge from individual behaviors,[13] one can only count at this time on computation by an empire and acceptance by the parties on rationality grounds. In that limited

---

[12] An alternative but equivalent formulation of the CT transfers is provided in Lecture 8, in the framework of a dynamic simulation model of the GEG.

[13] A bit in the spirit of the so-called "tâtonnement processes" of the economic theoretic literature of the years 1980–1990. A tempting research topic for the future, isn't it? Here, I am alluding again to a possible extensive form of the GEG, still to be formulated.

sense I feel one can assert that the CT solution is a voluntary outcome of the GEG.

Seventh, the transfers (6.19) play a role in the model as "lump sum" ones, that is, they are paid or received by the countries without this affecting any behavioral variable other than the countries' utility levels. Non-lump sum transfers, which by definition would be based on some variable describing a behavior, would modify the level of this variable, in equilibrium or its optimal value, and therefore the entire outcome. This could be the case if, for instance, the transfers were earmarked to finance adaptation expenditure on the receivers side, whereas on the payers side they would be collected by income taxation. Entering in such a fascinating development would require abandoning the one commodity world of the economic-ecological model used thus far. I can only leave it for another occasion.

Note finally that formula (6.19) implies that in the case of identical players-countries all transfers equal to zero, in line with Theorem 6.3.

How is the ecological surplus being shared at the CT solution?

The form (6.18) of the γ-core imputation, together with the seven comments just given on the transfers (6.19), provides the answer to the question left unanswered at the end of Section 6.2. At the CT solution the surplus goes exclusively to the pollutes and this corresponds to point B of Fig. 6.1 as was announced.

What is that surplus made of, for each country i? In Lecture 3, the total surplus before transfers is defined in (3.42) as

$$\widehat{u}^* - \widehat{u} \underset{\text{def}}{=} \sum_{i \in N} (g_i(e_i^*) - d_i(z^*)) - \sum_{i \in N} (g_i(\bar{e}_i) - d_i(\bar{z}))$$

and shown in Proposition 3.10 to be strictly positive. Here, at the CT solution with transfers T_i, each country i gets from that total

$$u_i^{**} - \bar{u}_i = (g_i(e_i^*) - d_i(z^*)) + T_i - (g_i(\bar{e}_i) - d_i(z)).$$

Using (6.11), this reduces to

$$(d_i(\bar{z}) - d_i(z^*)) - \frac{d_i'}{\sum_{j\in N} d_j'} \left(\sum_{j\in N} g_j(\bar{e}_j) - \sum_{j\in N} g_j(e_j^*) \right) \qquad (6.20)$$

where the first term between parentheses is the amount of damage cost avoided by i thanks to the reduction of the ambient pollutant from $\bar{z}$ to z^* and the second term is the amount borne by i of the total world cost of the reduced world output due to that move — an amount proportional to d_i' that is, to the country's willingness to pay to avoid the damages of ambient pollutant. The individual rationality of the CT solution ensures that (6.20) is positive for any country i where $d_i' > 0$.

The respective positions of polluters vs. pollutees at the CT solution: Graphical illustration

Illustrating the γ-core solution for the standard GEG where the number of countries-players is larger than two is done at the end of Lecture 5: with the three-dimensional Fig. 5.1 the role of coalitions is identified. But the figures of Lecture 3 also permitted to further distinguish the specific roles of the economic agents *qua* emitters *vs.* *qua* recipients of the externality. How about the CT solution in that context? This is done in Fig. 6.2.

The game with 1 polluter and 2 pollutees

For the particular 3 players GEG with one polluting country (indexed 1 in this section) and two polluted countries (indexed 2 and 3),[14] consider the space of payoffs drawn in Fig. 6.2. By convention, let the origin be set at the payoff levels of the Nash equilibrium in the case where the right to emit pollutant is exerted by the polluter, the equivalent of point M in the two countries case. The coordinates of every point of the triangular surface ABC are those of an imputation,

---

[14]The respective payoff functions of the polluter and the pollutees are the same as those specified in the appendix of Lecture 3.

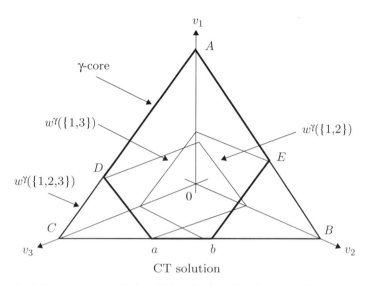

CT solution

Fig. 6.2   The γ-core and the CT solution in the payoffs space of the one polluter (1)–two pollutees (2,3) economy.

Notes: (i) The imputations in the triangle CDa can be improved upon by coalition $\{2, 1\}$.

(ii) The imputations in the triangle BEb can be improved upon by coalition $\{1, 3\}$.

(iii) The coalition $\{2, 3\}$ cannot improve upon the Nash equilibrium payoffs.

so that the entire surface constitutes the payoff possibility frontier of the all players set $N = \{1, 2, 3\}$. The ecological surplus defined in Lecture 3 for the two players case, is transposed here into a path of payoff gains that goes from the origin to some efficient point on that surface.

As in the general case of Figs. 4.2–4.4, the payoff possibility frontiers of coalitions $\{1, 2\}$ and $\{1, 3\}$ are represented here by lines in their respective two-dimensional payoff spaces, and then again by their projection on the surface ABC as the line segments Da and Eb, respectively. They each correspond to what the polluter can achieve with either one of the pollutees taken separately. The payoff frontier of coalition $\{2, 3\}$ reduces to one point, the origin, because both players are deprived of any emissions strategy that they could coordinate to do better.

The γ-core of the game is the set of points in the polygon *ADabEA*. The CT solution, that is, the γ-core imputation (6.1)–(6.2), is some point on the line segment *ab*, where the payoff of the polluting country 1 is at the level of the Nash equilibrium, and all the ecological surplus is captured by the pollutee countries 2 and 3. The precise point on the segment *ab* is determined by the relative values of the marginal disutilities d_1' and d_2'.

Comparing, *mutatis mutandis*, with the one polluter–one pollutee game of Fig. 3.5 in Lecture 3, the CT solution point just located here is of the same nature as point A in that previous case, where the Nash equilibrium is point M and the core of the game is the entire segment AB. The CT solution for this two players game is actually point A on that segment, with the transfer received by player (r) from player (e) being represented by a segment of the horizontal axes extending between point H and the abscissa of point A.

The game with 2 polluters and 1 pollutee

In Fig. 6.3, the triangle ABC is again the set of imputations for $N = \{1, 2, 3\}$. Players 1 and 2 are both polluters, whereas player 3 is only a pollutee and the only one. The payoff frontiers of what coalitions $\{2, 3\}$ and $\{1, 3\}$ can do are projected on the triangle ABC as DG and EF, respectively. The payoff frontier of coalition $\{1, 2\}$ reduces to one point, the origin.

The γ-core of the game is in this case the set of points in the polygon $AERDA$. The CT solution, i.e. the γ-core imputation (6.1)–(6.2) is point A, where the pollutee country 3 captures all of the ecological surplus. This point is again of the same nature as point A in the 2 players game of Fig. 3.4, where the Nash equilibrium is point M and the transfer from the pollutee to the polluter is as in the previous case.

Do polluters pay at the CT solution?

The answer to this question is simply: No! It is the pollutees who "pay", and they are the only ones. Let me explain why, and why it is realistic that it be so in the context of international externalities

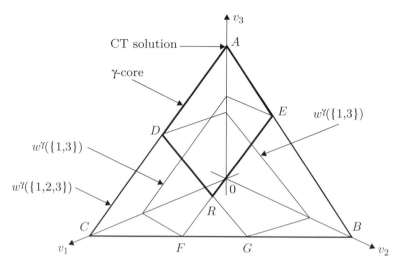

Fig. 6.3   The γ-core and the CT solution in the payoffs space of the two polluters (1,2)–one pollutee (3) economy.

Notes: (i). The imputations in the triangle DGC can be improved upon by coalition $\{2,3\}$.

(ii). The imputations in the triangle EFB can be improved upon by coalition $\{1,3\}$.

(iii). The coalition $\{1,2\}$ cannot improve upon the Nash equilibrium payoffs.

in general, and of climate change in particular. First, beware of the difference between the *solution of the game*, on the one hand, and the *transfer payments* that help ensuring it, on the other hand. While the interest is of course in the solution of the game, confusion often arises in the mind of some readers when for a player the net payment is negative although the payoff is higher than at the Nash equilibrium.

Let us see first what the CT solution implies in terms of payments by the players. It has been seen above that the components of the transfer in formula (6.19) are two-fold:

(a) An amount $g_i(\bar{e}_i) - g_i(e_i^*)$ that corresponds to the change in country i's output level entailed by the move to the Pareto efficient outcome. It is based on the country's production function $g_i(e_i)$, *thus as a polluter only*. It is a compensatory payment for the change from emitting $\bar{e}_i$ to emitting e_i^*, received if positive,[15] and paid if negative. This part of the transfer is thus not really a "payment"; actually, it is more of the nature of a subsidy. Its role is to make the country's participation neutral as an emitter.

(b) The other amount is negative for all those players who are recognized as benefiting from the ambient pollution being reduced, that is, for which $d'_i > 0$, and are thus *pollutees*. In that role the formula proposes that all of them take a share in the total cost of the aggregate reduction of emissions from $(\bar{e}_1, \ldots, \bar{e}_n)$ to $(e_1^*, \ldots, e_n^*)$, the share being proportional to their respective relative individual marginal benefit.

Most if not all countries are both a polluter and a pollutee. For those that are just one of the two, only the relevant part of the formula applies. For those that are both, one sees that *as polluters*, their situation remains neutral in the move from Nash to Pareto,[16] whereas *as pollutees*, but as pollutees only, they do pay their share $\frac{\pi_i}{\sum_{j \in N} \pi_j}$ of the global cost of that move.

The logic of the γ-core ignores any other motivation than willingness to pay to avoid damage.[17]

The CT solution and the benefit principle of public finance

Once it is admitted as a fact that, prior to any treaty, the polluting regions have arrogated[18] themselves the right to emit pollutants, the

---

[15]In the unlikely but not impossible case that for some country i the Pareto efficient emission level e_i^* would be larger than the Nash non-cooperative level $\bar{e}_i$, the formula takes away the gain in output so secured by country i. It thus prevents a player to take an advantage from the move from Nash to Pareto on the sole changes in emissions. This is parallel to the compensation mentioned above for the output loss entailed by this move for most of the other players.

[16]This thus recognizes the fact that they arrogated themselves the right to pollute.

[17]The lecture dealing with dynamics will amplify this statement to avoid present and future damage.

[18]Recall the discussion of the rights assignment issue in general terms in Lecture 3 as well as in the relation between the γ-core solution and the Coase theorem in the third subsection of Section 6.2.

CT transfers and for that matter the entire γ-core solution are to be seen as an implementation of the "benefit principle", often opposed to the "ability to pay principle" in the design of taxation and pricing systems in public economics theory.[19] The benefit principle applies here because the solution rests entirely upon the self interest of the parties.

Yet, in the climate change problem a parallel could be similarly drawn between the alternative ability to pay principle and the notion of responsibility, given the wealth that the dynamic context of past growth has brought to the currently developed economies. Clearly, that growth makes them able to compensate the current and future damages they are responsible for.

However, transposing to the international sphere the distinction between these two principles is not immediate, because — once again — of the absence of an authority that could choose between them, and in particular evaluate abilities to pay in an "objective" way and impose its implication. As unanimity is inescapable in international affairs it is more likely to be obtained under the benefit principle than under the alternative principle of ability to pay, in spite of the obvious moral justification of the latter. The dynamic context of Lecture 8 (see Section 8.3) gives an occasion to come back to this issue in a more constructive way.

On free riding and γ-core stability

In Lecture 3, two forms of free riding have been presented, respectively, called "preference revelation (PR) free riding" and "non-participatory (NP) free riding". Both forms are potentially present in the solution presently developed. I consider the latter first.

(a) *Free riding vs. blocking*

Participatory free riding is an aspect, among many, of instability of a group. Let me concentrate for the time being on the one at stake in the γ-core, leaving for consideration in Lecture 9 the discussion of an alternative concept of coalitional stability.

---

[19]The classical presentation is Musgrave (1959).

Transposing to the GEG the typical spirit of the theory of the core, the notion of blocking a proposed agreement has been presented in Chander and Tulkens (1995, 1997) as attempting to free ride against it. I wish to abandon this view that I now feel to be simply incorrect. Blocking is not free riding, because the players who block are by definition emitters of the externality and the reason invoked is not the enjoyment of an externality from the other players but rather the recourse to their own resources only. And the γ-assumption on singletons expresses, just as a secondary argument, a supposed reaction from the other players, like the α- and β-assumptions do. These reactions are of the nature of a deterrence, where no free riding is involved.

(b) *The γ-assumption and coalition formation*

A particularly troublesome case is the one where the defecting S happens to be just one player, say $S = \{j\}$. In this case, applying strictly the logic of the γ-core , the outcome is simply... the non-cooperative Nash equilibrium! Admittedly this extreme disintegration of $N\backslash\{j\}$ into singletons is hardly credible. It is not realistic either, as it clearly does not occur in the case of the Kyoto Protocol where one observes that no "disintegration" occurs within the complement of the defecting $S = \{j\}$ which is the US. But one may ask: why should the Kyoto Protocol at its pre-ratification stage, be seen as a γ-core strategy profile? And why interpret j's behavior as a "blocking" one?

Focusing less on the γ-*core* solution and more on the γ-coalitional *function*, another approach may be adopted to justify the γ-assumption. This is the point of view of coalition *formation* sketched out at the end of Lecture 4. Rather than seeing S as forming *against an imputation*,[20] one may think of S as forming against the "no coalition" state of the system, namely the Nash equilibrium. Then the γ-assumption consists in assuming just the formation of S, given the prevailing situation of the other players as

---

[20] A view relayed by Barrett (2003, p. 213, put somewhat questionably under the title of "collective rationality"), and still mentioned by Nordhaus (2015, online Appendix p. 1).

singletons. In this view, the players of S do not form a coalition as free riders, since there is nothing to free ride about. Instead, it is the singleton players who are free riding on the externality created by the formation of S! No other assumption needs to be made to characterize their behavior, except for the absence of any group-wise reaction. With this view of the γ-coalitional function, no other argument than spontaneous generation is provided to explain why S forms, leaving the other players where they are. Implications of this view[21] for the conceptualization of free riding in the context of the GEG are taken up in Lecture 9 and developed at the policy level in Lecture 10.

(c) *Preference revelation free riding and the CT solution*

While the CT solution has all the core properties outlined thus far, it allows one to see in addition the effect of a party i joining but incorrectly revealing preferences, through the $\dfrac{d_i'(z^*)}{\sum_{j \in N} d_j'(z^*)}$ coefficients in the transfers formula. Understating $d_i'(z^*)$ implies a lesser contribution of country i to the coverage of the aggregate abatement cost. But that understatement also induces a less than optimal level of aggregate abatement since the optimality criterion is based on the sum of the $d_i'(z^*)$'s. Thus, the CT solution to the GEG is vulnerable to "informational" free riding of the preference revelation type, at least away from the optimum.

The proviso just made has the following source. When the optimum is reached, there is an argument due to Drèze and de la Vallée Poussin (1971, Section 3) establishing that it is a Nash equilibrium of a (local) preference revelation game that all parties reveal correctly their preferences. Away from the optimum, this is not the case, but the bias in misrepresentation can be identified as done in Roberts (1979).[22]

---

[21] My change of opinion came from the subsequent theoretical dynamic analysis of the GEG, here presented in the last sections of Lecture 7, and from the Chander and Tulkens joint reinterpretation of the Kyoto Protocol, first put forward in their 2011 Discussion Paper. It now constitutes the backbone of the policy Lecture 10 hereafter.

6.4   Whither the γ-core solution for the GEG?

The last section of Lecture 4 has highlighted many of the virtues of the core solution concept for cooperative games in general, without externalities first and then with externalities. All these virtues apply as well to the GEG of the just completed Lectures 5 and 6 where the externality has the special physical form of being "diffuse" as I like to call its public good property. Let me take stock of what is gained with this application.

On the nature of the game: A negociation on a diffuse externality

My insistence on calling upon the core of a game to conceptualize international environmental agreements may be seen by some game theorists as being at odds with what is often considered as *the* natural economic application of the core, namely the competitive market equilibrium. The property of the core to "shrink" towards the set of competitive equilibria with large numbers of players reinforces this assimilation of the two concepts. But it is known that this shrinking property towards (Lindahl equilibria) does not hold in pure public goods theory and it is doubtful it would hold with the GEG. More importantly, the shrinking idea is irrelevant since in the GEG the number of players is fixed by definition. Can other arguments beproposed in defense of a core theory of international environmental agreements?

Consider the process[23] whereby a core outcome can conceivably be reached. Contrary to an exchange where the *quid pro quo* transmission of property of commodites between seller and buyer is essentially a *bilateral* one, the negotiation of a treaty bearing on the mitigation of a diffuse externality must by nature be *multilateral*

---

[22]The Drèze and de la Vallée Poussin (1971) results, complemented by those of Roberts (1979) are very early ones in the fields of the economics of information and incentives theory, that were just emerging at that time.

[23]Refer to Buchanan's (1968) theory of voluntary bargaining on public goods, described as a process in Tulkens (1978).

because the *quid pro quo* consists in a payment against a change in the general non-appropriable state of a system, not in receiving the possession of a physical good. The collective decision takes place under the two conditions that each payer is confident that the others do their contribution, and that the change occurs. All this makes the process necessarily a multilateral one.

The announcement of individual emissions and transfer payments strategies as postulated by core theory, followed by a joint decision on them by all parties concerned, seems to be a natural, if not unescapable way to proceed to handle this multilateral reality.

The γ-partition

The γ-assumption has two components: a partition of the players set, and the strategies chosen by the players given the partition. As far as the first component is concerned — let me call it the γ-partition — why retain this partition and not another one? Current cooperative game theory offers no compelling general argument explaining the formation of a coalition in general.[24] With the γ-partition, one may argue that the purpose is to specify the framework for what a coalition can best do by itself, before and independently of the externalities (i.e. strategies) possibly exerted on the other players, as well as of those possibly exerted by the others on itself. In particular, it permits to minimize the coalitional externality possibly exerted by non-members.

By contrast, the α- and β- assumptions consist in presuming that with the formation of coalition S the complement $N\backslash S$ also forms as a coalition, which is assuming another particular partition. Again, why this partition and not another one? It is difficult to find another justification than an analyst's care for a formal symmetry between the two subsets of players.

---

[24]In the particular context of the application to climate change, an idea of "climate clubs" has emerged recently as one possible source of effective coalition formation. Refer to Lecture 10 on that development.

The γ-strategies of the non-members

Given any partition, theorizing on the behavior of non-members of a coalition must specify strategies that take two aspects into account: the externality exerted on the non-members of S as a result of S's formation as a coalition,[25] and the reciprocal externality exerted on the members of S as a result of the strategies adopted by the outsiders of S.

In that respect, the main virtue of the concept of PCNE r.t. S resides in its general property, independent of the GEG, of *being an equilibrium* between the coalition and the rest of the players, as mentioned in Lecture 4. According to the γ-assumption, the members of coalition S, while maximizing their common interests, presume that each one of the rest of the players also maximizes his own individual interest. This results in a strategy profile chosen *by all players* according to utility maximization. In Lecture 9 this property is shown to provide a deeper theoretical basis for characterizing free rider behaviors.

The PCNE and the γ-coalitional function

As already mentioned, the $w^\gamma(S)$ function and the PCNE's behind it are independent of whether or not the formation of S is motivated by a "deviating" attitude *vis-à-vis* a proposed imputation. The interest of the alternative view of coalition formation suggested above appears to be major, both theoretically in the dynamic context of Lecture 7 and policy-wise in the proposed interpretation of the UNFCCC process and of the Kyoto Protocol in Lecture 10. Within the temporal sequence of successive PCNE's defined there the γ-coalitional function offers a flexibility that allows one to see the γ-core as an ideal limit not necessarily achieved at all times.

Very recently, Kóczy (2018) offers a discussion of the γ-assumption, the PCNE concept (pp. 76–77), the γ-core (dubbed "s-core", p. 79), and its application to international environmental

---

[25] An effect that will be called "the coalitional externality" in Lecture 9.

agreements (see his Section 12.2). A wealth of conceptual variants and/or extensions is also presented, that unfortunately time and space constraints prevent me to consider presently.

The γ-core is self-enforcing

"Self-enforcement" is an intuitively quite attractive expression, very often used by authors when dealing with international environmental agreements. It evokes the absence of an external authority, which is at the root of the problems raised by this type of agreements. It also contains an implicit reference to incentives. After its introduction in the international environmental agreements literature by Barrett (1994), the appearance of a book (Barrett, 2003) entirely devoted to that idea has positioned the author as its most articulate advocate.

For cooperative game-minded theorists, there is a bit of mystery with it: it is difficult to find in the standard literature a commonly received definition of self-enforcement. It does not appear in the index of most game theory textbooks, and when it does (e.g. in Myerson, 1991), it is only to refer to a property of occasional interest. In fact, it is not a received game theoretic concept!

Yet, there is a need for it and Scott Barrett, an economist, fills up that gap by stating that self-enforcement is a property of a treaty that "must satisfy three conditions: individual rationality, collective rationality and fairness" (2003, pp. xiii–xiv). In Chapter 8 of Chander and Tulkens (2009) I have discussed briefly these three dimensions by sticking (too) closely to the way they are presented by the author in his book. By now, seeing the issues in a broader perspective and pushing the discussion more rigorously, I come to the opinion that there are aspects of γ-core imputations that do meet what Barrett has in mind, even if the wording differs. Yet, there are disagreements remaining, perhaps more in terminology than on matters of substance, so that a clarification may be useful for all. Let me cover briefly each of the three properties Barrett requires for self-enforcement.

"Individual rationality" is a property of a solution[26] of a cooperative game which, according to most textbooks,[27] is such that each player's payoff is at least as high as it is at the start of the game (the NCNE, in the case of the GEG). This is quite different from what Barrett writes on p. xiii. What he describes as individual rationality of a treaty is actually an outcome of the game that has the property of "internal and external stability".[28] This switch in terminology would be innocuous if there were only a slight difference of content, but this is unfortunately not the case. The notions of internal and external stability of coalitions are much more demanding than the standard meaning of individual rationality reminded above and in addition they are plagued with existence problems, as shown in the discussion of Lecture 9. Here the disagreement is complete.

Barrett's description of "collective rationality" of a treaty focuses on the presence or not of credible threats that can deter signatories from possible "deviations" by signatories. Here one gets closer to the kind of coalitional rationality present in the γ-core concept, if one sees the "disintegration" in singletons as such a threat. Barrett dismisses this threat as non-credible, but he does not specify which other strategy would be credible by anything more than just examples. But I feel that this is of secondary importance: behind the deterrence issue, there is implicit the consideration that the stability of the coalition is a desirable virtue. Stability for what purpose? Efficiency within the coalition, of course, *and achievable by its own means.*[29]

---

[26]Not necessarily an imputation, but well a strategy profile.

[27]See, for instance, Straffin (1993, p. 151), Maschler, Solan and Zamir (2011, p. 674). More to the point here at stake, Osborne and Rubinstein (1994, p. 143) call "enforceable" an individually rational solution that they define like everybody else in this list.

[28]See Lecture 9 for a formal definition and discussion of this alternative concept of stability.

[29]In that spirit, Shapley (1973) writes: "...if the core is described in terms of 'improving' or 'recontracting' rather than 'blocking' (...) [it] expresses what coalitions can or cannot do for themselves, not what they can or cannot do to

Applying this to the coalition of all players, collective rationality in Barrett's sense is actually aggregate efficiency in the fullest sense of the notion, that is, including coalitional stability.

"Fairness", finally, is not formally dealt with, but presented as a requirement that the treaty "be perceived by the parties as being legitimate" (p. xiv). I like to submit, albeit immodestly, that there is a strong virtue of justice in the fact that the CT solution concentrates all the gain from curbing the externality in the hands of its recipients, that is, the victims. Is it not legitimate that there be no net gain grabbed by emitters, in a solution that nevertheless yields them exact compensation for the effort required?

In spite of the considerable differences in our writing styles and perhaps in our ways of practicing economic science, I feel that convergence of ideas, and even more of ideals dominate our decades long controversies. Yes, the γ-core is self-enforcing.[30]

Where do we stand now with respect to the seven problems "left open" at the end of Lecture 3? I would claim that the first four have received explicit answers in the preceding pages. They concerned the really basic issues, while two of the remaining last three deal with extensions and implementation. This will complete the background for a by then sufficiently documented answer to the very last question.

---

their opponents." With this view, PCNE's in the GEG is not to be seen as threats but rather as a description of the coalitions' opportunities.

[30]After having written the above, I have been reminded by Caparros and Péreau (2017) that Telser (1980) presents for cartels "a theory of self-enforcing agreements" based on the core concept (see Chapter 6 of Telser (1987). Self enforcement is presented there as a property of the core).

Lecture 7

THE DYNAMIC GLOBAL EXTERNALITY GAME

The purpose and the message

The purpose now is to formulate and implement the extension over time of the static analysis made thus far, by introducing the temporal components of the economic-ecological problem, by defining the associated dynamic game, and by constructing for the latter a solution inspired by γ-core theory. I am thus combining Lectures 3, 5 and 6 in a dynamic setting.

The developments that follow are more than just an extension: a genuine component of climate change is introduced, namely the stock nature of the externality. Two methodologies of dynamic systems are considered successively, optimal control and dynamic programming. Because of rigidities of the former, only the latter is found to be suited for our purpose of dealing with negotiations.

The message is that a cooperative, i.e. an efficient and coalitionally stable solution extending over time can be formulated. It takes the natural and plausible form of a discrete time sequence of subgames where at each stage the alternative of cooperation vs. non-cooperation is the object of choice for the players, that is, the countries. Negotiations are thus modeled as an ongoing process and not as a one shot event as the static model or the optimal control method might lead one to believe.

Plan

The dynamic economic-ecological reference model

The associated dynamic global externality game

Equilibrium concepts in the DGEG

Coalitional functions, efficient and alternative cooperative paths

The γ-core stable path of the DGEG: optimal control formulation

The γ-core stable path as a sequence of negotiations: dynamic programming

Lecture 7

The Dynamic Global
Externality Game

7.1 The dynamic economic-ecological
reference model

Components of the system

Time and commodities

Time is formulated in discrete "intervals" denoted $t = 1, 2, \ldots, T$, where T is called the "horizon". A sequence of intervals $1, 2, \ldots, T$ is called a "time period". Why discrete intervals?[1] Because in the international negotiations I am interested in, decisions are taken at successive moments of time, and always imply some duration for their implementation until the next one. Formally intervals are assumed to be of equal length, but this specification may be modified.

All variables are "dated", that is, they are formulated, respectively, as:

- $x_{it} \geq 0$, the amount of consumption in country i — a flow occurring during the time interval t;
- $y_{it} \geq 0$, the amount of production in country i — also a flow occurring during the time interval t;
- $e_{it} \geq 0$, the amount of emissions in country i — a flow occurring during the time interval t;
- $z_t \geq 0$, the amount of ambient pollutant diffused all over the world — a stock present during the time interval t.

---

[1]This is at variance with the alternative of continuous time, which is much used in other areas of dynamic economics, in particular descriptive ones.

229

Taken together over all countries $i \in N$ and over all time intervals of a given time period $(1, \ldots, T)$ these variables form the following:

Definition 7.1. **A discrete time path** (or trajectory) of the economic-ecological system is a $(3n + 1) \times T$ dimensional vector denoted

$$(x_t, y_t, e_t, z_t)_{t=1}^{T} \equiv (x_{1t}, \ldots, x_{nt}, y_{1t}, \ldots, y_{nt}, \ e_{1t}, \ldots, e_{nt}, \ z_t)_{t=1}^{T}.$$
$$(7.1)$$

Production

Production in country i at time t is now specified as $y_{it} = g_i(e_{it})$ where the function g_i has the same properties as in the static case.

Admittedly, this minimal specification ignores many characteristics of the temporal dimension of production activities, such as the role of capital and its accumulation, as well as the possibilities of technical changes — thus of changes in the form of the function. Deliberately so, because my first and main purpose in this lecture is to capture the role that time can play in the game theoretic argument set forth previously. Introducing other time related characteristics[2] can be done afterwards.[3]

Utilities and discounting

What utility for country i does the consumption time path $(x_{it}, z_t)_{t=1}^{T}$ generate? Alternative formulations are conceivable, which I present in increasing order of complexity. A first one, directly extended from the static utility functions of Lecture 2 could be

$$u_{it} = u_i(x_{it}, z_t), \quad t = 1, 2, \ldots, T. \tag{7.2}$$

Country i 's utility at time t is then considered to be generated separately in each time interval t from the consumption and ambient

---

[2] Broader views on economies over time, dealing with sustainability and development, and offered by a game theorist, can be found in Ray (1998).
[3] As shown in the extension of the present model to capital accumulation made in Germain, Tulkens and Magnus (2011).

pollutant of that moment, and therefore denoted u_{it}. Over a period $(1, \ldots, T)$ the utility is then represented by a T-dimensional vector of the successive utility levels u_{it}.

By contrast, utility may be considered to result from the entire consumption stream occurring over the time period $(1, \ldots, T)$, and to be represented by a function of the form

$$U_i = \sum_{t=1}^{T} u_i(x_{it}, z_t). \tag{7.3}$$

Here, utility over the whole period is measured by a single number U_i. It is also time neutral, i.e. it attaches equal weights to the time intervals where the successive components x_{it}, z_t take place.

To take into account the intuitively plausible notion that time is not neutral, in the sense that utility is more appreciated early than late, the previous formulation can be amended by formulating it as

$$U_i = \sum_{t=1}^{T} \beta^{t-1} u_i(x_{it}, z_t), \quad 0 < \beta < 1, \tag{7.4}$$

where β, a constant called discount factor, dampens the utility impact of consumptions and damages the more distant in time they take place.[4] This is the formulation I adopt, and I apply to it the quasi-linear form assumed since Lecture 2. A country's utility over a period $(1, \ldots, T)$ is thus defined in this lecture as:

$$U_i = \sum_{t=1}^{T} \beta^{t-1} u_i(x_{it}, z_t) \equiv \sum_{t=1}^{T} \beta^{t-1} (x_{it} - d_i(z_t)). \tag{7.5}$$

In which units is utility measured in this case? In Lecture 2, the expression $x_i - d_i(z)$ in the function (2.2) is said to be an amount of the composite (GDP) good, called green consumption. This remains valid in (7.5). However, the aggregation over time with discounting introduces another magnitude, U_i, for the value of the function which is now a *weighted* sum of GDP units. For

---

[4]For an exemplary exposition, including its advanced developments, of the economics of discounting in a context such as mine here, refer to Gollier (2011).

this accounting magnitude the units are logically called "discounted utility" or "discounted consumption" and expressed in monetary terms.

Disutility of a stock or of a flow?

In global warming, which is a major motivation of this research, the dynamic component is an essential one, modeled from now on by means of the stock variable z_t. However, temperature — the source of disutility — is a flow and not a stock. Shouldn't temperature change, caused by the size of the stock of accumulated CO_2, be the argument of the functions d_i instead of the stock?

In fact, it is implicitly so according to the following reasoning. Let ΔT_t be a temperature change at time t, z_t be the CO_2 stock at t and let the function $\Delta T_t = F(z_t)$ represent the causality just mentioned. One may then redefine $d_i(z_t)$ as $d_i(\Delta T_t)$ and substitute $F(z_t)$ for ΔT_t which gives $d_i(F(z_t))$. The function $F(z_t)$, a climatic transfer function in the sense of Lecture 1, is thereby embedded in the disutility function d_i.[5]

Feasible paths

Definition 7.2. **A feasible time path** is a discrete time path $(x_t, y_t, e_t, z_t)_{t=1}^{T}$ which at every time interval $t = 1, \ldots, T$ satisfies the technological constraints

$$y_{it} = g_i(e_{it}) \quad \forall i \in N, \tag{7.6}$$

the scarcity constraints

$$\sum_{i \in N} x_{it} = \sum_{i \in N} y_{it} \tag{7.7}$$

---

[5]A similar presentation is used in Lecture 8 where the disutility of temperature change takes the form of reduced consumable production. These alternative presentations lead to identical results, as long as one sticks to the separability assumption made above on the utility function.

and the ecological constraints

$$z_t = [1 - \delta]z_{t-1} + \sum_{i \in N} e_{it} \qquad (7.8)$$

given some initial value $z_0 > 0$.

Note that (7.7) allows for transfers across countries within each time interval t, but not across intervals.

Steady states

A special category of feasible paths is steady states, where all variables that define a path remain constant over time. For such states one has from (7.8):

$$z_t = z_{t-1} \Leftrightarrow \sum_{i \in N} e_{it} = \delta z_{t-1} \qquad (7.9)$$

or more generally

$$\delta z_t \begin{Bmatrix} > \\ = \\ < \end{Bmatrix} z_{t-1} \Leftrightarrow \sum_{i \in N} e_{it} \begin{Bmatrix} > \\ = \\ < \end{Bmatrix} \delta z_{t-1} \qquad (7.10)$$

which shows the role of the decay parameter δ in the evolution of the stock z_t. Notice also that constant emissions do not necessarily imply a constant stock, as the time evolution of the latter depends on the stock's initial value.

Finally, the static model of Lectures 3, 5 and 6 corresponds to $\delta = 1$ in (7.8). It is worth remarking that with such a parameter value the dynamic model looses much of its interest. Indeed, it does not contain links anymore between actions having effects across several time intervals through a physical accumulation process. It just adds up utility levels reached independently of one another.

Intertemporal equilibria

Individual behavior of a country over time

Using the modeling tools proposed in the previous subsection, an extension over time of the individual behaviors assumed for the countries in Lecture 3 is fairly straightforward. Definition 3.2 may be reproduced quasi-*verbatim*.

Definition 7.3. A country's behavior is an **environmentally nationalistic individual equilibrium over time** if it consists in the consumption, production, emissions and ambient pollution that maximize the country's discounted utility of domestic consumption over the period $(1, \ldots, T)$ diminished by the value of the damages incurred from the global emissions over that period, and taking as given the emissions of the other countries.

Formally, this behavior is described by the solution of the following optimization problem

$$\max_{(x_i^t, y_i^t, e_i^t, z^t)} \hat{U}_i = \sum_{t=1}^{T} \beta^{t-1} [x_{it} - d_i(z_t)] \tag{7.11}$$

subject to the technological constraints

$$y_{it} = g_i(e_{it}), \quad t = 1, \ldots, T, \tag{7.12}$$

the scarcity constraints

$$x_{it} = y_{it}, \quad t = 1, \ldots, T, \tag{7.13}$$

the ecological constraints

$$z_t = [1 - \delta] z_{t-1} + e_{it} + \sum_{j \in N \backslash i} \hat{e}_{jt}, \quad t = 1, \ldots, T, \tag{7.14}$$

where for all $j \in N \backslash i$ and all $t, \hat{e}_{jt}$ are given constants, and given some initial value $z_0 > 0$.

This is a problem in optimal control theory, where the e_{it}'s are called "control variables" and the z_t's are "state variables". After simplification, the problem reduces to:

$$\max_{(e_{it})_{t=1}^{T},(z_t)_{t=1}^{T}} U_i = \sum_{t=1}^{T} \beta^{t-1} [g_i(e_{it}) - d_i(z_t)], \tag{7.15}$$

where

$$z_t = [1 - \delta]z_{t-1} - e_{it} - \sum_{j \in N \setminus \{i\}} \hat{e}_{jt}, \quad t = 1, \ldots, T,$$

and $z_0 > 0$ is given.

The solution of the problem consists of a time path $((\bar{e}_{it}), (\bar{z}_t))_{t=1}^{T}$ of the variables that satisfy (7.15), as well as (7.12) and (7.13) by construction of (7.15). Clearly this path depends on what the other countries do, that is, the solution is a function of the value of the path

$$\left(\sum_{j \in N \setminus \{i\}} \hat{e}_{jt} \right)_{t=1}^{T}.$$

First-order conditions

The conditions that characterize this behavior are of the same spirit as (3.11)–(3.12) in the static case, but they involve additional elements that establish important links between the behaviors at successive time intervals. They are established as follows. With $\lambda_{it} \geq 0$ Lagrange multipliers, the lagrangian of the optimization problem reads:

$$L_i = \sum_{t=1}^{T} \beta^{t-1}[g_i(e_{it}) - d_i(z_t)]$$

$$+ \sum_{t=1}^{T} \lambda_{it} \left(z_t - [1 - \delta]z_{t-1} - e_{it} - \sum_{j \in N \setminus \{i\}} \hat{e}_{jt} \right).$$

For $(\bar{e}_{it})_{t=1}^{T}, (\bar{z})_{t=1}^{T}$ and $(\bar{\lambda}_{it})_{t=1}^{T}$ to be a solution one must have

$$\partial L_i / \partial e_{it} = \beta^{t-1} g_i'(\bar{e}_{it}) - \bar{\lambda}_{it} = 0, \quad t = 1, \ldots, T \qquad (7.16)$$

$$\partial L_i / \partial z_t = -\beta^{t-1} d_i'(\bar{z}_t) + \bar{\lambda}_{it} - \bar{\lambda}_{it+1}[1 - \delta] = 0,$$

$$t = 1, \ldots, T - 1, \qquad (7.17)$$

$$\partial L_i / \partial z_T = -\beta^{T-1} d_i'(\bar{z}_T) + \bar{\lambda}_{iT} = 0, \qquad (7.18)$$

$$\bar{z}_t = [1 - \delta]\, z_{t-1} + \bar{e}_{it} + \sum_{j \in N \setminus \{i\}} \bar{e}_{jt}, \quad t = 1, \ldots, T. \qquad (7.19)$$

Substituting for $\bar{\lambda}_{it}$ and $\bar{\lambda}_{it+1}$ from (7.16) into (7.17) and dividing by β^{t-1} yields

$$g_i'(\bar{e}_{it}) - \beta[1 - \delta] g_i'(\bar{e}_{it+1}) = d_i'(\bar{z}_t), \quad t = 1, 2, \ldots, T - 1. \qquad (7.20)$$

This expression is known as the *Euler equation* in optimal control theory. It shows a link that holds at the solution between the variables of any two successive time intervals. An economic interpretation is given below.

Standard economic properties of an individual equilibrium over time

Proposition 7.1. *The solution $((\bar{e}_{it}), (\bar{z}_t))_{t=1}^T$ is unique.*

Proof. Uniqueness is implied by the concavity of the objective function, as in Proposition 5.2 of the static case.   □

Proposition 7.2. *The solution $((\bar{e}_{it}), (\bar{z}_t))_{t=1}^T$ satisfies*

$$g_i'(\bar{e}_{it}) = \sum_{\tau=t}^T (\beta[1 - \delta])^{\tau-t} d_i'(\bar{z}_t) \quad t = 1, \ldots, T. \qquad (7.21)$$

Proof. In the Euler equation (7.20) consider the similarity between the first and the second terms of the LHS. Multiplying each subsequent equation of this sequence of equations by $\beta(1 - \delta)$ and then summing over the equations after cancelling the second terms on the left with the first term on the left of the subsequent equation, one gets (7.21).   □

The system (7.21) of T equations derived from the first order conditions characterizes the emissions policy of a country all over the period $(1, \ldots, T)$, according to its preferences as expressed by the objective function (7.11). In this form (7.21), they are the dynamic counterparts of conditions (3.12) in the static model. Dasgupta's decision oriented expression of "country i's individual benefit–cost rule" applies here as well.

In words these equations say that at every time interval t the equilibrium emissions policy of a country consists in pushing them up to the point where the gain in output for the country from a marginal increase in its emissions (the LHS of (7.21)) equals the stream of discounted additional damages the country would incur from this increase, at that same time t and up to the horizon T (the RHS of (7.21)). Alternatively, taking derivatives to the left, emissions abatement at each t is pushed down to the point where the marginal abatement cost equals the stream of future discounted damage costs avoided in country i by this marginal reduction. One or the other of these two interpretations applies best according to whether at any time t along its equilibrium path the country has to increase or decrease its emissions.

The Euler equation (7.20) also has an economic interpretation of its own: the link it shows is between the country's marginal abatement costs of its emissions at any two successive points in time and its marginal damage cost at the first of these points. In other words, the change in marginal abatement cost between t and $t+1$ is equal to the marginal damage cost at t.

Other general properties of an individual equilibrium over time

- *Durability*: Notice that in the equalities (7.21) the dynamics is present only on the RHS i.e. the damages side. This is implied by the "durability" of the stock pollutant: once a flow is emitted (or abated) at some time t, it generates (respectively, reduces) detrimental effects of the stock across all time intervals τ that follow t.

- The *environmentally nationalistic* character of the behavior is expressed by the fact that the conditions (7.21) only involve in their RHS the country's own damages, present and future, in the determination of its emissions. The country gives no consideration whatsoever to the damages it inflicts on other countries.

- *Autarky*: As far as the rest of the economy is concerned, this individual behavior is one of complete autarky: the conditions (7.12)–(7.13) imply that the country consumes at each time t only what it produces at that time. Note that this has no "nationalistic" character, contrary to the environmental characterization just commented: the autarky only results from the assumption of a single private good in the formulation of the economic-ecological model, which of course precludes including a description of world trade relations in the economic part. As already mentioned, there is no logical objection to such an extension, but the increased complexity of the model would render it less accessible, letting the reader perhaps miss the forest (the environment) for the trees (the world trade).

Time profile of the emissions along individual equilibrium path

With T finite and under linearity of the damage function, it is possible to characterize how the individual emissions $(\bar{e}_{it})_{t=1}^{T}$ evolve over time according to the model. Formally, with $d_i'(z_t) = \pi_i, \pi_i > 0$ for all z, (7.21) reduces to

$$g_i'(\bar{e}_{it}) = \pi_i(1 + \beta(1 - \delta) + (\beta(1 - \delta))^2 + \cdots + (\beta(1 - \delta))^{T-t},$$
$$t = 1, \ldots, T, \tag{7.22}$$

where the RHS appears to be a constant, entirely determined by the time related parameters β and δ of the economic-ecological model. This equation has the following three implications:

(i) The country's emissions $(\bar{e}_{it})_{t=1}^{T}$ are steadily increasing with t, the reason being that while g_i' is a decreasing function of e_{it} the fact that the RHS of (7.22) decreases with t implies that $\bar{e}_{it}$ is increasing. Eventually at $t = T$ this RHS reduces to just π_i.

(ii) The farther is the horizon T, the lower are the emissions $\bar{e}_{it}$ at all t, but they are still increasing.

(iii) The path $(\bar{e}_{it})_{t=1}^{T}$ is independent of the evolution of the state variable z_t, that is, of the pollutant stock.

It is hard not to have a feeling that these "profiles" are really simplistic. Their mechanistic form is not entirely due to the extremely schematic structure of the economic-ecological model, of which they nevertheless show a severe limit. A critical evaluation done below does also reveal limitations of the optimal control methodology that eventually call for an alternative treatment of time, allowing for a widening of the perspectives. In the meantime there is some interest in pursuing what this quite common method in economics has to offer on our economic-ecological model.

International equilibrium over time

Definition 7.4. An **environmentally nationalistic international equilibrium over time** is a path $(\bar{x}_t, \bar{y}_t, \bar{e}_t, \bar{z}_t)_{t=1}^{T}$ of the system where each country behaves according to its individual equilibrium over time, and which is such that $\forall i \in N$ the country's choice level of z_t is $\bar{z}_t$ at every t.

Standard economic properties of the international equilibrium over time

These simultaneous paths of discrete time intervals constitute a sequence of feasible states of the system, linked to one another through the evolution of the stock pollutant variable z. All countries behave according to the solution of their individual problem (7.11)–(7.14). Hence one has at the global level:

Proposition 7.3. *The international equilibrium* $(\bar{x}_t, \bar{y}_t, \bar{e}_t, \bar{z}_t)_{t=1}^{T}$ *satisfies the* $n \times T$ *equalities*

$$g_i'(\bar{e}_{it}) = \sum_{\tau=t}^{T} (\beta[1-\delta])^{\tau-t} d_i'(\bar{z}_t) \quad t = 1, \dots, T, \quad i = 1, \dots, n.$$

$$(7.23)$$

The characterizations made above after Proposition 7.2 and equation (7.21) of the individual country behaviors do all apply, by construction, to this sequence of sates.

Other general properties of the international equilibrium over time

- *Compatibility* and *uniqueness*. The proviso that for every $i \in N$ the chosen level of z_t be equal to $\bar{z}_t$ at every t raises the same problem of compatibility (i.e. existence of the equilibrium) that was mentioned after Definition 3.4 in Lecture 3. Here too, I postpone its examination to the game theoretic formulation of the problem further down in this lecture (see Section 7.3).

- *Non-cooperation*. More generally, the purpose of this equilibrium concept is to describe the evolution of the economic-ecological system as long as no country decides to reduce its emissions below the level of its individual equilibrium path as stated in Definition 7.3 and in the absence of any internationally decided alternative mitigation policy.[6] In terms of the analysis presented in the policy Lecture 10, one can say that the concept of environmentally nationalistic international equilibrium over time of Definition 7.4 is a description of what the world evolution would have been if the Kyoto Protocol had not existed.[7]

Time profile of the stock along the international equilibrium path

Given what is known from above on the individual emission variables $((\bar{e}_{it})_{i \in N})_{t=1}^T$ of all countries over time, the (now endogenous) evolution of the ambient pollutant variable $\bar{z}_t$ along the international equilibrium can be characterized as follows.

---

[6]In Lecture 8, the "NCNE" scenario reported from the computations done in Eyckmans and Tulkens (2003) is a numerical representation of the environmentally nationalistic international equilibrium concept here discussed, using the CWS economic-ecological model instead of the present dynamic extension of the reference model of Lecture 2.

[7]Which international equilibrium is actually prevailing under the Kyoto Protocol is another story, also covered in Lecture 10, but on the basis of another game theoretic concept, to be introduced below with Definition 7.11.

Under linearity of the damage functions and with T finite:

(i) Given that (7.22) holds in all countries, the total $\sum_{i \in N} \bar{e}_{it}$ and hence $\bar{z}_t$ must be increasing as t gets closer to T since the number of constant terms in the expression decreases with time.

(ii) Over the entire time period $(1, \ldots, T)$ the evolution of the stock depends upon de starting level z_0 of ambient pollutant. At the beginning, if z_0 is large enough so that at $t = 1$ one has $\sum_{i \in N} \bar{e}_{i1} < \delta z_0$, then $\bar{z}_t$ decreases according to (7.10). This occurs until some time τ where one must have $\sum_{i \in N} \bar{e}_{i\tau} = \delta \bar{z}_{\tau-1}$. Then, for $t > \tau$, $\bar{z}_t$ increases. When exactly the time interval τ falls over the period $(1, \ldots, T)$ depends on z_0 and δ. By contrast, if z_0 is small enough so that $\sum_{i \in N} \bar{e}_{i1} > \delta z_0$, then $\bar{z}_t$ increases uniformly up to its horizon value $\bar{z}_T$.

The time profile of the state variable $\bar{z}_t$ along the environmentally nationalistic international path is hardly less simplistic than the emission paths characterized above for the individual equilibrium path, for obviously similar reasons. The critical evaluation I shall present in Section 7.5 widens the perspectives on this point too.

Intertemporal international efficiency

Definition 7.5. **A Pareto efficient path** of the economic-ecological system is a time path $(x_t^*, y_t^*, e_t^*, z_t^*)_{t=1}^T$ feasible in the sense of satisfying (7.6)–(7.8), such that there exists no other feasible path $(x_t', y_t', e_t', z_t')_{t=1}^T$ in which $\sum_{t=1}^T \beta^{t-1} u_i(x_{it}', z_t') \geq \sum_{t=1}^T \beta^{t-1} u_i(x_{it}^*, z_t^*)$ for all $i \in N$, with $>$ for at least one i.

As was the case in Lecture 3 when dealing with efficiency in the static model, an efficient path of the dynamic model can be obtained as the solution of a mathematical programming problem. In those terms, a path is efficient if it maximizes the sum, over all countries and over the whole time period $1, \ldots, T$, of their discounted utilities from domestic consumption diminished by the value of the damages incurred from the global emissions.

After substituting $x_{it} - d_i(z_t)$ for $u_i(x_{it}, z_t)$ in Definition 7.5 the problem reads[8]

$$\underset{\{x_{it}, y_{it}, e_{it}, z_t\}}{\text{Max}} \ \widehat{U} =_{\text{def}} \sum_{i \in N} U_i \equiv \sum_{i \in N} \sum_{t=1}^{T} \beta^{t-1}[x_{it} - d_i(z_t)] \qquad (7.24)$$

subject to, at each $t = 1, \ldots, T$,

$$\sum_{i \in N} x_{it} = \sum_{i \in N} y_{it}, \qquad (7.25)$$

$$y_{it} = g_i(e_{it}) \quad i \in N, \qquad (7.26)$$

$$z_t = [1 - \delta]z_{t-1} + \sum_{j \in N} e_{jt}, \qquad (7.27)$$

$$z_0 > 0 \text{ given.}$$

Substituting (7.26) in (7.25), and then (7.25) in (7.24), the problem reduces to the simplified form

$$\underset{\{e_{it}, z_t\}}{\text{Max}} \ U = \sum_{i \in N} \sum_{t=1}^{T} \beta^{t-1}[g_i(e_{it}) - d_i(z_t)] \qquad (7.28)$$

where

$$z_t = [1 - \delta]z_{t-1} + \sum_{j \in N} e_{jt} \quad t = 1, \ldots, T, \qquad (7.29)$$

and

$$z_0 > 0 \text{ is given.}$$

This is again an optimal control problem with $n \times T$ control variables e_{it} and T state variables z_t. The solution $((e_{it}^*)_{i \in N}, (z_t^*))_{t=1}^{T}$ induces values $((x_{it}^*)_{i \in N}, (y_{it}^*))_{t=1}^{T}$ of the other variables of the

---

[8]The optimization problem that follows is the closest equivalent in the present dynamic reference model of the "EFF" scenario computed in Eyckmans and Tulkens (2003), on which I report in Lecture 8 with the acronym of PESP.

economic-ecological model through (7.26) as well as (7.25) and (7.27). The world welfare for the entire period $1, \ldots, T$ reads:

$$\widehat{U}^* = \sum_{i \in N} \sum_{t=1}^{T} \beta^{t-1} [g_i(e_{it}^*) - d_i(z_t^*)]. \tag{7.30}$$

First-order conditions

With $(\lambda_t)_{t=1}^{T}$ a vector of non-negative Lagrange multipliers associated with the T equalities (7.29) treated as constraints, the Lagrangian reads:

$$L = \sum_{i \in N} \sum_{t=1}^{T} \beta^{t-1} [g_i(e_{it}) - d_i(z_t)] + \sum_{t=1}^{T} \lambda_t \left[z_t - [1-\delta] z_{t-1} - \sum_{j \in N} e_{jt} \right].$$

For $(e_t^*, z_t^*)_{t=1}^{T}$ and $(\lambda_t^*)_{t=1}^{T}$ to yield an (interior) optimum we must have

$$\partial L / \partial e_{it} = \beta^{t-1} g_i'(e_{it}^*) - \lambda_t^* = 0, \quad i \in N, \tag{7.31}$$

$$t = 1, \ldots, T,$$

$$\partial L / \partial z_t = -\beta^{t-1} \sum_{i \in N} d_i'(z_t^*) + \lambda_t^* - \lambda_{t+1}^* [1-\delta] = 0, \tag{7.32}$$

$$t = 1, \ldots, T-1,$$

$$\partial L / \partial z_T = -\beta^{T-1} \sum_{i \in N} d_i'(z_T^*) + \lambda_T^* = 0, \tag{7.33}$$

$$z_t^* = [1-\delta] z_{t-1}^* + \sum_{i \in N} e_{it}^*, \quad t = 1, \ldots, T. \tag{7.34}$$

Substituting for λ_t^* and λ_{t+1}^* from (7.31) into (7.32) and dividing by β^{t-1} yields

$$g_i'(e_{it}^*) - \beta [1-\delta] g_i'(e_{it+1}^*) = \sum_{j \in N} d_j'(\bar{z}_t), \quad i \in N, \ t = 1, \ldots, T-1, \tag{7.35}$$

i.e. $n + T - 1$ Euler equations. Their economic interpretation follows shortly.

Standard economic properties of an efficient path

As a preliminary, an alternative specification of the model (7.21)–(7.24) must first be pointed out. The scarcity constraints written as in (7.25) do leave at every t a degree of freedom in terms of the variables $((x_{it}^*)_{i \in N})_{t=1}^T$ of which only the sum is constrained. As was the case in Lecture 3 with the openness comment on (3.16), implicit commodity transfers between countries are assumed to occur, in this case at every t. An alternative specification of (7.25) could be

$$x_{it} = y_{it} \quad \forall i \in N, \quad t = 1, \dots, T. \tag{7.36}$$

In this way, the paths $((x_{it}^*)_{i \in N})_{t=1}^T$ are well defined, but commodity transfers of the kind just discussed are excluded.

I can now characterize the paths

$$[(e_{it}^*)_{t=1}^T, \ (x_{it}^*)_{t=1}^T, \ (y_{it}^* = g_i(e_{it}^*)_{t=1}^T), i \in N, \ \text{and} \ (z_t^*)_{t=1}^T] \tag{7.37}$$

of the solution of the problem (7.24)–(7.27), that is, a Pareto efficient time path of the dynamic international economic-ecological model. They enjoy properties that are parallel to or expand on the properties of the static version of the model that were stated in Lecture 3 (Section 3.2).

Proposition 7.4. *The path* $((e_{it}^*)_{i \in N}, \ (z_t^*))_{t=1}^T$, *which solves the problem (7.28), is unique.*

Proof. Concavity of the objective function (7.28) is a sufficient condition for the values of the variables that achieve a maximum to be unique. □

This uniqueness does not extend to all components of an efficient path $(x_t^*, y_t^*, e_t^*, z_t^*)_{t=1}^T$ that solves problem (7.24)–(7.27) because of the degree of freedom left to the variables $((x_{it}^*)_{i \in N})_{t=1}^T$, but it does if the specification (7.36) is substituted for (7.25). This remark is of importance below in a discussion to come on the multiplicity of efficient paths and inter-country transfers.

Proposition 7.5. *The Pareto efficient path* $(x_t^*, y_t^*, e_t^*, z_t^*)_{t=1}^T$ *satisfies the* $n \times T$ *equalities*

$$g_i'(e_{it}^*) = \sum_{\tau=t}^{T} [\beta[1 - \delta]]^{\tau-t} \sum_{j \in N} d_j'(z_\tau^*) \quad \forall i \in N, \ t = 1, \ldots, T.$$

$$(7.38)$$

Proof. The Euler equations (7.35) are shown above to be derived from the first order conditions to which they are equivalent. Given the concavity of the objective function (7.28), they are thus necessary and sufficient for $((e_{it}^*)_{i \in N}, (z_t^*))_{t=1}^T$ to be the solution of the problem. By applying the same reasoning as above (that is, consider the similarity between the first and the second terms of the LHS, multiply each subsequent equation of this sequence of equations by $\beta(1 - \delta)$ and then sum over the equations after cancelling the second terms on the left with the first term on the left of the subsequent equation) one gets (7.38). $\square$

In words, the proposition says that at every t the emissions of each i are such that the gain in output from a marginal increase of them (LHS of equation (7.38)) equals the sum of the stream of discounted additional damages that all countries would incur up to T (the RHS). Alternatively, with derivatives taken to the left, marginal abatement cost of each i at every t equals the sum over time of discounted damage costs avoided by all countries. The reader surely recognizes Dasgupta's "international benefit–cost rule".

Here, also the Euler equations (7.35) establish a link, when the emissions are optimal, between the marginal abatement costs of emissions at any two successive points in time in each country i and the sum over all countries of their marginal damage cost at the first of these points.

Proposition 7.6. *Along the Pareto efficient path* $(x_t^*, y_t^*, e_t^*, z_t^*)_{t=1}^T$ *the marginal abatement costs of all countries are equal to one another at every time interval* t. *Formally,*

$$g_i'(e_{it}^*) = g_j'(e_{jt}^*) \quad \forall i, j \in N, \ t = 1, \ldots, T.$$

$$(7.39)$$

Proof. In (7.38), the RHS are identical for all $i \in N$. Therefore, Proposition 7.5 implies (7.39). □

Notice that this international efficiency condition holds across countries at every t, but not across periods. For conditions holding across periods remember and compare with (7.35) the Euler equations.

Other general properties of an efficient state

As to the other three general properties of efficiency recorded in Lecture 3 for the static case, two of them translate fairly unchanged in the dynamics context, while the third one raises more complex issues.

- *Cooperation and the nature of decisions.* Being prescribed courses of action, the emissions paths do not describe spontaneous behavior of the economic agents. Instead they specify what is being sought for. Their achievement requires cooperation sustained all over the period $1, \ldots, T$.
- *Compatibility.* By construction no problems arise of compatibility between the individual paths.
- *Openness thanks to transfers.* Here also, as in Lecture 3, the uniqueness of the efficient path vector $((e_{it}^*)_{i \in N})_{t=1}^T$ as well as of the variables $(z_t^*)_{t=1}^T$ and $(y_{it}^*)_{t=1}^T$ through (7.27) and (7.26) does not prevent efficiency preserving transfers to occur and thus extend the flexibility of the Pareto efficiency concept. However, the possibility of the two alternative specifications (7.25) *vs.* (7.36) does matter as can be seen in the following paragraphs.

Multiple efficient outcomes

How to transpose to the present dynamic context the developments that followed Proposition 3.7 on the multiplicity of efficient states in the static model? In Lecture 3, this possible multiplicity results from varying the countries' individual consumption levels x_i^* by means of transfers between them. In statics, the transfers are specified in units of the commodity x which are also the units in which utilities u_i are measured, under the quasi-linearity Assumption 2.1 I am working with. Thus it is indifferent whether the transfers are said to be in commodity or in utility units: they are identical. This identity is maintained in the game theoretic developments throughout Lectures 4–6, where the model and its associated game are both static.

In the present intertemporal context, another dimension of utilities appears with their aggregation over time and discounting. As pointed out in Section 7.1 when introducing dynamics, this aggregation lumps together the utilities generated at each time interval t along the path where they are generated and forms for the whole period $1, \ldots, T$ a single accounting magnitude of discounted utility. A direct transposition of the multiplicity of efficient outcomes can be conceived of by defining transfers in these same units of discounted utility. This is expressed as follows.

Proposition 7.7. *Given a Pareto efficient path $(x_t^*, y_t^*, e_t^*, z_t^*)_{t=1}^T$ and its aggregate discounted utility outcome*

$$\widehat{U}^* = \sum_{i \in N} \sum_{t=1}^T \beta^{t-1}[g_i(e_{it}^*) - d_i(z_t^*)],$$

for any vector of transfers $\Psi = (\Psi_1, \ldots, \Psi_n) \in R^n$ satisfying $\sum_{i \in N} \Psi_i = 0$, the alternative aggregate discounted level of utilities

$$\widehat{U}^*(\Psi) =_{def} \sum_{i \in N} \left(\sum_{t=1}^T \beta^{t-1}[g_i(e_{it}^*) - d_i(z_t^*)] + \Psi_i \right)$$

is also an efficient utility outcome.

Notice that no physical component of the time path $(x_t^*, y_t^*, e_t^*, z_t^*)_{t=1}^T$ itself is modified by the introduction of such transfers, contrary to what was the case in (3.3) for the consumption variables. Only the discounted utilities are transferred as they result from the unique Pareto efficient path of the economic-ecological model. This allows one to illustrate Proposition 7.7 by just transposing here Fig. 3.1 without any other change than the notation for the labeling of the axes and transfers.

Proposition 7.7 applies to the model (7.24)–(7.27), using (7.25) as the worldwide scarcity constraints that links the countries' consumptions and productions at every time t. The alternative specification (7.36) allows for another formulation of transfers. It suffices to specify at each t a vector

$$\Psi_t = (\Psi_{it}, \ldots, \Psi_{it}) \in R^n \text{ such that } \sum_{i \in N} \Psi_{it} = 0, \quad t = 1, \ldots, T,$$

and to add each Ψ_{it} to x_{it}^* in the RHS of the relevant it'th equality (7.36). Clearly, given a Pareto efficient path $(x_t^*, y_t^*, e_t^*, z_t^*)_{t=1}^T$ satisfying (7.36), alternative vectors Ψ_t generate utility levels that constitute alternative Pareto efficient solutions of the problem (7.24)–(7.27).[9]

Time profiles of the emissions and the stock along the efficient path

With T finite and under linearity of the damage functions, the evolution of the individual emissions along the efficient path can be characterized as follows. Formally, letting $d_i'(\bar{z}) = \pi_i, \pi_i > 0$ for all values of z, the equalities (7.38) reduce to

$$g_i'(e_{it}^*) = \sum_{j \in N} \pi_j (1 + \beta(1-\delta) + (\beta(1-\delta))^2 + \cdots$$

$$+ (\beta(1-\delta))^{T-t}) \quad \forall i \in N, \ t = 1, \ldots, T \quad (7.40)$$

where the RHS is a sum of constants that declines with t. These equations imply:

(i) Emissions e_{it}^* in all countries increase with t for the same reason as was argued above for $\bar{e}_{it}$ on the basis of (7.22).
(ii) The farther the horizon T, the lower e_{it}^* for all $t = 1, \ldots, T$, and $i = 1, \ldots, n$ but still increasing with t.
(iii) At every t the emissions e_{it}^* do not depend on the stock (state) variables z_t^*.

---

[9]This provides the economic theoretic basis for the transfers computed in Eyckmans and Tulkens (2003) and reviewed in Lecture 8. The connection with the γ-core game theoretical role of these transfers is made in Section 7.4.

As to the evolution of the stock along the efficient path,

(iv) In general, a lower z_T^* obtains with uniformly higher marginal damage functions, and a lower z_T^* also obtains with a higher discount factor β and a higher durability rate $(1 - \delta)$.

(v) The initial value of the stock z_0 plays an important role in the evolution of z_t. Thus, under linearity of the damage functions, at time $t = 1$, if z_0 is such that $\sum_{i \in N} e_{i1}^* < \delta z_0$, then z_t^* decreases with time up to some time interval τ where $\sum_{i \in N} e_{i\tau}^* \geq \delta z_{\tau-1}^*$, after which z_t^* increases. The time τ depends on z_0 and δ.

The rationale for cooperation in the dynamic setting

Proposition 7.8.   *The path $(\bar{x}_t, \bar{y}_t, \bar{e}_t, \bar{z}_t)_{t=1}^T$ of the environmentally nationalistic international equilibrium is not a Pareto efficient path.*

Proof.   For the equilibrium path the equalities (7.23) are necessary first order conditions for every $i \in N$ For the efficient path the necessary first order conditions are (7.38) which differ from (7.23). Therefore the two paths must be different.   □

Proposition 7.9.   *Assuming linearity of the damage functions, the Pareto efficient emissions e_{it}^* are uniformly lower[10] than the nationalistic equilibrium ones $\bar{e}_{it}$.*

Proof.   Given that the equilibrium emissions solve (7.23) whereas the efficient emissions solve (7.40), the assertion results from the concavity of g_i and the fact that $\sum_{j \in N} \pi_j > \pi_i$ for each $i \in N$.   □

With the above two propositions, the extension over time of the economic-ecological model has produced results that parallel very much those of the static version: characterization of a sequence of

---

[10]It is interesting to know already, anticipating on Lecture 8, that this property is observed in numerical simulation models where damage functions are nonlinear, such as RICE of Nordhaus and Yang (1996), CWS of Eyckmans and Tulkens (2003) and Bréchet, Gerard and Tulkens (2011), as well as WITCH (De Cian, private communication).

autarkic international equilibria that are environmentally nationalistic, identification of a Pareto efficient path of the system, complemented with the possibility of intercountry transfers, culminating
with the observation that the path of equilibria is not Pareto efficient
(Proposition 7.8).

This last statement implies that for the whole period $1, \ldots, T$
one has in global terms:

$$\bar{U} = \sum_{i \in N} \sum_{t=1}^{T} \beta^{t-1} [g_i(\bar{e}_{it}) - d_i(\bar{z}_t)]$$

$$< \sum_{i \in N} \sum_{t=1}^{T} \beta^{t-1} [g_i(e_{it}^*) - d_i(z_t^*)] = \widehat{U}^*, \qquad (7.41)$$

that is, the sum of the countries' utilities obtained along the path
that constitutes an equilibrium is lower than the sum of these utilities
along the efficient path. The difference between the two expressions
is the intertemporal version of the ecological surplus, expressed this
time in units of discounted green GDP of the countries. The graphical
illustration of Fig. 3.2 in Lecture 3 applies here too, after due change
in the labeling of the axes.

In addition, Proposition 7.9 confirms over time the environmental
non-friendliness of the international nationalistic equilibrium by
hinting at the difference between the respective time profiles of the
ambient pollutant variables $(\bar{z}_t)_{t=1}^T$ and $(z_t^*)_{t=1}^T$.

Therefore, the same question arises as in Lecture 3: can an appropriate cost sharing scheme be devised, possibly implying transfers,
to induce all countries not to stick to their individual nationalistic
equilibria in the foreseeable future and to follow, instead, the path
of world efficient and environmentally more friendly emissions?

Here as in the static case, the mathematical formulations of
equilibria and optima show clearly where the difficulty lies: individual
behaviors at nationalistic equilibria rest on considering environmental care in a different way than what a Pareto efficient behavior would
require: in each individual objective function (7.11) only $\beta^{t-1} d_i(z_t)$
is present at each t whereas $\sum_{i \in N} \beta^{t-1} d_i(z_t)$ appears at each t in
the collective objective function (7.24). The challenge of achieving

a world environmental optimum is to convince countries to regulate their emissions according to the latter instead of the former.

Parallel to the modalities and obstacles to achieving worldwide efficiency that were covered at length in the closing Sections 3.4 and 3.5 of the static exposition of the economic-ecological model, one might consider at this point whether or not these modalities and obstacles remain in the dynamic setting presently covered. As this examination may benefit from new tools brought about by dynamic game theory, I better postpone it until after Section 7.2 where they are now introduced.

7.2 The associated dynamic global externality game

Formulation of the dynamic global externality game (DGEG)

As done in Section 5.1 with the static modeling of Lecture 3, I now associate a dynamic game with the dynamic economic-ecological model just specified. Remember from Lecture 4 that a game in strategic form is, in general, a triplet comprising the players set, the set of strategy sets, and the players' payoffs. In the present case I denote the triplet by $(N, \hat{E}, V)$ and specify as follows its components together with the corresponding elements of the model:

- $N = \{i = 1, 2, \ldots, n\}$, the players set, is the set of countries,
- $\hat{E} = \{\hat{e} \in R_+^{nT} | \hat{e} \in \hat{E}_1 \times \cdots \times \hat{E}_i \times \cdots \times \hat{E}_n\}$ is the set of joint strategies where for each $i = 1, \ldots, n$, $\hat{E}_i = \{\hat{e}_i \equiv (e_{it})_{t=1}^T : 0 \leq e_{it} \leq e^o \, \forall t\}$ is the set of T vectors of emission strategies $(e_{it})_{t=1}^T$ accessible to player i at each time interval t over the period $t = 1, 2, \ldots, T$,
- $V = (V_1, \ldots, V_n)$ is a vector of payoffs each component of which is a function from $\hat{E}$ to R of the form

$$V_i(\hat{e}) \equiv \sum_{t=1}^T \beta^{t-1} [g_i(e_{it} - d_i(z_t))]$$

where $z_t = [1 - \delta] z_{t-1} + \sum_{j \in N} e_{jt}$, $z_0 > 0$ is given, (7.42) defined over the entire period $t = 1, 2, \ldots, T$, and called the payoff function of player i.

With these components one has:

Definition 7.6. The **dynamic global externality game** (henceforth **DGEG**) in strategic form is the triplet $(N, \hat{E}, V)$ just specified.

The game so formulated is in strategic form. A *strategy profile*, that is, a specification of a strategy for each one of the players, is denoted $((e_{1t}))_{t=1}^{T} \ldots, (e_{nt})_{t=1}^{T})$ or, for short, $((e_{it}))_{i \in N})_{t=1}^{T}$ or occasionally even $\hat{e}$ as above. Any such profile induces the individual payoffs (7.42) and corresponds in the economic-ecological model to a feasible time path as defined in (7.6)–(7.8) and vice versa.

In the terminology of optimal control theory the emission strategies e_{it} are the *control* variables of the DGEG, the resulting levels of the pollutant stock z_t are the *state* variables, and the ecological transfer function, here presented in the dynamic form (7.8), is the *transition equation* of the dynamic game.

Antecedents and alternative categories of dynamic games

In the same way that static game theory has a place in economics and other social sciences, dynamic games are part of the literature on dynamic systems, which extends over various areas of science and engineering. Therefore the expression of "dynamic games" covers many things, much beyond what can be found under that name in the mathematically oriented social sciences. Within this last field, the topic is sometimes simply ignored, as in the basic texts of Myerson (1991), Osborne and Rubinstein (1996) as well as Maschler, Solan and Zamir (2011). At another extreme one finds in Friedman (1986) under the general heading of "supergames" the expressions of repeated games, multiperiod games, multistage games, time-dependent games, etc. Which one of these should one use in order to develop in game theoretic terms the temporal dimension of the economic-ecological model just presented?

The answer happens to be: none of them! How come? The reason is that none of these games has a form that suits the dynamic economic-ecological model of our concern. The game models reviewed and developed by Friedman (and actually also in the basic texts referred to above) have all in common the characteristic that over time, the game remains the same: it is *repeated*, and the object of enquiry is the influence of time, *per se*, on the game's outcome. The notion of "dynamic" is thus taken in a very specific sense. Now, in the dynamic economic-ecological model that motivates my enquiry, the time element comes from the fact that the successive emissions result in a pollutant stock that accumulates, which implies a change in the state variable at each point in time in the specification of the game. The game to be defined is therefore *not* a repeated game.

There exists another category of dynamic games that covers this reality, under the terminologies of *differential* and *difference games* (respectively for continuous and discrete time formulations). This distinct category, also called *state-space games* is introduced in the important paper by de Zeeuw and van der Ploeg (1991). In those games, the objectives depend on the values of both the state variables and the chosen controls, and the state variables change over time under influence of the controls, which are the decision variables of the players. This is exactly what is specified with the triplet $(N, \hat{E}, V)$ of Definition 7.6 labeled DGEG. Being formulated in discrete time, the DGEG thus belongs to the category of difference games.

Basar and Olsder (1995) is a basic general reference in this field, dealing with non-cooperative games only, unfortunately. For the present application, Houba and de Zeeuw (1995) and especially de Zeeuw (1998) are a first source of inspiration. The cooperative game solution to the DGEG presented in this lecture was initiated at about the same time, and materialized in a series of three papers: Germain, Toint, and Tulkens (1998) for the optimal control (so-called "openloop") part, Germain, Tulkens and de Zeeuw (1998) and Germain, Toint, Tulkens and de Zeeuw (2003) for the dynamic programming ("feedback") part. Later on Germain, Tulkens and Magnus (2010) added another dimension to the economic-ecological model.

7.3 Equilibrium concepts in the DGEG

Having specified the dynamic form of the economic-ecological model as well as its game theoretic counterpart, I follow now again, in this expanded context, the successive steps of enquiry through which the static model of Lecture 5 has been studied, namely: equilibria, efficiency, reasons for negotiations, and finally construction of an efficient and stable cooperation scheme that can inspire an international environmental agreement. While such transposition may seem quite natural at first sight, and thus easy, the implementation reveals it to be a complex task. With the mathematics of game theory, those of dynamic systems are now to be called upon, and the combination of the two must be done without losing sight of the primary goal: an understanding of the logic of international agreements.

This should not discourage the reader, though: there is an undeniable intellectual beauty in the insights brought about by the so broadened framework. Some nice discoveries can be expected!

Non-cooperative Nash equilibrium paths

I begin by retaining for the DGDG all four assumptions made in Lecture 5 on the components of the static GEG prior to introducing the equilibrium concepts. These assumptions specify that for each individual player the choices are made from strategy sets covering the entire time period $(1, \ldots, T)$. Strategy profiles thus consist in the simultaneous such specifications by all players. It is, in a sense, a complete description of all possible actions of all the players for the entire future.

There are reasons to depart from this extreme form of farsightedness, which I shall do in due time and for reasons not only of realism, but rather linked with our specific objective. Yet, for the time being, I prefer to stick to a formulation based on the stated assumptions because this allows me to introduce the reader to game dynamics in a way methodologically as close as possible to the statics.

Accordingly, and using terms parallel to those of Definition 5.2, I have now:

Definition 7.7. A non-cooperative Nash equilibrium path (NCNE path) of the DGEG in strategic form $(N, \hat{E}, V)$ is a strategy profile $((\bar{e}_{it})_{i \in N})_{t=1}^{T}$ such that

for all $i \in N$, $(\bar{e}_{it})_{t=1}^{T} = \arg \max_{(e_{it})_{t=1}^{T}} V_i(e_{it})$

$$= \sum_{t=1}^{T} \beta^{t-1}[g_i(e_{it}) - d_i(z_t)] \qquad (7.43)$$

where

$$z_t = [1 - \delta]z_{t-1} + e_{it} + \sum_{j \in N \setminus \{i\}} \bar{e}_{jt}, \quad t = 1, \ldots, T, \qquad (7.44)$$

and

$$z_0 > 0 \text{ is given.}$$

This strategy profile corresponds to the environmentally nationalistic international equilibrium over time of the dynamic economic-ecological model (Definition 7.4).

Existence and uniqueness

This equilibrium is the simultaneous solution of the n optimal control[11] problems (7.43)–(7.44), one for each i. Under our assumptions, each of these problems has a well defined solution. As in the static case, the issue arises here too of the compatibility between these n solutions: indeed, they are interdependent through the transition equation (7.14), which is common to all of them. One therefore must prove existence of the Nash equilibrium of a DGEG, which can be done by using an argument similar to the proof of proposition 4.3: it follows from properties of the strategy sets $\hat{E}_i$ and of the payoff functions V_i.

---

[11]In some mathematical literature on dynamic systems the optimal control optimization methodology is often dubbed "open loop", and contrasted with an alternative one called "feedback". The distinction is of paramount importance for my present purpose and the reason for introducing it and developing the stated alternative are given in Section 7.5.

Proposition 7.10. *For the game* $(N, \hat{E}, V)$, *given* $z_0 > 0$ *and* $T > 1$, *there exists a Nash equilibrium.*

Proof. The argument made to prove the similar Proposition 5.1 in the static case can be used presently because the conditions are identical: each player's strategy space is a compact and convex set of a Euclidean space and each player's payoff function is defined and continuous for all $e \in E$ and concave with respect to his own strategy $e_i \in E_i$. Hence, Proposition 5.1 establishing the existence of a Nash equilibrium applies. $\quad\square$

As in the static case, uniqueness of the Nash equilibrium path is necessary for developing the dynamic cooperative theory of the γ-core. This can be done, again, by means of a contradiction argument where use is made of the properties of concavity of the functions g_i, convexity of the functions d_i, as well as of the first order conditions of.

Proposition 7.11. *For the game* $(N, \hat{E}, V)$, *given* $z_0 > 0$ *and* $T > 1$, *the Nash equilibrium is unique*

Proof. Suppose that given the same initial stock z_o there exists two Nash equilibria $\bar{e} = (\bar{e}_{1t}, \ldots, \bar{e}_{nt})_{t=1}^{T}$ and $\hat{e} = (\hat{e}_{1t}, \ldots, \hat{e}_{nt})_{t=1}^{T}$ and let $(\bar{z}_t)_{t=1}^{T}$ and $(\hat{z}_t)_{t=1}^{T}$ be the associated sequences of the stock. Consider the last time interval T. If $\bar{z}_T = \hat{z}_T$, then $\bar{e}_{iT} = \hat{e}_{iT}$ using (7.23) and therefore $\bar{z}_{T-1} = \hat{z}_{T-1}$ (using (7.44)). Repeating this argument one obtains $\bar{z}_t = \hat{z}_t$, and $\bar{e}_{it} = \hat{e}_{it}$ for all $t = 1, \ldots, T$. This means that the game can have more than one Nash equilibrium only if $\bar{z}_T \neq \hat{z}_T$.

Suppose without loss of generality that $\bar{z}_T > \hat{z}_T$. Since each d_i is an increasing and convex function, $d_i'(\bar{z}_T) > d_i'(\hat{z}_T)$ for all i. In view of (7.23), $g_i'(\bar{e}_{iT}) = d_i'(\bar{z}_T)$ and $g_i'(\hat{e}_{iT}) = d_i'(\hat{z}_T)$. Therefore, $g_i'(\bar{e}_{iT}) \geq g_i'(\hat{e}_{iT})$ for all i. As a consequence, $\bar{e}_{iT} \leq \hat{e}_{iT}$ for all i because the function g_i is increasing and concave. Thus, $\sum_{i \in N} \bar{e}_{iT} \leq \sum_{i \in N} \hat{e}_{iT}$.

Combining this last property with the fact that

$$\bar{z}_T = [1 - \delta]\bar{z}_{T-1} + \sum_{i \in N} \bar{e}_{iT} > \hat{z}_T = [1 - \delta]\hat{z}_{T-1} + \sum_{i \in N} \hat{e}_{iT}$$

one obtains

$$\bar{z}_{T-1} > \hat{z}_{T-1}.$$

On the other hand, by the Euler equation (7.20) and using condition (7.23) one has

$$g_i'(\bar{e}_{1T-1}) = d_i'(\bar{z}_{T-1}) + \beta(1 - \delta)d_i'(\bar{z}_T)$$

and

$$g_i'(\hat{e}_{1T-1}) = d_i'(\hat{z}_{T-1}) + \beta(1 - \delta)d_i'(\hat{z}_T).$$

Together, $\bar{z}_T > \hat{z}_T$ and $\bar{z}_{T-1} > \hat{z}_{T-1}$ just established imply $g_i'(\bar{e}_{iT-1}) > g_i'(\hat{e}_{iT-1})$. Thus, $\bar{e}_{iT-1} < \hat{e}_{iT-1}$ for all i. Repeating this argument for all $t < T - 1$, we eventually have

$$\sum_{i \in N} \bar{e}_{it} < \sum_{i \in N} \hat{e}_{it} \quad \text{and} \quad \bar{z}_t > \hat{z}_t \quad \text{for all} \quad t = 1, \dots, T.$$

However, this is a contradiction since it implies that at $t = 1, \bar{z}_t > \hat{z}_t$, but

$$\bar{z}_1 = [1 - \delta]z_0 + \sum_{i \in N} \bar{e}_{i1}, \quad \hat{z}_1 = [1 - \delta]\hat{z}_0 + \sum_{i \in N} \hat{e}_{i1}, \quad \text{and}$$

$$\sum_{i \in N} \bar{e}_{i1} < \sum_{i \in N} \hat{e}_{i1}.$$

Thus, we must have $\bar{z}_t = \hat{z}_t$ and hence the Nash equilibrium is unique. □

Other properties of the non-cooperative Nash equilibrium path

Since every joint strategy of the players in the associated game is a feasible path of the dynamic economy, its economic properties, now confirmed by the existence proof, are similar to those listed in Section 7.1 for the international equilibria over time of the economic-ecological model. In view of (7.13) there are neither transfers nor any form of cooperation among the countries and in each period each country consumes only what it produces. This non-cooperative path is also "environmentally nationalistic" as in the static case of

Lecture 5: indeed, conditions (7.23) involve only each country's own marginal damages, present as well as future, in the determination of its emissions.

From the same conditions it can be inferred that $\bar{e} = (\bar{e}_{1t}, \ldots, \bar{e}_{nt})_{t=1}^{T}$ remains a Nash equilibrium of the subgame of the dynamic game that would start at time t with initial value of stock $\bar{z}_{t-1}$. In other words, the Nash equilibrium satisfies a *time consistency* property.

A higher discount factor[12] β or a higher durability rate $(1 - \delta)$ also imply a lower terminal stock $\bar{z}_T$. However, no general conclusion can be drawn about the entire time profile of the emissions except that they must be lower in at least some periods, since the terminal stock is lower. Sharper results can be obtained in special cases such as the following.

Linear damage functions: Equilibrium in dominant strategies

With linear damage functions, that is, if $d'(z) = \pi_i > 0$, a constant, equation (7.23) reduce to:

$$g_i'(\bar{e}_{it}) = \pi_i(1 + \beta(1 - \delta)) + (\beta(1 - \delta))^2 + \cdots + (\beta(1 - \delta))^{T-t},$$

$$t = 1, \ldots, T, \quad i = 1, \ldots, n.$$

This expression allows one to state for the international equilibrium:

(i) Decisions by other players than i do not play any role in this expression. Therefore for each $i \in N$, the Nash equilibrium strategy is a dominant strategy. This property was also holding for the Nash equilibrium of the static game in Chapter 4 under linearity of the damage functions.

(ii) Finally, in contrast with (7.23) where the damage functions are strictly convex, the equilibrium level of emissions when damage functions linear as above does not depend on the level of the stock $\bar{z}_t$. In other words, the equilibrium control variables are independent of the state variables.

---

[12]That is, a lower discount rate.

Coalitions and utilities

Just as I did in Lecture 5 for statics, I now introduce coalitions, partially cooperative Nash equilibria and coalitional functions, paving the way for a conceivable subsequent introduction of dynamic cooperative solution concepts. The methodology remains that of optimal control.

Coalitions

The appearance of coalitions in a dynamic game raises all the issues that have been handled in Lecture 4 (Section 4.2) and 5 (Section 5.2) for static games, leading by and large to the same conclusions. What is genuine to the dynamic framework is the question of how long coalitions last in time. In this section, I assume the mathematically simplest case that any coalition lasts for the entire time period $(1, \dots, T)$. Let me explore how far it leads.

Transferability of utilities

In Sections 7.1 and 7.2, I have discussed individual utilities and payoffs in the dynamic context, including discounting. This is to be pursued with the specification of the behavior of coalitions over time. The introduction of the γ-assumption in Lecture 4 led first to proposing in Lecture 5 for the GEG the expression (5.8)–(5.9) as an objective function for a coalition, which includes transferability of payoffs. Such transferability is retained here, with the same justifications applying between individual players within each time interval t.

Paths of partially cooperative Nash equilibria

With these two assumptions now introduced in the dynamic setting the extension can be pursued with solution concepts, among which the following:

Definition 7.8. Given a coalition $S \subset N$, a **partially cooperative Nash equilibrium path relative to a coalition** S (PCNE path r.t.S) **of the DGEG** is a strategy profile$((\tilde{e}_{it}^S)_{i\in N})_{t=1}^T$ such that

$$((\tilde{e}_{it}^S)_{i\in S})_1^T = \underset{((e_{it}^S)_{i\in S})_1^T \in E_S}{\arg\max} \sum_{i\in S} V_i = \sum_{i\in S}\sum_{t=1}^T \beta^{t-1}[g_i(e_{it}^S) - d_i(z_t^S)],$$

$$(7.45)$$

where

$$z_t^S = [1-\delta]z_{t-1}^S + \sum_{i\in S} e_{it}^S + \sum_{j\in N, j\notin S} \tilde{e}_{jt}^S, \quad t=1,\ldots,T,$$

and

$$\forall j \in N, j\notin S, (\tilde{e}_{jt}^S)_1^T = \underset{(e_{jt}^S)_1^T \in E_j}{\arg\max} V_j = \sum_{t=1}^T \beta^{t-1}[g_j(e_{jt}^S) - d_j(z_t^S)],$$

$$(7.46)$$

where

$$z_t^S = [1-\delta]z_{t-1}^S + \sum_{i\in S} \tilde{e}_{it}^S + \sum_{j\in N, j\notin S} e_{jt}^S, \quad t=1,\ldots,T,$$

with $z_o^S > 0$ given.

This definition implies that along the path of a PCNE r.t. S, the strategy profile $((\tilde{e}_{it}^S)_{i\in N})_{t=1}^T$ induces for the state variable a path $(\tilde{z}_t^S)_{t=1}^T$ such that at every time interval t

$$\tilde{z}_t^S = \sum_{i\in N} \tilde{e}_{it}^S. \tag{7.47}$$

Existence and uniqueness

As argued in the existence proof of Proposition 5.4 for the PCNE r.t. S, the coalition S once formed may be considered as behaving as a single player, with an objective function and strategy set having identical properties. For that same reason, the present PCNE path r.t. to S is also the Nash equilibrium path of a game with $n - s + 1$ players. To this game, the existence and uniqueness of proofs of Propositions 7.10 and 7.11 may be applied.

Behavioral economic and environmental characteristics

The need of transposing to the dynamic setting the other characteristics of the static PCNE relative to coalitions (Propositions 5.6–5.8)
will soon appear to be less pressing because of the little use that
will be made of these properties in the sequel. That little use itself is
due to an excessive rigidity of the optimal control methodology when
dealing with coalitions over time — a point to be fully developed in
Section 7.5.

7.4   Coalitional functions, efficient and alternative cooperative paths

The γ-coalitional function, the efficient path, and the imputations set

From Lectures 4 and 5, each at its level of generality, one learns
that with the instrument of PCNE r.t. S coalitional functions can
be defined that allow one to characterize the behavior of alternative
coalitions in a game with externalities in general and in the GEG in
particular. This possibility remains with the dynamic version of the
GEG, as can be seen from the following straightforward transposition
from the static case of Lecture 5.

Let $S \subset N$ be some coalition and let $((\tilde{e}_{it}^S)_{i \in N})_{t=1}^T$ be the path of
the PCNE relative to that S of Definition 7.8. The strategy profile
corresponding to that definition and the induced state variables yield
for each $i \in N$ a payoff

$$\tilde{V}_i^S \underset{\text{def}}{=} \sum_{t=1}^T \beta^{t-1} \left[g_i(\tilde{e}_{it}^S) - d_i \left(\sum_{j \in N} \tilde{e}_{jt}^S \right) \right]. \tag{7.48}$$

Limiting oneself to the payoffs of the members of S only,[13] and
considering now all coalitions including N, one may propose the
following notion:

---

[13]Thus, as I did in Lecture 5, leaving out of consideration the payoffs of the non-
members of S. But do remember that, as announced, they will reappear in the
further theoretical discussion of coalition stability in Lecture 9.

Definition 7.9. The γ-**coalitional function of the DGEG** in strategic form is the function that associates with every coalition $S \subseteq N$ the value

$$W^\gamma(S) \underset{\text{def}}{=} \sum_{i \in S} \tilde{V}_i^S = \sum_{i \in S} \sum_{t=1}^T \beta^{t-1}[g_i(\tilde{e}_{it}^S) - d_i(\tilde{z}_t^S)] \quad \forall \ S \neq N,$$

(7.49)

$$\underset{\text{def}}{=} \sum_{i \in N} V_i^* = \sum_{i \in N} \sum_{t=1}^T \beta^{t-1}[g_i(e_{it}^*) - d_i(z_t^*)] \quad \text{if } S = N,$$

(7.50)

where $\tilde{z}_t^S$ is as in (7.47) above and

$$((e_{it}^*)_{i \in N})_{t=1}^T = \underset{((e_{it})_{i \in N})_{t=1}^T \in E}{\arg\max} \sum_{i \in N} \sum_{t=1}^T \beta^{t-1}[g_i(e_{it}) - d_i(z_t)],$$

(7.51)

with at each t

$$z_t = [1 - \delta]z_{t-1} + \sum_{j \in N} e_{jt} \quad \text{and } z_0 > 0 \text{ given.}$$

Clearly, in (7.49), the T terms under the second summation sign solve, for each S, the component (7.45) of the PCNE relative to that coalition. Similarly in (7.50) the T terms that make up $W^\gamma(N)$ solve the optimal control problem (7.28)–(7.29). In economic terms, the strategies $((e_{it}^*)_{i \in N})_1^T$ so determined are the emissions of the Pareto efficient path of the dynamic economic-ecological model, and the payoffs $(V_1^*, \dots, V_n^*)$ represent the discounted utilities $(U_1^*, \dots, U_n^*)$ of all countries at the solution of (7.24), each summed over the entire period $1, \dots, T$.

These same magnitudes being such that $\sum_{i \in N} V_i^* = W^\gamma(N)$, they also satisfy, in game theoretic terms, the definition of an imputation of the game $(N, \hat{E}, V)$. If I denote as

$$\{\Phi \in R^n | \sum_{i \in N} \Phi_i = W^\gamma(N)\}, \tag{7.52}$$

the set of imputations of the DGEG in coalitional function form that are defined in (7.50), each component of the payoff vector Φ is equivalent to the utility

$$U_i^*(\Psi) \underset{\text{def}}{=} \left(\sum_{t=1}^{T} \beta^{t-1}[g_i(e_{it}^*) - d_i(z_t^*)] \right) + \Psi_i.$$

It appears in each term under the summation sign of the last expression of Proposition 7.7. The connection is thus complete between the dynamic versions of the economic-ecological model and of the game, respectively.

Alternative cooperative paths

With the γ-coalitional function so extended to dynamics, what about cooperative solutions for the DGEG? In the corresponding paragraph of the static model, several alternatives to the γ-coalitional function have been recorded. Performing the formal exercise of extending to the present dynamic model the α-coalitional function and the β-coalitional function is an easy matter, but its interest is probably limited by the fact that the dynamic context renders all the less acceptable the threatening behaviors on which they rest as far as players non-members of a coalition are concerned. These behaviors hardly could be considered to hold for long periods. To my knowledge, no such attempted extension can be found in the literature, neither game theoretical, nor environmentally motivated. By contrast, the equilibrium behaviors of coalition non-members implied by the γ-assumption makes the dynamic extension of the γ-coalitional function less irrealistic.

7.5   The γ-core stable path of the DGEG: Optimal control formulation

The optimal control approach

The way I have presented the components of the DGEG thus far make it essentially a multi-dimensional extension of the GEG, with an unchanged structure. With the concept of γ-coalitional function thus extended over time in Definition 7.9, one may transpose as follows to the DGEG the Definition 5.6 of the γ-core of the GEG:

Definition 7.10.   For the DGEG in strategic form **the γ-core stable path** is the set of strategy profiles $((e_{it}^*)_{i \in N})_{t=1}^T$ inducing imputations $(V_1^*, \ldots, V_n^*)$ such that there exists no coalition $S \subset N$ for which the PCNE path r.t. it is an alternative strategy profile $((\tilde{e}_{it}^S)_{i \in N})_{t=1}^T$ that yields payoffs $(\tilde{V}_1^S, \ldots, \tilde{V}_n^S)$ by means of which S improves the payoffs of its members over the period $(1, \ldots, T)$ in the sense that $\sum_{i \in S} \tilde{V}_i^S > \sum_{i \in S} V_i^*$ in (7.49)–(7.50).

In more compact terms, the γ-core is the set of strategy profiles that no coalition $S \subset N$ can block by means of the PCNE path r.t. S.

Establishing existence analytically, either in the general sense of balancedness or in the particular way of exhibiting appropriately designed transfers to accompany a Pareto efficient strategy profile, should follow suit. The second way is followed in Germain, Toint and Tulkens (1998) as well as in the numerical simulation made by Eyckmans and Tulkens (2003), where a γ-core CT solution (with transfers) in the sense of Definition 7.10 is computed. Lecture 8 is entirely devoted to that.

However, I shall not presently go farther in such direction, for two reasons: (a) The critical evaluation made below strongly suggests that the methodology followed thus far is not well suited for dealing with our main objective of dealing with negotiations; and (b) There exists an alternative methodology of economic dynamics, not used to my knowledge for the objective just mentioned, whose exploration reveals to be more promising in that respect. This is the subject matter of Section 7.6 that follows the critique.

Critical evaluation

What was the purpose of extending to dynamics the theory of international environmental agreements developed in Lectures 3, 5 and 6? A first an immediate objective of that exercise was to test the ability of this theory to handle stock externalities, which involve in an essential way a time dimension absent from the static models. This seems to be reasonably well achieved in Sections 7.1–7.4 and in the beginning of the present one. The modeling tools have shown to have flexibility and the dynamic game has been introduced smoothly. But does the outcome contribute to the overall aim of these lectures, namely the understanding of the logic on which international environmental agreements are built? At that level, does the introduction of time the way I have done it bring about essential new ingredients? I believe there are several reasons to give negative answers to these questions.

Let me distinguish between economic and game theoretic reasons for that judgment, focusing on the point of view of decision making.

Economic considerations

(i) As determined by Definition 7.4, the path of an environmentally nationalistic equilibrium of the economic-ecological model has the characteristic of being determined at the initial time interval $t = 1$, and for the entire time period $(1, \ldots, T)$. It specifies the future as a function of the data and parameters known at time 1 and remains fixed from then on. On that basis it amounts to a *sheer description* of the parties' parallel behaviors as they result from a single decision taken once and for all. There is very little social science reasoning to support that description.

(ii) In other contexts,[14] such rigidity is interpreted as *commitments* of economic agents *vis-à-vis* one another, the Nash equilibrium inducing thereby some kind of stability. But in the present context, the idea of commitment is inappropriate: why would a

---

[14]Such as oligopoly theory whose early dynamics started with optimal control.

country commit itself on an emissions policy which is the one it prefers anyway, taking due account of what the other countries' do during the same time period?

(iii) The economic variables whose role is most artificial are transfers, be they implicit as in Definition 7.10, or explicitly used as in the two (1998) and (2003) papers mentioned in p. 264. The artificiality is with their *timing*. While they are defined in units of green consumption discounted at time interval 1, the model does not specify at what point in time these amounts should be paid and received.

Game theoretic considerations

(i) According to Definition 7.5, the consideration of alternative *coalitions* occurs only at the initial point in time $t = 1$ after which they are fixed for the entire future. In other words, coalitions are permanent. As a corollary, the singletons are treated as remaining singletons for ever. Thus, the concept of PCNE r.t. S is at best an instrument of exploration of the future in that rigid context. How and why coalition structures might evolve over time cannot be handled.

(ii) As just said, the optimal control NCNE does not allow for *transfers* between players. However, in addition to their real-locative role in the economy, voluntary transfers may have also a strategic role in the design of solution concepts, as shown in Lecture 6 for the static γ-core. The possibility of such a role is ignored in the dynamic extension of the equilibrium concept.

(iii) If at some time t along the actual path of the economy the state of the system is z_t and for some reason not $\bar{z}_t$, that is, the state implied by the equilibrium path $(\bar{e}_{1t}, \ldots, \bar{e}_{nt})_{t=1}^{T}$ predicted by the model, then this strategy profile is not an equilibrium any more that can serve at time t as a *reference* describing the non-cooperative behavior of the countries — for instance to justify transfers between countries according to a formula such as (6.19) in the previous lecture. Indeed in this formula *the equilibrium nature of the reference point* is an essential ingredient for the solution constructed with it to have the γ-core property.

All the above six causes of rigidity characterizing the solution offered by the optimal control methodology prevent one to formulate dynamics that are adequate to deal with the issue of our concern, namely negotiations on a stock externality which cannot be concluded once and for all. For that purpose, it is not sufficient that time be represented in the model by just dating the variables. The role of time must be modeled in such a way that time be a component the decision process itself all along the period $1, \ldots, T$.

7.6 The γ-core stable path as a sequence of negotiations: Dynamic programming formulation

The GTTZ alternative approach[15]

The issue of cooperation vs. non-cooperation
in an intertemporal context

When I invoke negotiations on international environmental agreements what exactly do I have in mind? Quite simply and basically: the search for a logical explanation of why cooperation *vs.* non-cooperation can prevail between the parties. In this lecture, this central question is restated in the intertemporal context of the DGEG. The mention of time triggers two subquestions: *when* is cooperation going to prevail — if at all? And if so, *for how long* does it last?

The answers given to these two subquestions by the optimal control approach just reviewed are, respectively: "at time $t = 1$"

---

[15]The contents of this section is inspired for its essential part by two papers: Germain, Toint and Tulkens (1999) and Germain, Toint, Tulkens and de Zeeuw (2003). The last part of the section also benefited of some inputs from private exchanges in 2010 with Professor Chander. For an excellent introduction to dynamic programming in economic terms, independent of the particular "negotiations" motivation invoked here, consult Adda and Cooper (2003).

and "for the whole period $1, \ldots, T$". While clear-cut, these answers actually beg the questions because they eliminate time from the decision making *process*. The modeling formalizes just a one shot decision, taken at one moment of time namely the beginning of the period. Admittedly the content of that decision consists of actions that take place over time, present and future, but it is organized in a way that excludes the possibility of any decision taken after time 1 along the time path. Although bearing on a wider content, the nature of the decision as to the cooperation *vs.* non-cooperation alternative is in that framework not different from what it was in Lectures 5 and 6. Up to here there is thus hardly any gain achieved in this lecture towards understanding whether the elapsing of time may have any effect on the decision concerning the central issue mentioned above.

As argued in the preceding section the reason for this poor outcome lies in the too restricted timing possibilities that the optimal control formulation of decisions allows for. Against this lack of flexibility, an alternative technique in dynamic systems theory is offered by dynamic programing, which allows for considering intermediate decision stages along the temporal path as well as to evaluate the direction being followed, and finally to possibly modify the path in function of the ultimate objective being pursued. This is what I now turn to.

State variables and value functions:
Dynamic programming in lieu of optimal control

The relevance of allowing for decision making along the temporal path of a solution to a dynamic system is best highlighted by argument (iii) of the above game theoretic critique: the state of the system may evolve differently from what can be anticipated at time $t = 1$ only, and if taken into account, such changes in the state variables may determine at any time $t > 1$ choices of the control variables that are different from those declared optimal at time 1. The changes may be exogenous, as can easily be imagined, but they may also be endogenous, due to particular characteristics of the model.

Optimal control and dynamic programming are different instruments of dynamic optimization that can compute the efficient strategy profile $((e_{it}^*)_{i\in N})_{t=1}^T$ of the DGEG $(N, \hat{E}, V)$. While the two methods differ (linked together by the well known Bellman equation) the efficiency solutions they generate are identical. By contrast, if the two instruments are used to compute the Nash equilibrium of that same game, the solutions are not identical,[16] for a reason that exactly meets argument (iii): For the game $(N, \hat{E}, V)$ the Nash equilibrium generates endogenous changes in the state of the system along its temporal unfolding that cannot be anticipated at the initial time of the period $1, \dots, T$. What are these endogenous changes? Why are they unpredictable?

Characteristically, the computation of the Nash equilibrium of a n−players game is a multiobjective optimization problem. Each objective, one for each player, is subject to its own constraints while some constraints make the objectives interdependent. In the present dynamic case, interdependence comes from the transition equations that determine the state variables. The controls, i.e. the strategies, are specific to each player and chosen by them independently. Such structure implies that at every time interval, the level of the state variable that each player is facing results not only from his own optimal choice of his controls but also from the individual control choices of the other players. But these are foreign to his own decision power at time $t = 1$ and thus are *for him* an "exogenous" and unpredictable element in the determination of the states all along the optimization period. Yet, these so determined state variables are an argument in the payoff functions of all players, they thus understandably influence the choice of individual controls, in a "feed back" effect so to speak. Therefore, optimal choice of controls at each t cannot be the same under optimal control and under an alternative algorithm that would take into account for each i of the evolution of the state variable beyond what this evolution owes to i. By allowing

---

[16]A point already made in Germain, Tulkens and de Zeeuw (1998) and also by Germain, Toint, Tulkens and de Zeeuw (2003, Section 5.3, pp. 95–96) where it is illustrated with a numerical example. Another example where the argument is analytical, is presented in Khiem Nguyen Tho (2015, p. 44, equation (4.60)), inspired by Long (2010).

for this exogenous effect, dynamic programming makes room for the flexibility needed in the negotiations model presently constructed.

Turning now to the modeling of the cooperation *vs.* non-cooperation decision, consider at any time interval t the alternative payoffs that can be obtained by each player from the decisions to adopt *at that moment* either a cooperative or a non-cooperative strategy. How are the strategies and payoffs to be defined in such case? As far as cooperation is concerned, those of the tth stage of the efficient strategy profile $((e_{it}^*)_{i \in N})_1^T$ and payoffs $(V_1^*, \ldots, V_n^*)$ specified by (7.50)–(7.51) are natural candidates, if it is known that no exogenous causes of changes in z have occurred prior to t. Thus due account is taken of the state of the system at every time t. This is a virtue of time consistency of the optimal control method when used to solve (7.50)–(7.51). Let me observe that for the efficient solution dynamic programming and optimal control produce the same solution when no exogenous causes of changes in z can be assumed.

As for non-cooperation, it would be contradictory with the above critique to consider in a similar fashion the NCNE strategy profile $((\bar{e}_{it})_{i \in N}))_{t=1}^T$ and payoffs that solve in the optimal control fashion the family of problems (7.43)–(7.44) above. The reson is due to the unavoidable endogenous feedback effect described above[17].

Instead, an instrument is proposed by dynamic programming, called the *value function,* that allows to simultaneously (a) generate a joint decision on cooperation *vs.* non-cooperation at each time interval t given the state of the system at that time, given all exogenous and endogenous influences, *and* (b) take into account the future implied by that decision, from that moment on. The decision consists of a strategy profile for time t (and time t only), and the ensuing payoffs are those induced by that profile *and* the future ones, as anticipated by the value function to be defined shortly.

---

[17]One may think of the proposal of Yang (2003) which consists of respecifying the dynamic game at each t, with its open loop NCNE relative to the initial state taken as the value of z at that moment. This does not resolve the rigidity problem as to the future, however. In addition, the proposal does not specify in which intertemporal direction the system taken as a whole is driven by the sequence of decisions generated by such successive respecifications.

The fallback position and the Houba-de Zeeuw assumption on expectations

There remains to specify whitch point of reference, other than the open loop NCNE path, can be conceived of as a "fallback position" in case one or several players opt for a non-cooperative strategy along a solution path $((e_{it})_{i \in N}, (z_t))_{t=1}^{T}$. Such position should be in the nature of a Nash equilibrium of some game, now determined by modified payoff functions — thus a new game, the modification reflecting the possibility for the players to express at each time t their preferences *vis-à-vis* the cooperative *vs.* non-cooperative courses of action given the prevailing state of the system. One way to do that in a *non*-open loop spirit is to assume the players' attitude with respect to time to be the one summarized by the expression: "possibly non-cooperation at time t, followed by cooperation afterwards". The authors[18] of this assumption call it a *rational expectations* attitude, i.e. expectations based on the subjective view that even if only a non-cooperative individual attitude can be taken immediately, the knowledge that cooperation in the future is conceivable, possible and favorable for all parties makes it worth betting on. It is not just a form of optimism opposed to the pessimism of the open loop dynamics of the previous paragraphs. It rather rests on the idea that when a collectively favorable outcome can be identified and justified for the future, there is rationality in expecting its realization, in spite of a possible current non-cooperation. This idea[19] is now going to be couched in terms of payoffs of the players in a new kind of games defined at each time interval t, linked to one another over time by means of a value function generated by the dynamic programming handling of the DGEG.

---

[18]Houba and de Zeeuw (1995), who conceived of the concept in a modeling context different from mine here on two counts: their modeling is not explicitly an environmental one, and the game theoretic solution concept they are considering is not the core but the "Nash bargaining solution" (see Nash (1950)) not to be confused with the NCNE.

[19]It was originally transposed to the present context in Germain, Tulkens and de Zeeuw (1998) and further developed in Germain, Toint, Tulkens and de Zeeuw (2003) as well as in Germain, Tulkens and Magnus (2010).

Rational expectations games: Introducing the concept

Assume T finite, and consider the last time interval T: the DGEG then reduces to the static coalitional game of Lecture 5. However, a full description of cooperation prevailing at time T as a γ-core solution e_T^* of this reduced DGEG comprises two novelties:

(a) that the γ-core efficient vector of emissions e_T^* is now seen as a vector-valued function of z_{T-1}, the state of the system at the beginning of time T, and is thus to be denoted as

$$e_T^*(z_{T-1}) \underset{\text{def}}{=} (e_{1T}^*(z_{T-1}), \dots, e_{nT}^*(z_{T-1})),$$

(b) that a γ-core imputation of the game now reads

$$v^{**}(z_{T-1}) = (v_1^{**}(z_{T-1}), \dots, v_n^{**}(z_{T-1})),$$

where

- the payoff of player i is

$$v_i^{**}(z_{T-1}) = g_i(e_{iT}^*) - d_i(z_T^*) + \theta_{iT}(z_{T-1})$$
$$= g_i(e_{iT}^*(z_{T-1}))$$
$$-d_i \left[(1-\delta)(z_{T-1}) + \sum_{j \in N} e_{jT}^*(z_{T-1}) \right] + \theta_{iT}(z_{T-1})$$

and

- $\theta_{iT}(z_{T-1})$ is a transfer ($>, =$, or < 0) ensuring for player i the core property of the imputation $v^{**}(z_{T-1})$.

Existence of this γ-core imputation of the game results from the balancedness of the identical static game shown in Lecture 5 as well as from the core property of the "CT solution with transfers" (6.18), presented in Lecture 6. The rationale for selecting this core imputation is the same as in these lectures. Arguments justifying cooperation in the static model can equally be invoked to assert cooperation prevailing at time T.

Consider now the next to last time interval $T - 1$ and define another strategic coalitional game at that time, with for each player i a new payoff function $v_i(e_{T-1}, z_{T-2})$ and a vector of strategies $e_{T-1}(z_{T-2})$ both valid at $T - 1$ only. These are of the form:

$$v_i(e_{T-1}, z_{T-2}) = g_i(e_{iT-1}) - d_i(z_{T-1}) + \beta a_i(z_{T-1}) \qquad (7.53)$$

where

$$e_{T-1} = (e_{1T-1}, \ldots, e_{nT-1})$$

is the strategy profile chosen at time $T - 1$,

$$z_{T-1} = [1 - \delta] z_{T-2} + \sum_{j \in N} e_{jT-1}, \quad z_{T-2} > 0 \text{ given,}$$

and

$$a_i(z_{T-1}) = v_i^{**}(z_{T-1}). \qquad (7.54)$$

As said, in this game the strategies are formulated for the time interval $T - 1$ only. One more novelty in (7.53) is the presence of the term $a_i(z_{T-1})$, which bears on the future. It is the heart of the argument: (7.54) sets it equal to $v_i^{**}(z_{T-1})$, that is, the γ-core payoff of player i at the *next* time interval which is T. It plays the role of what is called a value function in dynamic programming. In this way, the game played at $T - 1$ integrates in its payoff functions the Houba-de Zeeuw "cooperation afterwards" assumption that I have announced.

Now, to answer the question "cooperate or not cooperate?" at time interval $T-1$, consider a γ-core solution of the game just stated, with its new payoff function (7.53). If adopted, this solution means that cooperation prevails at $T - 1$, and it induces a corresponding value for the magnitude z_{T-1}, which will be a parameter in the next time interval of the game. If the γ-core solution is not adopted, non-cooperation prevails at $T - 1$ in the sense of the fallback position announced earlier in this section, which is the NCNE of the game. It nevertheless induces another value for the parameter z_{T-1} in the next time interval of the DGEG. In either case, the emissions at $T-1$

are well defined, and they determine a key parameter, z_{T-1}, of the game which is played at T.

Thus, either outcome constitutes a step forward in the time path of the dynamic game solution, and this solution has the property of subgame perfectness since the last game solution is a function of the state induced by the next-to-last game solution.

The argument in general terms and existence

Definition 7.11. Given z_{t-1}, a **rational expectations GEG at time** t is a strategic game (N, E_t, v_t) where

- $N = \{1, 2, \ldots, n\}$ is the set of players, indexed $i = 1, 2, \ldots, n$,
- $E_t = E_{1t} \times \cdots \times E_{nt}$ is the set of strategy profiles at time t where $E_{it} = \{e_{it} : 0 \leq e_{it} \leq e^0\}$ is the set of strategies accessible to player i at time t,
- $v_t = (v_{1t}, \ldots, v_{nt})$ is the vector of the players' payoffs at time t.

Given a strategy profile $e_t = (e_{it}, \ldots, e_{nt}) \in E_t$ and the state z_{t-1}, the payoff of player i is the image of the function:

$$v_{it}(z_{t-1}, e_t) = g_i(e_{it}) - d_i(z_t) + \beta a_i(z_t)$$

$$= g_i(e_{it}) - d_i \left([1 - \delta]z_{t-1} + \sum_{j \in N} e_{jt} \right)$$

$$+ \beta a_i \left([1 - \delta]z_{t-1} + \sum_{j \in N} e_{jt} \right)$$

where $a_i(z_t) = a_i([1 - \delta]z_{t-1} + \sum_{j \in N} e_{jt})$ is a value function representing player i's γ-core payoff in the rational expectations game (N, E_{t+1}, v_{t+1}) defined in the next period.

But does this game have a γ-core solution? If not, cooperation cannot be asserted, neither at $T - 1$, nor at any other earlier time interval t. The answer is as follows.

Theorem 7.1. *The rational expectations GEG (N, E_t, v_t) has a unique Nash equilibrium, is balanced, and hence has a non-empty* *γ-core, if in its payoff function the value function*

$$a_i(z_t) = a_i \left([1 - \delta]z_{t-1} + \sum_{j \in N} e_{jt} \right)$$

is decreasing and concave in $\sum_{j \in N} e_{jt}$.

Proof. If the condition stated in the theorem is satisfied, then the function

$$d_i \left([1 - \delta]z_{t-1} + \sum_{j \in N} e_{jt} \right) - \beta a_i \left([1 - \delta]z_{t-1} + \sum_{j \in N} e_{jt} \right)$$

is increasing and convex in $\sum_{j \in N} e_{jt}$. If so, the rational expectations GEG (N, E_t, v_t) has exactly the same mathematical structure and properties than the static GEG (N, E, v) associated in Lecture 5 with the static form of the reference economic-ecological model. Therefore, existence of a Nash equilibrium and balancedness, which are established for this game in Lectures 5 and 6 (based on Chander and Tulkens (1997) and Helm (2001)) apply equally to the present game. □

The cooperative solution of the dynamic global environmental game

Definition and existence

The implications of Theorem 7.1 for the design of a solution for the basic DGEG of Definition 7.6 (Section 7.2) are considerable. Indeed, it offers support for the key building block of a solution for the dynamic game for the whole period $1, \ldots, T$, namely a sequence of solutions, non-cooperative or cooperative, to rational expectations games defined at the successive time intervals t, $1 < t < T$, each parameterized by z_{t-1}. Along the path so induced the solution of each such game is a function of the state of the system in the previous time interval, which plays the same role as the feedback notion in dynamic programming. More precisely, conceive of a process of successive γ-core imputations of the rational expectations game (N, E_t, v_t) at each time interval t, each of which dominates the fallback Nash equilibrium of that same game.

Definition 7.12.   For the DGEG $(N, \hat{E}, V)$ in strategic form, **a γ-core stable solution path** consists of a sequence of γ-core imputations which solve at each period t a rational expectations game (N, E_t, v_t).

Intuitively, the source of cooperation lies in the fact that at each time interval t the γ-core solution dominates the fallback NCNE of the rational expectations game defined at that time, as well as the partially cooperative Nash equilibria relative to all possible coalitions that might form.

Theorem 7.2.   *For the DGEG $(N, \hat{E}, V)$, there exists a γ-core cooperative solution, that is, a world efficient emissions path which is at every t coalitionally stable against the alternative of non-cooperation.*

Proof.   Existence follows from the existence of γ-core imputations of the rational expectations games at each time t, established by Theorem 7.1.   ☐

The existence invoked in Theorem 7.1 is conditioned on the property of the value function $a_i(z_t) = a_i([1 - \delta]z_{t-1} + \sum_{j \in N} e_{jt})$ to be decreasing and concave in $\sum_{j \in N} e_{jt}$. In the two following subsections, the analytical solution of the game is computed explicitly for DGEGs where the damage functions are linear or quadratic, showing that in these cases the property is satisfied. Theorem 7.2 is thereby given a logical foundation.

Computing the solution by backward induction — Linear damage functions

I now apply the methodology of backward induction to solve the DGEG problem (7.28)–(7.29) where the damage functions of the economic-ecological model are assumed to be linear, i.e. $d_i'(z) = \pi_i$, $\pi_i > 0$, for all z and $i \in N$.

At the last time interval T, for the rational expectations game (N, E_T, v_T) the payoff functions of the players are, for each $i \in N$,

$$v_{iT}(z_{T-1}, e_T) = g_{iT}(e_{iT}) - \pi_i z_T,$$

$$\text{where } z_T = (1 - \delta)z_{T-1} + \sum_{j \in N} e_{jT},$$

thus

$$v_{iT}(z_{T-1}, e_T) = g_{iT}(e_{iT}) - \pi_i \left[(1 - \delta)z_{T-1} + \sum_{j \in N} e_{jT} \right]$$

$$= g_{iT}(e_{iT}) - \pi_i[(1 - \delta)z_{T-1}] - \pi_i \sum_{j \in N} e_{jT},$$

$$z_{T-1} > 0 \text{ given.}$$

Note that these functions are decreasing and affine in $\sum_{j \in N} e_{jT}$ with the constant term being $\pi_i[(1 - \delta)z_{T-1}]$.

The γ-core (CT) solution, that is, an imputation of this[20] game, is the vector of n functions

$$v_{iT}^{**}(z_{T-1}) = x_{iT}^{**}(z_{T-1}) - \pi_i z_T^*(z_{T-1}), \quad i = 1, \ldots, n$$

where, remembering (6.2) in the previous lecture,

$$x_{iT}^{**}(z_{T-1}) = g_i(\bar{e}_{iT}(z_{T-1}))$$

$$- \frac{\pi_i}{\sum_{j \in N} \pi_j} \left(\sum_{j \in N} [g_j(\bar{e}_{jT}(z_{T-1})) - g_j(e_{jT}^*(z_{T-1}))] \right)$$

and by definition

$$z_T^*(z_{T-1}) = (1 - \delta)z_{T-1} + \sum_{j \in N} e_{jT}^*(z_{T-1}).$$

---

[20]The payoff functions being affine rather than linear, a slight modification is needed in order to use here Theorem 6.1. It boils down to having the constant term appear in the expression that defines the γ-core imputation.

In these expressions all magnitudes $\bar{e}_{1T}(z_{T-1}), \dots, \bar{e}_{nT}(z_{T-1})$ (that constitute the NCNE strategy profile) and $e_{1T}^*(z_{T-1}), \dots, e_{nT}^*(z_{T-1})$ (constituting the Pareto efficient strategy profile) are defined and can be computed from the respective first order conditions $g_i'(\bar{e}_{iT}) = \pi_i$ and $g_{iT}'(e_{iT}^*) = \sum_{j \in N} \pi_j, i = 1, \dots, n$. As indicated, they all are functions of the given state z_{T-1}.

At variance with the solution of the static game of Section 6.1, one has for the imputation

$$v_{iT}^{**}(z_{T-1}) = x_{iT}^{**}(z_{T-1}) - \pi_i z_T^*(z_{T-1}), \quad i = 1, \dots, n$$

$$= x_{iT}^{**}(z_{T-1}) - \pi_i \left[(1-\delta)z_{T-1} + \sum_{j \in N} e_{jT}^*(z_{T-1}) \right] \quad (7.55)$$

a form which shows that the γ-core imputation functions $v_{iT}^{**}(z_{T-1})$ are themselves decreasing and affine in $\sum_{j \in N} e_{jT}$ with constant term $\pi_i \cdot (1-\delta)z_{T-1}$. They will serve as value functions in the next stage.

Indeed, *at time interval $T-1$*, for the rational expectations game (N, E_{T-1}, v_{T-1}) the payoff functions of the players are, for each $i \in N$,

$$v_{iT-1}(z_{T-2}, e_{T-1}) = g_i(e_{iT-1}) - \pi_i z_{T-1} + \beta\, v_{iT}^{**}(z_{T-1}),$$

$$z_{T-2} > 0 \text{ given}, \quad (7.56)$$

where by definition

$$z_{T-1} = (1-\delta)z_{T-2} + \sum_{j \in N} e_{jT-1}. \quad (7.57)$$

After replacement of $v_{iT}^{**}(z_{T-1})$ by its value as defined in (7.55) above and using (7.57) twice, the payoff functions (7.56) become

$$v_{iT-1}(z_{T-2}, e_{T-1}) = g_i(e_{iT-1}) - \pi_i \left[(1-\delta)z_{T-2} + \sum_{j \in N} e_{jT-1} \right]$$

$$+ \beta \cdot (x_{iT}^{**}(z_{T-1}) - \pi_i(1-\delta)$$

$$\times \left[(1-\delta)z_{T-2} + \sum_{j \in N} e_{jT-1} \right] - \pi_i \sum_{j \in N} e_{jT}^*(z_{T-1}) \bigg),$$

$$z_{T-2} > 0 \text{ given}.$$

In these expressions the only variables are e_{jT-1}, $j = 1, \ldots, n$, since z_{T-2} is given and all the rest is decided at time T. But their payoff maximizing values are functions of z_{T-2}. Notice also that the functions v_{iT-1} are, again, decreasing and affine in $\sum_{j \in N} e_{jT-1}$.

The NCNE strategy profile $\bar{e}_{1T-1}(z_{T-2}), \ldots, \bar{e}_{nT-1}(z_{T-2})$ and the Pareto efficient strategy profile $e^*_{1T-1}(z_{T-2}), \ldots, e^*_{nT-1}(z_{T-2})$ can be computed from the respective first order conditions, as well as the ensuing state variable $z^*_{T-1}(z_{T-2})$. Then, the γ-core (CT) solution that is, an imputation of the game (N, E_{T-1}, v_{T-1}) is the vector of n functions

$$v^{**}_{iT-1}(z_{T-2}) = x^{**}_{iT-1}(z_{T-2}) - \pi_i z^*_{T-1}(z_{T-2}) + \beta v^{**}_{iT}(z_{T-1}),$$

$$i = 1, \ldots, n$$

where the first term is

$$x^{**}_{iT-1}(z_{T-2}) = g_i(\bar{e}_{iT-1}(z_{T-2})) - \frac{\pi_i}{\sum_{j \in N} \pi_j}$$

$$\times \left(\sum_{j \in N} [g_j(\bar{e}_{jT-1}(z_{T-2})) - g_j(e^*_{jT-1}(z_{T-2}))] \right),$$

and the second term is such that

$$z^*_{T-1}(z_{T-2}) = (1 - \delta)z_{T-2} + \sum_{j \in N} e^*_{jT-1}(z_{T-2}). \tag{7.58}$$

Using (7.55) in the third term, one gets for each component i of the imputation vector at $T - 1$

$$v^{**}_{iT-1}(z_{T-2}) = x^{**}_{iT-1}(z_{T-2}) - \pi_i \left[(1 - \delta)z_{T-2} + \sum_{j \in N} e^*_{jT-1}(z_{T-2}) \right]$$

$$+ \beta \left(x^{**}_{iT}(z^*_{T-1}) - \pi_i(1 - \delta)z^*_{T-1} - \pi_i \sum_{j \in N} e^*_{jT}(z^*_{T-1}) \right) \tag{7.59}$$

In this expression, all z_{T-1} are now to be replaced by (7.58), thus becoming functions of z_{T-2}. So, the value function (7.55) present

in the last term of (7.59) is to be taken as adjusted implicitly, in
(7.59), to the change of z_{T-1} into $z^*_{T-1}(z_{T-2})$. In this form (7.59) the
function appears to be decreasing and affine in $\sum_{j \in N} e_{jT-1}$.

Thus, the two rational expectations games (N, E_T, v_T) and
(N, E_{T-1}, v_{T-1}) have the same mathematical structure and properties as those of the static GEG, which are established in Lecture 6.
By applying this reasoning to all time intervals $1 < t < T$ a solution

$$([(e^*_{iT})_{i \in N}, z^*_T], [(e^*_{iT-1})_{i \in N}, z^*_{T-1}],$$

$$[(e^*_{iT-2})_{i \in N}, z^*_{T-2}], \dots, [(e^*_{i1})_{i \in N}, z^*_1])$$

as stated in Definition 7.2 is exhibited for the DGEG, whose existence
is established in general terms by Theorem 7.2.

The infinite horizon case

Finally, the approach to solving a dynamic game above for the finite
horizon case can be extended to the infinite horizon case. The key
instrument to do that is what is introduced above as the concept of
a rational expectations game (N, E_t, v_t) in Definition 7.11, that is,
a game dealing at each period with the alternative cooperation *vs.*
non-cooperation. That concept was constructed by considering the
static game that is played in the final period of the finite horizon
model, and the definition of the game at each t reflected that in its
recursive formulation. However, there is no final period in the infinite
horizon case: so how can the game be defined at all?

In fact, the essential element in the definition is not that the
horizon be finite: this was used only to motivate the introduction
of the function $a_i(z_t)$ in the payoff functions $u_{it}(z_{t-1}, e_t)$ in the
spirit of a value function as used in dynamic programming. What
is essential for defining the game is that such a function exists,
for any t. If so, and assuming its concavity, we can now similarly
proceed to establish existence and uniqueness properties of the non-
cooperative and cooperative solutions of any rational expectations
game (N, E_t, v_t) defined along a path with an infinite horizon.

To illustrate, consider again the case of the linear damage
functions. The rational expectations game (N, E_t, u_t) at any time

t has **payoff functions** of the form

$$u_{it}(z_{t-1}, e_{it}) = g_i(e_{it}) - \pi_i z_t + \beta a_i(z_t)$$

$$= g_i(e_{it}) - \pi_i \cdot \left((1 - \delta)z_{t-1} + \sum_{j \in N} e_{jt} \right)$$

$$+ \beta a_i \left((1 - \delta)z_{t-1} + \sum_{j \in N} e_{jt} \right), \qquad (7.60)$$

$i \in N$, z_{t-1} given, where the value of the function $a_i(z_t)$ is player i's payoff at a γ-core imputation of the rational expectations game played at the next period, namely $t + 1$. This function is unknown, but if we suppose it to be of the general (affine and decreasing) form $a_i(z) = c_i z + b_i$, $z \geq 0$, $c_i < 0$, $i \in N$, we then have in the last term of the previous expression

$$a_i(z_t) = c_i z_t + b_i, \qquad (7.61)$$

that is,

$$a_i \left((1 - \delta)z_{t-1} + \sum_{j \in N} e_{jt} \right) = c_i \left((1 - \delta)z_{t-1} + \sum_{j \in N} e_{jt} \right) + b_i$$

$$\qquad (7.62)$$

and player i's payoff function (7.60) now reads

$$u_{it}(z_{t-1}, e_{it}) = g_i(e_{it}) - \pi_i z_t + \beta(c_i z_t + b_i)$$

$$= g_i(e_{it}) - (\pi_i - \beta c_i) \left((1 - \delta)z_{t-1} + \sum_{j \in N} e_{jt} \right) + \beta b_i.$$

$$\qquad (7.63)$$

Since this payoff function is decreasing and affine in $\sum_{j \in N} e_{jt}$, Theorem 6.1 extended to affine functions (see footnote 20) implies that the following is player i's payoff **at a γ-core imputation** of the game (N, E_t, v_t):

$$a_i(z_t) = g_i(\bar{e}_{it}) - \frac{\pi_i - \beta c_i}{\sum\limits_{j \in N}(\pi_j - \beta c_j)} \sum\limits_{j \in N}[g_j(\bar{e}_{jt}) - g_j(e_{jt}^*)]$$

$$- (\pi_i - \beta c_i)\left[(1 - \delta)z_{t-1} + \sum\limits_{j \in N} e_{jt}^*\right], \qquad (7.64)$$

$i \in N$. To find out what the parameters c_i and b_i are in this expression, they can be identified by substituting $c_i z_t + b_i$ for $a_i(z_t)$ in the LHS of the above equation, and then solving for them, taking advantage of the fact that $\bar{e}_{it}$ and e_{jt}^* are all independent of the stock z_{t-1}. After some elaborate manipulations one gets:

$$c_i = -\pi_i \frac{(1 - \delta)}{1 - \beta(1 - \delta)} \qquad (7.65)$$

and

$$b_i = g_i(\bar{e}_{it}) - \frac{\pi_i}{\sum_{j \in N}\pi_j}\sum\limits_{j \in N}[g_j(\bar{e}_{jt}) - g_j(e_{jt}^*)] - \frac{\pi_i}{1 - \beta(1 - \delta)}\sum\limits_{j \in N} e_{jt}^*. \qquad (7.66)$$

This gives for the ith component (7.64) of the γ-core imputation, using (7.65),

$$a_i(z_t) = g_i(\bar{e}_{it}) - \frac{\pi_i}{\sum\limits_{j \in N}\pi_j}\sum\limits_{j \in N}[g_j(\bar{e}_{jt}) - g_j(e_{jt}^*)]$$

$$- \frac{\pi_i}{1 - \beta(1 - \delta)}\left[(1 - \delta)z_{t-1} + \sum\limits_{j \in N} e_{jt}^*\right]. \qquad (7.67)$$

With this expression of $a_i(z_t)$ when assumed as in (7.61), player i's payoff function (7.63) of the rational expectations game played at time t is now identified, using again (7.65) for c_i, as

$$u_{it}(z_{t-1}, e_{it}) = g_i(e_{it}) - \pi_i z_t + \beta \left[-\pi_i \frac{(1-\delta)}{1 - \beta(1-\delta)} z_t + b_i \right] \quad (7.68)$$

and, using in addition (7.66) for b_i and the transition equation for z_t, as

$$
\begin{aligned}
u_{it}(z_{t-1}, e_{it}) = {} & g_i(e_{it}) - \pi_i \left[(1-\delta)z_{t-1} + \sum_{j \in N} e_{jt} \right] \\
& + \beta \left[-\frac{\pi_i(1-\delta)}{1 - \beta(1-\delta)} \left[(1-\delta)z_{t-1} + \sum_{j \in N} e_{jt}^* \right] \right. \\
& \left. + \left(g_i(\bar{e}_{it}) - \frac{\pi_i}{\sum_{j \in N} \pi_j} \sum_{j \in N} [g_j(\bar{e}_{jt}) - g_j(e_{jt}^*)] - \frac{\pi_i}{1 - \beta(1-\delta)} \sum_{j \in N} e_{jt}^* \right) \right].
\end{aligned}
$$

As a result, along the γ-core stable solution of the dynamic game and applying again the extension of Theorem 6.1 to affine payoff functions, the payoff of player i at the imputation reads at each t:

$$
\begin{aligned}
u_{it}(z_{t-1}, e_{it}^*) = {} & \left[g_i(\bar{e}_{it}) - \frac{\pi_i}{\sum_{j \in N} \pi_j} \left(\sum_{j \in N} [g_j(\bar{e}_{jt}) - g_j(e_{jt}^*)] \right) - \pi_i z_t^* \right] \\
& + \beta \left[g_i(\bar{e}_{it}) - \frac{\pi_i}{\sum_{j \in N} \pi_j} \left(\sum_{j \in N} [g_j(\bar{e}_{jt}) - g_j(e_{jt}^*)] \right) - \frac{\pi_i}{1 - \beta(1-\delta)} z_t^* \right],
\end{aligned}
$$

where $z_t^* = (1-\delta)z_{t-1} + \sum_{j \in N} e_{jt}^*$.

One recognizes within the first square brackets the structure of player i's payoff at the γ-core solution (6.3) of the static model, this being the utility level actually reached by player i at time t. This structure is reproduced within the second square brackets, discounted at the rate β, but here it is not an actual utility level: it is only the one anticipated according to the assumption of cooperation after t that we have called rational expectations. In that anticipation, there is also the proviso that the valuation π_i of the stock variable is increased by a factor $1/1 - \beta(1-\delta) > 1$: this increase corresponds to the taking account in the solution of the future damages discounted over an infinite time horizon.

It is interesting to observe that the payoff function (7.68) implies

$$\frac{\partial u_{it}}{\partial e_{it}} = g_i'(e_{it}) - \pi_i - \beta c_i$$

$$= g_i'(e_{it}) - \pi_i(1 + \frac{\beta(1-\delta)}{1-\beta(1-\delta)}$$

$$= g_i'(e_{it}) - \pi_i \frac{1}{1 - \beta(1-\delta)}.$$

If set equal to zero, this expression is the first order condition of the NCNE of the rational expectations game at any time t. If one turns back to the optimal control optimization method and recalls the first order conditions (7.22) that hold for the linear damages case, it turns out that the conditions that determine the emissions strategy at any t are exactly the same when t is extended to $T = \infty$.

Similarly, taking the sum over all i's of the payoff functions (7.68), and thus writing a coalitional function for $S = N$ in the rational expectations game at any t, say $W_t^\gamma(N)$, one gets for each $i \in N$:

$$\frac{\partial W_t^\gamma}{\partial e_{it}} = g_i'(e_{it}) - \sum_{j \in N}(\pi_i - \beta c_i)$$

$$= g_i'(e_{it}) - \sum_{j \in N}\pi_i\left(1 + \frac{\beta(1-\delta)}{1 - \beta(1-\delta)}\right)$$

$$= g_i'(e_{it}) - \sum_{j \in N}\pi_j \frac{1}{1 - \beta(1-\delta)}.$$

Equated to zero this expression is identical to (7.40) when T is extended to $T = \infty$. Here, the two methods thus coincide.

7.7 Concluding considerations

The cooperative solution of the DGEG presented in Section 7.6 of this lecture may be called no less than a "decision-oriented, sequential, flexible and cooperative, international optimum". The solution is an optimum, because efficient. It is cooperative because immune of coalitional deviations. It is decision-oriented because it specifies actions to be taken immediately. It is sequential because formulated in terms of successive stages over time. It is flexible because it allows for reconsidering at each stage whether or not to cooperate and thereby not imposing the course of future events.

The paper by Germain, Tulkens and de Zeeuw (1998) (GTZ, 1998) is the first to present this frame of thought for theorizing on the process of formation of international environmental agreements, with both finite and infinite horizon models. It was initially motivated by the severe *economic* shortcoming of the optimal control modeling of the problem, namely the artificiality in the treatment of transfers that had been reported in an earlier contribution of Germain, Toint and Tulkens (1998) (GTT, 1998).[21] It is only later that Germain, Toint, Tulkens and de Zeeuw (2003) (GTTZ, 2003) conceived of the idea of converting each stage t of the dynamic programing solution of the DGEG into a game specific to that time interval. And for this game, the authors called on the Houba-de Zeeuw assumption which provided the ground for meaningful payoff functions and eventually coalitional functions, by means of which the CT solution could be implemented dynamically.

Thus, GTT (1998) and GTTZ (2003) are probably the first papers where *dynamic cooperative* games with $n > 2$ players are introduced and applied to a major economic *stock* externality problem, with infinite as well as finite horizon. Only the italicized words

---

[21]As described in the critical part of Section 7.5.

are valid in this claim, since of course other dynamic approaches of international environmental problems have been proposed in parallel if not previously. But none of the so mentioned specifications of the games, treated simultaneously, can be found in the literature of the time.

The exposition of Section 7.6 is of course not the final word on the ambitious topic of modeling the construction process of international environmental agreements. Among the many contributions that have appeared after the two initial ones just mentioned, Germain, Tulkens and Magnus (2011) explore the issue of a possible impact on the cooperative solution of enlarging the economic dynamic model to capital accumulation occuring in parallel to the pollutant stock. They find that apart from an increased complexity of the model, the conceptual game theoretic framework is hardly modified.

It is of interest to contrast the above with alternatives to the assumed γ-coalitional function for the solution concept and to the rational expectations games at each t for the treatment of time. For instance, Kranich, Perea and Peters (2005) propose no less than three other core concepts for cooperative dynamic games, called, respectively, the "classical", the "weak sequential" and the "strong sequential" cores. Each one of these core concepts derives from a different form of the characteristic function, the differences residing in the assumptions made on how "deviations" from the efficient path by coalitions may (or may not) occur over time. Coalitions are supposed to decide from the beginning whether to cooperate of not, and if a cooperating coalition decides to deviate later on, the deviation is supposed to be permanent.

In Filar and Petrosyan (2000) it is assumed that if a coalition deviates, it deviates forever. Both of these approaches include state variables as well as controls but the fact that they accept the time rigidities mentioned in the above critique of the optimal control methodology implies that their models describe essentially fixed long term evolutions with no room, or very little of it, for decisions on the cooperation *vs.* non-cooperation issue along the temporal path.

For the sake of completeness let me mention that the review by Benchekroun and Long (2012) covers the dynamic game part of this lecture in much the same spirit. More recently — but too late for inclusion in these lectures — Zaccour (2017) presents remarkable developments, while Chander (2017) provides reinforced and expanded theoretical basis for the approach that I have shown to have been initiated in the early 2000s.

Lecture 8

THE DYNAMIC GLOBAL EXTERNALITY GAME

IN NUMBERS: THE CWS MODEL

The purpose and the message

The purpose is to show how the theory constructed thus far can be implemented in the reality it concerns. This requires calling upon another standard tool of economic analysis, namely numerical simulation. Some new vocabularies as well as computational expertise and equipment are necessary for that purpose. The emphasis is on the procedure rather than on the numbers themselves, which serve only as illustrations.

Based on the kind collaboration with coauthors and the parallel work of colleagues, I present below an "integrated assessment" model of the world economic-ecological system, to which I associate a game, called the CWS game, in order to implement in it the γ-core concept.

The message is simply: it works! A γ-core solution is identified and computed for the CWS game. It is also used to evaluate, as an example, the Kyoto Protocol and conceivable alternative post Kyoto policies. A more encompassing study of climate policy issues, still in the economic-game theoretic spirit, is done in Lecture 10.

Plan

The ClimNeg World Simulation (CWS) model

Key numerical results

Cooperation beyond efficiency in the CWS model

An example of policy use of CWS and its associated game

Concluding consideration

Lecture 8

The Dynamic Global Externality Game in Numbers: The CWS Model

8.1 The ClimNeg World Simulation (CWS) model

Informal description of purpose, vocabulary and origin

What is a "model" in this case? In Lecture 2, I have referred to ecological models, as a descriptive tool of the natural phenomena that occur between emission and reception of externalities. I called them "transfer functions". Now the reader is invited to think at a level where the word model designates a much wider kind of reality. The language remains mathematical but its scope is widened so as to encompass the functioning of the entire Society. I should say, Society as it is seen by economic theorists, summarily illustrated by the well known picture of the "economic circular flow" presented in most elementary economic textbooks, and of which the economic-ecological model constructed in Lecture 2 is an example. The model then represents "states" of the world, "decisions" by the agents, including possibly game theoretic "strategies" and "solutions", with the considerable addition of numerical specification of all the magnitudes involved. This last feature then allows for computational simulation of conceivable "scenarios" describing properties as well as the evolution, fictitious or realistic, of the system.

The CWS model is an *Integrated Assessment Model*[1] (IAM) of climate change, representing the overall activity of the world over a

---

[1] It belongs to a class of economic-ecological models designed with the specific purpose of assessing policy options. They are interestingly surveyed in Kelly and Kolstad (1999). In that paper, a basic distinction is made between policy

period of 300 years, with the world being partitioned in 6 regions, each evolving according to its own determinants. The population's welfare of each region is represented by the value of a collective utility function derived from its domestic green consumption. Similarly, produced output is described as deriving from an aggregate domestic production function where the inputs are labor and capital, these two factors evolving over time according to demographic pressure and investment decisions within each region. Characteristically, given our context, production is also described as generating CO_2 emissions in each region, this giving rise to costly damages that result from the impacts of temperature rise on the one hand, as well as, on the other hand, to equally costly CO_2 abatement activities. At the world level, a climate model represents the link that prevails at each time interval between the CO_2 emissions from all regions and the carbon accumulation in the atmosphere as well as the resulting rise in world temperature.

The acronym CWS stands for "Climneg World Simulation", where **ClimNeg** (for "**Clim**ate **Neg**otiations) is the name chosen by the research group established at CORE, Louvain-la-Neuve in 1996 when a large interdisciplinary, multiannual, research program on climate issues was launched by the author in collaboration with his colleagues at Louvain, the physicist Jean–Pascal van Ypersele, and at Leuven, the economist Johan Eyckmans, with the support of the Belgian government. Among the many outputs of that research program, a main one for the purpose of this lecture is Eyckmans and Tulkens (2003),[2] on which the presentation below is based.[3]

---

evaluation models and policy *optimization* models, which differ according to the purpose sought by their authors. Section 8.1.3 will make clear that CWS belongs to the second category. In a recent state of the art, Weyant (2017) reviews a quite large number of IAMs that have been developed in many countries since 1990.

[2]Initially circulated as two working documents in 1999 (*Core Discussion paper* 9926 and *CLIMNEG Working paper* no. 18) and presented at a workshop held at FEEM Milan in January 1999.

[3]Another essential output of the CLIMNEG research program is the paper on the Kyoto Protocol by Chander, Tulkens, van Ypersele and Willems, issued in 1999 and eventually published in 2002. Its thesis is taken up in a large part of Lecture 10.

By a happy coincidence the September issue of that same year 1996 of the *American Economic Review* contained a paper, Nordhaus and Yang (1996), in which a model dubbed RICE was presented, disaggregating into multiple regions the global climate-economy growth model DICE that Nordhaus had published in 1994.[4] That regionally disaggregated model, the first of its kind to my knowledge, was an obvious and perfect instrument allowing my research project — the application of cooperative game theory to the climate change problem — to turn from analytical theory to the reality of numbers. The extreme generosity of Professor Nordhaus in sharing the computer code of his model facilitated considerably the access to it for my colleague Johan Eyckmans and myself, as well as later on for the update of the CWS model contained in Bréchet, Gerard and Tulkens (2011).

At about the same time a major European IAM was created at the Fondazione ENI Enrico Mattei (FEEM) in Milan, Italy under the acronym of WITCH.[5] Also inspired by the RICE model, it developed first the energy sector of the model and later on several other aspects of the climate change issue such as adaptation, R & D and innovation.[6] An exercise similar to the one presented hereafter can of course be done with WITCH, but this extension is still to come.[7]

Components of the model

Directly inspired from RICE, the CWS model modifies RICE in order to make it suitable for handling the game theoretic concepts of the

---

[4]RICE is the acronym for *Regional Integrated Climate-Economics* and DICE for *Dynamic Integrated Climate-Economy*.
[5]The acronym WITCH stands for *World Induced Technical Change Hybrid*.
[6]Unfortunately neither CWS nor WITCH are included in the Weyant (2017) review quoted above.
[7]The early source for this model is Bosetti *et al.* (2006). A more recent paper is Bosetti *et al.* (2013). The papers showing the many uses of the WITCH model are listed in http://www.witchmodel.org/publications/ and a most recent model documentation is given in http://www.witchmodel.org/documentation/.

previous lectures, and doing it in a way that makes it as close as possible to the DGEG. This specific objective requires and justifies some simplifications,[8] the main ones being omission of international trade, extending the length of the period covered by the analysis, linearization of the green consumption utility function and of part of the consumption budget feasibility constraint.

Here below, the equations (8.1)–(8.7) are economic, while (8.8)–(8.11) are ecological, that is, climatic. These last four are the models of Lecture 1 and commented there.

As far as the seven first equations are concerned, (8.1) is the *t*th term of an objective function to be formulated below, whose variable consists in the discounted value of consumption X_{it} of the region at the time interval t. Equation (8.2) specifies the budget that this consumption should satisfy within region i, that is, that it be equal to production Y_{it} minus what is distracted from it by the resources allocated to investment I_{it} and to the coverage of emissions abatement cost C_{it}, as well as by the losses D_{it} entailed by climatic damages.

Next comes, for each time interval t and each region i, a traditional Cobb–Douglas production function of GDP Y_{it} (8.3) with global productivity parameter A_{it}, and capital K_{it} and labor L_{it} as arguments. Equation (8.4) specifies capital accumulation over time as a result of investment decisions. Equation (8.5) is central in the overall architecture of the model. It specifies both the region's carbon emissions E_{it} as a linear function of its GDP, and the region's abatement decision by its choice of the rate μ_{it} whereby it modifies the value of the GDP's carbon intensity parameter σ_{it}.

The abatement cost function (8.6) as well as the damage cost function (8.7) are both specified as including GDP, reflecting an assumption that these costs increase with a region's development level.

---

[8]For details and motivations see Section 2.2 of Eyckmans and Tulkens (2003).

The assumed evolution over time of the productivity, population and carbon intensity parameters is the same in CWS as in Nordhaus and Yang (1996) whereas the differentiation of the countries' discount rate (see last column of Table 8.2), introduced in CWS, is justified by an assumption of more value attached to present income by low GDP regions relative to high GDP ones.

Finally, concerning equations (8.10) and (8.11), let us recall that the unidimensionality of the temperature variable ΔT is by no means a logical necessity of the CWS model. Models yielding two-dimensional as well as three-dimensional representations of regional temperature changes, as alluded to in Lecture 1, could replace equations (8.8)–(8.11), with some adjustments in (8.7) however.

- *Functions and equations*

$$V_{it} = \beta_i^{t-1} X_{it} \text{ utility function as discounted consumption} \tag{8.1}$$

$$X_{it} = Y_{it} - I_{it} - C_{it}(\mu_{it}) - D_{it}(\Delta T_t) \text{ consumption budget from}$$
$$\text{output } Y_{it} \text{ minus investment, abatement and damage}$$
$$\text{costs} \tag{8.2}$$

$$Y_{it} = A_{it} K_{it}^{\gamma} L_{it}^{1-\gamma} \text{ production function} \tag{8.3}$$

$$K_{it} = (1 - \delta_k) K_{it-1} + 10 \, I_{it} \text{ capital accumulation} \tag{8.4}$$

$$E_{it} = \sigma_{it} \left[1 - \mu_{it} \right] Y_{it} \text{ emissions generation} \tag{8.5}$$

$$C_{it}(\mu_{it}) = Y_{it} b_{i1} \mu_{it}^{b_{i2}} \text{ abatement cost function} \tag{8.6}$$

$$D_{it}(\Delta T_t) = Y_{it} \theta_{i1} \left(\tfrac{\Delta T_t}{2,5} \right)^{\theta_{12}} \text{ damage cost function} \tag{8.7}$$

$$M_t = \bar{M} + [1 - \delta_M] (M_{t-1} - \bar{M}) + \beta_E \sum_{j \in N} E_{jt}$$
$$\text{carbon concentration accumulation} \tag{8.8}$$

$$H_t = H_t^c(\log(M_t/M_0)) + H_t^x$$
$$\text{radiative forcing of gas concentrations variations} \tag{8.9}$$

$$\Delta T_t^{oc} = \Delta T_{t-1}^{oc} + \tau_3 [\Delta T_{t-1} - \Delta T_{t-1}^{oc}]$$
$$\text{ocean temperature change} \tag{8.10}$$

$$\Delta T_t = \Delta T_{t-1} + \tau_1 \left[\lambda H_t - \Delta T_{t-1} \right] - \tau_2 \left[\Delta T_{t-1} - \Delta T_{t-1}^{oc} \right]$$
$$\text{atmospheric temperature change} \tag{8.11}$$

- *Indexes*: $i = 1, \ldots, 6$ regions, $t = 1, \ldots, 30$ time intervals of 10 years.

- *Variables computed (All billions US\$ yearly macroeconomic aggregates)*

  X_{it} : Green consumption

  Y_{it} : Output of production, i.e. GDP

  I_{it} : Investment

  K_{it} : Capital stock

  C_{it} : Cost of abatement

  D_{it} : Damage from ambient pollutant

  E_{it} : Carbon emissions (billions tons of C)

  μ_{it} : Carbon emission abatement rate $0 \le \mu_{it} \le 1$

  M_t : Atmospheric carbon concentration (billions tons of C)

  F_t : Radiative forcing of gas concentrations (Watts per m^2)

  ΔT_t : Temperature increase in the atmosphere ($^\circ$C)

  T_t^{oc} : Temperature increase in the deep ocean ($^\circ$C)

- *Exogenous data (See Tables 8.1 and 8.2 for others)*

  A_{it} : Global productivity.

  L_{it} : Population (million people)

  σ_{it} : Carbon intensity of GDP (kgC/1990 US\$)

  K_{i0} : Initial value of the capital stock

  M_0 : Initial value of worldwide carbon concentration

  H_t^x : Radiative forcing of non-CO$_2$ gas concentrations

  β_i : Discount factor ($= 1/(1 + \rho_i)$)

  ρ_i : Discount rate

- *Acronyms for the regions*

  USA: USA   CHN: China

  EU: 15 European Union members (as of 1990)   FSU: Former Soviet Union

  JPN: Japan   ROW: Rest of the world

• *Calibration*

Table 8.1. Global parameter values.

δ_k	Capital depreciation rate	0.10
γ	Capital productivity parameter	0.25
β	Airborne fraction of carbon emissions	0.64
δ_M	Atmospheric carbon removal rate	0.0833
τ_1	Parameter temperature relationship	0.226
τ_2	Parameter temperature relationship	0.44
τ_3	Parameter temperature relationship	0.02
λ	Parameter temperature relationship	1.41
M_0	Initial carbon concentration	590
ΔT_0	Initial temperature change atmosphere	0.50
T_0°	Initial temperature change deep ocean	0.10

Table 8.2. Regional parameter values.

	$\theta_{i,1}$	$\theta_{i,2}$	$b_{i,1}$	$b_{i,2}$	ρ_i
USA	0.01102	2.0	0.07	2.887	0.015
JPN	0.01174	2.0	0.05	2.887	0.015
EU	0.01174	2.0	0.05	2.887	0.015
CHN	0.01523	2.0	0.15	2.887	0.030
FSU	0.00857	2.0	0.15	2.887	0.015
ROW	0.02093	2.0	0.10	2.887	0.030

The CWS game

What is the game associated with the economic-ecological model specified above? Recalling from the beginning of Lecture 7 how a dynamic game is defined in general, one has to find here the triplet $(N, \hat{E}, V)$ consisting of the players set, the players' strategy sets and the payoffs, by means of which strategy profiles and finally solutions are determined. Where are all these elements in the CWS model? The articles on which this exposition is based do in fact contain answers to all these questions, but in a somewhat hidden way. To identify explicitly the structure of the game associated with the CWS model I now propose the following:

Reducing the economic-ecological model to its decision variables

The economic-ecological model (8.1)–(8.11) comprises 6 regions indexed $i = 1, \ldots, 6$. It consists of $(7 \times 6) + 4 = 46$ equations. Equation (8.1) presents the objective at time t, $\beta^{t-1} V_{it}$, which results from total production in the country, Y_{it}, diminished by the resources it devotes, respectively, to investment I_{it}, to coverage of its emissions abatement cost $C_i(\mu_{it})$ and of its damage cost $D_i(\Delta T_t)$ (all of these expressed in terms of forgone output). Making use of (8.6) and (8.7) one has for (8.2)

$$X_{it} = Y_{it} - I_{it} - Y_{it} b_{i1} \mu_{it}^{b_{i2}} - Y_{it} \theta_{i1} \left(\frac{\Delta T_t}{2,5} \right)^{\theta_{i2}},$$

where, as mentioned, the presence of Y_{it} in the abatement and damage cost functions expresses an assumption that both of these costs are proportional to the country's GDP level. Using (8.3), one further gets

$$X_{it} = (A_{it} K_{it}^{1-\gamma} L_{it}^{\gamma}) - I_{it} - (A_{it} K_{it}^{1-\gamma} L_{it}^{\gamma}) b_{i1} \mu_{it}^{b_{i2}}$$
$$- (A_{it} K_{it}^{1-\gamma} L_{it}^{\gamma}) \theta_{i1} \left(\Delta T_t / 2, 5 \right)^{\theta_{i2}}. \tag{8.12}$$

Viewed in this way, the objective X_{it} appears to be entirely determined by the following four variables: K_{it}, L_{it}, μ_{it} and ΔT_t. Among these four, the population variable, L_{it}, taken as exogenous to the model, is given for all i's and t's. Of the remaining three, K_{it} is determined by I_{it} in view of (8.4).

As to ΔT_t, it appears to be a function of $\sum_{j \in N} E_{jt}$ through the carbon concentration M_t as specified by (8.11), (8.10), (8.9) and (8.8). But through (8.5) $\sum_{j \in N} E_{jt}$ is a function of all Y_{jt}'s, themselves determined by all K_{jt}'s (and L_{jt}'s) and finally by the investment variables I_{jt} through (8.4). Parallel to that, $\sum_{j \in N} E_{jt}$ is also a function of all μ_{jt}'s in (8.5). Thus, ΔT_t is at every time t

a function of both all investments $I_{jt}, j = 1, \ldots, n$ and all emission abatement rates μ_{jt}. Let me write this chain of dependencies as the function of functions

$$\Delta T_t \left[M_t \left(\sum_{j \in N} E_{jt}[Y_{jt}(K_{jt}(I_{it}), \mu_{jt})] \right) \right]. \qquad (8.13)$$

Eventually the two categories of variables $((I_{jt})_{j \in N})_{t=1}^{T}$ and $((\mu_{jt})_{j \in N})_{t=1}^{T}$ are the only ones of the model that remain "free", that is, once chosen, all the others follow suit.[9]

Considering the model as a whole, the emissions are actually governed, in absolute amounts, by the investment decisions I_{it} made in each country, of which they are a consequence by becoming capital and thereby contributing to output. At the same time, abatements occur at rates μ_{it} which are distinct decisions made in each country. The model thus describes each country as simultaneously generating the externality by its investments in production, and reducing it through its abatements.

Growth comes from the growth of population, L_{it}, assumed to be exogenous and taken from UN demographic projections.

Specifying the dynamic game

The above allows one to associate now a game $(N, \hat{E}, V)$ — let me call it from now on the "**CWS game**" — to the so reduced form of the CWS model. In the terms of the general Definition 7.6 of a dynamic game the CWS game is specified by the following components:

- The **players set** N, which is the set of regions $\{i \mid i = 1, \ldots, 6\}$.
- The **strategy sets**, which are two-fold:
  (a) $\hat{I} = \hat{I}_1 \times \cdots \times \hat{I}_i \times \cdots \times \hat{I}_n$, a set of joint strategies where for each $i = 1, \ldots, n$, $\hat{I}_i = \left\{ (I_{it})_{t=1}^{T} : 0 \leq I_{it} \leq I_{it}^{o} \forall t \right\}$ is the set of

---

[9]In standard mathematical programming terminology these are the decision variables. Nordhaus and Yang (1996) call them "policy variables".

paths of *investment* strategies $(I_{it})_{t=1}^{T}$ chosen by player i at each time interval t over the period $t = 1, 2, \ldots, T$,

(b) $\hat{\mu} = \hat{\mu}_1 \times \cdots \times \hat{\mu}_i \times \cdots \times \hat{\mu}_n$, a set of joint strategies where for each $i = 1, \ldots, n$, $\hat{\mu}_i = \{(\mu_{it})_{t=1}^{T} : \ 0 \le \mu_{it} \le 1 \ \forall t\}$ is the set of paths of *abatement rate* strategies$(\mu_{it})_{t=1}^{T}$ chosen by player i at each time interval t over the period $t = 1, 2, \ldots, T$,

- The **vector of payoffs** $V = (V_1, \ldots, V_n)$, where for each $i \in N$

$$V_i(\hat{I}, \hat{\mu}) \underset{\text{def}}{=} \sum_{t=1}^{T} \beta^{t-1} X_{it}$$

$$= \sum_{t=1}^{T} \beta^{t-1} \left(A_{it} K_{it}^{1-\gamma} L_{it}^{\gamma} - I_{it} - A_{it} K_{it}^{1-\gamma} L_{it}^{\gamma} b_{i1} \mu_{it}^{b_{i2}} \right.$$

$$\left. - A_{it} K_{it}^{1-\gamma} L_{it}^{\gamma} \theta_{i1} \left(\frac{\Delta T_t}{2,5} \right)^{\theta_{i2}} \right), \tag{8.14}$$

where ΔT_t is the function (8.13),

$$K_{it} = (1 - \delta_k) K_{it-1} + I_{it}, \quad K_{i0} > 0 \text{ given}, \tag{8.15}$$

$$M_t = \bar{M} + [1 - \delta_M] (M_{t-1} - \bar{M})$$

$$+ \beta \sum_{j \in N} \sigma_{jt} [1 - \mu_{jt}] A_{jt} K_{jt}^{1-\gamma} L_{jt}^{\gamma}, \tag{8.16}$$

$M_0 > 0$ given,

is the payoff (utility) function of player (region) i defined over the entire period $1, \ldots, T$.

As N covers the entire world, the game is effectively a DGEG.[10] The individual payoff functions V_i correspond to the theoretical specification (7.42) of the regions' utility functions, with two transition equations instead of one: (8.15) stands for the accumulation of capital, and (8.16) governs the accumulation of carbon, the ambient pollutant. M_t plays here the role of z_t in (7.42).

---

[10]Recall from Lecture 5: a game that no player can "leave"!

Finally, a **strategy profile** for the CWS game is thus a family of n pairs of T-dimensional vectors $((\boldsymbol{I}_{it}, \boldsymbol{\mu}_{it})_{t=1}^{T})_{i \in N}$.

In establishing this correspondence between the DGEG and the CWS game, a possibly surprising feature is that emissions, which are strategies and denoted e_{it} in the former, are not treated as strategies in the latter. This reflects the fact that in the underlying economic-ecological model the emissions' role is split into, on the one hand, the emissions *sensu stricto*, that is, production of the physical amounts E_{it} of pollutant as a by-product of production Y_{it} — and on the other hand, the activity of abatement which consists in reducing the fixed link σ_{it} that is, the coefficient of carbon intensity of produced output. Thanks to this ingenious distinction, the environmental variables emissions E_{it} and abatement σ_{it} as well as the key variables of economic dynamics I_{it} are operating simultaneously in the model.

Thus, the CWS economic-ecological model, like its predecessor RICE, is converted into a dynamic game in strategic form, meeting rigorously the terms of Definition 7.6 of Lecture 7.[11] For this game, the solution concepts covered in Lecture 7 can now be defined and evaluated numerically. This is done for the first time in Eyckmans and Tulkens (2003) and again with updated data in Bréchet, Gerard and Tulkens (2011). On this couple of works I now wish to report in some detail.

The "scenarios"

Once a game is defined, the matter of interest lies of course in the solution concepts it offers for dealing with the social science problem with which it is associated. Yet, the term "solution concept" is not much in use in the literature devoted to numerical simulations of climate change modeling. Instead, the term of "scenario" has been used first by Nordhaus and Yang (1996), and has been taken up in

---

[11]The same exercise is performed for the models MICA, STACO and WITCH in the unpublished note Tulkens (2013). It could also be made on the original RICE model of Nordhaus and Yang provided adequate care be taken of the components that are deleted in CWS.

the early 1999 version of the joint 2003 paper by Eyckmans and the author.

Prior to engaging in a detailed presentation and to prevent confusions, I should remark that a few years later, the IPCC instances picked the same term for reporting on what essentially describes future factual behaviors, taking into account the influence of some well-defined exogenous factors, regrouped in various categories. Each such category is called a "scenario". This is the methodology inspiring the SRES 2006 document developed by the IPCC parallel to its 4th and 5th assessment reports. But these scenarios are essentially descriptive *extrapolations* of facts, given some assumptions. One is tempted to add "without theory", which is half true and in fact worse than that, because it is in fact an illusion. As every experienced scientist knows, there is always an underlying theory, no matter how simple or minimal, behind any extrapolation. Unfortunately, the implicit theories involved in the IPCC SRES are never made explicit. Methodologically, this is an essential difference with what is being done in the present lectures.

To facilitate reference to the literature on which this lecture is based, I shall nevertheless stick in this section to the "scenario" expression to designate the outcomes of the particular solution concepts being put to numerical tests in what follows.

Description of the BAUE, NCNE, PCNE's, PESP and CS scenarios

The scenarios presented below are essentially paths of the economic-ecological system, or equivalently strategy profiles of the game, that have properties of being solutions of the dynamic game associated with that system. All scenarios are of optimal growth, an expression where optimality refers to the fact that the values of the variables are solutions of some well-defined optimization problems. In such problems, some of the variables play a key role — the "decision" variables, whose values determine the other ones. The problems differ according to the way the regions are treated as well as to the choice of the decision variables. The five scenarios listed in detail below are direct applications of the four solution concepts proposed by the theory gradually developed in Lectures 3, 5 and 6 in static form, and in Lecture 7 for the dynamic form. Thus,

- In the case of the *business as usual equilibrium* scenario (dubbed below BAUE): the optimization bears only on domestic investments, which induce capital accumulation and growth of the output if the utility of the population requires it. No domestic climate policy and hence no international agreement either. The outcome is a dynamic version of the international equilibrium of Definition 3.3 (not made explicit in Lecture 7).

- In the case of the *non-cooperative Nash equilibrium* (NCNE) scenario: the optimization bears, in each region separately, on both domestic investments (which induce capital accumulation and growth of output) *and* domestic emissions abatements, taking as given the amount of investments and abatement done by the other regions. The outcome is not a treaty, but just a description of the temporal paths generated by the parallel nationalistic decisions of the regions.

- In the case of each scenario called *partially cooperative Nash equilibrium* (PCNE) r.t. some coalition S (there are 56 of them): for the members of S, the optimization of both domestic investments and emissions abatement occurs jointly, while each one of the other regions optimizes individually on both counts. The outcome is a treaty, this time, whose content is the coalition's jointly determined emissions path as specified in Definition 7.8, letting the outsiders follow a freely chosen environmentally nationalistic individual path of their own.

- In the case of the *Pareto-efficient strategy profile* scenario (PESP): the optimization bears on the jointly determined investment and emissions abatement rates that maximize the sum total of all regions' utilities. Outcome: a global treaty the content of which is an explicit quantitative specification of the efficient emissions to be implemented by each signatory region.

- In the case of the *Core stable* (CS) scenario: the model specifies the same joint investment and emissions abatement rates policy as in the PESP scenario supplemented by a scheme of inter-country transfers of resources. Outcome: a global treaty with the quantitative specification of efficient emissions and of transfers ensuring coalitional stability of the policy.[12]

The optimization problems and their solutions

Each scenario in the sense retained here above is the solution of some specific optimization problem or family of such problems. The first three listed below are called an equilibrium because they are in fact joint, and compatible[13] solutions of several parallel optimizations, one for each player or coalition. The fourth scenario is the solution of just one optimization problem. Differences lie in the number and forms of the objective functions in each case. Specifically:

- The BAUE scenario is a family of n solutions $((\bar{\bar{I}}_{it})_{t=1}^{T})_{i \in N}$ with value $(\bar{\bar{V}}_i)_{i \in N}$, one for each i, which together solve the n simultaneous problems

$$\max_{(I_{it})_{t=1}^{T}} V_i = \sum_{t=1}^{T} \beta^{t-1} V_{it}$$

subject to the economic and climatic constraints (8.2)–(8.11), with all variables μ_{it} set identically equal to zero.

- The NCNE scenario is a family of n solutions $((\bar{I}_{it}, \bar{\mu}_{it})_{t=1}^{T})_{i \in N})$ with value $(\bar{V}_i)_{i \in N}$, one for each i, which together solve the n simultaneous problems

$$\max_{(I_{it}, \mu_{it})_{t=1}^{T}} V_i = \sum_{t=1}^{T} \beta^{t-1} V_{it}$$

subject to the constraints (8.2)–(8.11).

---

[12]Recall that fifth feature of the CT solution in the economic interpretation given in Lecture 6, Section 6.3.

[13]An essential property, as the reader has realized in the comments preceding and accompanying Nash equilibria in Lectures 5 and 7.

- The PCNE scenarios are 56 in number,[14] each of which corresponds to a coalition $S \subset N$, $|S| \geq 2$, and consists of a family of solutions to $(1 + |N \backslash S|)$ problems, that is, for each coalition S:
- one solution $((\tilde{I}_{it}, \tilde{\mu}_{it})_{t=1}^{T})_{i \in S}$ with value $\tilde{V}_S$ solving

$$\max_{((I_{it},\mu_{it})_{t=1}^{T})_{i \in S}} V_S = \sum_{i \in S} \sum_{t=1}^{T} \beta^{t-1} V_{it}$$

for the members of S, given $((\tilde{\boldsymbol{I}}_{jt}, \tilde{\boldsymbol{\mu}}_{jt})_{t=1}^{T})_{j \in N, j \notin S}$ and
- $|N \backslash S|$ solutions $((\tilde{I}_{jt}, \tilde{\mu}_{jt})_{t=1}^{T})_{j \in N, j \notin S}$ with values $\tilde{V}_{\{j\}}$ solving

$$\max_{(I_{jt},\mu_{jt})_{t=1}^{T}} V_{\{j\}} = \sum_{t=1}^{T} \beta^{t-1} V_{jt}$$

for each j non-member of S, given $((\tilde{I}_{it}, \tilde{\mu}_{it})_{t=1}^{T})_{i \in N, i \neq j}$ all problems subject to the constraints (8.2)–(8.11) in all these 56 cases.
- The PESP scenario is the solution $((I_{it}^{*}, \mu_{it}^{*})_{t=1}^{T})_{i \in N}$ with value $\hat{V}^{*}$ that solves the single problem

$$\max_{((I_{it},\mu_{it})_{t=1}^{T})_{i \in N}} \hat{V} = \sum_{i \in N} \sum_{t=1}^{T} \beta^{t-1} V_{it}$$

subject to the constraints (8.2)–(8.11).
- The CS scenario is identical to the PESP scenario supplemented by payoffs transfers $(\psi_i)_{i \in N}$ defined in (8.14) to yield the imputation vector

$$(\hat{V}_i^{*} + \psi_i)_{i \in N} \in \gamma \text{ core of } (N, (\hat{I}, \hat{\mu}), V).$$

For all these problems the set of economic and climatic constraints is identical. The alternative scenarios, which differ essentially in the form and degree of cooperation assumed among the regions, are thus formalized only in terms of alternative objective functions, which are behavioral, rather than in terms of constraints, which are a given.

---

[14]From $2^6 = 64$, the number of subsets of N for $n = 6$, subtract the empty set, 6 singletons and the all players set to get 56.

These alternative forms of cooperative behaviors and their effects on the outcome of the game are now illustrated with the numbers and diagrams that follow.

8.2 Key numerical results

Details of the computational procedure are given in Section 5.2 of Eyckmans and Tulkens (2003). It was implemented using the optimization software GAMS. For the computation of Nash equilibria, which are all fixed points whether non-cooperative or partially cooperative, the use of this software requires iterated optimizations that may present convergence problems. This was not the case however.

From the wealth of results generated by the CWS model the very few singled out below graphically are the essential ones for my present purpose as they perfectly illustrate the skeleton of the economic-ecological model that CWS consists of. They indeed show:

- The physical magnitudes that are the source of the problem, from emissions to temperature change, (Figs. 8.1(a)–8.1(c))
- The economic magnitudes involved at the macro levels, (Figs. 8.1(d) and 8.1(e))
- The break down, in terms of economic magnitudes at the micro levels, of
  - the individual abatement efforts (Figs. 8.1(f) and 8.1(g))
  - the utilities-payoffs between coalitions at all conceivable outcomes (Tables 8.3–8.5, in Section 8.3 below).

In the first four cases, the distinction is made between non-cooperative and efficient outcomes. The last table gives utilities for PCNEs relative to all coalitions.

While the main interest is in the last two tables let me comment first the more general characteristics of the results obtained with the model.

Given the (exogenously) predicted growth of the population, the CWS model generates a growing evolution of the world GDP in all scenarios. The global emissions that are mechanically entailed by this

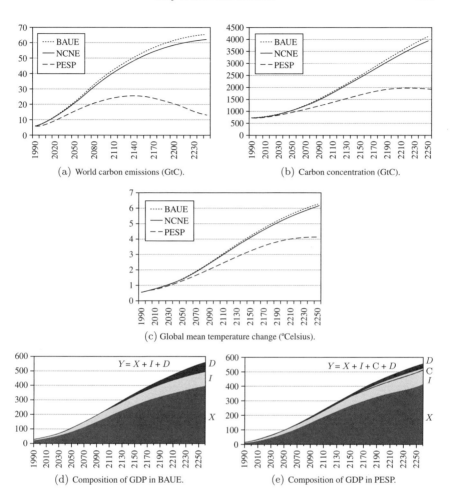

Fig. 8.1 **Key results from the CWS model.**

Notes:

(i) Paths of emissions, concentration and temperature in the BAUE and PESP scenarios (Figs. 8.1(a)-(c)).

(ii) Paths of macroeconomic variables in the BAUE and PESP scenarios: $Y =$ production, $X =$ consumption, $I =$ investment, $C =$ abatement costs, $D =$ damage costs (Figs. 8.1(d)-(e)). (all in trillions of 1990 US\$, discounted)

(iii) Paths of abatement rates μ_{it} by region in the NCNE and PESP scenarios (Figs. 8.1(f)-(g)).

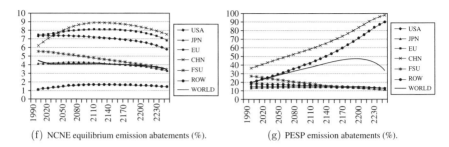

(f) NCNE equilibrium emission abatements (%).   (g) PESP emission abatements (%).

Fig. 8.1 (*Continued*)

output growth (remember the parameters σ_{it} in equation (8.5)) are mitigated by the abatement decisions (μ_{it}, also in equation (8.5)) except in the BAUE where they are excluded. The resulting effective emissions and temperature change are those reported in Fig. 8.1(c). Overall these results suggest the following comments.

Together, Figs. (8.1(a)) and (8.1(e)) show that decoupling economic growth from the evolution of CO_2 emissions characterizes an efficient policy, in contrast with the *laissez faire* and *nationalistic* scenarios. Thus, the structure of the model makes economic growth and environmental protection compatible to a large extent, especially in the long run. And this compatibility is in addition a property of the efficient character of the policy action on emissions that inspires the PESP scenario.

Figures (8.1(d)) and (8.1(e)) show an interesting shift in the allocation of the produced output in its alternative uses: in the former diagram, the BAUE scenario allocates GDP, apart from consumption X and capital investment I, exclusively to losses due to damages D, whereas under the PESP scenario of the latter diagram, an amount of GDP approximately equal to damage losses in the previous case is now split between abatement costs C and remaining damage losses D, consumption and investment remaining also approximately the same. Clearly such substitution makes very good sense since in the process total green consumption is roughly not affected and environmental quality is enhanced.

The breakdown between regions of the emissions abatement strategies shown in Figs. (8.1(f)) and (8.1(g)) is a crucial information for policy purposes. However, the numbers obtained in this case are obviously unrealistic, due to parameter values that were probably erroneous. They have been corrected substantially in the subsequent updating of Gerard (2007) part of which is reported in Bréchet, Gerard and Tulkens (2011). Let me recall that this is a presentation exercise of the kind of material that can be made available. Attaching credibility to the values of the numbers presented is only admissible if they constitute converging results from repeated experiments.

8.3 Cooperation beyond efficiency in the CWS model

Efficient utility levels at the time horizon and the ecological surplus

Table 8.3 shows the utility levels reached in 2300 according to the CWS model under the BAU, NCNE and PESP scenarios (columns 2, 3, 4) as well as the differences between them (columns 5, 6, 7). It reveals what aggregate magnitudes are at stake.

Table 8.3. CWS 2003: Utility levels and differences at horizon time.

	Total utilities in each scenario			Utility differences between scenarios		
	2	3	4	5	6	7
Column number	BAUE	NCNE	PESP	NCNE-BAUE = Domestic ecological surplus	PESP-NCNE = International ecological surplus	PESP-BAUE = Total ecological surplus
World Regions' shares	337,692	338,065	339,837		1,772	2,146
USA	78,270	78,353	78,986	83	633	716
Japan	42,867	42,909	43,222	42	313	355
EU	102,612	102,731	103,650	119	919	1038
China	9,131	9,141	8,862	10	−279	−269
FSU	23,763	23,794	24,025	31	231	262
ROW	81,049	81,137	81,093	88	−44	44

Note: All figures in billions of 1990 discounted $ of green consumption

Source: Eyckmans and Tulkens (2003, Table 4, p. 319).

Table 8.4. Individual payoffs and transfers in the CWS game (billions 1990 US\$).

Key	$V_i^{\{i\}}$	V_i^*	$V_i^* - V_i^{\{i\}}$	%	ψ_i	$V_i^* + \psi_i$	$V_i^* + \psi_i - V_i^{\{i\}}$	%
1	2	3	4	5	6	7	8	9
100000	78353	78986	633	0.808	-282	78704	351	0.448
010000	42909	43222	313	0.729	-121	43102	192	0.448
001000	102731	103650	919	0.895	-423	103226	496	0.482
000100	9141	8862	-279	-3.057	333	9195	54	0.591
000010	23794	24025	231	0.969	-123	23902	108	0.452
000001	81137	81093	-44	-0.054	616	81709	572	0.705

Key: See p. 313 and p. 315 for comment.

Individual and coalitional blockings of the Pareto efficient scenario

Table 8.3 has the interesting feature that while at the aggregate world level the PESP scenario (339.8 billions) improves upon the NCNE scenario (338.1 billions), at the regional level the scenario does not similarly improve for all regions. This is revealed by the negative entries for China (-279 billions) and ROW (-44 billions).[15] Thus, global efficiency does not imply acceptability for all. Of course, the fact that the regions are not the same in the two cases is due to the differences between the two models, differences in both their structure and in their parameter values. Irrespective of these differences, the point of interest lies in the repeated observation that world efficiency may not *per se* be beneficial for every individual country — beneficial in comparison with the relevant alternatives, which in this case are taken as the environmentally nationalistic international equilibrium or the BAU equilibrium in both CWS and RICE. Regions in that situation understandably reject — or "block", or can improve upon — the strategy assigned to them by the Pareto efficient scenario, and therefore this strategy profile cannot be called "cooperative".[16]

---

[15]In Nordhaus and Yang (1996), the same kind of result is observed, but for just one country: the US.

The teachings of cooperative games in the previous lectures prompt a widening of that remark. Not only individual regions may object to the outcome of a proposed PESP strategy profile but also groups of regions might do the same, claiming that a strategy of their own is better for themselves. In the CWS game such claims can be verified by examining all coalitions and computing for each of them the outcome of the best strategy profile its members can afford, namely the PCNE relative to itself.

This is done in columns 2–5 of Table 8.5 where coalitions are ranked in increasing size. Thus, column 2 entitled $\hat{V}_S^S$ lists, for each coalition S, the value of its γ-coalitional function, that is, the aggregate payoff the coalition can achieve for its members at the PCNE r.t. itself. Next, column 3 entitled $\hat{V}_S^*$ lists for every S the sum of the payoffs that the members of S obtain at the PESP solution.

Column 4 then lists the differences between the former and the latter. It shows that while most coalitions are better off with the PESP scenario than at the PCNE relative to themselves, for 12 coalitions of two or more regions the difference is negative: these coalitions do by themselves better for their members at their PCNE than what they are offered by the PESP scenario. The existence of this preferred and feasible alternative is an understandable reason for them to block the PESP scenario.

Transfers inducing cooperation

The blockings so revealed by the CWS game imply that the Pareto efficient path computed by the CWS economic-ecological model may be unstable, individually and coalition wise. This is a quite undesirable feature, if one remembers that the determination of such path is being sought for in order for it to become the content of an international treaty. Technically, the efficient path does not

---

[16]Nordhaus and Yang (1996) use interchangeably the terms "efficient" and "cooperative", as well as many other authors after them in the field. This confusion between efficiency and cooperation regrettably masks the much harder difficulty to achieve the latter compared to the former.

Table 8.5. Coalitions' worths and transfers in the CWS game (billions 1990 US$).

Key	V_S^S	V_S^*	$V_S^* - V_S^S$	%	ψ_S	$V_S^* + \psi_S$	$V_S^* + \psi_S - V_S^S$	%
1	2	3	4	5	6	7	8	9
coalitions of 2 countries								
110000	121264	122208	945	0.779	−403	121806	542	0.447
101000	181090	182636	1546	0.854	−706	181930	841	0.464
100100	87535	87848	312	0.357	51	87899	364	0.416
100010	102151	103011	860	0.842	−405	102605	455	0.445
100001	159829	160079	250	0.156	334	160413	584	0.365
011000	145642	146872	1230	0.845	−544	146328	686	0.471
010100	52062	52084	22	0.043	213	52297	235	0.451
010010	66705	67247	542	0.813	−244	67003	299	0.448
010001	124262	124315	53	0.043	495	124811	548	0.441
001100	111946	112511	566	0.505	−90	112421	476	0.425
001010	126531	127674	1143	0.903	−546	127128	597	0.471
001001	184315	184743	427	0.232	192	184935	620	0.336
000110	32944	32886	−58	−0.175	210	33097	153	0.463
000101	90467	89955	−512	−0.566	949	90904	437	0.483
000011	105134	105118	−17	−0.016	493	105610	476	0.453
coalitions of 3 countries								
111000	224007	225858	1851	0.826	−826	225032	1024	0.457
110100	130486	131070	584	0.448	−69	131001	515	0.394
110010	145067	146233	1166	0.804	−526	145707	641	0.442
110001	202879	203301	422	0.208	213	203514	635	0.313
101100	190415	191497	1083	0.569	−372	191125	711	0.373
101010	204903	206660	1757	0.857	−829	205832	928	0.453
101001	263009	263729	719	0.274	−90	263639	630	0.239
100110	111367	111872	505	0.453	−72	111800	433	0.389
100101	169139	168941	−199	−0.117	667	169608	468	0.277
100011	183752	184103	352	0.191	211	184314	562	0.306
011100	154905	155734	829	0.535	−211	155523	618	0.399
011010	169448	170897	1448	0.855	−667	170230	781	0.461
011001	227376	227965	589	0.259	72	228037	661	0.291
010110	75880	76109	229	0.301	90	76198	318	0.420
010101	133513	133177	−336	−0.252	829	134006	492	0.369
010011	148160	148340	180	0.121	372	148712	552	0.372
001110	135788	136536	748	0.551	−213	136323	535	0.394
001101	193681	193604	−76	−0.039	526	194130	450	0.232
001011	208255	208767	512	0.246	69	208837	582	0.279
000111	114376	113979	−397	−0.347	826	114805	429	0.375

(*Continued*)

Table 8.5. (*Continued*)

Key	V_S^S	V_S^*	$V_S^* - V_S^S$	%	ψ_S	$V_S^* + \psi_S$	$V_S^* + \psi_S - V_S^S$	%
1	2	3	4	5	6	7	8	9
coalitions of 4 countries								
111100	233398	234720	1322	0.566	−493	234227	829	0.355
111010	247830	249883	2053	0.828	−949	248933	1104	0.445
111001	306113	306951	838	0.274	−210	306741	628	0.205
110110	154332	155095	763	0.494	−192	154902	571	0.370
110101	212255	212163	−92	−0.043	546	212710	454	0.214
110011	226825	227326	501	0.221	90	227416	591	0.261
101110	214285	215522	1237	0.577	−495	215027	741	0.346
101101	272543	272590	48	0.018	244	272834	292	0.107
101011	286996	287753	757	0.264	−213	287540	544	0.190
100111	193119	192965	−154	−0.080	544	193509	390	0.202
011110	178761	179758	998	0.558	−334	179425	664	0.372
011101	236817	236827	10	0.004	405	237232	415	0.175
011011	251338	251990	652	0.259	−51	251938	600	0.239
010111	157457	157202	−255	−0.162	706	157907	451	0.286
001111	217685	217629	−57	−0.026	403	218032	346	0.159
coalitions of 5 countries								
111110	257284	258744	1461	0.568	−616	258129	845	0.328
111101	315738	315813	75	0.024	123	315936	198	0.063
111011	330123	330976	853	0.258	−333	330642	519	0.157
110111	236267	236188	−79	−0.033	423	236611	344	0.146
101111	296612	296615	3	0.001	121	296736	124	0.042
011111	260851	260881	1	0.000	282	261134	283	0.108
coalitions of 6 countries								
111111	339837	339837	0	0.000	0	339837	0	0.000

Key indicates the presence of regions in a coalition:
"1" in position 1 means USA is in; "1" in position 2 means JPN is in; "1" in position 3 means EC is in; "1" in position 4 means CHN is in; "1" in position 5 means FSU is in; "1" in position 6 means ROW is in. Reproduced from Table 7.3 (pp. 321–322) of Eyckmans and Tulkens (2003).

belong to the core of the game, a desirable property for the treaty's sustainability.

But does the CWS game have a non-empty core in the first place? Lectures 5 and 6 have shown that there are mathematical conditions — balancedness — for answering that question at the abstract level by just yes or no. But this qualitative answer is not very helpful for the writing of an international treaty. However, an alternative is provided by the CT solution to the DGEG presented in Lecture 7. It consists in keeping unchanged the structure of the PESP scenario as it is, while modifying the payoffs by means of transfers appropriately defined so as to meet the coalitional stability criterion of the γ-core. Whether that is feasible has been proved analytically[17] for the optimal control version of the DGEG of Lecture 7. That proof may not hold for the CWS game because its underlying economic-ecological model is more complex than the one underlying the DGEG. Yet, one may experiment numerically with the GTT transfers formula mentioned in Lecture 7 inspired from the CT one of Lecture 6.

This is done in Eyckmans and Tulkens (2003). Consider transfers specified as follows: for each $i \in N$, where the amount (> 0 if paid by region i, < 0 if received) is

$$\psi_i = -(\hat{V}_i^* - \bar{V}_i) + \frac{\tilde{\pi}_i}{\sum\limits_{j \in N} \tilde{\pi}_j} \left(\sum_{j \in N} \hat{V}_j^* - \sum_{j \in N} \bar{V}_j \right), \qquad (8.17)$$

where $\hat{V}_i^*$ and $\bar{V}_i$ are the values of player $i's$ payoff respectively at the PESP and the Nash solution as specified in Section 8.1.3(b), and the ratio $\frac{\tilde{\pi}_i}{\sum_{j \in N} \tilde{\pi}_j} \in [0, 1]$ is defined and commented a few lines below. Notice that the accounting budget of these transfers is balanced, i.e. $\sum_{i \in N} \psi_i = 0$.

Individual rationality

Adding the transfer (8.17) to the outcome $\hat{V}_i^*$ of each $i \in N$ results in the modified individual payoffs

$$\hat{V}_i^* + \psi_i = \bar{V}_i + \frac{\tilde{\pi}_i}{\sum\limits_{j \in N} \tilde{\pi}_j} \left(\sum_{j \in N} \hat{V}_j^* - \sum_{j \in N} \bar{V}_j \right) \geq \bar{V}_i, \qquad (8.18)$$

where the inequality on the right holds by construction of (8.17) since the expression within parentheses is positive: recall from Lecture 3

---

[17]In Germain, Toint and Tulkens (1999).

that it measures the "ecological surplus" generated in the economic-ecological system by the move from the environmentally nationalistic (Nash) equilibrium to the (Pareto) efficient state. These modified payoffs thus appear to be equal, for each $i \in N$, to the Nash equilibrium payoff augmented by a fraction of the global gain of the ecological surplus.

This transfer scheme solves the *individual* blocking problem raised by the regions CHN and ROW in Table 8.3. Indeed, the columns 6–9 of Table 8.4 now show that with the transfers listed in column 6, the inequality (8.18) is satisfied for all six regions. This is the property usually called, in the cooperative game literature, "individual rationality".[18]

Coalitional rationality

What about the coalitions of more than one member? A coalition S blocks the imputation $\hat{V}^* = (\hat{V}_1^*, \ldots, \hat{V}_n^*)$ if

$$\hat{V}_S^S \underset{\text{def}}{=} \sum_{i \in S} \hat{V}_i^S > \hat{V}_S^* \underset{\text{def}}{=} \sum_{i \in S} \hat{V}_i^*,$$

where $\hat{V}_i^S$ is player $i's$ payoff at the PCNE r.t. S of which i is a member and $\hat{V}_S^S$ is the coalitional payoff. Consider now for each coalition S a transfer ψ^S made up of the sum over the members of S of the individual transfers (8.17), that is:

$$\psi^S \underset{\text{def}}{=} \sum_{i \in S} \psi_i. \tag{8.19}$$

Adding this amount to $\hat{V}_S^*$, which is what the members of coalition S obtain at the PESP solution, results in the modified coalitional payoffs $\hat{V}_S^* + \psi^S$ of column 7 in Table 8.5. These appear in column 8 to be all larger than the coalitional payoffs $\hat{V}_S^S$ achieved at the respective PCNE's (column 2). Thus, none of these modified

---

[18]Some game-theoretically inspired literature on climate change economics speaks of "profitability", a dubious terminology in the current context, in my opinion.

payoffs is blocked anymore by any coalition. Therefore one may state:

Proposition 8.1. *The vector whose components are the numerical values of the lines 1–6 of column 7 in Table 8.5 is a payoff vector which is both efficient and coalitionally stable. It is thus an imputation that belongs to the γ-core of the CWS game.*

It should be noted that to make possible in these computations the extension to the DGEG of the CT formula for transfers, it is needed to adapt it not only to the intertemporal context but also to the nonlinearity[19] of the CWS model. To that effect, use is made of the following expression for the surplus sharing coefficients:

$$\frac{\tilde{\pi}_i}{\sum\limits_{j \in N} \tilde{\pi}_j} \underset{\text{def}}{=} \frac{\sum_{0 \le t \le T} \beta^{t-1} D'_{it}(\Delta T^*_t)}{\sum\limits_{j \in N} \sum_{0 \le t \le T} \beta^{t-1} D'_{jt}(\Delta T^*_t)'}, \quad i = 1, \ldots, n, \qquad (8.20)$$

that is, the relative discounted sums over the entire period of the regions' marginal damages from temperature changes along the PESP solution.

Transfers in the CWS game vs. in the DGEG

Finally, it may not be evident to the reader that the transfers (8.17) are the same as those of formula (5.24) in Lecture 5, or correspond to those mentioned in the optimal control part of the dynamics presented in Lecture 7 (Section 7.5). In fact, they are similar in substance because the DGEG in its rigid open loop formulation is of the same structure as the static GEG. There is however a difference which is of some interest of its own, as shown in what follows.

Referring to their respective economic-ecological models, the individual payoffs V_i^* of the CWS game correspond to the payoffs $g_i(e_i^*) - d_i(z^*)$ of the GEG. Indeed, the explicit damage terms $d_i(z^*)$ of the latter are embedded in the former, V_i^*, which through (8.2) contain the damage functions D_i of (8.7). Similarly, V_i corresponds

---

[19]The linear case, where the surplus sharing coefficients are constants, is treated in Germain, Toint and Tulkens (1998).

to $g_i(\bar{e}_i) - d_i(\bar{z})$. Then, turning to the modified payoffs (8.18) of the CWS game, one has that they correspond to the similarly modified payoffs (5.23) of the GEG, which are recalled to be:

$$v_i^{**} = g_i(e_i^*) - \pi_i(z^*) + T_i \qquad (5.23)$$

with

$$T_i = (g_i(\bar{e}_i) - g_i(e_i^*)) - \frac{\pi_i}{\sum\limits_{j \in N} \pi_j} \left(\sum_{j \in N} g_j(\bar{e}_j) - \sum_{j \in N} g_j(e_j^*) \right). \qquad (5.24)$$

Given the correspondences just identified, the CWS payoffs (8.18) may be rewritten in the terms of the DGEG payoffs as

$$V_i^* + \psi_i = [g_i(e_i^*) - d_i(z^*)]$$
$$+ \Bigg(- ([g_i(e_i^*) - d_i(z^*)] - [g_i(\bar{e}_i) - d_i(\bar{z})])$$
$$+ \frac{\pi_i}{\sum\limits_{j \in N} \pi_j} \left(\sum_{j \in N} [g_i(e_j^*) - d_j(z^*)] - \sum_{j \in N} [g_i(\bar{e}_j) - d_j(\bar{z})] \right) \Bigg) \qquad (8.21)$$

or, after regrouping the g and d functions:

$$V_i^* + \psi_i = [g_i(e_i^*) - d_i(z^*)]$$
$$+ \Bigg(- (g_i(e_i^*) - g_i(\bar{e}_i)) + (d_i(z^*) - d_i(\bar{z}))$$
$$+ \frac{\pi_i}{\sum\limits_{j \in N} \pi_j} \sum_{j \in N} \left([g_j(e_j^*) - g_j(\bar{e}_j)] - \sum_{j \in N} [d_j(z^*) - d_j(\bar{z})] \right) \Bigg) \qquad (8.22)$$

If in this formulation of the GEG payoffs, damage functions are linear, that is, if $d_i(z) = \pi_i z$, $\pi_i > 0$ $\forall i$, then (8.22) reduces to:

$$V_i^* + \psi_i = [g_i(e_i^*) - \pi_i z^*]$$

$$+ \left(- ([g_i(e_i^*) - g_i(\bar{e}_i)]) + ([\pi_i z^* - \pi_i \bar{z}]) \right.$$

$$\left. + \frac{\pi_i}{\sum_{j \in N} \pi_j} \left(\sum_{j \in N} [g_j(e_j^*) - g_j(\bar{e}_j)] - \sum_{j \in N} [\pi_j z^* - \pi_j \bar{z}] \right) \right)$$

$$(8.23)$$

or, after simplifying,

$$V_i^* + \psi_i = [g_i(e_i^*) - \pi_i z^*] + \left(- ([g_i(e_i^*) - g_i(\bar{e}_i)]) \right.$$

$$\left. + \frac{\pi_i}{\sum_{j \in N} \pi_j} \left(\sum_{j \in N} [g_j(e_j^*) - g_j(\bar{e}_j)] \right) \right)$$

or still

$$V_i^* + \psi_i = [g_i(e_i^*) - \pi_i z^*] + ([g_i(\bar{e}_i) - g_i(e_i^*)])$$

$$- \frac{\pi_i}{\sum_{j \in N} \pi_j} \left(\sum_{j \in N} g_j(\bar{e}_j) - \sum_{j \in N} g_j(e_j^*) \right) \qquad (8.24)$$

an expression where the transfer is exactly the one specified in (5.24) and recalled here above.

Beyond the consistency shown by this exercise, notice that one formula, (8.15), consists in taking as a basis for the transfer of each country its payoff at the Nash equilibrium and adding upon that a share in the ecological *surplus*, whereas the other one, (5.24), takes as basis the amount of output from efficient emissions and subtracts from it a share of the aggregate *cost* entailed in the economy by the move from non-cooperation to coalitionally stable efficiency. The role of the transfers thus appears to be only one of modifying the structure of the sharing of the cost among the players, without any effect on the levels of individual emissions.

One may note also that the transfer is equal to zero if a country i happens to have the parameters of its production function such that the difference $g_i(\bar{e}_i) - g_i(e_i^*)$ is just equal to the fraction $\frac{\pi_i}{\sum_{j \in N} \pi_j}$ of the global ecological surplus. In that case, the region does not object to the strategy assigned to it within the PESP without transfers. Transfers are thus not *necessary* for achieving core stability, in general. But they are sufficient as soon as an efficient outcome is blocked by some individual player and/or coalition of players. Note finally that if regions are identical, the transfer is zero with both formulae, and the PESP scenario nevertheless belongs to the core.

A provisional stocktake

The main interest of the above presentation of the CWS model is not in the absolute numbers contained in Tables 8.3–8.5. It is instead in their structure, which allows one to obtain numerical confirmations (some of which for the first time) of several claims made thus far by the theory only. Let me take up again the issues considered in the second half of Lecture 3, some of which were left open.

On the ecological surplus

The overall picture

For the domestic, international and total surpluses, the order of magnitude at the world level is respectively of 373, 1,772 and 2,146 in billions of 1990 US\$, as given by the top line of Table 8.4, columns 5–7. Column 3 reveals that this amounts to 0.5% of the discounted value of the world GDP accumulated over the period covered by the analysis, that is, 1990–2250. Parallel to that, Fig. 8.1(a) reveals that emissions end up at the end of the period at a level approximately equal to the one of 1990 and that temperature eventually stabilizes at about 4°C. Thus, the size of the surplus is rather modest, but the environmental achievement is substantial. While physically the externality is large, the economic loss appears to be a limited one relative to the size of the world economy.[20]

However, this estimate is made by means of a tool that ignores the threat of catastrophic events that may occur in the future, as announced by more than one climate scientist. Such kind of phenomena has been left out of my enquiry, regretfully, my only excuse being that I do not see what game theory could bring about concerning them. But economics of course has a lot to offer on catastrophes. As entering that literature would bring me too far afield, I shall limit myself to referring to just one work by economists who deal with catastrophic climate events, namely Keller, Bolker and Bradford (2004).

Pre-transfer surplus sharing

The numbers mentioned in column 4 of Table 8.4 show the respective individual payoffs of the regions at the Pareto solution, and the numbers in column 6 are the difference with what these payoffs are at the NCNE. Most numbers in col 6 are positive, meaning a gain, but two are negative (-279 for China and -44 for the rest of the world), reflecting a loss. Upon noticing that the sum of the four positive numbers is equal to $2,096 billions one realizes that these four regions gain together, in the move from Nash to Pareto, *more* than the aggregate $1,772 billions mentioned above for the world total surplus. This is possible only because the two other regions, China and Rest of the world, loose in the move, by the amounts of 279 and 44, respectively, thus a total of $323 billions. Thus, with the world efficient emissions as determined by the respective production and damage functions, the first four regions not only exhaust the aggregate surplus made available, but they actually benefit of more value than what the collective move generates.[21]

---

[20]In a later version of the RICE model, Nordhaus and Boyer (2000, p. 127) estimate the surplus at $198 billion. With the update figures used in Bréchet, Gerard and Tulkens (2011) the surpus is estimated at $997 billion.

[21]Similar consequences of the PESP scenario without transfers are obtained in the RICE model of Nordhaus and Yang (1996), and again in the updated version of the CWS model by Bréchet, Gerard and Tulkens (2011).

Cooperation-enhancing surplus sharing

That feasible transfers can serve to induce *individual* rationality of a Pareto efficient outcome for all countries in the economic-ecological model was a well-established economic result before the game theoretic considerations were introduced in the model.[22] The extension of that claim for transfers to achieve the much stronger property of *coalitional* stability required the other tools that have been reexposed in the above lectures. This objective is achieved with the numbers produced in Table 8.5 (first six lines of columns 6–8): the efficient scenario of column 2 is converted, by means of the transfers of column 6, into the one of column 7, which is cooperative in the γ-core sense (no coalition has an interest in switching to another scenario).

CT transfers in CWS and time: The feasibility issue

The transfers (8.17), and their numerical values reported in column 6, are formulated in the same units as those of the objective function of the CWS model, that is, in yearly ($\times 10$) units of green consumption discounted and added up over the period 1990–2310.

The model does not specify when these amounts are supposed to be paid. But can they physically be paid at all? Figure 8.2 below shows what the surplus is made of, that is, the difference between the NCNE and the PESP scenarios with all values discounted back to 1990, formally $(\sum_{j \in N} \hat{V}_{jt}^* - \sum_{j \in N} \bar{V}_{jt})(1 + \rho_j)^{-t}$. The ordinate of the curve measures at each time interval the surplus generated at that moment, which is negative at the beginning of the period and positive thereafter. The sum of these differences, that is, the surface under the curve, represents the total world surplus available over the period of analysis and is summarized by the figure of 1,772 billions mentioned on Table 8.4 (column 6). The transfers are not equal to the total surplus but are drawn from that amount.

---

[22]In Tulkens (1979), followed by Chander and Tulkens (1991/1992), all inspired by the literature on the optimal provision of public goods reviewed in Tulkens (1978).

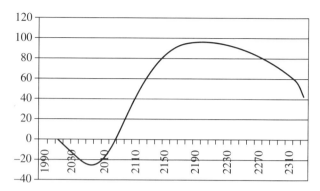

Fig. 8.2 **World green consumption difference PESP–NCNE in optimal control scenarios (billions 1990 US$).**

The sums involved can obviously not be paid in one shot, neither at the beginning of the period since the value they represent has not yet been created, nor at the end: how could countries trust each other to hold that promise for such a long period? Having the transfers paid by slices at each time interval is not a solution either since it faces the difficulty of the negative components of that sum in the early decades. These difficulties are all due to the open loop methodology used to cope with the dynamics of the CWS game. They come as additional arguments reinforcing the critical ones developed in Section 7.3 of Lecture 7. Thus, the transfers (8.14) of the Eyckmans and Tulkens (2003) paper can only be considered as virtual ones. Yet, they are far from being without interest to the extent that they confirm the role assigned to them by the theory.

The alternative methodology of formulating the dynamics of our model by means of dynamic programming, as exposed in Section 7.6 and dubbed GTTZ, has been put to the test of numerical implementation by means of a variant of the CWS model in Germain and van Ypersele (1999) (an unpublished paper, to my knowledge). Transfers of the CT type (non-linear version (6.9)) are defined at each time interval t and introduced in the value function. The model is solved by backward induction. With these transfers, the PESP scenario is claimed to achieve coalitional stability at each t. In the later paper by Germain *et al.* (2003) a similar test is performed, solving by backward induction a version of CWS aggregated into three regions. Feasible transfers are computed for each time interval and the PESP scenario shown to achieve coalitional stability.

A more complete version (six regions) is still in an awaiting stage. Pursuing with more than six regions and with the method of coalition enumeration such as the one used to produce Table 8.5, one quickly faces the problem of computing PCNE's for excessively large numbers of coalitions : with 6 players, that was only 64 but with 10 players, there are 1,024 coalitions to consider, and with 20, 1,048,576. A note written to facilitate this task is available from the author (Tulkens, 2015).

On distributional equity and responsibility in the CT solution

As was already mentioned in Lecture 6, there is nothing distributional in the CT transfers: they are only determined by the objective of cooperation towards efficiency, and exclusively so. This is what was in fact sought for, answering the question: can efficient cooperation result logically from only the self-interest of the parties? I think the answer as provided by the γ-core concept is a positive one. But I also think that the concept, and especially in its CT formulation, can be supplemented with elements that go beyond self-interest.

Consider, for instance, the notion of responsibility. It is also absent from the formulation of γ-core solution. Again, this is because cooperation towards efficiency is the primary objective of the theoretic construct. Yet, the notion of responsibility can be given a role in the CT solution, through the transfers it implies. This will be argued quite explicitly and more forcefully in the policy Lecture 10, after the instrument of tradable permits is introduced and its close connection is established with transfers. At this stage however the intuition of the argument can be given by referring to how the size of the CT transfers is a function of the reference that the Nash equilibrium consists of. Tilting this reference upwards or downwards allows the transfers to be respectively more or less beneficial to some players in the game, be it to acknowledge responsibility or for purely redistributive reasons. The virtue of this possibility is even considerably reinforced when it is considered in the dynamic context, and in particular the one of dynamic programming: successive decisions can give an increasing dimension to the distributional and/of responsibility factors.

The CT solution and the ability to pay principle of public finance

In Section 6.3, it has been pointed out that in the climate change problem a parallel could be drawn between the ability to pay principle and the notion of responsibility, given the wealth that the dynamic context of past growth has brought to the currently developed economies.

Here again, the remarks made above on tilting the terms of reference of the negotiations in favor of some countries may be called upon. In particular, if the institutional framework of tradable permits is introduced, polluters can be made to pay. And the proceeds of this trade can be used to the benefit of those who deserve to be favored, using some of the many versions of the "polluter pays" principle proposed in Tulkens and Schoumaker (1975).

The computational nature of the CT solution

The *raison d'être* of the present lecture is not only in the pride of showing the applicability of the theory and in the pleasant intellectual feeling this application may give. It is also and foremost in the conviction that willy-nilly the modeling methodology will continue to exert an increasing and eventually dominant role in the mastering of the climate change problem.

Implementing the CT solution thus requires computation of its main components. First, a dynamic economic-ecological model must be available, that is, a model of the world economy coupled with a model of climatic phenomena linking emissions to temperature change, both covering several decades. Essential ingredients of the former are that on the one hand production activities be formulated in a way that makes explicit the pollutant emissions they generate, and that on the other hand, damages be formulated in functional forms of amounts of measurable ambient pollutants — all these components being disaggregated by countries. With all these ingredients, there just remains to perform the computation of the efficient emissions $(e_1^*, \ldots, e_n^*)$, of the reference emissions $(\bar{e}_1, \ldots, \bar{e}_n)$, of the transfers $(T_1, \ldots, T_n)$ (and/or, anticipating on Lecture 10, of the initial allowances $(e_1^o, \ldots, e_n^o)$). It would be naïve to believe that the knowledge of these numbers is sufficient for the reality to conform readily to them. But it is equally necessary that reality conforms to them for improvement to prevail in our societies.

8.4   An example of policy use of CWS and its associated game

Under the heading of "coalitional analysis" alternative Kyoto and post-Kyoto policies such as the following can be discussed and evaluated. Each one of these policies is actually a "scenario" in the sense defined in Section 8.1.3 and is thus the solution of a well-defined PCNE relative to the formation of some assumed coalition.

An important cautionary note: All numbers below are taken from Table 8.5, which date back to the time of publication of the Eyckmans and Tulkens (2003) paper. While all absolute values have, by now, little significance, the interest remains in their structure, which is theoretically consistent and therefore illustrates well the concepts.

(1) *The "Kyoto Annex B countries" scenario*
Here the coalition S corresponds to the row keyed as $\{1\,1\,1\,0\,1\,0\}$ in Table 8.5 (see coalitions of four countries, row 2). Referring to Table 8.4 reveals that for this coalition:

$$V_S^S = 247.830 > \sum_{i \in S} V_i^{\{i\}} = 247.787,$$

that is, the aggregate payoff for Annex B coalition in terms of discounted aggregate consumption is higher than if each of its members chooses the NCNE scenario. Thus, although this coalition does not achieve optimality at the world level, its formation is preferable for all its members compared to isolated domestic actions by them. It is thus collectively rational for Annex B countries to act together as specified in the Kyoto Protocol, in spite of the fact that the rest of the world sticks to an individualistic, non-cooperative policy.

(2) *The "George W. Bush" scenario*

In this case, the coalition S corresponds to the row keyed as $\{100000\}$. Table 8.4 reveals that for this coalition:

$$V_{\text{USA}}^{\{\text{USA}\}} = 78.353$$
$$< V_{\text{USA}}^* + \Psi_{\text{USA}}^* = 78.704$$
$$< V_{\text{USA}}^* = 78.986,$$

that is, sticking to a domestic optimization policy only — actually the NCNE — is for the USA less beneficial than its payoff in the world optimal policy, both with and without transfers.

(3) *The "Annex B without USA" scenario*

Here, the coalition S corresponds to the row keyed as $\{011010\}$ (coalitions of three countries, row 12). For this coalition:

$$V_S^S = 169.448 > \sum_{i \in S} V_i^{\{i\}} = 169.434,$$

meaning that, in spite of the Bush policy of staying out of the Protocol, the Annex B group of regions would benefit from the partial cooperation achieved among the non-USA countries. This comes as a support of the policy initiated by the EU in the Spring of 2001.

Other simulations not reported here also show that the USA gains only very little from leaving the Kyoto coalition. By renouncing the Kyoto coalition (and free riding on the effort of the remaining Kyoto members), the USA's pay off would be $V_{\text{USA}}^S = 78.367$ for S $= \{011010\}$, which is only slightly more than what it would achieve if it would stick to its Kyoto commitment $(V_{\text{USA}}^S = 78.366$ for $S = \{111010\})$.[23]

---

[23]Moreover, in Eyckmans (2001), it is shown that the deviation of USA from the Kyoto Protocol is not credible in the farsighted sense as defined by Chwe

8.5 Concluding consideration

This lecture shows conditions for world cooperation in a game theoretic sense, obtained in the framework of a dynamic, multiregional integrated assessment model of stock externalities, and developed all the way to numerical verification. This last feature should arguably give credibility to the cooperative approach advocated by its authors for tackling the climate change problem. In Lectures 9 and 10, this approach is pursued at the policy level.

(1994). The initial deviation of the USA would trigger subsequent deviations by, among others, the FSU, making the USA in the end worse off than under the original Kyoto Protocol. Further coalitional analysis of the CWS model is offered in Eyckmans and Finus (2003), as well as in Bréchet, Eyckmans, Gerard, Marbaix, Tulkens and van Ypersele (2010).

Lecture 9

INTERNAL COALITIONAL STABILITY
AND THE GLOBAL EXTERNALITY GAME

The purpose and the message

"Internal and external coalitional stability" is a branch of the game theoretically inspired literature on international environmental negotiations that rests on assumptions concerning behaviors in the presence of coalitions that are substantially different from those used to construct γ-core theory.

After a summary introductory presentation, this stream of thought is studied here with the conceptual apparatus, the vocabulary and the notation of the preceding lectures. Specifically, using the PCNE concept, a motion of "coalitional externality" is introduced and an equilibrium relation is identified between internal stability of the grand coalition and individual free riding behavior vis-à-vis this particular coalition. However, for reasons of non-existence and inconsistent expectations, it appears that such equilibrium cannot exist simultaneously with all players.

The message is that internal–external coalitional stability is essentially a partial equilibrium concept, not suited for characterizing an outcome of the GEG, let alone policy implications, which are postponed to the next lecture.

Plan

An alternative theory of coalitional stability

The "internal and external" stability concepts: An informal presentation

Internal coalitional stability in the GEG

Concluding considerations

Lecture 9

Internal Coalitional Stability and the Global Externality Game

9.1 An alternative theory of coalitional stability

Since the early 1990's the game theoretically inspired literature that deals with international environmental agreements is dominated by a controversy on the notion of coalitional stability. Parallel to "core stability" (CS) which is developed at full length in the preceding lectures, an alternative concept called "internal stability" (IS) has been proposed by Carraro and Siniscalco (1993) as well as Barrett (1994), who borrowed it from oligopoly theory.[1]

The first parallel presentation of the two approaches occurred at the initiative of Professor Carraro at the European meeting of the European Economic Association in Cambridge, UK, in August 1991.[2] Later, the two concepts were contrasted at the theoretical level in two occasions,[3] without the comparison leading to sufficient characterizations to show their interrelation — if any. Bréchet, Gerard and Tulkens (2011) proposed a first comparison by means of the CWS numerical simulation model of Lecture 8. It confirmed the theoretical intuitions explained below, but a logical reason for the differences is lacking in that paper. A next step in the theoretical direction is attempted in Tulkens (2014a). However, this papers'

---

[1] To be found in d'Aspremont and Gabszewicz (1986). The concept is actually two-fold, comprising "external stability" as a second facet. I explain below why I deal here only with internal stability.

[2] See the two papers, Carraro and Siniscalco (1992) and Chander and Tulkens (1992a), published in the same issue of the *European Economic Review*.

[3] Namely in the papers by Tulkens (1998) and Chander and Tulkens (2009), with a discussion in Thoron (2009, p. 191.).

thesis of reconciliation is now quasi-reversed, after convincing and creative discussions with a critical reader led to an equilibrium concept — developed below — whose relevance was overlooked so far. The 2014a paper should thus be ignored being superseded by the content of the present lecture.

9.2   The "internal and external" stability concepts: An informal presentation[4]

Rather than focusing on the grand coalition N only, the internal–external stability theory deals with *any* coalition $S \subseteq N$. It considers essentially the difference in the individual payoffs that any player can reach according to whether he is inside or outside of a coalition. Being inside means for the player to follow the strategy he is assigned to within the coalition, whereas being outside means behaving as a singleton. A coalition S is said (i) to be internally stable if no insider prefers to stay out of the coalition than remain inside, and (ii) to be externally stable if no outsider prefers to join the coalition than to stay outside. The coalition S is called "internally and externally stable" if these two conditions are met. Stability of a coalition in this case is not by reference to the absence of alternative blocking coalitions as in the γ-core concept, but instead by reference to a difference in *individual* payoffs that affects each player depending upon his being inside or outside the coalition.

Formally, the usual presentation runs as follows. For a game of the GEG type, letting $v_i(S)$ denote[5] the individual payoff of player i when i belongs to some coalition $S \subseteq N$, one has that the **coalition** S

---

[4]The relevant literature is for a very large part reproduced in the book edited by Finus and Caparrós (2015). The most elaborate analytical exposition of the theory in probably by Diamantoudi and Sartzetakis (2006).

[5]Here I am using momentarily a simplified notation to be close to the one used by the authors (see e.g. Barrett (1994) expression (8), p. 882, or Carraro and Siniscalco (1993) Definition 2, p. 314). It is to be put later in connection with the notation of the rest of the present book.

is **internally–externally stable** if for the players of that coalition, the payoffs of are such that:

$$\forall i \in S, \quad v_i(S) \geq v_i(S \backslash \{i\}) \text{(Internal stability)} \qquad (9.1)$$

and for the players not in that coalition the payoffs are such that

$$\forall i \notin S, \quad v_i(S) \geq v_i(S \cup \{i\}) \text{(External stability).}[6] \qquad (9.2)$$

As mentioned earlier, the theory is formulated for any coalition, but since my main interest in these lectures is in the grand coalition, N, for which external stability is meaningless, I develop below only internal stability of N.

9.3 Internal coalitional stability in the GEG

Let me take up the issue in terms of the tools used thus far, namely Definition 4.1 for a game in strategic form in general (Lecture 4), Definition 5.1 for the GEG (Lecture 5), as well as their graphical illustrations presented in these two lectures.

Coalitional externality and coalitional free riding

Recall from Fig. 4.1 in Lecture 4 that in a general cooperative game with players set $N = \{1, 2, 3\}$, the presence of a coalition is accounted for by specifying its worth, denoted, for instance, $w^{\gamma}(\{1, 2\})$ for coalition $\{1, 2\}$, and represented by a payoff possibility line drawn in the (v_1, v_2) space. In this setting, the payoff of player 3 is simply ignored. That ignorance would be innocuous if there were no externalities in the game. However, if there are, as with the GEG throughout this book, the externality exerted by the members of the coalition does have an effect on player 3's payoff. Shouldn't this effect be taken into account more explicitly in the determination of

---

[6]No confusion should be made with the concept of "stable set" of Von Neumann and Morgenstern (1944), covered in Osborne and Rubinstein (1994) Section 14.2. By the way, Proposition 279.2a of these last two authors establishes that the core is a stable set in the Von Neumann and Morgenstern sense.

the solution of the game, and how? The answer to that question has two aspects.

Recall first that in the three-dimensional diagrams of Figs. 4.3, 4.4, or 5.2 and 5.3 the origin $(0,0,0)$ is conventionally set at the payoff levels reached by *all three* players at the NCNE. In that outcome, each one of them fully exerts the externality generated by his individual behavior equilibrium. Thus, and this is the first aspect, the externality is well taken into account at the NCNE, including all effects from individual players on player 3, as well as those from the latter on the former.

Now, in the present cooperative game context where characteristically coalitions have strategies of their own, possibly distinct from the individual equilibrium ones, the formation of a coalition modifies the payoff levels of the other players in the following way. Suppose that players 1 and 2 form a coalition and choose the joint strategy that maximizes the sum of their payoffs. This yields $w^\gamma(\{1,2\})$ as reminded above and induces the line so designated in the space (v_1, v_2) now redrawn in Fig. 9.1. The second aspect of the question is that this strategic choice of $\{1,2\}$ has *per se* an effect on player 3, reinforcing the externality. This effect is favorable to 3 because the externality is of the "positive" type in the GEG. Graphically, in the $(v_1,\ v_2, v_3)$ space, the windfall benefit that player 3 so receives from $\{1,2\}$'s strategic choice *as a coalition* can be measured along the v_3 axis by a segment extended from the origin to point G, for instance, as shown in Fig. 9.1. As said, the occurrence of this effect is entirely due to the *concerted jointness* of the strategies of the coalition members. If coalition $\{1,2\}$ were not to form and not to maximize its joint payoff, the reinforced externality described here would not occur: all players' payoffs would remain at the origin, i.e. at the NCNE of the game where only the first effect takes place.

This extra benefit is for player 3 a windfall benefit from external cooperation or, for short, a "coalitional externality" that player 3 is the recipient of.[7] I call it *external* because it comes to 3 from the

---

[7]Notice that in fact, this benefit is an enhancement of the external effect, within the game and the economy, generated by the coalition formation process.

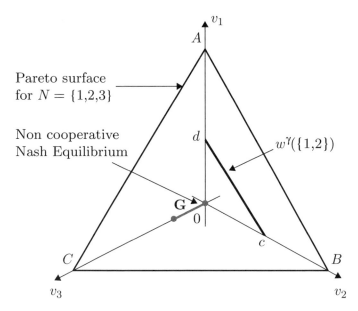

Fig. 9.1 A coalitional externality: Player 3's benefit (point G) generated by cooperation within coalition $\{1,2\}$.

cooperation occurring within a coalition $N\backslash\{3\}$ of which $\{3\}$ is not a member. It is also one component of the phenomenon of free riding which, given its source, can also be called "coalitional free riding".

In order to make explicit the recognition of the existence of player 3 when coalition $\{1,2\}$ forms and leaves 3 outside, I denote from now on the coalition's worth as $w^{\gamma}(\{1,2\}|\{3\})$. I modify accordingly the way the γ-coalitional function of Definition 5.4 is denoted, replacing henceforth $w^{\gamma}(S)$ by $w^{\gamma}(S;\{\{j\}\}_{j\in N\backslash S})$.

The equilibrium size of the coalitional externality

To appreciate whether or not taking into account of the particular benefit just identified has an influence on conceivable outcomes of the game, and thereby on possible states of the economic-ecological model, one needs an instrument. It turns out that, to play that role, the concept of PCNE r.t. a coalition[8] reveals itself to be, once again, appropriate.

Consider the extreme point G of the segment just identified in Fig. 9.1. One may see it as the outcome in payoff terms of the simultaneous effects of two factors determining player 3's payoff: (a) his utility maximizing individual strategic choice and (b) the reception of the coalitional externality from cooperation within $\{1, 2\}$. Added up, the utilities obtained by player 3 from each of these two factors allow one to see point G as an individual equilibrium payoff.

Taken together, the values represented by point G and the line $w^\gamma(\{1, 2\}|\{3\})$ appear now as being the components, in payoff terms, of an equilibrium state of the game. Indeed it satisfies the definition of a PCNE, for the case where the equilibrium is relative to the coalition $N\backslash\{3\}$, with player 3 as the only outside singleton. In the notation of Lecture 5, referring to the payoff function (5.16–5.17) of Definition 5.4 as well as to the strategy profiles (5.8) and (5.9) of Definition 5.3, the strategy profile of the PCNE so identified reads

$$\tilde{e}^{N\backslash\{3\}} = \left((\tilde{e}_j^{N\backslash\{3\}})_{j\in N\backslash\{3\}}, \tilde{e}_3^{N\backslash\{3\}} \right), \tag{9.3}$$

where

$$(\tilde{e}_j^{N\backslash\{3\}})_{j\in N\backslash\{3\}}$$

$$= \arg\max \sum_{j\in N\backslash\{3\}} \left(g_j(e_j) - d_j \left(\sum_{k\in N\backslash\{3\}} e_k + \tilde{e}_3^{N\backslash\{3\}} \right) \right) \tag{9.4}$$

and

$$\tilde{e}_3^{N\backslash\{3\}} = \arg\max \ g_3(e_3) - d_3 \left(\sum_{j\in N\backslash\{3\}} \tilde{e}_j + e_3 \right). \tag{9.5}$$

---

[8]For a reminder of its formulation in a general cooperative game, please refer to Definition 4.7 of Lecture 4, and, in the GEG context, to Definition 5.3 of Lecture 5.

At this equilibrium the payoffs are

$$\left(\sum_{j \in N \setminus \{3\}} \tilde{v}_j^{N \setminus \{3\}}, \tilde{v}_3^{N \setminus \{3\}} \right), \tag{9.6}$$

where for the coalition $N \setminus \{3\}$

$$\sum_{j \in N \setminus \{3\}} \tilde{v}_j^{N \setminus \{3\}} = \sum_{j \in N \setminus \{3\}} \left(g_j \left(\tilde{e}_j^{N \setminus \{3\}} \right) - d_j \left(\sum_{k \in N} \tilde{e}_k^{N \setminus \{3\}} \right) \right) \tag{9.7}$$

$$= w^\gamma(\{1,2\}|\{3\}) \text{ in alleviated notation}$$

and for the singleton $\{3\}$

$$\tilde{v}_3^{N \setminus \{3\}} = g_3 \left(\tilde{e}_3^{N \setminus \{3\}} \right) - d_3 \left(\sum_{k \in N} \tilde{e}_k^{N \setminus \{3\}} \right) \tag{9.8}$$

$$\underset{\text{def}}{=} w^\circ(\{3\}|\{1,2\}).$$

Notice that in (9.8), the superscript $^\circ$ instead of γ means that w° is *not* the same function as the γ-coalitional function w^γ, familiar since Lecture 5. It is instead just the value of the payoff of player 3 when coalition $\{1,2\}$ forms and 3 remains outside: as mentioned, the payoff is the one resulting from the choice of his best strategy — $\tilde{e}_3^{N \setminus \{3\}}$ as mentioned in 9.5 — and from receiving the windfall benefit generated by $\sum_{k \in N \setminus \{3\}} \tilde{e}_k^{N \setminus \{3\}}$, that is, the emissions of coalition $\{1,2\}$.

Properties of the strategies prevailing in general at a PCNE relative to any S are described in detail in Chander and Tulkens (1997) (Proposition 4 (iii) and (iv), p. 389)[9] and supplemented by Helm (2001) (first part of proof of Lemma 1, p. 144). They typically characterize the strategies of PCNEs in their relation with what they are at the NCNE. They imply that in the present case where

---

[9]Reproduced in Propositions 5.6–5.8 of Lecture 5.

$S = N\backslash\{3\}$ one has simultaneously

$$\sum_{j \in N\backslash\{3\}} \tilde{e}_j^{N\backslash\{3\}} \leq \sum_{j \in N\backslash\{3\}} \bar{e}_j \tag{9.9}$$

and

$$\tilde{e}_3^{N\backslash\{3\}} \geq \bar{e}_3, \tag{9.10}$$

where for all $i \in N$, $\bar{e}_i$ denotes player i's strategy at the NCNE. In words, (9.10) asserts that the equilibrium emissions of player 3 at the PCNE are larger than (or equal to) what they are at the NCNE. These larger emissions combined with the coalitional externality unquestionably induce $\tilde{v}_3^{N\backslash\{3\}} \geq \bar{v}_3$ which justifies the segment (0,G) drawn along player 3's axis of Fig. 9.1.

Parallel to that, since coalition $\{1,2\}$ is formed, the PCNE r.t. $\{1,2\}$ prevails. The worth of the coalitional function, $w^\gamma(\{1,2\}|\{3\})$, is illustrated on the same Fig. 9.1 by the line dc drawn in the payoffs space of players 1 and 2, as was done in Fig. 5.2 of Lecture 5.

Thus, the simultaneous existence of the coalition $N\backslash\{3\}$ and of the singleton $\{3\}$, with the respective payoff values $w^\gamma(\{1,2\}|\{3\})$ and $w^\circ(\{3\}|\{1,2\})$ interpreted in terms of utility maximization on either side, constitutes a *pairwise* PCNE of the game. Referring to a terminology used above, it can also be called an "*equilibrium with one free riding player*". In what follows I use these two expressions interchangeably.

This interpretation in terms of a PCNE gives an answer to the question implicit in the title of this subsection: the size of the coalitional externality is determined endogenously as an equilibrium of the game. It is therefore a fixed[10] magnitude.

---

[10]In the successive versions of the research discussion paper Tulkens (2014a) that have preceded the present exposition, the size of the benefit from external cooperation was systematically considered to be an exogenous magnitude, *assumed* to satisfy some consistency requirement. This was ignoring the equilibrium feature pointed out here.

"Outside option payoff" and possible outcomes
of negotiations

As to terminology, the expression of "outside option payoff" will
henceforth be attached to an individual situation such as the one
of player 3 at the pairwise PCNE for the following reason, best
suggested graphically as follows.

The windfall benefit that has just been described by point G
along the v_3 axis in Fig. 9.1 can also be expressed on the Pareto
surface of Fig. 9.2 by projecting point G on any point of the surface
that lies at the same distance $w^{\circ}(\{3\}|\{1,2\})$ of the $(v_1,\ v_2)$ plane, a
distance represented by the segments a, a^3 and b, b^3. This is done in
Fig. 9.2, where to the point representing the outside option of player 3
corresponds now to the entire dashed line labeled a^3b^3 on the Pareto
surface. The location of this line on the surface is determined by the
size of the windfall benefit $w^{\circ}(\{3\}|\{1,2\})$. It is a fixed magnitude
because, as just shown, it is part of the equilibrium between $N\backslash\{3\}$
and the singleton $\{3\}$: it is a datum of the game.

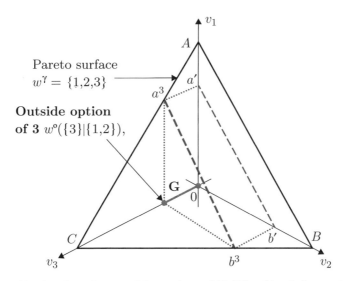

Fig. 9.2 Projecting the outside option $w^{\circ}(\{3\}|\{1,2\})$ **of player 3 as the
line** a^3b^3 **on the Pareto surface** $w^{\gamma}\{1,2,3\}$.

In a negotiation process where the solution sought for is supposed to be an imputation of the game, that is, a point on the Pareto surface, the set of accessible imputations now appears to be restricted to the area a^3b^3C in Fig. 9.2. Indeed, if an imputation is proposed that for player 3 does not reach at least $w°(\{3\}|\{1,2\})$, this player logically rejects this imputation, because he is better off by leaving the coalition $\{1,2,3\}$ and playing outside as a singleton: the outcome is then the PCNE r.t. $\{1,2\}$ where his payoff is for sure $w°(\{3\}|\{1,2\})$. In other words, staying in the grand coalition is only possible for player 3 if the proposed solution is an imputation that does *not* belong to the area a^3ABb^3. Otherwise player 3 declines being a member of the coalition $\{1,2,3\}$ as he prefers to stay outside: hence the expression of "outside option".

Graphically, player 3's requirement of $w°(\{3\}|\{1,2\})$ in a negotiation "bites" the chunk a^3ABb^3 off the set of points of the Pareto surface that player 3 can accept to stay in $\{1,2,3\}$. Notice that if that bite is big enough, that is, if $w°(\{3\}|\{1,2\})$ is larger than $w^\gamma(\{1,2,3\})$ — with point G lying beyond point C — the restricted accessible area a^3b^3C does not exist because player 3 requires for himself more than the worth that the entire Pareto efficient coalition can possibly generate: cooperation with player 3 within $\{1,2,3\}$ cannot even be envisaged in that case.

Properties of an equilibrium with one free riding player

(i) One can see that the Pairwise PCNE r.t. $\{1,2\}$ is not a Pareto efficient outcome by comparing its first-order conditions (5.10) and (5.11) with the Paretian ones of (3.33).

(ii) This implies that the following inequality holds at that PCNE r.t. $\{1,2\}$:

$$w^\gamma(\{1,2\}|\{3\}) + w°(\{3\}|\{1,2\}) < w^\gamma(\{1,2,3\}). \quad (9.11)$$

(iii) From this inequality it also appears that the case evoked above of point G lying beyond point C cannot logically occur and that the relative positions of the lines a^3b^3 and d^3c^3 on the Pareto

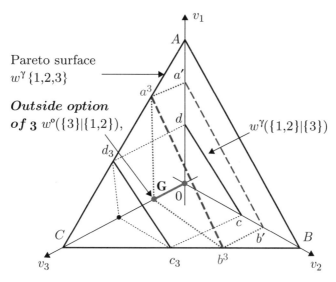

Fig. 9.3 **Relative positions of player 3's outside option payoff and of the joint payoff of coalition** $\{1,2\}$ **at the PCNE rt** $\{1,2\}$.

surface must be as shown in Fig. 9.3. This further characterizes the fixed link already mentioned between the three components of an equilibrium with one free riding player.

(iv) Moving to the RHS the first term on the left of (9.11) shows that the size of $w^\circ(\{3\}|\{1,2\})$ is less than the difference $w^\gamma(\{1,2,3\}) - w^\gamma(\{1,2\}|\{3\})$: this means that the value that the free riding player obtains in equilibrium with his outside option is necessarily smaller than the value he could get by remaining within N at Pareto. This is particularly visible in the numerical GEG 9.1 presented a few pages below, where $\frac{3}{8} < \frac{8}{8} - \frac{2}{8}$.

(v) The preceding point implies that the grand coalition $N = \{1,2,3\}$ is always *potentially* internally stable *vis-à-vis* any single player $i \in N$ taken separately, in the following sense: (9.11) implies that for the grand coalition N of the GEG, there always exists a feasible strategy profile e^* that yields player i a higher payoff by staying in rather than by opting out, that is, such that $v_i^*(e^*) > w^\circ(\{i\}|N\backslash\{i\})$.

(vi) For exactly the same reason, for any single player $i \in N$ taken separately the pairwise PCNE r.t. $N \backslash \{i\}$ is such that the coalition $N \backslash \{i\}$ is *not* potentially externally stable *vis-à-vis* player i: (9.11) implies that coalition N can choose a strategy profile that yields the outsider i a higher payoff by joining rather than by staying out.

(vii) Finally, a crucial element in the above reasoning is that it rests on player i expecting that the coalition he leaves does survive without him, that is, that $N \backslash \{i\}$ stays formed. Without assuming that i makes his choice on the basis of this expectation, we are back on the γ-assumption: indeed the only opposite belief is that $N \backslash \{i\}$ breaks apart into singletons.

Equilibria with multiple free riding players: Problems

The concept of "equilibrium with one free riding player" designates the strategy profile of *one* particular PCNE of the GEG which is also a state of the underlying economic-ecological model. It characterizes a relation between one specific country and the rest of the world. This relation corresponds to a feasible state. How about such relation holding for many countries?

An existence issue

Consider now the externality generated by coalition $\{1,3\}$ on player 2. Repeating the above graphical argument, player 2's windfall benefit from the coalitional externality generated by the formation of $\{1,3\}$ is measured and represented in Fig. 9.4 by the level of the payoff $w^{\circ}(\{2\}|\{1,3\})$ along the v_2 axis, as well as by its projection as the line $a^2 b^2$ on the Pareto surface. Here, only the imputations in the triangular area $a^2 b^2 B$ remain accessible for the coalition $\{1,2,3\}$ as far as player 2 is concerned. But if the two externalities are assumed to occur simultaneously and both 1 and 2 require to be granted a payoff at least equal to their respective outside option, the accessible set of imputations reduces to the points in the intersection of the triangles $a^2 b^2 B$ and $a^3 b^3 C$. Introducing the third player leads to Fig. 9.5 where each coalition generates a coalitional externality on its non-member, with the windfall coalitional benefits being $w^\circ(\{1\}|\{2,3\})$, $w^\circ(\{2\}|\{1,3\})$ and $w^\circ(\{3\}|\{1,2\})$, respectively. If all players require at least their outside option, the imputations accessible for $\{1,2,3\}$ then further reduce to the intersection of the triangles a^1b^1A, a^2b^2B and a^3b^3C, that is, the points in the subset CEF of the Pareto surface.

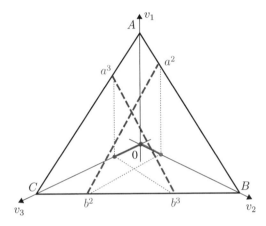

Fig. 9.4 Two coalitional externalities with the respective outside option lines of the benefiters.

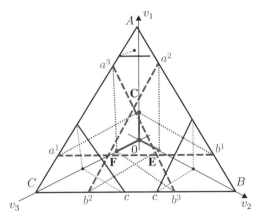

Fig. 9.5 Three conceivable coalitional externalities with the respective outside option lines of the benefiters.

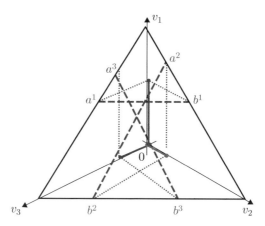

Fig. 9.6 An impossible equilibrium: three simultaneous coalitional externalities.

Now, the next Fig 9.6 is constructed in exactly the same way, but the equivalent of the set CEF happens to be empty, as revealed by the fact that the three tri-angular areas a^1b^1A, a^2b^2B and a^3b^3C do not intersect. The position of the dashed line a^1b^1, which is "higher" along the v_1 axis than it is in the previous figure, seems to be the cause of this emptiness. But it is not exactly so. The cause lies in the positions of all three dashed lines, relative to one another: the non-intersection reveals an impossibility of *simultaneous* feasibility of *all* these individual requests for compensation for their outside option *vis-à-vis* N.

Returning to the GEG 9.1, one reads there that

$$\sum_{i \in N} w_i^o(\{i\}|N\backslash\{i\}) = \frac{9}{8} > 1 = \sum_{i \in N} v_i^* = w^\gamma(N),$$

which means that summed together, the values of the three outside options cannot be covered by the value that the grand coalition generates. In GEG 9.1 an equilibrium with simultaneous three individual free riders, being impossible, cannot not exist. A logical reason for this impossibility is identified below when I turn to the general case.

GEG 9.1. A game with a set $N = \{1,2,3\}$ of identical players all with linear damage functions, and payoff functions: $v_i = e_i^{\frac{1}{2}} - (e_1 + e_2 + e_3) + \frac{1}{4}$, $i = 1, 2, 3$.

Outcomes	Individual emissions	Total emissions	Individual payoffs	Aggregate payoffs
NCNE	$\forall i, \, \bar{e}_i = \frac{1}{4}$ $(= 0.250)$	$\sum_{i \in N} \bar{e}_i = \frac{3}{4}$ $(= 0.750)$	$\forall i, \, \bar{v}_i = 0$	$\sum_{i \in N} \bar{v}_i = 0$
PCNE r.t. $N\backslash\{i\}, i = 1, 2, 3$ and outside option for $(\{i\}|N\backslash\{i\})$	$\forall j \in N\backslash\{i\}$, $\tilde{e}_j^{N\backslash(i)} = \frac{1}{16}$ $(\cong 0.063)$ $\tilde{e}_i^{N\backslash\{i\}} = \frac{1}{4} (= 0.250)$	$\sum_{j \in N\backslash(i)} \tilde{e}_j^{N\backslash(i)}$ $= \frac{1}{16} + \frac{1}{16}$ $(= 0.125)$ $\sum_{j \in N} \tilde{e}_j^{N\backslash\{i\}}$ $= \frac{1}{16} + \frac{1}{16} + \frac{1}{4}$ $(= 0.375)$	$\forall j \in N\backslash\{i\}$, $\tilde{v}_j^{N\backslash\{i\}} = \frac{1}{8}$ $(= 0.125)$ $\tilde{v}_i^{N\backslash\{i\}}$ $\underset{def}{=} w^o(\{i\}|N\backslash\{i\})$ $= \frac{3}{8} (= 0.375)$	$\sum_{j \in N\backslash\{i\}} \tilde{v}_j^{N\backslash\{i\}}$ $\underset{def}{=} w^\gamma(N\backslash\{i\}|\{i\})$ $= \frac{1}{8} + \frac{1}{8} (= 0.250)$ $\sum_{j \in N} \tilde{v}_j^{N\backslash\{i\}}$ $= \frac{1}{8} + \frac{1}{8} + \frac{3}{8}$ $= \frac{5}{8} (= 0.625)$
All outside options	$\forall i, \, \tilde{e}_i^{N\backslash\{i\}}$ $= \frac{1}{4} (= 0.25)$	$\sum_{i \in N} \tilde{e}_i^{N\backslash\{i\}}$ $= \frac{3}{4} (= 0.750)$		$\sum_{i \in N} w^o(\{i\}|N\backslash\{i\})$ $= \frac{3}{8} + \frac{3}{8} + \frac{3}{8}$ $= \frac{9}{8} (= 1.125)$
PESP	$\forall i, \, e_i^*$ $= \frac{1}{36} (\cong 0.028)$	$\sum_{i \in N} e_i^*$ $= \frac{3}{36} (\cong 0.083)$	$\forall i, \, v_i^*$ $= \frac{1}{3} (\cong 0.333)$	$\sum_{i \in N} v_i^*$ $= w^\gamma(\{1,2,3\}) = 1$

One may verify the following properties:

- superadditivity and balancedness: yes
- internal stability of coalition N: no $(9/8 > 1)$,
- the PEP and its payoff vector (without transfers) belong to the γ-core, as well as, e.g.
  - the payoff vector $(3/8, 3/8, 2/8)$ (also satisfying two outside option payoffs),
  - the payoff vector $(1/2, 1/2, 0)$ (this GEG is "anchored" — see Lecture 5).
- coalitional externalities:
  in strategies: none,
  in payoffs: $3/8 - 0$ for each i.

A chain of contradictory expectations

Remember at this point the "crucial element" mentioned above in introducing the pairwise PCNE, namely that the concept rests on the assumption that the free riding player 3 is *expecting* that the coalition he leaves does survive without him, that is, that $\{1,2\}$ remains formed. Now, when one takes into account that other players in the game might consider also to be a free rider, one runs into the following troublesome chain of expectations.

Take the case of player 2 being this additional free rider, *vis-à-vis* the coalition $\{1,3\}$. It is assumed that 2 *expects* that $\{1,3\}$ remains formed. But this differs from the just mentioned assumed expectation by 3 that $\{1,2\}$ remains formed. Take next the case of player 1 being a free rider *vis à vis* coalition $\{2,3\}$; it is now assumed that 1 *expects* that $\{2,3\}$ remains formed. But this differs from the just assumed expectation by 2 that 3 remains in coalition with 1. And finally, the initial expectation by player 3 that $\{1,2\}$ remains formed, thus that 1 will not free ride, is inconsistent with the assumed expectation by 1 that 2 remains in coalition with 3!

In summary, at an equilibrium with multiple free riding players, when such equilibrium exists, all free riders are acting on the basis of expectations that are different from one another. Related to this troublesome inconsistency, one may feel uneasy at noting that in the GEG 9.1 the very *same* strategies, $e_i = \frac{1}{4} \forall i \in N$, that yield individual payoffs of 0 at the NCNE, would yield the larger payoff of $\frac{3}{8}$ for each player at an equilibrium with multiple free riding players if feasible, due to the sole effects of these *expected* coalitional externalities.

Analytical exploration of more general cases

To understand the source of the possible non-existence fact revealed by GEG 9.1 one may look at the details of the model's properties, as they are stated in the table. While confirming expression (9.11) in the sense that for some individual i one has the outside option payoff $w^\circ(\{i\}|N\backslash\{i\}) < w^\gamma(N)$, implying feasibility for N, the table also shows that if for two players i, $i = 1,2$, their individual outside option payoffs are considered simultaneously, one has $\sum_{i=1}^{2} w^\circ(\{i\}|N\backslash\{i\}) < w^\gamma(N)$ implying thus feasibility for N of granting their outside option to at least these two free riding players. But infeasibility prevails if the outside option is also considered for the third players simultaneously with the two previous ones. Indeed, one then finds that $\sum_{i=1}^{3} w^\circ(\{i\}|N\backslash\{i\}) > w^\gamma(N)$.

In fact, such infeasibility is more general in GEGs than what can be claimed from only this 3-players numerical example, as shown by the following statement.

Proposition 9.1. *For any GEG in coalitional function form* $[N, w^\gamma(S; \{\{j\}\}_{j \in N \backslash S})]$ *with* n *identical players indexed* $i = 1, \ldots, n$ *and for each of them linear damage cost functions* $d_i(z) = \pi z$, $\pi > 0$, *the maximal number* ν *of players, whose individual outside option payoff* $w^\circ(\{i\}|N \backslash \{i\})$ *can be satisfied simultaneously by the worth* $w^\gamma(N)$ *of the all players coalition* N, *is necessarily smaller than* n. *Formally,* $\nu \in [1; n[$.

Proof. For a game as specified, consider for some player $i \in N$ the pairwise PCNE denoted by its pair of payoffs $[w^\circ(\{i\}|N \backslash \{i\}), w^\gamma(N \backslash \{i\}|\{i\})]$. Knowing that such equilibrium is not efficient, one has

$$w^\circ(\{i\}|N \backslash \{i\}) + w^\gamma(N \backslash \{i\}|\{i\}) < w^\gamma(N) \qquad (9.12)$$

and *a fortiori* since $w^\gamma(N \backslash \{i\}|\{i\}) > 0$,

$$w^\circ(\{i\}|N \backslash \{i\}) < w^\gamma(N). \qquad (9.13)$$

In strategic terms, and given the assumptions of linearity of the damage functions and identical players, the last inequality may be written as

$$g_i(\tilde{e}_i^{N \backslash \{i\}}) - \pi[(n-1)\tilde{e}_j^{N \backslash \{i\}} + \tilde{e}_i^{N \backslash \{i\}}] < n(g_i(e_i^*) - \pi n e_i^*). \qquad (9.14)$$

For player i, linearity of the damage function implies furthermore that when acting as a singleton, as in (9.14), his strategy $\tilde{e}_i^{N \backslash \{i\}}$ is a dominant strategy and thus the same as his Nash equilibrium one, which was denoted $\bar{e}_i$ above. Expression (9.14) then reads

$$g_i(\bar{e}_i) - \pi[(n-1)\tilde{e}_j^{N \backslash \{i\}} + \bar{e}_i] < n(g_i(e_i^*) - \pi n e_i^*). \qquad (9.15)$$

Now if two players, say i and j, claim to obtain simultaneously their outside option payoff, this amounts to require $w^\circ(\{i\}|N \backslash \{i\}) + w^\circ(\{j\}|N \backslash \{j\})$ to be covered by the worth of the grand coalition N.

This is the case in GEG 9.1 where $3/8 + 3/8 < 1$, but the reason invoked with the property (9.12) of the game for asserting the feasibility of the outside option of a single claimant cannot be invoked for two. With a third such claimant, infeasibility now prevails in the example, as noted above, but why now and not for two? And can anything general be said for games with $n \geq 3$?

Letting the integer $\nu \geq 1$ be the number of players, whose individual outside option payoffs can be satisfied simultaneously by the aggregate payoff $w^\gamma(N)$, the question boils down to determining from (9.15) values of ν for which the following inequality holds:

$$\nu(g_i(\bar{e}_i) - \pi[(n-1)\tilde{e}_j^{N\setminus\{i\}} + \bar{e}_i]) < n(g_i(e_i^*) - \pi n e_i^*). \qquad (9.16)$$

From (9.16) one can derive that for the stated GEG, ν cannot be equal to n because such equality would imply that the expressions between parentheses on either side be equal. But this is also not possible because

(a) for each $i \in N$ the NCNE strategy $\bar{e}_i$ is larger than the PESP strategy e_i^*, as is known from (3.24) in Proposition 3.3 compared to (3.33) in Proposition 3.5, in Lecture 3, which imply $g_i(\bar{e}_i) > g_i(e_i^*)$ by concavity of the functions g_i; and

(b) $-\pi[(n-1)\tilde{e}_i^{N\setminus\{i\}} + \bar{e}_i] < -\pi[(n-1)e_i^* + e_i^*]$, in view of Proposition 6.1 in Lecture 6 (expression (6.10): total emissions at a NCNE are always larger than total Pareto efficient ones).

□

More generally, for GEGs with non-identical players but still linear damage functions, the heterogeneity makes the feasibility conditions (9.16) for multiple free riding claims take a more complex form. Yet, the impossibility of accommodating the free riding option of all players remains established by showing:

Proposition 9.2. *For any GEG in coalitional function form* $[N, w^\gamma(S; \{\{j\}\}_{j \in N\setminus S})]$ *with* $n \geq 3$ *players indexed* $i = 1, \ldots, n$ *and for each of them linear damage cost functions* $d_i(z) = \pi_i z, \pi_i > 0$, *the largest set of players, whose individual outside option payoff* $w^\circ(\{i\}|N\setminus\{i\})$ *can be satisfied simultaneously by the worth* $w^\gamma(N)$, *is necessarily a proper set of N. Formally, the expression*

$$\sum_{i \in S} \left(g_i(\bar{e}_i) - \sum_{j \in N \setminus i} \pi_j \bar{e}_j^{N \setminus \{i\}} + \pi_i \bar{e}_i] \right) < \sum_{i \in N} \left(g_i(e_i^*) - \sum_{j \in N} \pi_j e_j^* \right).$$

(9.17)

does not hold for $S = N$.

Proof. The argument made in the proof of the preceding proposition on the impossible similarity of the expressions under parentheses in either side of (9.17) if $S = N$ applies without change. □

Attempts to further extent the thesis of these two propositions by substituting convexity to the linearity assumption on damage functions were discouraged when Maurice Queyranne produced (in private communication) the interesting 3-players GEG 9.2 stated below, where non linearity prevails for all components of the payoff functions. In this game, the sum of the individuals outside option payoffs 3.584 is less than 4.630, the worth of the grand coalition, thus allowing for N to cover the outside options of all players.

A further interest of the GEG 9.2 lies in the observation that the vector of outside option payoffs does belong to the γ-core of this balanced game!

Notice that the GEG 9.2 is not superadditive. The reader may remember that this is also the case of the 3-players game presented in the appendix of Lecture 5. For that game too, the vector of outside option payoffs belongs to the γ-core.

From these examples, there thus appears that for some GEGs there is a possible compatibility between the two properties of *internal stability of N* and *γ-core stability*. Comparing with CEG 9.1, these two examples have properties in common, that makes them different in substantial ways from 9.1: heterogeneity of the players, non linearity of damage functions, and non-superadditivity of the game. Does that mean that for the GEG in general, existence of internal stability of N, possibly together with the well established γ-core property, can only be considered as holding in special cases?

GEG 9.2 (Queyranne). **A game with a set $N = \{1,2,3\}$ of non-identical players, all with quadractic production and damage functions, and payoff functions $v_i = 10e_i - 20e_i^2 - (e_1 + e_2 + e_3)^2, i = 1,2$, low productivity and low sensitivity to damages, $v_3 = 10e_3 - 5e_3^2 - 10(e_1 + e_2 + e_3)^2 + 3$, high productivity and high sensitivity to damages.**

Outcomes	Individual emissions	Total emissions	Individual payoffs	Aggregate payoffs
NCNE	$\forall i = 1,2$ $\bar{e}_i = \frac{7}{31}(\cong 0.226)$ $\bar{e}_3 = \frac{1}{31}(\cong 0.032)$	$\sum_{i \in N} \bar{e}_t$ $= \frac{15}{31}(\cong 0.484)$	$\forall i = 1,2$ $\bar{v}_i = \frac{965}{961}(\cong 1.004)$ $\bar{v}_3 = \frac{938}{961}(\cong 0.976)$	$\sum_{i \in N} \bar{v}_i$ $= \frac{2.868}{961}\ (\cong 2.984)$
PCNE r.t				
$N \backslash \{1\}$ $= \{2,3\}$ and outside option for $(\{1\}|N\backslash\{1\})$	$\tilde{e}_2^{N \backslash \{1\}} = \frac{5}{152}$ $(\cong 0.033)$ $\tilde{e}_3^{N \backslash \{1\}} = \frac{5}{38}$ $(\cong 0.013)$ $\tilde{e}_1^{N \backslash \{1\}} = \frac{35}{152}$ $(\cong 0.230)$	$\sum_{j \in N} \tilde{e}_j^{N \backslash (1)}$ $= \frac{15}{38}(\cong 0.395)$	$\tilde{v}_2^{N \backslash \{1\}} = \frac{875}{5776}$ $(\cong 0.151)$ $\tilde{v}_3^{N \backslash \{1\}} = \frac{203}{76}$ $(\cong 2.671)$ $\tilde{v}_2^{N \backslash \{1\}}$ $\underset{def}{=} w^o(\{1\}|N\backslash\{1\})$ $= \frac{6275}{5776}(\cong 1.086)$	$\sum_{j \in N \backslash \{1\}} \tilde{v}_j^{N \backslash \{1\}}$ $= w^\gamma(N\backslash 1|\{1\})$ $= \frac{875}{5776} + \frac{203}{76}$ $= \frac{16303}{5776}(\approx 2.822)$ $\sum_{j \in N} \tilde{v}_j^{N \backslash \{1\}}$ $= 2.822 + 1.086$ $= 3.908$
$N \backslash \{2\}$ $= \{1,3\}$ and outside option for $(\{2\}|N\backslash\{2\})$	$\tilde{e}_1^{N \backslash \{2\}} = \frac{2}{152}$ $(\cong 0.033)$ $\tilde{e}_3^{N \backslash \{2\}} = \frac{5}{38}$ $(\cong 0.013)$ $\tilde{e}_2^{N \backslash \{2\}} = \frac{35}{152}$ $(\cong 0.230)$	$\sum_{j \in N} \tilde{e}_j^{N \backslash \{2\}}$ $= \frac{15}{38}(\cong 0.395)$	$\tilde{v}_1^{N \backslash \{2\}} = \frac{875}{5776}$ $(\cong 0.151)$ $\tilde{v}_3^{N \backslash \{2\}} = \frac{703}{76}$ $(\cong 2.671)$ $\tilde{v}_2^{N \backslash \{2\}}$ $\underset{def}{=} w^o(\{2\}|N\backslash\{2\})$ $= \frac{6275}{5776}(\cong 1.086)$	$\sum_{j \in N \backslash \{2\}} \tilde{v}_j^{N \backslash \{2\}}$ $= w^\gamma(N\backslash 21\{2\})$ $= \frac{875}{5776} + \frac{203}{76}$ $= \frac{16303}{5776}(\cong 2.822)$ $\sum_{j \in N} \tilde{v}_j^{N \backslash \{2\}}$ $\frac{16303}{5776} + \frac{6275}{5776}$ $(\cong 3.908)$
$N \backslash \{3\}$ $= \{1,2\}$ and outside option for $(\{3\}|N\backslash\{3\})$	$\tilde{e}_1^{N \backslash \{3\}} = \frac{13}{64}$ $(\cong 0.203)$ $\tilde{e}_2^{N \backslash \{3\}} = \frac{13}{64}$ $(\cong 0.203)$ $\tilde{e}_3^{N \backslash \{3\}} = \frac{1}{16}$ $(\cong 0.062)$	$\sum_{j \in N} \tilde{e}_j^{N \backslash \{3\}}$ $= \frac{15}{32}(\cong 0.469)$	$\forall j \in N \backslash \{3\}$ $\tilde{v}_j^{N \backslash \{3\}} = \frac{505}{8512}$ $(\cong 0.986)$ $\tilde{v}_3^{N \backslash \{3\}}$ $\underset{def}{=} w^o(\{3\}|N\backslash\{3\})$ $= \frac{721}{512}(\cong 1.408)$	$\sum_{j \in N \backslash \{3\}} \tilde{v}_j^{N \backslash \{3\}}$ $= w^\gamma(N\backslash 3|\{3\})$ $= \frac{505}{512} + \frac{505}{512}$ $= \frac{1010}{512}(= 1,973)$ $\sum_{j \in N} \tilde{v}_j^{N \backslash \{3\}}$ $= \frac{1010}{512} + \frac{721}{512}$ $= \frac{1731}{512}(\cong 3.381)$
All outside options	$\forall i = 1,2$ $\tilde{e}_i^{N \backslash \{i\}} = \frac{35}{152}$ $(\cong 0.230)$ $\tilde{e}_3^{N \backslash \{3\}} = \frac{1}{16}$ $(\cong 0.062)$	$\sum_{i \in N} \tilde{e}_i^{N \backslash \{i\}}$ $= \frac{159}{304}$ $(\cong 0.523)$		$\sum_{i \in N} w^o(\{i\}|N\backslash\{i\})$ $= \frac{6275}{5776} + \frac{6275}{5776} + \frac{721}{512}$ $= \frac{661881}{184832}(\cong 3.584)$

(Continued)

GEG 9.2. (*Continued*)

Outcomes	Individual emissions	Total emissions	Individual payoffs	Aggregate payoffs
PESP	$\forall i = 1, 2$ $e_i^* = \frac{5}{92}$ $(\cong 0.054)$ $e_3^* = \frac{5}{23}$ $(\cong 0.217)$	$\sum_{i \in N} e_i^*$ $= \frac{15}{46}(\cong 0.326)$	$\forall i = 1, 2$ $v_i^* = \frac{200}{529}(\cong 0.378)$ $v_3^* = \frac{4099}{1058}(\cong 3.874)$	$\sum_{i \in N} v_i^*$ $= w^\gamma(\{1, 2, 3\})$ $= \frac{200}{529} + \frac{200}{529} + \frac{4099}{1058}$ $= \frac{213}{46}(\cong 4.630)$

One may verify the following properties:

- balancednes: yes, but no superadditivity ($\{1, 2\}$ is a weak coalition: $1.973 < 2.008$)

- internal stability of coalition N: yes ($3.584 < 4.630$)

- the PESP (without transfers) does not belong to the γ-core (coalition $\{1, 2\}$ with 1.973 improves on $0.378 + 0.378$), but the imputation $(1.086, 1.086, 2.458)$ does belong to the γ-core and also satisfies all outside option payoffs

- coalitional externalities:
  in strategies: positive from all coalition and for all receivers
  in payoffs: positive from all coalitions and for all receivers (largest $i = 3$: 1.408-$0{,}976$).

The *Transferable Utility Games* laboratory at the University of Vigo provided effective computational help.

This compatibility issue between the two concepts remains, at this stage, a challenging open topic for further research.

The Propositions 9.1 and 9.2 constitute, in spite of their limitations, a serious argument for excluding internal stability of N, the grand coalition, as a solution concept for the GEG. While this has been known from the start, many years ago, analytically for identical players only and otherwise by means of simulations, what is brought about here is a wider conceptual basis, namely the equilibrium concept of a pairwise PCNE, allowing for the further results stated above.

Numerical experiments with CWS

After Eyckmans and Tulkens 2003 tested for the first time γ-core stability theory in an integrated assessment model, Eyckmans and Finus (2006) did the same with internal-external stability theory, with an updated and slightly modified IAM. In either case this was the CWS model, here reviewed in Lecture 8. Next, Bréchet, Gerard and Tulkens (2011) pursued with a further updated version of the

CWS model where they present a first numerical comparison between the two stability theories.

The absence of the grand coalition as an internally stable one in Table 6.3 of Eyckmans and Finus (2008) (p. 123, first column), as well as in Table 2 of Bréchet, Gerard and Tulkens (2011) (p. 62, column *IS*, last line) does illustrate, with simulations of a "real world" model[11], the impossibility of internal stability for N which had been found repeatedly in previous fictitious examples. The above argument offers analytical cues for identifying conditions under which compatibility can prevail.

9.4   Concluding Considerations

On the scope of the internal coalitional stability concept

Internal coalitional stability theory provides a solution concept which is, in a quite essential way, of partial equilibrium nature: by being an equilibrium, it offers a consistent and well-defined logical structure that characterizes the behavior *some* economic agents. But extending it to all agents, and using it to characterize states of the whole economy as a general equilibrium concept, is shown to be problematic by Propositions 9.1 and 9.2.

A planet-wide problem such as climate change can hardly miss being handled otherwise than by general equilibrium concepts. Given the object of these lectures, namely international environmental agreements with particular attention to climate change, the methodological choice made explicitly from the start explains itself.

---

[11] A similar illustration can be found in the comparison of six integrated assessment simulation models made in Lessman *et al.* (2015). Probably due to the known impossibility of internal stability of N, the focus of this paper is on which smaller coalitions can possibly be internally (and externally) stable. The idea of including γ-core stability in the comparison was lost in that query. Testing for γ-core stability with these six models thus remains an unfinished take in that imperfectly cooperative project.

On achieving cooperation: By surplus grabbing vs. surplus sharing?

While the two concepts rest on the idea of sharing the "ecological surplus", that is, the surplus generated by the move from the no agreement Nash equilibrium to an efficient Pareto outcome in an environmental externality framework, they organize that sharing on quite different grounds. Internal coalitional stability is based on the bargaining ability of a player to grab for himself a part of the global surplus achieved in common within the grand coalition. By contrast, γ-core coalitional stability rests on each coalition comparing what it gets from sharing the common surplus with what it gets from relying on its own resources.

Put in another way, internal stability is obtained by granting the potential free riding player the payoff he could secure *by not cooperating*, that is, his outside option. This payoff is of the nature of a carrot to keep him in the coalition he considers leaving[12] On the other hand, core stability is obtained, instead, by comparing what deviating coalitions could get using their own resources, with a solution that results from the coalitions' resources *being pooled with those of all the other players in the game*. Arguably, this is a stricter form of cooperation and, I submit, a potentially more fruitful form.

On internal vs. γ-core stability and efficiency

Free riding is a special form of instability of a group. Depending upon the stability concept one uses, what free riding designates will vary. Thus, if a core allocation is declared not to be internally stable,

---

[12]At an admittedly higher level of motivation, Weikard (2009) finds to be "a natural assumption to grant each member a *right* (my emphasis) to a position no worse than his outside option" (p. 580), based on a rights-egalitarian sharing theory where "individual claims have priority and it is a collective responsibility to meet them". I do not think that this collective responsibility extends to the appropriation of the individual benefit from *external* cooperation identified in this paper.

that is, lets some i leave the grand coalition, it is because the non-stability statement implicitly rests on the assumption that if i leaves N, $N\backslash\{i\}$ remains as a coalition, possibly reoptimizing its strategy, and *tolerates* i's free riding, that is, it tolerates the global inefficiency induced by i's defection.[13]

By contrast, the γ-core stability concept preserves efficiency in the first place, and does not contain any reference to free riding. As mentioned above, it refers instead, and only, to the resources that deviating (blocking) coalitions can possibly use by themselves, with an aim at improvement, without counting on those of the other players.[14]

Briefly stated, a strategic weakness of the γ-core concept in dealing with the free rider problem is thus that it ignores it. A moral weakness of internal stability is, instead, in that it legitimates free riding.

---

[13]Eyckmans and Finus (2004) do even reward free riding and call it "ideal". Note that to offer his outside option to a possible defector, it is needed to know his preferences. Is there any reason to believe that he will reveal them truthfully, in bargaining on a possible defection?

[14]I have dismissed in Lecture 6 (Section 6.3, pp. 219 and ff.), as unnecessary and misleading, the "disintegration" interpretation of the γ-assumption.

Lecture 10

THE UNFCCC PROCESS: AN ECONOMIC AND GAME THEORETIC INTERPRETATION

The purpose and the message

This lecture is intended to show that, how, and to what extent, the theoretical construct developed in this course is policy relevant. While this theory could be used in many applications, I concentrate on only one, namely climate change.

What I call "the UNFCCC process" is the overall organizational and institutional framework within which the climate change problem is handled at the world level. Its work consists in preparing, facilitating the conclusion of treaties. The Kyoto Protocol, the post-Kyoto evolution of the process and the texts of the Paris Agreement of 2015 are lucidly analyzed in the light of the relevant theoretical concepts.

For the process taken as a whole, the lecture develops the thesis that there is an internal logic in the sequence of these multistage negotiations, and that this logic can be reasonably explained and even supported by current advanced theory.

Plan

The United Nations Framework Convention on Climate Change, Rio 1992

The Kyoto Protocol of 1997

Appraising and the first commitment period, 2005–2012

The Durban ADP, the Doha amendment and the second commitment period: 2013–2020

The Paris agreement of December 2015 (COP 21)

The UNFCCC Process: An Economic and Game Theoretic Interpretation

Introduction

For the last lecture of June 2015, I introduced the topic in the following terms:

"After the 1992 Rio *Convention* and the 1997 Kyoto *Protocol,*

followed by the 2009 Copenhagen *Accords,*

then by the 2010 Cancun *Arrangements,*

then by the 2011 Durban *Platform,*

then by the 2012 Doha *Gateway,*

then by the 2013 Warsaw meeting [no name],

then by the 2014 Lima *Call for Climate Action,*

and now, by the *Paris Agreement* of COP 21 under preparation, does this evolution of the vocabulary reveal a chaotic institutional mess, an unstructured "favela"[1] in the negotiations process? Or can one uncover in it some architecture that shapes the international climatic regime? For an answer, see you at the end of the class..."

From science to policy and diplomacy

In the four-fold interdisciplinary voyage of these lectures, I am entering now a leg that is most typical of the social science stage, namely policy. Here, the obvious challenge is: can, and does, such a sophisticated construct have any impact on actual collective action? More precisely, how about the connection between what science has

---

[1]An expression I am borrowing from Professor Henry (Jake) Jacoby from MIT who used it in a presentation he made at a Stanford, RFF, FEEM conference in Venice 2006 (incidentally, held in the architectural splendor of Palladio's room in the San Giorgio Maggiore monastery). Most of the contents of my discussion of his talk is taken up in this lecture.

to say on climate change and what societies of the world do achieve in this area through their processes of collective decision?

The worldwide dimension of the climate change problems has raised up much governmental activity at the international level, where diplomacy is the main channel of interaction between the actors. To proceed to a scientific analysis of that activity one has to move from "hard" to "soft" forms of science. While the scientific status of economics is, as of today, not much disputed (any more), the status of diplomacy is certainly less clear. But diplomatic activity may of course be an *object* of science, and as such it is probably to be considered as a field of application of political science. Rather than daring to call myself a political scientist, which I am not, I intend in this final lecture to introduce as explicitly as possible the student-reader into the diplomatic, thus political, dimension of the problems that have caught the attention thus far.

This is in the spirit of the Nobel Prize distinction for peace awarded jointly in 2007 to the scientific institution IPCC and the politician Al Gore. Such simultaneously crowning of the scientific and the political dimensions of the climate change problem, materialized in a quite unique and deep going form of international cooperation, was an exceptional way of showing science at its best to the service of mankind, that is, covering the full spectrum that goes from knowledge to action. Notice that the Prize goes to all sciences involved in the IPCC's Assessment Reports. As social sciences are present in quite a large proportion, they have their share in the Prize's appreciation of a contribution to peace. Now, a few years later, do they really deserve it? ... See you at the end of the lectures!

10.1 The United Nations Framework convention on climate change, Rio 1992

Worldwide, governmental negotiations on climate change have been taking place since the late 1980s at the initiative of the General Assembly of the United Nations Organization. From the start all countries of the world are thus potentially concerned by them.

These negotiations led to an international treaty officially called *United Nations Framework Convention on Climate Change* (UNFCCC) signed by the executive delegates of 165 countries in 1992 in Rio de Janeiro and subsequently ratified by the competent legislative bodies of all 193 countries of the world members of the UN.[2] It entered into force on March 21, 1994.

The text is essentially a declaration of intent. For this purpose no mention is made of specific physical actions of environmental relevance such as, e.g. amounts of emissions reductions, but the Convention instead establishes essentially a framework for action in climate matters. The negotiations that have taken place within this framework between governments of the 193 countries have consisted in defining, comparing and evaluating a large variety of possible courses of effective action. In the words of these lectures, negotiations by governments means exploring the players' strategy sets in the game.

For the implementation of any policy, an essential and pre-liminary component was that emissions be known. To that effect, the signatories first committed themselves to submit information regarding inventories of their emissions, annually for the countries listed in Annex 1 of the Convention, less frequently for the others. An administration has been set up, located in Geneva and Bonn, which is in charge of receiving, reviewing, compiling and publishing "national communications" containing these inventories (which did not exist before) as well as other reports on actions taken towards the reduction of emissions.

The other negotiations that take place within the UNFCCC, are accompanied by the scientific body of The Intergovernmental Panel on Climate Change (IPCC),[3] as well as by two technical bodies called

---

[2]193 is the number of members according to the UNFCCC website at the time of completing this manuscript, that is, October 2017. The number of members has varied over the years I am covering in this lecture.

[3]The IPCC was established in 1988 under the joint auspices of the United Nations Environment Programme and the World Meteorological Organization for the purpose of assessing "the scientific, technical and socioeconomic information relevant for the understanding of the risk of human-induced climate change. It

SBI and SBSTA. Last but not least, the UNFCCC also organizes the successive "Conference Of the Parties" (COP)'s. They have met annually since 1995 in various parts of the world.

These are the actors of the process, accompanying the governments in their ambitious but complex multilateral enterprise. The UNFCCC is the place where to find out how are prepared climate relevant *strategies* in the technical sense of these lectures and what they consist of.

10.2   The Kyoto Protocol, 1997

The Kyoto Protocol, signed at COP 3 in December 1997, is a major development in the post-Rio evolution of the negotiations. It may be considered as the main achievement, thus far, that the UNFCCC has produced. Its importance lies mainly in the fact that it specifies that a list of countries decide to achieve numerically defined emission reductions before a precise time deadline, reductions that they consider binding for them once they ratify the text.

Taking the Protocol as it was signed, I present in this section a series of its characteristics, features and properties. Independently of the subsequent developments of its actual implementation I consider it as a very useful benchmark for understanding the many various issues raised by the climate change problem in general. A theoretical reference similar to the one I am to follow here below had led me, with three colleagues, to offer at the time[4] an essentially constructive view of the Protocol. As this view still inspires the presentation made here I restate many of its arguments. It remains in sharp contrast with more critical views offered by other commentators.[5]

---

does not carry out new research nor does it monitor climate-related data. It bases its assessment mainly on published and peer reviewed scientific technical literature." See in the References the list of *Assessment Reports* issued periodically from 1992 until 2014. A sixth one is currently in preparation.

[4]In a paper written and circulated in 1998. It was eventually published as Chander, Tulkens, van Ypersele and Willems (2002).

[5]For instance, Nordhaus and Boyer (1999) have argued under the no less than dismal title of "Requiem for Kyoto" that

Main features of the Protocol

Let me briefly note the main features of the Protocol[6] that are important from the point of view of our analysis:

1. The Protocol establishes *dated caps* of yearly maximal emissions allowed, expressed in percentages of their 1990 emissions, for countries listed in an Annex labeled "B", to be met on average over the period 2008–2012.
2. It establishes the principles of (a) an *emissions trading system* (ETS) by the countries (or by their entities) and of (b) a *joint implementation* (JI) *mechanism* between Annex B countries.
3. It establishes a *clean development mechanism* (CDM) as a way to involve the non-Annex B countries (especially developing ones) in some particular form of JI and emissions trading.
4. It allows for trade in emissions *only among those countries that ratify* the Protocol. It also proposes that trade in emissions be suspended with countries that do not fulfill their obligations under the Protocol.

"the strategy behind the Kyoto Protocol has no grounding in economics or environmental policy. The approach of freezing emissions at a given level for a group of countries is not related to a particular goal for concentrations, temperature, or damages. Nor does it bear any relation to an economically oriented strategy that would balance the costs and benefits of greenhouse-gas (GHG) reductions."

Thus, while the "Requiem" was celebrated a long time ago, the current survival of the Protocol until 2020 (see Section 10.4) clearly suggests that "the rumors of [its] death have been much exaggerated". On balancing costs and benefits, see a method based on integrated models, but leading to less pessimistic views, presented in Bréchet and Tulkens (2015).

[6]In Kyoto, the text of the protocol was adopted and signed unanimously by the delegates of the 84 countries, including the US, who participated in the negotiations, with ratification by parliaments to take place later on. The Protocol was to enter into force only if 55 countries, representing 55% of the world total emissions ratified it. This occurred in February 2005, but ratifications by more countries continued and by October 2009, 189 countries had ratified the Protocol. In spite of the signature of the US government, the US Congress never ratified, letting the USA be the only non-ratifying member of the United Nations Organization.

5. It recognizes a *Financial Mechanism* established by Art 11 of the UNFCCC to provide funds to finance activities of developing country Parties, and provides guidance for the operation of special Funds established for that purpose.

In summary, a "cap and trade" scheme, where the rigidity of the caps is mitigated by the flexibility of the ETS, JI and CDM mechanisms, accompanied by the confirmation of an earlier promise of financial support to developing countries.

One may also note some features that the Protocol does not have:

- The Protocol does not set targets in terms of the accumulated stock of greenhouse gas (GHG), nor does it specify a world temperature target. Its object is not a trajectory of the stock of GHG or of the temperature, but well maximum emission flows per year at some point in time by Annex B countries.
- No explicit emission caps are proposed for non-Annex B countries; such caps, if at all, have to be negotiated in future rounds of negotiations.
- The parties to the Protocol are expected to enforce the commitments made by them within their own countries. But the text does not specify sanctions if a ratifying country does not fulfill its obligations under the Protocol, except for the above provision on being excluded from emissions trading.

Finally, a compliance regime, including details of sanctions for non-compliance with commitments, has been set up in subsequent negotiations and eventually established by the Marrakech Accord signed at COP 7 in December 2001, which is binding for all ratifying countries.

Economic and game theoretic ideas supporting the Protocol

The cap and trade scheme in the reference model

How does this cap and trade scheme fit in the reference model of the above lectures? Quite simply, the connection is readily made as

soon as actions by the parties explicitly specified in the Protocol
do correspond to what is defined as decision variables in the
economic-ecological model, or equivalently as strategies in the global
externality game. This correspondence is obvious as far as emissions
of GHG are concerned: they are mentioned explicitly in the Protocol's
texts summarized under item 1 above.

One major element is new, however, namely trade in emissions,
which is absent from Lectures 2 and 3. Thus a market must be
introduced in our model. Before entering into a formal description
of it, let me explain what justifies its presence in the Protocol. The
fundamental reason comes from a teaching of pure economic theory,
namely the argument that *trade is, in general, an organizational
instrument that contributes to the achievement of efficiency.* While
widely accepted today by most professional economists throughout
the world, this argument is nevertheless often put in doubt, on the
one hand by those professionals whose attention is blindly focused
on market "failures" (which are admittedly real, but not always
overwhelming) and, on the other hand, by those non-professionals
who at best ignore the efficiency enhancing property of market
allocations or at worst simply confuse markets with capitalism. It
is therefore worthwhile to spend some time on a detailed explanation of what market forces can contribute, in the international
environmental context of climate change, to the achievement of the
societal objective of efficiency. To that effect, let me backup a few
steps.

*Efficiency and coalitional stability: A reminder on the
role of transfers*

Let $(\bar{e}_1, \ldots, \bar{e}_n)$ be some vector of emissions of all countries called
henceforth *reference emissions.* These may be taken as simply
the currently observed ones, or thought of as those of the Nash
equilibrium, or of the business-as-usual equilibrium, or those of any
other outcome of national concerns for the use of energy. In the sense
used below the term designates emission levels that parties are willing
to agree upon at the start of the negotiations, *not* as an objective, but
instead as the levels they would return to in case of non-agreement.

In the spirit of Lecture 3, these are likely to be higher than the world efficient emissions $e^* = (e_1^*, \ldots, e_n^*)$ defined there.

Given my assumption that negotiations on climate change aim at achieving world efficient emissions, the obvious question to consider now is whether and how the Kyoto Protocol, as part of the UNFCCC, does contribute to that objective by having all countries reduce their emissions from what they accept to be the reference levels to what is recognized as the world efficient levels — formally that each country i reduces its emissions by $\bar{e}_i - e_i^*$. As this entails abatement costs, i.e. $g_i(\bar{e}_i) - g_i(e_1^*)$, as well as benefits[7], i.e. $-d_i(\sum_{j=1}^{n}(\bar{e}_j - e_j^*))$, the latter should exceed the former for each country i — call this the *"benefit minus cost test"*[8] — in order to ensure that the emission reductions be agreed upon voluntarily. Now this is unlikely to be the case *in all countries*, for two reasons ignored by Dasgupta: (a) some may have high abatement costs and low benefits, while others may have low abatement costs and high benefits. How to coordinate international action in such case? And (b) some groups of countries might have structures of costs and benefits such that instead of moving to the proposed e_i^* they might benefit more from moving to some other emission target $\tilde{e}_i$ with lower costs $g_i(\bar{e}_i) - g_i(\tilde{e}_i)$ These two reasons are the rationales justifying the scheme of transfers (6.19) introduced in Lecture 6: it guarantees that benefits after transfers exceed costs for all individual countries as well as for all coalitions of countries.

Recall that the scheme consists of amounts, expressed in units of GDP, given by the formula

$$T_i = \{g_i(\bar{e}_i) - g_i(e_i^*)\} - \frac{d_i(z^*)}{\sum_{j=1}^{n} d_j(z^*)} \left\{ \sum_{j=1}^{n} g_j(\bar{e}_j) - \sum_{j=1}^{n} g_j(e_j^*) \right\},$$

for each $i = 1, \ldots, n$, (10.1)

where $T_i > 0$ means a receipt by country i, while $T_i < 0$ means a payment by i. Recall from Lecture 6 that the first expression within

---

[7]That is, damage costs avoided.
[8]Alternatively called "benefit-cost rule" by Partha Dasgupta — recall Proposition 3.5. of Lecture 3.

braces on the RHS is equal to country i's total abatement cost, and the second expression within braces is equal to the world's total abatement cost of the move from the reference emissions to the world efficient ones. The scheme thus requires country i not to bear its own abatement cost $g_i(\bar{e}_i) - g_i(e_i^*)$ but to bear instead a damage-weighted proportion, $d_i(z^*)(/ \sum_{j=1}^{n} d_i(z^*)$, of the world's total abatement cost (where $z^* = \sum_{i \in N} e_i^*$).

Clearly, $\sum_{i=1}^{n} T_i = 0$, which ensures a balanced budget if an international agency were established to implement the scheme. Notice the role played by the reference emissions $(\bar{e}_1, \ldots, \bar{e}_n)$ in the calculation of the transfers $(T_1, \ldots, T_n)$. In Lecture 6, I assumed the reference emissions to be equal to the Nash equilibrium emissions and showed that the scheme enjoys the game theoretic properties of coalitional stability in the sense of the core of a game.

But what if the reference emissions are not equal to the Nash equilibrium emissions? In particular, if these are equal to the business-as-usual emissions of the type discussed in Lecture 3? It turns out that the game theoretic properties of the scheme are robust with regard to the reference emissions. If $(\bar{e}_1, \ldots, \bar{e}_n)$ are equal to the business-as-usual emissions of Definition 3.3, then the corresponding transfers $(T_1, \ldots, T_n)$ have the same game theoretic properties as when they are equal to the Nash equilibrium emissions. This is seen intuitively as follows: (a) the business-as-usual emissions are generally higher than the Nash equilibrium emissions, and (b) given (a) the payoff that a coalition can achieve for itself is lower, since the emissions of members not in the coalition are higher. The core is thus larger and includes more imputations.

Competitive emissions trading in lieu of transfers

Unlike the scheme of transfers specified in equation (10.1), the Kyoto Protocol does not specify explicit transfers among the countries. It only[9] proposes the caps just described on the emissions. For the

---

[9]The *amounts* of the funds referred to under item 5 of my Protocol's summary presentation above are not mentioned in the Protocol's text. The role of these

purposes of the present lectures, the major intellectual interest of
the Protocol resides in the fact that these caps, together with the
trade they induce, constitute a scheme that may be shown to be *an
instrument for implementing **both** world efficient and coalitionally
stable emissions.* To see this, one has to redefine the above scheme
of transfers in terms of emission caps and trades, which can be
done by introducing the concept of a "competitive emissions trading
equilibrium".

**Definition 10.1. A competitive emissions trading equilib-
rium relative to emission caps** $(e_1^0, \ldots, e_n^0)$ is a vector of emissions
permits $(\hat{e}_1, \ldots, \hat{e}_n), \hat{e}_i \geq 0 \; \forall i$, and a price $\hat{\gamma} > 0$ such that

$$\hat{e}_i = \arg\ \max(g_i(e_i) + \hat{\gamma}(e_i^0 - e_i)) \quad \text{for each country } i = 1, \ldots, n,$$

$$(10.2)$$

and

$$\sum_{i=1}^{n} \hat{e}_i = \sum_{i=1}^{n} e_i^0. \tag{10.3}$$

The price $\hat{\gamma}$ is expressed in units of the composite GDP good
(as defined in Lecture 2) per unit of emissions. Notice that the first-
order conditions for a maximum of (10.2) imply, assuming an interior
solution:

$$g_i'(\hat{e}_i) = \hat{\gamma}, \quad i = 1, \ldots, n. \tag{10.4}$$

At such a competitive equilibrium in emissions, the countries
choose freely the amounts of their production and emission activities
$\hat{e}_i$ so as to maximize their domestic output. At the solution of (10.2)–
(10.3) if for some i the difference $(e_i^0 - \hat{e}_i)$ is positive then the country
sells on the market that amount of permits, which is in excess of what
it needs. At the price $\hat{\gamma}$ this yields a receipt of $\hat{\gamma}(e_i^0 - \hat{e}_i)$ whereas
if $(e_i^0 - \hat{e}_i)$ is negative, country i spends the amount of $\hat{\gamma}(e_i^0 - \hat{e}_i)$

---

funds is logically independent of the cap and trade mechanism and of the implicit
transfers they contain, discussed in the present subsection. A connection with the
funds committed under the Financial Mechanism is made in Sections 10.3 for the
Kyoto Protocol and 10.5 for the Paris Agreeement.

to purchase the amount of permits it needs to reach its individual equilibrium.

At the world level and price $\hat{\gamma}$, the total demand and supply of emission permits are equal and the total emissions remain restricted to $\sum_{i=1}^{n} e_i^0$, since by construction $\sum_{i=1}^{n} \hat{e}_i = \sum_{i=1}^{n} e_i^0$. Finally, by (10.4), the single world price achieves that

$$g_i'(\hat{e}_i) = g_j'(\hat{e}_j) \text{ for all countries } i, j = 1, \ldots, n,$$

which is a necessary condition for international efficiency in the allocation of emissions among countries (recall Proposition 3.6 of Lecture 3).

Now, let the chosen emission caps $(e_1^0, \ldots, e_n^0)$ be computed from the world efficient emissions $(e_1^*, \ldots, e_n^*)$ and from the reference emissions $(\bar{e}_1, \ldots, \bar{e}_n)$ so as to satisfy for each country i the condition

$$(e_i^0 - e_i^*) \sum_{j=1}^{n} d_j'(z^*) = \{g_i(\bar{e}_i) - g_i(e_i^*)\}$$

$$- \frac{d_i'(z^*)}{\sum_{j=1}^{n} d_j'(z^*)} \left\{ \sum_{j=1}^{n} g_j(\bar{e}_j) - \sum_{j=1}^{n} g_j(e_j^*) \right\}$$

$$(10.5)$$

and let the permits price be computed as $\gamma^* = \sum_{j=1}^{n} d_j'(z^*)$, that is, the aggregate marginal abatement cost used to compute the efficient level of emissions $(e_1^*, \ldots, e_n^*)$. Then one may assert:

Proposition 10.1. *If an emissions vector $(e_1^*, \ldots, e_n^*)$ and a permits market price γ^* together constitute a competitive emissions trading equilibrium relative to caps $(e_1^0, \ldots, e_n^0)$ and are such that for all $i \in N$ (10.5) is satisfied, then the induced state of the economic-ecological system is coalitionally stable in the sense of the γ-core.*

Indeed, the RHS of (10.5) specifies an amount (paid or received) equal to the transfer T_i advocated in (10.1) as sufficient to induce coalitional stability of the world efficient emissions. Operated in this way, *the cap and trade scheme does achieve the objectives of environmental and global efficiency as well as coalitional stability* enounced in Lecture 3.

Note that while the world efficient emissions $(e_1^*, \ldots, e_n^*)$ are independent of the reference emissions $(\bar{e}_1, \ldots, \bar{e}_n)$, and thus fixed, the emission caps $(e_n^0, \ldots, e_n^0)$ proposed in (10.5) are not. Therefore, once $(\bar{e}_1, \ldots, \bar{e}_n)$ is agreed upon, the formula (10.5) specifies a one-to-one correspondence between $(e_1^*, \ldots, e_n^*)$ and $(e_1^0, \ldots, e_n^0)$. This means that if the countries are agreeable to the reference emissions $(\bar{e}_1, \ldots, \bar{e}_n)$, and wish to achieve the optimum $(e_1^*, \ldots, e_n^*)$, then they should also be agreeable to the assignment of emission caps $(e_1^0, \ldots, e_n^0)$ together with the resulting competitive trade in emissions. Indeed, this would not only lead to the world efficient emissions $(e_1^*, \ldots, e_n^*)$, but also to transfers, implicit in the trade, having the property of coalitional stability with respect to the reference emissions. This shifts the argument from an agreement on emission caps $(e_1^0, \ldots, e_n^0)$ to an agreement on reference emissions $(\bar{e}_1, \ldots, \bar{e}_n)$.[10]

The shift just mentioned amounts to replace a zero sum game — negotiating the caps directly — by a more complex one that has all characteristics of a non-zero sum game, that generates global payoffs higher than those of the pre-negotiation situation.

---

[10]Some clarification on the vocabulary I am using may be in order:

- *"caps"* = *"allowances"* = *"quotas"* = e_i^0 are initially assigned amounts of emittable pollutant to country i, whereas

- *"permits"* = *"QELROS"* = $\hat{e}_i$ are effectively emitted pollutant, for the amount of which country i must own an equal amount of permits minus its cap e_i^0.

  The amount of permits which are *traded* by country i is thus $(\hat{e}_i - e_i^0)$, bought if that difference is positive, sold if negative.

- *"Reference"* emissions is a vocabulary used in Chander and Tulkens (2002, Section 6; 2011, Section 3.1) as a basic component of their formulae to compute the transfers of the CT solution as well as the corresponding caps $(e_1^0, \ldots, e_n^0)$ of Proposition 10.1, as determined by equation (10.5).

Agreeing on reference emissions

However, reaching an agreement on reference emissions might not be easy, for at least the following two reasons. First, the current Nash or business-as-usual reference emissions $(\bar{e}_1, \ldots, \bar{e}_n)$ that determine the pollution caps $(e_1^0, \ldots, e_n^0)$ and the transfers $(T_1, \ldots, T_n)$ may be considered unfair, especially by those countries which are in the early stages of their economic development. They currently have comparatively low emissions, while the emissions of developed countries are high, and formula (10.5) implies that the higher the reference $\bar{e}_i$ the higher the cap e_i^0 obtained by country i. As in the future, when they will have developed, the currently developing countries will have higher emissions, they might argue that those should be used already now as reference emissions instead of the current ones. Second, if the reductions to be achieved in the emissions, i.e. $\bar{e}_i - e_i^*$, are very large (as proposed by some countries), they are politically infeasible, at least in the short run.

The Kyoto Protocol can be seen to address both issues. While the emissions of the non-Annex B (developing) countries have not been subjected to caps, these emissions will rise over time as a result of their ongoing economic development and those of the Annex B countries will fall as a result of the abatements they are committed to. With time the emissions of the former will become comparable to those of the latter — likely to be sooner in China than in India — and these might *then* be subjected to caps. As to the second point, the Kyoto Protocol only requires relatively small reductions for the immediate future, leaving further reductions to later periods. In other words, the Kyoto Protocol as it stands is not inconsistent with the ultimate goal of reaching an agreement on appropriate reference emissions $(\bar{e}_1, \ldots, \bar{e}_n)$ in some future round of negotiations.

What this means in policy terms is that the developing countries should not oppose the Kyoto Protocol and leave the issue of the initial allocation of pollution rights to future negotiations. In the meantime, implementation of the Kyoto Protocol will not only reduce the emissions of Annex B countries and thus improve the global environment, but will also strengthen the position of the developing countries in future rounds of negotiations as their emissions will continue to rise as their economies grow and become comparable to those of Annex B countries.

Showing the efficiency and coalitional stability of the trading equilibrium

Let me observe first that when meeting its Kyoto assignment cap e_i^0, every Annex B country gains in trading in the way just described, compared with meeting this cap on its own. This follows from the inequality

$$g_i(\hat{e}_i) + \hat{\gamma}(e_i^0 - \hat{e}_i) \geq g_i(\hat{e}_i + (e_i^0 - \hat{e}_i)) = g_i(e_i^0), \qquad (10.6)$$

where $\hat{e}_i \geq 0$ in the LHS is the amount of country i's actual equilibrium emissions generated by the production $g_i(\hat{e}_i)$ and $\hat{\gamma}(e_i^0 - \hat{e}_i)$ is the value of the permits sold by i if positive, or bought by i if negative, in equilibrium. This inequality holds true irrespective of whether $(e_i^0 - \hat{e}_i)$ is positive or negative. It is implied by the concavity of the production function if one takes into account the property (10.4) of the said equilibrium. Figure 10.1 illustrates.

As a consequence if each Annex B country were to meet its Kyoto assigned cap e_i^0 on its own, the world output would be equal to $\sum_{i=1}^{n} g_i(e_i^0)$ which by the above argument is less than $\sum_{i=1}^{n} g_i(\hat{e}_i)$, the world GDP amount that can be reached with the competitive trading equilibrium emissions relative to the same caps $(e_1^0, \ldots, e_n^0)$. Equivalently, the aggregate Kyoto commitment $e^0 = \sum_{i=1}^{n} e_i^0$ is reached at a lower cost than it would without trading emissions. So much for efficiency.

However, this does not imply that each *coalition* of countries would be willing to participate in competitive emissions trading. For that to be true one must show further that no grouping of countries can gain even more by forming a separate bloc and trade emissions only among themselves. The following argument, based on the theory of market games, does the job.

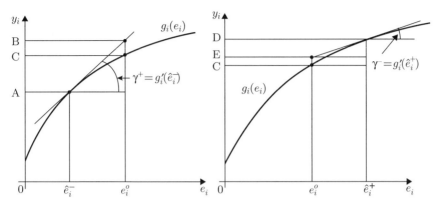

(a) *A permit selling country.* Given an international price γ^+ for tradable permits, country i, by choosing equilibrium emissions $\hat{e}_i^-$ instead of emissions equal to its assigned cap e_i^0 and selling as permits the difference, reduces its output by a value of CA but gets a revenue of BA $= (e_i^0 - \hat{e}_i^+)\gamma^+$ from that sale.

(b) *A permit buying country.* Given an international price γ^- for tradable permits, country i, by choosing equilibrium emissions e_i^+ instead of emissions equal to its assigned cap e_i^0 and buying permits for the difference, increases its output by a value of DC while paying only DE $= -(e_i^+ - e_i^0)\gamma^-$ for that purchase.

Fig. 10.1 **A country's gain by trading *in lieu* of meeting its cap e_i^0 on its own.**

Let $S \subset N$ be a bloc of countries whose members decide, given their aggregate emission cap $\sum_{i \in S} e_i^0$, to adopt some joint policy restricting the trade among them only. The maximum payoff such a bloc of countries can achieve is

$$w(S) = \max \sum_{i \in S} g_i(e_i) \text{ subject to } \sum_{i \in S} e_i = \sum_{i \in S} e_i^0, \qquad (10.7)$$

given the aggregate emissions caps assigned to them.[11]

Consider again $(\hat{e}_1, \ldots, \hat{e}_n)$, the competitive trading equilibrium emissions relative to $(e_1^0, \ldots, e_n^0)$. It is shown below that the payoff of the members of S under the competitive equilibrium is not lower than their payoff when they form a separate bloc (as defined in (10.7)). To that effect, I have to show that $\sum_{i \in S} g_i(\hat{e}_i) \geq w(S)$.

---

[11]I ignore the damages in the payoffs because they remain the same, the aggregate emission cap $\sum_{i \in N} e_i^0$ being fixed.

Using (10.6), this is equivalent to

$$\sum_{i \in S} \left(g_i(\hat{e}_i) + \hat{\gamma}(e_i^0 - \hat{e}_i) \right) \geq \sum_{i \in S} g_i(\tilde{e}_i),$$

where $(\tilde{e}_i)_{i \in S}$ is the solution to (10.7). Since $\sum_{i \in S} \tilde{e}_i = \sum_{i \in S} e_i^0$, there remains to show that

$$\sum_{i \in S} g_i(\hat{e}_i) + \hat{\gamma} \left(\sum_{i \in S} \tilde{e}_i - \sum_{i \in S} \hat{e}_i \right) \geq \sum_{i \in S} g_i(\tilde{e}_i).$$

Using the same argument as above, this inequality is true with each g_i concave and $\hat{\gamma} = g_i'(\hat{e}_i)$ in competitive emissions trading equilibrium. Therefore, and irrespective of whether $(\tilde{e}_i - \hat{e}_i)$ is positive or negative,

$$g_i(\hat{e}_i) + \hat{\gamma}(\tilde{e}_i - \hat{e}_i) \geq g_i(\tilde{e}_i), \quad i \in S.$$

This leads to the conclusion that no coalition of countries has an incentive to form a separate bloc instead of not participate in worldwide competitive emissions trading. I am thereby rediscovering — in fact, just applying — a general property of competitive equilibria known as their "core" property, which says that competitive equilibria belong to the core of an appropriately defined cooperative game.[12]

Desirability of free trade in emissions

While the Kyoto Protocol allows trade in emissions among the Annex B countries, it leaves open the questions of the extent and the nature of such trading. Economic and game theoretic considerations can be further called upon to deal with these issues.

As to the extent of trading, that is, the number of participants in the trade, the market equilibrium theory generally favors trade among the largest number of economic agents. This is also implied

---

[12]The present game is a pure market game where externalities play no role, since, once the emission caps are fixed, the public good aspect of the problem disappears. Strategies are e_i and payoffs $g_i(e_i)$. One is left with only the private goods-type problem of allocating the emissions (which are the strategies here also) between the countries. Note, however, that this game is formulated for a production economy and is not the standard pure exchange economy.

by the previous argument against the formation of separate trading blocs. Thus, it is in the world's overall economic interest that non-Annex B countries, whose emissions are not subject to caps, be nevertheless allowed to participate in the trading process. I shall argue below that the CDM contains provisions to that effect. A policy implication is that this mechanism be designed so as to make it as open as possible to the largest number of countries. The fact that no caps were assigned to these countries is irrelevant if the full benefits of trade in emissions are to be realized.[13]

As to the nature of trading, the same body of theory advocates that the institutions governing the trades be designed so as to ensure that they be as competitive as possible — competitiveness meaning here that all participants behave as price takers. It is indeed only for markets with that property that efficiency, coalitional stability and worldwide maximal benefits are established.

Regulatory provisions that restrict competitiveness in the emissions trading process are thus to be avoided. Such as, for instance, provisions allowing for market power to be exerted by some traders so as to influence price formation to their advantage, as well as regulatory controls that would impede sufficient price flexibility; or still, as proposed by some, limiting the quantities that can be traded.

As is well known, the larger the number of participants, the more competitive the market is likely to be: our argument favoring a large extent of the market is thus also one that favors competition.[14] Large numbers are admittedly neither the only way nor a sufficient condition to ensure the competitive character of a market, but they are a powerful factor.

---

[13]One might even argue that it is similarly irrelevant whether or not a country ratifies the Protocol, or has not met its commitment under the Protocol. Excluding a country from trade in emissions on any pretext hurts *all*. However, exclusion from trade is the only threat that can be exerted against a non-complying country: the loss so incurred is thus to be seen as a cost to ensure compliance.

[14]The argument on the role of markets to achieve coalitional stability is also reinforced by a central result in economic theory (Debreu and Scarf, 1963; Edgeworth, 1881) according to which competitive equilibria are coalitionally stable only if the number of traders is large.

JI and CDM as alternative forms of emissions trading

For the reasons mentioned above, restricting trade in emissions among Annex B countries alone may affect both Annex B and non-Annex B countries. This raises the question of how to involve the non-Annex B countries in emission trade without having them committed to any emission caps? That seems difficult, but it is not impossible.

In fact, it is the main purpose of the CDM. In essence, trade occurs through "certified project activities"[15] located in non-Annex B countries. The certification determines the amount of emissions reduction ("certified units") that the project generates, in comparison to a baseline that specifies what the emissions would be in the absence of the project. The amount of the reduction so achieved can then be sold by the initiator of the project to any economic agent belonging to an Annex B country, with the certified amounts being credited to meet the commitment of the country to which the purchasing party belongs.

The price at which the certified units are sold and purchased is determined by supply and demand for them, which are in turn determined by the supply of project activities and the demand of those Annex B countries for which buying such units is cheaper than reducing their own emissions. That competitive conditions should prevail in the formation of this price is as necessary as in the formation of the price of the caps in the emissions trading scheme described above.

Developing countries often interpret the CDM as a form of trade that distributes the gains from trade entirely to the carbon credit importing (read Annex B) country and none to the carbon credit exporting (read non-Annex B) country. More specifically, it has been often proposed that rather than paying the credit-exporting developing country i the market value at the competitive price, i.e. $\hat{\gamma}(e_i^0 - \hat{e}_i)$, the credit-importing countries may pay only the actual cost of abatement, i.e. $g_i(e_i^0) - g_i(\hat{e}_i)$, which is strictly less than $\hat{\gamma}(e_i^0 - \hat{e}_i)$ given the strict concavity of the function. This form of

---

[15] As per the vocabulary of Article 12 of the Protocol.

trade in emissions can be given effect by the importing countries by systematically "offering" to cover the cost, and cost alone, of abatement activities in developing countries on a project- by-project basis. But the developing countries may not accept this form of trading if carbon credit importers collude so as to behave monopolistically. Against this bias, there is the countervailing force of competition among the project authors, if there are many.

In the CDM construct, the determination of the baseline is of fundamental importance. As with emissions trading, the reference to it in the operation of the mechanism points to the fact that the ultimate solution rests on the determination of reference emissions. It was shown above how these can lead to well-defined caps for each country. A similar reasoning may be applied to CDM projects. More generally by being part of the Protocol's architecture, CDM projects enhance its efficiency properties.

10.3   Appraising the first commitment period: 2005–2012

In this section, I proceed to an appraisal of the situation of the world climate regime that is actually prevailing during the first commitment period 2008–2012 given the non-unanimous ratification of the Protocol and the characteristic divide between Annex B and non-Annex B countries. The central question is whether the Kyoto Protocol is to be considered as just an Annex B agreement, or is it to be seen, beyond the appearances, as a worldwide agreement? In this section, I reproduce and defend the second thesis as it was developed in the joint paper of Chander and Tulkens (2011, Section 4).

Game theoretic interpretation of the post-ratification situation

Let me clearly distinguish between the text of the Protocol (1997) and the actual situation after it's of entry into force (2005). The *text* of the Protocol expresses a collective choice of specific actions to be taken by each one of the 190 countries which signed it. However, due to the non-ratification by the US, the *situation* that prevails after all

ratifications have taken place is different. It is this factual situation
that I now consider as an outcome of the negotiations involving the
190 countries.

The appropriate solution concept

It is a tempting interpretation to say that the Protocol is *an "Annex
B" agreement, partially cooperative among the Annex members, with
the rest of the world remaining outside of this "coalition".* This
interpretation is prompted by the view that the members of Annex
B "do something" (i.e. abate somewhat — from their 1990 levels),
whereas the others "do nothing" (i.e. remain at their BAU or non-
cooperative strategy).

Upon reflection, such a view neither corresponds to the full
specifications of the Protocol, nor is it a well-grounded application
of the game theoretical notion of "strategy". Rather, the situation
prevailing under the Protocol is more correctly interpreted if this is
done in terms of what *all* countries are effectively doing during the
first commitment period and for each of them in accordance with
their ratification decision. In other words, in terms of a precisely
identified *strategy profile*. In game theoretic technical language a
strategy profile[16] is a set of actions, not statements, not intentions.
So, one must look at the effective actions of the signatories.

During the period 2008–2012 these actions are the outcome of a
game with $n = 190$ players-countries, where:

- 189 form a coalition[17] because they are acting jointly as specified
  in the Protocol,
- 1 remains out of the Protocol, and is acting individually the way
  it wishes.

---

[16] Recall its precise sense in the general Definition 4.2 of Lecture 4, its application
to the GEG following Definition 5.1 for the static model in Lecture 5, and to the
DGEG following Definition 7.6 for the dynamic model in Lecture 7.

[17] Thus the term "coalition" refers, here, to a set of players said to act jointly
because they ratify a treaty. This is of course quite different from those groups of
countries who often form to prepare tactics in view of the treaty.

In terms of worldwide emissions, the strategy profile consists of actions that can be grouped in three categories:

(i) Emissions reduction to their QELRO[18] levels, for the 37 ratifying countries and for the amounts listed in Annex B,

(ii) Emissions not quantified but equal to the BAU or non-cooperative equilibrium levels, for the other 152 ratifying non-Annex B countries,

(iii) Emissions not quantified but equal to the BAU or non-cooperative equilibrium level, for the single non-ratifying country.

This situation has a coalition structure akin to what I call in the previous lectures a *partially cooperative Nash Equilibrium relative to a coalition* (PCNE),[19] in which the coalition in question is the set of 189 ratifying countries whose joint strategy is what they have committed themselves to do according to the provisions of the Protocol. The strategy of the singleton outside of the coalition, that is the US, is whatever emissions it decides to choose for itself. This describes in terms of the factual situation of the period 2008–2012, a "strategy profile" of the 190 players of the whole world, specifying (a) the jointly agreed upon strategies of the members of the coalition of 189, and (b) the individually decided strategy of the outsider.

The PCNE thus appears to be a concept whose structure describes fairly well what prevails during the commitment period 2005–2012. What about its properties?

On efficiency and coalitional stability of the prevailing situation

Since the situation, like any PCNE, is not a Pareto efficient one, it could logically be better for all, including the US. Less obvious is the property of stability, which I consider now in some more detail.

---

[18]On that vocabulary, recall Footnote 10.

[19]Recall Definition 5.3 of Lecture 5 for the static version and Definition 7.8 of Lecture 7 for the dynamic version. In our previous writings, this concept was called a "partial agreement Nash equilibrium with respect to a coalition".

As documented in Lecture 9, the issue of stability of an international environmental agreement has been a matter of debate in the literature since the early 1990s, between the two theses of "internal–external stability" and "core strategic stability".[20] To what extent are these two theories pertinent for interpreting the world climate regime effectively prevailing during the first commitment period?

The central claim of the internal–external stability theory[21] is to assert the intrinsic instability of large coalitions. This instability is attributed to the logical inevitability of free riding allowed by the public good characteristic of the externality involved. As a result, only small coalitions of countries[22] can prevail and be expected to sign an agreement improving on the *status quo*.

Clearly, this view is not supported by the facts since a coalition of 189 countries has formed to ratify the Protocol. Within that large coalition, the free riding temptation seems not to be at work. Admittedly, there is not much room for free riding on the part of those in this group whose strategy is their BAU, but even among the group of 37 countries of Annex B one does not observe free riding in spite of the wide possibilities they have for it.[23] Thus, contrary to the assertion of the internal–external stability theory, an unquestionably large coalition is holding together for the period 2008–2012, after the entry into force of the Protocol.

As mentioned, the prevailing situation for that period is better explained by calling upon the concept of partially cooperative Nash equilibrium of Lectures 5–7. There are two aspects to it. On the one hand, there is the point of view of coalition *formation*: a coalition of 189 countries has formed, leaving one player outside of it.

---

[20]Tulkens (1998) and Chander and Tulkens (2009) are successive stages of this ongoing debate.

[21]An excellent non-technical summary presentation can be found in Carraro (2008).

[22]Just one or several coexisting is left unprecise by the authors.

[23]After ratification, there does arise problems of non-compliance, typically with Canada and some others from 2010 on. But this is a different issue: the strategies I am interpreting now are the ratification decisions, not the subsequent decision of non-compliance with a duly ratified agreement.

That coalition appears not to dissolve before the expiry date of 2012, admittedly with some exceptions as the deadline approaches. Being a Nash equilibrium between the US and the rest of the world, the situation so described has thus some degree of stability. On the other hand, this PCNE is very close to the grand coalition since out of the 190 players of the game there is only one missing. Since the negotiations are still continuing within the framework of the UNFCCC, the situation may be seen as an intermediate stage towards the eventual formation of the grand coalition. Admittedly, the US in the meantime is pursuing its free riding policy with a current gain from not joining probably higher than from ratifying the Kyoto Protocol.

On caps and trades

The plural in the subtitle is not a typo: it reflects the institutional reality that followed 2005. According to the Kyoto Protocol, the traders are the states, and the states only. Within the European ETS however, the traders are other economic agents than the member states: private as well as public enterprises, private and public institutions and organizations, private and public bodies of all kinds. Several other ETS's have been created since 2010, among which one in California, one among a group of North American Eastern states, and most recently in China.

For a detailed and historical presentation of the European system, Delbeke and Vis (2015) is a first hand source. Further ones are Gronwald and Hintermann (2015) and especially Ellerman (2015).

Reflections in the wake of Kyoto, as of 2012

The above interpretation of facts and policies is inspired by referring only to the static model of Lectures 3, 5 and 6. The dynamic economic-ecological model and its associated dynamic game of Lecture 7 offer further insights, the main one of which is to suggest that there are good reasons to think of the Kyoto Protocol not as a one shot agreement but instead as being embedded in a sequence of successive such agreements, each of which initiating a distinct commitment period following the first one of 2008–2012. For conceiving this sequence the theory developed in Lecture 7 suggests the considerations that follow. I group my arguments into a series of six themes. Some views that they imply for the next commitment period 2012–2020 are taken up thereafter in Section 10.4.

The sequence of time intervals

I take now as reference model a dynamic game in discrete time where at each time interval the alternative of cooperation *vs.* non-cooperation is considered. It is resolved by applying γ-core theory at each stage of a dynamic version of the economic-ecological model. This structure is inspired by the methodology of dynamic programming in discrete time in contrast with open loop optimal control. This allows for redefining strategies at each stage of the solution path given what the state variables of the problem are, each of these stages being the solution of a one shot game that determines the course of the path for the next stage.

I thereby rationalize the view that the Kyoto Protocol is not to be seen as a single and fixed arrangement for the long term, but rather as being one step embedded in a sequence of one shot commitment periods, beginning with 2008–2012, and each of which in the future commanding a treaty of its own. In that framework, the meetings of Copenhagen (2009), Cancun (2010) and Durban (2011) have logically not led to treaties in the strict sense of the word; they were rather preparations for a 2012 second treaty which is the Doha Amendment to the Kyoto Protocol, covering 2013–2020. Similarly, the Paris 2015 COP 21 prepares strategies that, when adopted, will be the content of a third Protocol.

The players

It has been proposed to define the various caps or other forms of restrictions on emissions not by countries but rather by sectors and subsectors of the world economy, industrial (energy, chemical, etc.), agricultural (forestry, various forms of land use, etc.), a.s.o. At first sight this may be justified by the considerable differences by which the various sectors can proceed to emission reductions, as reflected by differences in their respective marginal abatement costs. A similar argument applies to the case of cities, a large number of which around the world have taken initiatives of their own, given the specific character of the damage costs they incur. In the modeling, should not these instances be considered as the actors in lieu of the states?

But this would ignore the fact that in international affairs conducted at the initiative and in the framework of the United Nations Organization, the key decision making units are the nation states. For this problem of international public good provision, sectors are to implement the states' decisions, not to make them. Of course, they can exert pressure, but the decision makers, that is, the players in the game theoretic model, remain the countries. Such pressures are more correctly interpreted as influencing the parameters of the payoff functions of the game, and more precisely, the damage cost and abatement cost functions[24] of the underlying economic-ecological model.

The nature of strategies

Let me first make clear that the term "strategies" is used here in its game theoretic sense, that is, what the countries' decisions effectively bear upon — what is also called "decision variables", e.g. in the optimization literature. How does the cap and trade mechanism, the corner stone of the architecture of the Kyoto Protocol, fare in this respect? It has been contested in many circles, the main alternatives being regrouped under the heading of "command and control". What can be said on these alternatives?

In the reference model of Lectures 2 and 7, the decision variables are the emission levels e_i whose effects on the environment were accounted for through a damage cost function $D_i = d_i(\sum_{j \in N} e_j)$. As the cap and trade mechanism directly bears on the actual individual

---

[24] And more generally the production functions in view of enhancing carbon free technologies.

emission levels e_i of each country i, the institutional structure specified by the Kyoto Protocol is closest to the reality at stake.

By contrast, what do "command and control" bear on? More precisely, what decisions do they consist of? In terms of the basic model, the answer to this question is that command and control essentially consist in modifying the production functions $y_i = g_i(e_i)$ in the sense of making it technically feasible to obtain reduced emissions e_i for various (possibly all) levels of output y_i. This means interfering with production processes throughout the economy. It may be formulated by denoting as $b_i > 0$ the quantity of resources devoted to technical progress (e.g. R and D expenditures) having the property just mentioned, and rewriting the production functions as $y_i = g_i(e_i, b_i)$ with $\partial g_i(e_i, b_i)/\partial b_i > 0$. If technically feasible, this represents a way to reduce emissions.

However, unlike with emissions e_i, the link between the decision variables b_i and the environmental target of temperature change (call it z) is only an indirect one and difficult to quantify. In addition, what is designated by b_i is an aggregate whose components may vary considerably. Therefore, the actions of the parties involved are hard to specify and monitor. In addition, in the multiagents setting that characterizes our problem, the environmental results eventually obtained in terms of z can hardly be traced back in a precise manner to actions taken on the variables b_i by the various countries. As a consequence, cooperative agreements are much more difficult to formulate and implement in terms of these variables.

Emissions abatement vs. temperature change

By 2009 a change in the negotiation "strategy" (the word being taken in the diplomatic, non-game theoretic sense — "tactics" is probably a better one) has put forward a form of agreement that bears on the ambient environmental variable z, namely the amount of temperature change (or an upper bound on it), rather than on the level of emissions, i.e. the amounts of CO_2 emitted. In the vocabulary of dynamic optimization and dynamic games of Lecture 7, this amounts to make the agreement bear on the state of the system instead of on the control variables that determine it.

Of course, the state of a system is not a control variable. Yet, the main element of the Copenhagen Accord of 2009 is the recognition by the heads of nation-states who signed it that an upper bound of $+2°C$ (above pre-industrialization time) is a necessity. Reference to emission reductions that could achieve that goal is left to an annex, containing promises to decide about them in the future.

It is unquestionable that the recognition by the US and China of the necessary $+2°C$ ceiling is a major step towards the world's protection against climate change. However, decision-wise, that is, in the technical sense of the expression of "decision variables" that I have been using since the beginning of this section, the accord is not a decision. Similarly, in game theoretic terms, it is not a joint strategy either. Therefore, the text of the Copenhagen Accord is by no means a solution of the game of climate change.

However the annex of the Accord invites submissions of "pledges" by countries of voluntary emission reductions. These are indeed strategies, or controls, in the technical sense. Whether these voluntary commitments are consistent with the goal of no more than $+2°C$ temperature change is another story. Yet, the very fact that these pledges are made, made publicly known, and thereby hopefully being actually undertaken is in the spirit of acting on controls. This 2009 change in the negotiation procedure has found its confirmation in the following COPs, culminating at the Paris COP 21. I elaborate on this point in Section 10.5.

A fragmented vs. global world climate regime?

Back in 2011, before the end of the first commitment period, the question was often raised whether a "fragmented" structure of multiple regional agreements could emerge, making unlikely the continuation after 2012 of the global cap and trade mechanism.

Lecture 9 has presented the theory of internal–external stability of coalitions, which questions the logical likelihood of a worldwide agreement on climate change, and concludes that only a fragmented structure of multiple regional agreements on climate change could ever emerge as an equilibrium outcome. As a corollary, this view directly objects to, or considers unlikely, the continuation after 2012 of the global cap and trade mechanism that was nevertheless established by the Kyoto Protocol.

However, I would argue that the multilateral and mutual recognition of these pledges is a clear indication of a will of cooperation among the countries that have expressed them, and not a sign of fragmentation. Similarly the silence of the countries which do not express any pledge is naturally interpreted as their choices of business as usual individual strategies, since there is no sign, among them, of countries seeking to establish separate groups of any kind. Moreover, it appears that a larger set of countries than those listed in Annex B of the Kyoto Protocol announce future emission levels in quantitative terms: they will thus be quantified *ex ante*, which was not the case under the Kyoto Protocol. This step is also to be considered as an increase in cooperative behavior since by doing so, these countries reduce the uncertainty regarding their future emissions, *vis-à-vis* the other players in the game.

These developments made Chander and I conclude in our 2011 last paper that our characterization of the situation under the Kyoto Protocol as an intermediate stage towards the formation of a world grand coalition, is not contradicted by the Copenhagen and Cancun events, and asserts instead that they are consistent steps in that direction.

The participation of developing countries

As in any global game with diffuse externalities, overall efficiency requires full participation of all concerned parties, that is, of all countries. In addition to the difficulties due to the temptations of free riding, participation by developing countries is further problematic for reasons specific to the climate change problem.

A first reason is summarized in the argument of "historical responsibility" of the countries which have polluted in the past. Let me recall first that this notion is not without connection with the externality phenomenon, a connection already mentioned in our review of externalities in Chapter 2: in addition to being a problem of stock externalities, climate change is also one of *intergenerational* externalities, because of the durability over centuries of the carbon that accumulates in the atmosphere. Emitters of today affect recipients of tomorrow, most of whom are not even born. And victims of today are similarly affected by emissions made in the past by generations that no more exist. To that extent, direct negotiation between polluters and pollutees as I described in Chapters 3 and 6 (let alone coasean bargaining) cannot take place. Pollutees of today cannot charge anything to the polluters of the past, and symmetrically, polluters of today cannot buy from their future victims the right to emit today.

There is however an indirect way to make the polluters of the past "pay", namely through their descendants. Indeed, as the emissions of the past have accompanied a glorious economic growth that some of today's populations are enjoying, it sounds as a natural application of the "polluters pay principle" that these populations take now a corresponding share in the responsibility for the current climate change.

The above argument is put forward when the determination of the time profile of abatement policies is under discussion. In particular, it takes the form of suggesting that developed countries "abate first", letting the developing ones join the effort only later, that is, when they will have reached a level of economic welfare comparable to the one of today's developed countries. In fact, this viewpoint was accepted at Kyoto in 1997, since according to the Protocol, no developing country is required to restrict its emissions at least up until 2012 while developed ones, that is, those listed in Annex B, are to have reduced globally theirs by the same deadline by an amount 5.2% with respect to their 1990 levels. In diplomatic discussions on post Kyoto strategies in Copenhagen and later COPs, this view was implicitly present in the insistence of some developing countries for a plain extension of the Kyoto Protocol after 2012.

In what form, to what extent, and at what speed is such participation to occur? In the spirit of the interpretation of the Protocol presented in Section 10.3, participation of a country may have two meanings, which are complementary. One meaning is that the country just makes known in the treaty the quantitative emissions path that it considers as its BAU path for the commitment period under discussion, and to which the country commits itself in the sense that it serves as its reference emissions in the trading scheme. Let me call this the passive form of participation. As argued above, this minimum form has essentially the merit of reducing uncertainty. The other meaning of participation is to make known a quantitative reference emissions path lower than the country's BAU path, to which the country voluntarily commits itself for the period under discussion. Let me call this the active form of participation.

Agreement on a (new) Annex B that lists the countries with their respective quantitative reference emission paths just stated, reflecting their participation commitments, is then the answer to the second question raised above.[25] As to the speed at which this evolving participation might occur, it is determined at each stage by the length of the next commitment period, a length that is part of the negotiations, as the Durban and post-Durban discussions have revealed.

Thus, the principle that "developed countries should abate first, letting the developing ones join the effort only later", takes the form of agreeing on gradually adjusted reference emissions in successive commitment periods which are all the more distant from the anticipated BAU emissions that the country is considered more "developed". This last point, i.e. development level, can be determined, for instance, on the basis of a comparison between the country's current GDP per capita and a "welfare threshold", to be negotiated. This is in the same spirit as the Jacoby rule[26] which proposes a formula linking the emissions reductions to a negotiated welfare threshold. However the proposal made here consists instead in using such a threshold for determining *the reference emissions* on which the ensuing emissions trading is based, as originally mentioned in Chander (2003) and restated here in the subsection of Section 10.2

---

[25] In fact, such a new Annex B would not be necessary because it would simply be identical to the list of all ratifying countries which by definition have announced an emissions path: BAU or lower.

[26] Presented in Jacoby, Schmalensee and Sue Wing (1999).

on agreeing on such references. In either case, the purpose is to implement over time switches of countries from passive to active participation in the sense described above, based on their evolving development levels. Comparable proposals are made in Frankel (2010).

Referring to another reason that makes problematic, in the mind of many, the participation of developing countries, is the quandary created by the often asserted trade-off between emission limitations and growth of the economy. On this trade-off, also faced by developed countries, the game theoretical construct described above, of gradual participation resulting from the solutions of a sequence of games played at successive commitment periods, does not bring any specific additional element. Growth considerations are just to be included in the specification of the BAU and other reference emissions to be agreed upon at the beginning of each Commitment period.

Concluding consideration on the Kyoto Protocol

In 2012, it was already possible to give an answer in the following terms to the question raised at the beginning of this lecture. Kyoto, being a "protocol", is an effective International Environmental Agreement, to the extent that it specifies a strategy profile that has been adopted by the countries and thereby constitutes a solution to a well defined game. This solution is interpreted here as conducive to worldwide cooperation, in a dynamic perspective. By contrast, Copenhagen, Cancun, Durban do not specify strategies, they are therefore not treaties, and they needed not be. This is why they are called *Accords*, *Arrangements*, or *Platform*. However they prepare for the next protocol, or other "treaty". And this one will be part of a sequence of treaties, each with its (possibly long) commitment period, during which some form of worldwide cooperation should prevail.

There is an *internal logic* in that itinerary, which is not a "favela" with no architecture. The logic is the one of a persistent strive towards efficiency and stability, that this lecture endeavors to uncover, using to the tools of game theory and of economics laid out in the previous lectures.

10.4 The Durban ADP, the Doha amendment and the second commitment period: 2013–2020

In the context of this interpretation of the UNFCCC process, two decisions taken and three facts that occurred towards the end of the first commitment period appear to be major ones, namely:

- At the Durban December 2011 (COP 17) meeting, the launching of a *Working Group* (dubbed ADP) of the UNFCCC with a mandate to develop *a protocol, another legal instrument, or an agreed outcome with legal force under the Convention, applicable to all Parties*, to be presented for adoption in December 2015, and to enter into force no later than 2020.
- At the Doha December 2012 (COP 18) meeting, the adoption of the *Doha amendment to the Kyoto Protocol* establishing as a second commitment period (January 2013–December 2020) a prolongation of the said Protocol.[27]
- In the meantime, compliance problems arose, which ended up with Japan and Russia announcing in 2011 that they did not intend to be under the obligation of quantitative emissions limitation or reduction for a second commitment period after 2012, and Canada formally withdrawing from the Protocol on December 15, 2012.

In summary: No collapse of the UNFCCC process, which since 1992 remains an "all parties" process explicitly reaffirmed as such. No collapse of the Kyoto Protocol either (in force since 2005): it is prolonged until 2020, with the same number of signatories and identity in the coalition, although with substantially different strategies of some of its members — thus: a modified PCNE.

In that perspective, the deadline of 2020 now becomes a new major occasion to reshuffle the cards, for which γ-core theory is

---

[27]An amendment requires no ratification but well "receipt by the Depositary of an instrument of acceptance by at least three fourths of the Parties to the Protocol". At this time (November 2018) 122 Parties have deposited such instrument. While the stated proportion requires 144 depositors, the Protocol survives on the basis of the 1969 Vienna Convention on the Law of Treaties.

saying, in a rough application: either the US joins the coalition of the 189 ratifying, and the *all* players' coalition forms to sign a new Protocol with coordinated emissions reductions and no outside free riders any more. Or the US still declines to join, in which case the prevailing partially cooperative coalition of the Kyoto Protocol collapses, and the whole game is repeated from scratch, in a new search for cooperation.

10.5   The Paris agreement of December 2015 (COP 21)

The Paris COP 21 took place after these lectures were completed. Publication delays and other circumstances make it possible, happily, to devote some space to it presently. I write "happily" for two reasons. First, because the Paris event is a landmark in the process studied here at length, and absence of coverage in this text would be frustrating for both the author and the reader. Second, what I wish and have to say on it, on the basis of these lectures, has already been invited for presentation as an article published in 2016 in a major economics journal in France.[28] Thanks to the courteous authorization of the publisher Dalloz, I am pleased to present here an extended summary of the main points of that paper, some of which are partly edited.

The texts of COP 21, officially denoted as ***Decision CP.21***[29] **and its *Annex*** (referred to henceforth as the "Paris texts") are scrutinized in what follows from the particular point of view of the extent to which economic and game theoretic concepts can be considered to inspire them. It will be shown here below that

---

[28]See Tulkens, H., "COP 21 and Economic Theory: Taking Stock", *Revue d'Economie Politique* (Paris, France) 126, 471–486, May 2016.

[29]That part consists of 140 paragraphs, which are the decisions taken by the Parties at the meeting. The Annex that follows, entitled "Paris Agreement", is a 29 articles document that the Parties decide to submit for ratification to their respective competent authorities. The ratification requirement distinguishes legally the annex (which is binding for the ratifying countries and is thus a treaty) from the decisions text (which is not a treaty).

this is partially the case in some of the intentions, but the texts themselves contain more diplomatically formulated promises than effective implementation of relevant mainstream and well established scientific concepts of the disciplines entertained in these lectures.

Let me announce the program with the following subtitles: (i) The grand coalition in sight? (ii) On strategies; (iii) On outcomes; (iv) On dynamics; (v) On mitigation, adaptation, loss and damage, and transfers; (vi) On carbon pricing as an instrument relegated to "voluntary cooperation". Then follow conclusions of this review as well as for the course.

The grand coalition in sight?

When learning about the Durban COP 17 decision recalled above to "launch a process to develop a protocol, another legal instrument, or an agreed outcome with legal force under the (UNFCCC) Convention *applicable to all Parties*[30]", I could not resist thinking that the economic rationality of public goods theory was going to prevail in international action on climate change. The problem being unanimously recognized in the profession as one of a "global public good", hence requiring an equally global joint decision framework for all countries of the world, the logic was thus confirmed that a full-fledged form of cooperation is called for — the one of the so-called "grand coalition" in game theoretic jargon — and here it was going to be implemented. In fact, more than 185 countries were present at the COP 21 meeting of 2015 in Paris, and eventually 195 signatures of the Paris texts followed. The required double threshold of ratification by 55 countries representing 55% of world CO_2 emissions was reached in October 2016 implying entry into force of the Annex on November 4 of that year.

For citizens of the planet, all this was very good news. Unfortunately, a detailed study of the texts motivated by economic theory is not that rejoicing.

---

[30]My italics.

On strategies

What contribution from game theory can one find in the Paris texts? After a first reading, one is tempted to answer "none", for the simple reason that there is missing one of the three components of a game, namely a specification of the strategies. While players are obviously the parties to the Convention and their payoffs are their individual development levels, there are no environmentally relevant actions to be taken by the players being specified. At variance with the Kyoto Protocol where actions were explicitly stated in great detail, most typically amounts of GHG emission reductions including the specification of units of measurement. The Paris texts contain no quantities, *a fortiori* no units. The game is incompletely defined. Let me elaborate a bit on this.

Stretching the nature of strategies?

There are only two numbers appearing in the texts under scrutiny (other than administrative ones): "2°C" and "1.5°C", in Art. 2(a). Couldn't these be called the strategies? Remembering Lecture 7, such vocabulary assimilation would be confusing a *state* variable with a *decision* variable.

But what should strategies be? In addition to emission reductions other decisions can be candidates for being strategies such as transfers, be they financial, or materialized in some specific physical resources, or still consisting in elements of information or knowledge, provided they are definable unambiguously and, when quantifiable, expressed in terms of well-defined units. Unlike the Kyoto Protocol,[31] the Paris texts cannot be considered as the outcome of a strategic game, simply because the strategies (if defined, as they should, as actions representing quantifiable magnitudes of components of the problem) are not specified.

---

[31]Typically, the Kyoto Protocol mentions three categories of magnitudes, each with well defined units of measurement: Assigned amount unit (AAU) for exchanges through emissions trading, Emission reduction unit (ERU) for emission reductions or emission removals from JI projects, and Certified emission reductions (CER) for emission reductions from CDM project activities.

Yet, the Paris texts are an outcome of something (other than a game), which one may find in a series of *commitments to action*. These can be regrouped in two main categories:

(1) Commitments by all Parties to adopt in the future some quantitatively defined *emission reductions*, individually determined: individual strategies for most countries, possibly coordinated for groups of countries such as, e.g. the EU.

(2) Commitments by some Parties (called "developed country Parties"), to provide *financial transfers* to other players (called "developing country Parties"), not in lump sum form but in relation with the adaption needs, loss and damage needs, capacity building needs, equity feelings, of the second group, to be determined by future COPs.

In this wider interpretation, fuzziness remains as to which Parties are "developing" and which ones are "developed". This distinction being clear in the Kyoto Protocol with the Annex B list, one knows who the players are. The Paris texts neither contain such list nor refer to one in some other document. Thus, the incompleteness in the formulation of the game extends even to the uncertainty on the identity of the players.

Now, let me attempt not to remain confined within purely classical forms of economic games, and think of the Paris texts as the outcome of a game where the strategies are not actions, but precisely these announced "commitments", or promises of actions. Not impossible: one may remember the example of games in public goods theory where strategies are not the physical goods, but instead preference revelation (Drèze and de la Vallée Poussin, 1971; Roberts, 1976; Henry, 1979): more precisely announcements of willingness's to pay per unit of the public good. In these games, strategies do not bear on amounts of the public good,[32] but they are nevertheless numerical values. To allow one to exploit the so suggested analogy,

---

[32]In fact, they are formulated in games whose solutions serve as information inputs in a resource allocation processes that determine the physical quantities of the public good.

the Paris Agreement should provide more precise indications of what the "commitment sets" could be. Otherwise no commitment announcement game can be formulated, no rational behaviors can be characterized, and no game theoretic solution concepts can be called for.[33]

In a further stretching of the strategies concept one could consider that the "mechanisms" to which it is repeatedly referred throughout the two Paris texts are in fact the strategies of the Paris COP 21 game. But again, the lack of definition in the texts of what a mechanism is makes this attempt illusory.

Changing the source of strategies

In general, the process of *formation* of strategies in a game situation is rather weakly covered in the literature that I know of: where do strategies come from? The history of climatic negotiations since their active beginnings with the Berlin mandate (COP 1, 1995) shows a recurrent debate on where proposals of action should initiate and then percolate until final adoption by the Assembly of Parties. A procedural distinction has often been made between two methods dubbed, respectively, "top down" *vs.* "bottom up". Up until the signature of the Kyoto Protocol and its generalized ratification, the former method dominated. The COP 15 in Copenhagen (2009) fundamentally changed this procedure into the latter one, when the US President and Chinese Prime Minister urged state negotiators to proceed by "pledges" voluntary expressed by the countries.[34] These eventually became what now appears as Nationally Determined Contributions (NDCs hereafter) in the Paris texts.

For logical arguments able to explain this important procedural evolution I know of no game theoretic explanation. Institutionally, top down methodology can be assimilated with "planning" imposed somehow by an external benevolent umpire, whereas bottom up

---

[33] Filling out all these requests may be seen as formulating the components of the extensive form of the game sketched out to at the outset.

[34] Called later and for some time "intended" NDCs.

is often considered to be an expression of autonomous individual decision making.

From a short enquiry on the preparation of past negotiations I learned that even during the top down years, Parties were always invited to submit initial proposals to the UNFCCC Secretariat, with this instance presenting syntheses in various subgroups of negotiators in view of final collective decisions. What is fundamentally changed with the bottom up methodology is at the synthesis stage. Ignoring "technocratic" concessions concocted among experts within UNFCCC subgroups, the Paris texts simply consider that NDCs, when received, are registered as they are and made publicly known. Period. *They are not an object of negotiation any more.*

This change of procedure in the formation of strategies should strike any economist familiar with public goods theory, because of the major implication for the result of the negotiation that I show in the next subsection on the outcome.

Implementing strategies: Stocktake, naming and shaming

Contrary to the Kyoto Protocol there are no sanctions mentioned in neither one of the two Paris texts. The achievement of the announced contributions is thus not mandatory. The ineffectiveness of sanctions is a known drawback in many international agreements in general, and the Kyoto Protocol is no exception, in spite of quite elaborate and innovative attempts made with the Marrakech Accords of 2002.

Rather than punitive sanctions, the Paris Agreement introduces in Art. 14 a mechanism sometimes informally dubbed "naming and shaming" that should induce implementation by creating a reputational risk — an essentially political cost — for those parties that would not implement their NDCs. Under the official denomination of "transparency" the main practical instrument of naming and shaming consists in repeated occasions of mandatory *reporting* on emissions and transfers of many kinds at the future COPs. These are called periodic "global stocktakes", that should start in 2018 and occur every 5 years thereafter.

There exist "reputation games" in the literature, but I am not aware of any environmental application that might have inspired the negotiators in this direction. Absent such information one may think that they have invented an innovative solution, in a compliance game otherwise rarely dealt with.[35]

On outcomes

Equilibrium with subscription

While the two Paris texts do not specify explicit strategies that would allow for a well grounded game theoretic interpretation, the framework they establish is structured enough to allow one to speculate on the state of the world that could prevail if the kind of strategies these texts announce were to be implemented. Let me go now into a bit of science fiction.

Here, economic and game theories combine nicely. For practitioners of public goods theory the logical outcome at the world level of the "bottom up" procedure of determining future emissions in terms of NDCs should evoke the concept of *equilibrium with subscription* first introduced by Malinvaud (1969, pp. 173–176, pp. 213–214 of the 1972 translation). This basically economic concept[36] is also shown to be of the nature of a Nash equilibrium in a game in which the decision variables (the emission strategies in the application below) are "voluntary contributions" of the players, and the sum of these contributions determine the quantity of the public good, i.e. a state variable. Being based on voluntary strategies, the concept may be seen as very democratic. Malinvaud[37] also shows, however, that an equilibrium with subscription is not Pareto efficient: away from it, with cooperation, things can go better for all.[38]

---

[35]The work of Hovi and Areklett (2004), who deal with the sanctions designed in the Marrakesh Accords is an exception. It might be a useful starting point for a game theoretic study of the name and shame sanction system.

[36]In the spirit of the Cournot equilibrium in oligopoly theory.

[37]As well as followers who dealt with that concept, among which Cornes and Sandler (1986 chapter 5) and Hirshleifer, Glazer and Hirshleifer (2005, pp. 521–527).

[38]Roberts (1976) later showed that the larger the number of consumers in the economy, the farther the equilibrium with subscription is from Pareto efficiency.

Application of that concept to the economic-ecological model[39] of Lecture 2 and its associated GEG of Lecture 5 is immediate and leads to the one of "environmentally nationalistic equilibrium" of Lecture 3.

Turning to the Paris texts of today, I hereby propose to interpret them as establishing a regime of successive equilibria with subscription. I elaborate below on the dynamics and focus now on characteristics of one typical stage of that sequence. First, while being inefficient in the Pareto sense, the world emissions are nevertheless not reduced to zero at any such equilibrium. This is in contrast with what is called "business as usual" equilibrium, that is, the equilibrium of the economy when no emissions abatement policy at all is in force. The subscription equilibrium concept rests, indeed, on assuming that each country does implement a domestic policy on the basis of only its own preferences *vis-à-vis* the environment. The interpretation proposed above thus consists in asserting that the NDCs, as filed by the countries with the Secretariat of the UNFCCC, are precisely the expression of these exclusively national policies. Environmentally, the sum of the NDCs is thus a *juxtaposition* of domestic policies. With this interpretation in terms of Malinvaud–Nash behavior, this sum of abatements needs not be zero. But its level is less than the efficient one — and possibly much less, given the Roberts (1976) result.

I am reaching here one of the main points of failure of our discipline in inspiring the negotiators at the Paris conference. While economic science is conceptually rich enough to characterize the (likely) contents of the texts and lucid enough to point out its efficiency deficit, it obviously has failed to play a role in orienting the design of this contents towards world efficiency. Diplomatic skills succeeded in getting an agreement but one which is devoid of part of its economically desirable contents.

Malinvaud (1969) pointed out that with cooperation, an economic state better than the equilibrium with subscription is

---

[39]The Malinvaud concept was formulated at least 10 years before international environmental problems started being considered in the economic literature.

reachable. Paradoxically, the Paris texts are full of requirements, expectations and demands for cooperation between Parties in the determination, the promotion and the facilitation of the NDC's. But these calls are just for the achievement of *their own* (Nash) abatement policies; there is no word in these texts on going beyond these policies. The cooperation that Malinvaud is calling for is instead one towards Pareto efficiency, which essentially consists in emission reduction levels that go beyond the Nash equilibrium levels. In the Paris texts, cooperation is not towards achieving efficiency, it is only towards ensuring a minimal environmental "cohabitation".[40]

Briefly stated, the Paris Agreement is an impressive worldwide cooperative achievement towards achieving a ... non-cooperative climatic regime of the Malinvaud–Nash equilibrium type. There is of course a reason for that: negotiators in Paris cared more for reaching at least some environmental progress in all countries and in particular where nothing has been done so far, rather than meeting economic theoretical standards.

PCNEs, climate clubs and little creeks

Lecture 9 was entirely devoted to the game theoretical controversy bearing on the issue whether the organization of the climate regime worldwide would be effectively a global one, gathering all countries of the world in a joint achievement of an efficient outcome, or a fragmented one with subgroups of countries ("coalitions") each adopting policies of their own. In Section 10.3, I have presented what is relevant from this stream of literature for the present confrontation between theory and the policy achievements under the UNFCCC process. Briefly (re-)stated, from the date of entry into force of the Kyoto Protocol (2005) until the end of the first commitment period (2012), it is claimed that a PCNE relative to a coalition is prevailing, the coalition consisting of the set of the

---

[40]In Bahn and Haurie (2008) an attempt is made to combine the non-cooperative equilibrium strategies with the countries meeting a global constraint on the state of the system, such as $2°C$. It would be of interest to explore its connection with the outcome implied by the Paris texts.

189 Parties that have ratified the Kyoto Protocol, with one country outside of that coalition pursuing its domestically preferred policy namely the USA. As noted in Section 10.4, from 2012 on, under the extension of the Protocol decided by COP 18 in Doha, the coalition of ratifiers has been changing: due to some defectors, there are by now more numerous non-ratifiers[41] of the Amendment, adopting their domestically preferred policy instead of complying with their previous Kyoto commitment.[42]

The Paris texts of COP 21 have no relevance for this characterization of the climate regime since they bear only on what will prevail after they will be ratified. For that period, and on the basis of these texts, one may venture that it could be another PCNE relative to some coalition. Typically an equilibrium with subscription with some "subscribers" being a coalition — e.g. the European Union — with abatements occurring both within and outside of that coalition. In any event, on the basis of these texts, it appears very illusory to expect an efficient state of affairs to ever prevail.

In his presidential address to the American Economic Association, Nordhaus (2015) has introduced the nicely chosen nickname of "climate club" for a coalition of the kind just discussed. But his reference to the Buchanan (1965) theory of clubs may be a source of confusion for students of public goods theory: Buchanan's clubs are defined for excludable public goods, thus, clubs of consumers who can deprive some others from access to the good, whereas climate change, a global public good,[43] is physically non-excludable. However, if one ignores that reference, then the Nordhaus clubs

---

[41] As reported above, only 122 countries have ratified the Doha Amendment. The current exact status is therefore unclear of those countries who have ratified the Kyoto Protocol but not yet the Doha Amendment.

[42] Notice that in making assertions of belonging or not of a country to the stated coalition I refer to the ratification decisions and not to whether or not the country belongs to the subset of those who are assigned abatements specified in Annex B of the Protocol. Recall that non-Annex B countries are also ratifiers: only in that capacity can they participate in emission reductions through the CDM.

[43] A public *bad*, for sure! This is why describing the problem as one of "a global externality with public good characteristics" is a better terminology.

are indeed coalitions of producers of the global public good — producers of CO_2 in our case, as the coalition is assumed to do at a PCNE.

Arts. 4.16–4.18 of the Paris texts allude to the European Union acting as a "climate club" under the overall scheme of the Paris texts. If this indeed materializes the result will clearly be a PCNE relative to the EU coalition. Now, the texts implicitly allow for possibly more than one such coalition forming in the future. Each coalition doing by definition some abatement, this suggests an equally nice picture drawn by my colleague at Collège de France Roger Guesnerie who sees and advocates PCNEs relative to several coalitions as "little creeks" eventually forming a large river[44]...

On dynamics

Compared with the Kyoto Protocol, the Paris texts contain many more provisions concerning the future, and more precisely, on the organization of that future. They are here, to some extent, more explicit on the characterization over time of the strategies than on the content of the strategies.[45] Basic in this respect are the provisions of Arts. 4.2 and 4.9, according to which *every 5 years* each Party shall communicate successive NDC's, and be informed of the "global stocktake" referred to in Art. 14. Various modalities accompany this disposition: in Art. 4.3 there is a "ratchet" clause saying that each time, the reported ndc is to represent a *progression* beyond the Party's current NDC. As to the strategies themselves, industrialized countries *shall* have economy-wide absolute targets of emission reduction (Art. 4.4), whereas developing countries *should*

---

[44]See Guesnerie (2015).

[45]As stated in the remarkable presentation of the Paris texts by Obergassel *et al.* (p. 3): "The question is (...) not whether the Paris Agreement will deliver the emission reductions necessary, but whether the agreement has the potential to catalyze further changes..."

only "move over time" towards economy-wide reduction or limitation targets (Art. 4.4).[46]

Turning now to economics, when dynamics has been introduced in the game theoretically inspired literature on international environmental problems, in the late 1990s and early 2000s, the methodology of optimal control has been brought in and dominated the scene. It focused on Pareto efficiency and Nash equilibria of trajectories of emissions, consumptions, investments, etc., that extend over very long periods of time (often centuries). This was the case with both analytical theoretical and simulation models (including mine, as in Lecture 8).

Compared with this methodology, one may observe that the time profile of the climate regime proposed and announced by the Paris texts lies ahead of optimal control. Ahead in the sense that the procedure of quinquennial communications and stocktake institutionalizes the necessity of taking into account the state of the system as it is at that point as well as the possibility of rethinking the strategies on that basis. This is not possible with the optimal control models used by, say, Nordhaus and Yang (1996) as well as Yang (2008) in the RICE model, by Bréchet, Gerard and Tulkens (2011) with the CWS model and more recently by Bréchet and Tulkens (2015), or still by Bosetti *et al.* (2013) with the WITCH model.

The alternative methodology of dynamic programming with feedback effects of state variables proposed in Germain, Toint, Tulkens and de Zeeuw (2003), and Germain, Tulkens and Magnus (2010) as well as in Lecture 7 lends itself better to a formulation of successive renegotiations over time. The concepts of PCNE r.t. a coalition, and of sequential γ-cores developed in these texts are in good agreement with the future proposed by the Paris texts. They could help in achieving their objectives.

---

[46]Incidentally, notice that the difference between "shall" and "should" in Art. 4.4 is intended, showing again a difference of commitment between developing and developed country Parties.

On mitigation, adaptation, loss and damage, and transfers

Since the early 2000s, adaptation has gained an important place in the overall thinking on the climate change problem and it is given a prominent place in the Paris texts: Art. 7 on adaptation now parallels Arts 3 and 4 on mitigation. It appears as an object of major concern and rightly so in general, and from the strict economic point of view in particular. Indeed, that kind of action will mobilize in the future large amounts of resources in many countries, and it is therefore worth considering with as much attention as mitigation. It was surely an error to have it absent from the Kyoto Protocol.

From the economic theoretic point of view, the reasons for international cooperative agreements on adaptation are different from those necessary for mitigation. Mitigation bears at reducing the amount of a public bad that affects all economic agents, whereas adaptation is more of the nature of a private good due to its essentially local character and therefore does not affect all. The former requires cooperation from all because without it an efficient provision cannot be reached. It bears on the total amount of mitigation. By contrast, an efficient level of adaptation essentially depends on who are the beneficiaries of it. Its appropriate level rests on a comparison of local costs and benefits. This does not tell, however, whether or not a country, where an adaptation investment is envisaged and justified, has the resources to over its cost. A recent paper by Bréchet Hritonenko, and Yatsenko (2016) deals with this issue in a dynamic general equilibrium setting.

The cooperation called for by the Paris texts on the issue of adaptation is dominated by this last consideration. Knowing that the major part of damages will occur in developing countries, covering the costs of large adaptation expenditures will be impossible for them, even for projects where the efficiency criterion — that benefits exceed the cost — is satisfied. Only transfers can ensure the desirable decision in such cases.

I purposely regrouped above, in Section 10.5 (p. 390), in two categories of decisions, the two kinds of strategies listed there: one bearing on magnitudes of physical emissions, the other on transfers of resources. Among the latter, financial transfers linked with emission reductions (e.g. Art. 4.5) do obviously contribute to financing the public good. The others (Art. 7), when taking a share in the finances of adaptation projects, also contribute to efficiency in achieving the proper balance between the respective roles of adaptation and mitigation[47] in the fight against climate change. When they are paid as compensation for loss and damage (as in Art. 8), they are essentially distributional.

In the game theoretic literature, transfers are seen as cooperation enhancing and stabilizing instruments whereas in the economic development perspective, which very much dominates the Paris texts, their distributional function is privileged.

On carbon pricing as an instrument relegated to "voluntary cooperation"

As is well known, the marginal abatement costs differ across countries at a Nash equilibrium of the global environmental game — thus at the equilibrium with subscription of the economy. There are thus social efficiency gains to be made through transfers if designed so as to equalize these marginal costs. And the simplest institutional form for this to occur is the one in which the countries transfer to one another emission units against some *numéraire*, through a competitive market. This elementary economics must have been present in the mind of the conceptors of Art. 6 of the Paris Agreement annex, because it is all in there — but, strangely enough, in a quite hidden way.

Indeed, under the expression of "voluntary cooperation schemes", Art. 6.2 of the Paris texts mentions the possible "use by the Parties of *internationally transferred mitigation outcomes* towards nationally

---

[47]Roles that are delineated in Tulkens and van Steenberghe (2009) in the benefit–cost perspective.

determined contributions ...", and Art. 6.4 pursues in announcing that "a mechanism (...) is established" to organize that instrument towards the mitigation of GHG emissions by the parties "on a voluntary basis". Commentators (Obergassel *et al.*, 2016) further observe that according to that article all countries can use the announced mechanism, which should combine features of CDM and JI[48], and that par. 38(f) of the CP.21 decision "recommends that this mechanism be designed on the basis of (...) experience gained and lessons learned from existing mechanisms and approaches adopted under the Convention and its related legal instruments."[49]

The good economics of the Kyoto Protocol are thus present — and there is perhaps even more, given the kind of vocabulary used — but in such terms that the words emission units, price of carbon, market are totally absent from the 9 sections of Art. 6 of the Agreement as well as from the entire par. 38–39 of the Decision. How come? Diplomatic language to have it in without saying it, I have been told, due to skeptic opposition to market mechanisms on the part of some delegations.[50] More constructively, Arts 6.8–6.9 of the Agreement and par. 40–41 of the Decision announce that a framework is defined to promote *non-market* approaches to sustainable development, "integrated, holistic and balanced", to assist the Parties in the implementation of their NDCs. Unfortunately the content of such framework is not as precisely specified than the mechanisms retained in par. 38(f).

Finally, the kind of emissions trading at a Nash equilibrium that might emerge in the wake of the Paris texts has an early theoretical precedent in the remarkable piece of Helm (2003), where the trading bears on allowances that are themselves a Nash equilibrium outcome of some game. There is probably a close connection to be made

---

[48]Acronyms of mechanisms established under the Kyoto protocol.

[49]These are CDM and JI just mentioned and, last but not least, cap and trade.

[50]The carbon price idea regained visibility among officials with the launching in mid April 2016 in Washington DC, just a few days before the signing ceremony of the Paris Agreement in New York, of a "Carbon Pricing Leadership Coalition", with Ms Segolène Royal as vice-chair.

between this Helm equilibrium and the equilibrium with subscription that I put forward in an earlier section of this note.

Concluding consideration on the Paris Agreement

In terms of both conceptual quality and substance of proposed action, the economics of the Paris texts is a real setback compared to the Kyoto Protocol. Nothing is destroyed, though: for instance, market mechanisms are still present as key instrument. But no progress is gained either. Environmentally speaking, nothing will change for several years, that is, the Kyoto regime will continue prevailing until 2020, admittedly as an inefficient partial agreement equilibrium "club". At its entry into force, the new "bottom up" (subscription) equilibrium prescribed by the Paris Agreement is known to be economically inefficient and environmentally insufficient. But at least better than "business as usual".

Diplomatically, COP 21 is a victory of immediate *savoir faire*. Its outcome, made of credible promises, may be a source of optimism for the planet. But, because of the fuzziness that dominates the texts as they are and the absence of decisions of material action, its economics cannot be characterized as "science driven policy", contrary to the physics of climatic science that clearly inspires and supports the whole UNFCCC process.

A conclusion for the course

My "introductory synthesis" to international environmental agreements seen through the lenses of economics and game theory, comes herewith to an end. I hope that my readers can see, as did many of my students after the classes, how widely open the subject matter remains, for both further research, theoretical, empirical and computational, as well as — perhaps even more — for diplomatic, administrative and political action. I know that some are engaged in either one of these directions, be it by achieving preparatory work for the IPCC and other thinking tanks, by attending COP's as experts in influential groups, or still in public administrations or private institutions where they devote their activity to environmental quality enhancement and/or protection. If the contents of these pages can be felt as a support to these readers' and students' professional efforts, probably Ca' Foscari's initiative in including this course in its PhD program shall have served its purpose.

References

- The references followed by (FC) are reprinted in Finus and Caparrós (eds.) 2015.
- The references followed by (CDLM) are reprinted in Chander, Drèze, Lovell, and Mintz (eds.) 2006.

Adda, J. and Cooper, R. 2003, *Dynamic Economics: Quantitative Methods and Applications*, The MIT Press, Cambridge, MA.

Alcamo, J., Shaw, R. and Hordijk, L. 1990, *The RAINS Model of Acidification: Sciences and Strategies for Europe*, IIASA, Kluwer Academic Publishers, Boston–Dordrecht.

Arrow, K. and Debreu, G. 1954, "The existence of an equilibrium for a competitive economy," *Econometrica* 22, 265–290.

Arrow, K.J. 1970, "The organization of economic activity: Issues pertinent to the choice of market versus non market allocation", in Haveman, R.H. and Margolis, J. (eds.), *Public Expenditure and Policy Analysis*, Markham Publishing Co., Chicago, pp. 59–73.

Arrow, K.J. and Hahn, F. 1971, *General Competitive Analysis*, Oliver and Boyd, Edinburgh.

Aumann, R. 1961, "The core of a cooperative game without side payments", *Transactions of the American Mathematical Society* 98, 539–552.

Aumann, R. 1985, "What is game theory trying to accomplish?" in Arrow, K. and Honkapohja, S. (eds.), *Frontiers of Economics*, Basil Blackwell, Oxford, pp. 28–76.

Aumann, R. 1987, "Game Theory", in J. Eatwell, M. Milgate, and P. Newman (eds.), *The New Palgrave: A Dictionary of Economics*, Volume 2, Macmillan, London, pp. 460–482.

Aumann, R. 1989, *Lectures on Game Theory*, Westview Press, Boulder.

Bahn, O. and Haurie, A. 2008, "A class of games with coupled constraints to model international GHG emission agreements", *International Game Theory Review* 10, 337–362.

Barone, E. 1908, "Il ministro della produzione nello stato collettivista", *Giornale degli economisti*, serie seconda, 37, pp. 267–293. English translation: *The Ministry of Production in the Collectivist State*, Routledge, London 1935.

Barrett, S. 1994, "Self-enforcing international environmental agreements", *Oxford Economic Papers* 46, pp. 878–894. (FC)

Barrett, S. 2003, *Environment and Statecraft: The Strategy of Environmental Treaty-Making*, Oxford University Press, Oxford (paperback edition 2005).

Basar, B. and Olsder, G. 1995, *Dynamic Non-cooperative Game Theory*, 2nd edition, Academic Press, London and San Diego.

Baumol, W. and W. Oates (1975), *The Theory of Environmental Policy*, Prentice Hall, Englewood Cliffs, NJ.

Benchekroun, H. and Long, N.V. 2012, "Collaborative Enviromental Mahagement: A review of the literature", *International Game Theory Review* 14(4).

Berger, L., Emmerling J. and Tavoni, M. 2017, "Managing catastrophic climate risks under model uncertainty aversion", *Management Science INFORMS* 63, 749–765.

Bloch, F. and van den Nouweland, A. 2014, "Expectation formation rules and the core of partition function games", *Games and Economic Behavior* 88, 339–353.

Boadway, R. and Bruce, N. 1984, *Welfare Economics*, Basil Blackwell, Oxford.

Bondareva, O. 1963, "Some applications of linear programming methods to the theory of cooperative games" (in Russian), *Problemy Kibernetiki* 10, 119–139.

Bosetti, V., Carraro, C., De Cian, E., Massetti, E., and Tavoni, M. 2013, "Incentives and stability of international climate coalitions: An integrated assessment", *Energy Policy* 55(44–56).

Bosetti, V., Carraro, C., Galeotti, M., Massetti, E. and Tavoni, T. 2006, "WITCH: A World Induced Technical Change Hybrid Model", *The Energy Journal*, Special Issue: Hybrid modelling, 27, pp. 13–38.

Bréchet, T., Eyckmans, J., Gerard, F., Marbaix, P., Tulkens, H. and van Ypersele, J.-P. 2010, "The impact of the unilateral EU commitment on the stability of international climate agreements", *Climate Policy* 10, 148–166.

Bréchet, T., Gerard, F. and Tulkens, H. 2011, "Efficiency vs. stability in climate coalitions: A conceptual and computational appraisal", *The Energy Journal* 32, 49–75. Reprinted in Carraro 2016.

Bréchet, T., Hritonenko, N. and Yatsenko, Y. 2016, "Domestic environmental policy and international cooperation for global commons", *Resource and Energy Economics* 44, 183–205.

Bréchet, T. and Tulkens, H. 2015, "Climate policies: a burden, or a gain?", *The Energy Journal* 36, 155–170.

Bréchet, T., Thénié, J., Zeimes, T. and Zuber, S. 2012, "The benefits of cooperation under uncertainty: The case of climate change", *Environmental Modeling Assessment* 17, 149–162.

Buchanan J. 1965, "An economic theory of clubs", *Economica* 32, 1–14.

Buchanan, J. 1968, *The Supply and Demand for Public Goods*, Rand McNally, Chicago.

Caparrós, A. and Péreau, J.-C. 2017, Multilateral versus sequential negotiations over climate change, *Oxford Economic Papers* 62(2), 365–387.

Carraro, C., Eyckmans, J. and Finus, M. 2006, "Optimal transfers and participation decisions in international environmental agreements", *The Review of International Organization* 1(4), 379–396.

Carraro, C. 2008, "Incentives and institutions: a bottom up approach to climate policy", *commentary* on the paper "Fragmented carbon markets and reluctant nations: implications for the design of effective architectures" by David Victor, in Aldy, J. and Stavins, R. (eds.), *Architectures for Agreement: Addressing Global Climate Change in the post-Kyoto World*, Cambridge University Press, 2008, pp. 161–172.

Carraro, C. (ed.) 2016, *Coalitions and Networks: 12 papers from 20 years of CTN workshops*, The FEEM Series on "Climate Change and Sustainable Development", FEEM Press, Milan.

Carraro, C. and Siniscalco, D. 1992, "The international dimension of environmental policy", *European Economic Review* 39, 379–387.

Carraro, C. and Siniscalco, D. 1993, "Strategies for the international protection of the environment", *Journal of Public Economics* 52, 309–328. (FC).

Carraro, C. and Siniscalco, D. 1995, "International coordination of environmental policies and stability of global environmental agreements", Chapter 13 in Bovenberg, L. and Cnossen, S. (eds.), *Public Economics and the Environment in an Imperfect World*, Kluwer Academic Publishers, Boston, London, Dordrecht.

Carraro, C., Eyckmans, J. and Finus, M. 2006, "Optimal transfers and participation decisions in international environmental agreements", *Review of International Organizations* I, 379–396. (FC).

Champsaur, P. and Laroque, G. 1981, "Strategic behavior in decentralized planning procedures", *Econometrica* 50, 325–344.

Chander, P. 1993, "Dynamic procedures and incentives in public good economies", *Econometrica* 61, 1341–1354.

Chander, P. 2003, "The Kyoto Protocol and developing countries: Strategic and equity issues", in Toman, M. (ed.), *India and Global Climate Change*, Routledge, London.

Chander, P. 2007, "The gamma-core and coalition formation", *International Journal of Game Theory* 35, 539–556.

Chander, P. 2017, "Sub-game — perfect cooperative agreements in a dynamic game of climate change", *Journal of Environmental Economics and Management*, March.

Chander, P. and Tulkens, H. 1991/2002, "Strategically stable cost sharing in an economic-ecological negotiation process", *CORE Discussion Paper no. 9135*, October 1991, published as Chapter 4 (pp. 66–80) in A. Ulph (ed.), *Environmental Policy, International Agreements, and International Trade*, Oxford University Press, Oxford, 2002.

Chander, P. and Tulkens, H. 1992a, "Theoretical foundations of negotiations and cost sharing in transfrontier pollution problems", *European Economic Review* 36, 288–299. (CDLM).

Chander, P. and Tulkens, H. 1992b, "Aspects stratégiques des négociations internationales sur les pollutions transfrontières et du partage des coûts de l'épuration", *Revue Économique* (Paris) 43, 769–781.

Chander, P. and Tulkens, H. 1994, "The core of an economy with multilateral environmental externalities", *CORE Discussion Paper 9550*, Louvain la Neuve, *FEEM Nota di Lavoro no. 69.94,* Fondazione ENI Enrico Mattei, Milan, and *Social Science Working Paper n° 886,* California Institute of Technology, Pasadena.

Chander, P. and Tulkens, H. 1995, "A core-theoretic solution for the design of cooperative agreements on transfrontier pollution", *International Tax and Public Finance* 2, 279–294. (CDLM).

Chander, P. and Tulkens, H. 1997, "The core of an economy with multilateral environmental externalities", *International Journal of Game Theory* 26, 379–401. Reprinted as Chapter 5 (pp. 81–103) in *Finus and Caparros,* 2015 (circulated in an earlier version as Chander and Tulkens 1994). (CDLM) (FC)

Chander, P. and Tulkens, H. 2008, "Cooperation, stability and self-enforcement in international environmental agreements: A conceptual discussion", Chapter 8 in R. Guesnerie and H. Tulkens (eds.), *The Design of Climate Policy,* CESifo Seminar Series, The MIT Press, Boston, pp. 165–186.

Chander, P. and Tulkens, H. 2011, "The Kyoto *Protocol*, the Copenhagen *Accord*, the Cancun *Agreements*, and beyond: An economic and game theoretical exploration and interpretation", *CORE Discussion Paper 2011/51* (October).

Chander, P., Drèze, J., Lovell, C.K. and Mintz, J. (eds.), 2006, *Public goods, environmental externalities and fiscal competition: Essays by Henry Tulkens,* Springer, New York.

Chander, P., Tulkens, H., van Ypersele, J-P., and Willems, S. 2002, "The Kyoto Protocol: An economic and game theoretic interpretation", Chapter 6 (pp. 98–117) in Kriström, B., Dasgupta P. and Löfgren K.-G. (eds.), *Economic Theory for the Environment : Essays in Honor of Karl-Göran Mäler,* Edward Elgar, Cheltenham (CDLM) (circulated earlier as *Climneg Working Paper no. 12* (December 1998), Center for Operations Research and Econometrics (CORE), Université Catholique de Louvain).

Chwe, M. 1994, "Farsighted coalitional stability", *Journal of Economic Theory* 63, 299–325.

Coase, R.M. 1960, "The problem of social cost", *Journal of Law and Economics* 3, 1–44.

Common, M. and Stagl, S. 2005, *Ecological Economics: An Introduction,* Cambridge University Press, Cambridge, U.K.

Connolly, J. 1972, "Trade in public goods: A diagrammatic analysis", *The Quaterly Journal of Economics* 86, 68–71.

Cornes, R. and Sandler, T. 1996, *The Theory of Externalities, Public Goods and Club Goods,* 2nd edition (1st edition 1986), Cambridge University Press, Cambridge, UK.

Currarini, S. and Tulkens, H. 2004, "Stable international agreements on transfrontier pollution with ratification constraints", Chapter 1 in Carraro, C. and Fragnelli, V. (eds.), *Game Practice and the Environment,* Edward Elgar, Cheltenham, pp. 8–36.

d'Aspremont, C. and Gérard-Varet, L. 1975 "Individual incentives and collective efficiency for anexternality gam with incomplete information", *CORE Discussion Paper no. 7519*, Center for Operations Research and Econometrics, Université catholique de Louvain.

d'Aspremont, C. and Gérard-Varet, L. 1976, "Un modèle de négociation internationale pour certains problèmes de pollution", *Revue d'Économie Politique* 80, 597–620.

d'Aspremont, C. and Jaskold Gabszewicz, J. 1986, "On the stability of collusion", Chapter 8 in Stiglitz, J.E. and Mathewson, G.F. (ed.), *New Developments in the Analysis of Market Structure*, The MIT Press, Cambridge, MA, pp. 243–264).

Dasgupta, P. 1982, *The Control of Resources*, Basil Blackwell, Oxford.

Dasgupta, P. and Heal, G. 1979, *Economic Theory and Exhaustible Resources*, Cambridge University Press, Cambridge, UK.

Davis, O. and Whinston, A. 1962, "Externalities, welfare and the theory of games", *The Journal of Political Economy* 70, 241–262.

de Zeeuw, A. 1998, "International dynamic pollution control", chapter 12 in Hanley, N. and Folmer, H., (eds.), *Game Theory and the Environment*, Edward Elgar, Cheltenham, pp. 237–254.

de Zeeuw, A. and van der Ploeg, F. 1991, "Difference games and policy evaluation: a conceptual framework", *Oxford Economic Papers* 43 1991, 612–636.

Debreu, G. 1959, *Theory of Value*, Wiley, New York.

Debreu, G. and Scarf, H. 1963, "A limit theorem on the core of an economy", *International Economic Review* 4, 235–246.

Dehez, P. 2017, *Théorie des jeux: Conflit, négociation, coopération et pouvoir*, Economica, Paris.

Delbeke, J. and Vis, P. 2015, (eds.), *EU Climate Policy Explained*, Routledge, Abingdon, Oxon.

Dequiedt, V., Durieu, J. et Solal, P. 2011, *Théorie des jeux et applications*, coll. Corpus Economie, Economica, Paris.

Diamantoudi, E. and Sartzetakis, E.S. 2006, "Stable international environmental agreements: An analytical approach", *Journal of Public Economic Theory*, 8, 247–263. (FC)

Drèze, J. 1995, "Forty years of public economics: A personal perspective", *Journal of Economic Perspectives* 9, 111–130.

Drèze, J. and de la Vallée Poussin, D. 1971, "A tâtonnement process for public goods", *Review of Economic Studies* 38, 133–150.

Edgeworth, F.Y. 1881, *Mathematical Psychics: An Essay on the Application of Mathematics to the Moral Sciences*, Kegan Paul, London.

Edmonds, H., Lovell, J. and Lovell, C. K. 2017, "A new composite index for greenhouse gases: Climate science meets social science", *Resources* (Resources for the Future, Washington), 6, 62, 11–16.

Ellerman, A.D. 2005, "A Note on tradable permits", *Environmental & Resource Economics* 31, 123–131.

Ellerman, D. 2015, "The EU ETS: what we know and what we don't know", Chapter 2 in Gronwald and Hinterman 2015, pp. 25–42.

Ellerman, D. and Decaux, A. 1998, "Analysis of post-Kyoto CO_2 emissions trading using marginal abatement curves", MIT Joint Program on the Science and Policy of Global Change, Report No. 40, Massachusetts Institute of Technology.

Eyckmans, J. 2001, "On the farsighted stability of the Kyoto Protocol", *ETE Working Paper* 2001–03, K.U. Leuven-CES-ETE and *CLIMNEG Working Paper 40*, CORE-UCL, Louvain-la-Neuve.

Eyckmans, J. and Finus 2004, "An almost ideal sharing scheme for coalition games with externalities", *FEEM Working Paper* 155.04.

Eyckmans, J. and Finus, M. 2006, "Coalition formation in a global warming game: how the design of protocols affects the success of environmental treaty-making", *Natural Resource Modeling* 19, 323–358. (FC)

Eyckmans, J., and Finus, M. 2007, "Measures to enhance the success of global climate treaties, international environmental agreements", *Politics, Law and Economics* 7, 73–97.

Eyckmans, J. and Finus, M. 2008, "Transfer schemes and institutional changes for sustainable global climate treaties", Chapter 6 (pp. 103–136) in Guesnerie R. and Tulkens, H. (eds.), *The Design of Climate Policy,* CESifo Seminar Series, The MIT Press, Cambridge, MA.

Eyckmans, J. and Tulkens, H. 2003, "Simulating coalitionally stable burden sharing agreements for the climate change problem", *Resource and Energy Economics,* 25, 299–327. Initially circulated in January 1999 as *CORE Discussion paper 9926* and *CLIMNEG Working Paper no 18*, CORE, Université catholique de Louvain, and in December 1999 as *CESifo Working Paper no 228*, Munich. First presented at the joint Workshop ClimNeg-FEEM in Milan November 12, 1999. (CDLM)

Finus, M. 2001, *Game Theory and International Environmental Cooperation,* Edward Elgar, Cheltenham.

Finus, M. and Caparrós, A. (eds.), 2015, *Game Theory and International Environmental Cooperation: Essential Readings,* Edward Elgar Publishing, Cheltenham, UK

Finus, M. and Caparrós, A. 2015a, "Introduction", pp. *xvii–xliv* of Finus and Caparrós 2015.

Frankel, J. 2009, "An elaborated proposal for global climate policy architecture: Specific formulas and emission targets for all countries in all decades", in Aldy, J. and Stavins, R. (eds.), *Post-Kyoto International Climate Policy,* Cambridge University Press, Cambridge, U.K., pp. 31–87.

Friedman, J. 1986, *Game Theory with Applications to Economics,* Oxford University Press, New York.

Gerard, F. 2007, "CWS 1.2, une mise à jour du modèle CWS", *CLIMNEG Working Paper no 80*, CORE, Center for Operations Research and Econometrics, Université catholique de Louvain.

Germain, M. and van Ypersele, J.P. 1999, "Financial transfers to sustain international cooperation in the climate change framework", *CLIMNEG Working Paper* no 19, and *CORE Discussion Paper* no 9936, Center for Operations Research and Econometrics, Université catholique de Louvain.

Germain, M., Toint, P. and Tulkens, H. 1996a, "International negotiations on acid rains in Northern Europe: a discrete time iterative process", Chapter 10 in Xepapadeas, A. (ed.), *Economic Policy for the Environment and Natural Resources*, Elgar, London, 1996, pp. 217–236.

Germain, M., Toint, P. and Tulkens, H. 1996b, "Calcul économique itératif pour les négociations internationales sur les pluies acides entre la Finlande, la Russie, l'Estonie", *Annales d'Economie et de Statistique* 43, 101–127 (July–September)

Germain, M., Toint, P. and Tulkens, H. 1998, "Financial transfers to sustain cooperative international optimality in stock pollutant abatement", in Duchin, F., Faucheux, S., Gowdy, J. and Nicolaï, I. (eds.), *Sustainability and Firms: Technological Change and the Changing Regulatory Environment*, Edward Elgar, Cheltenham, (available as CORE reprint 1369). pp. 205–219.

Germain, M., Toint, P. and Tulkens, H. 1999, "Transferts financiers et optimum coopératif international en matière de pollutions-stocks", *L'Actualité économique. Revue d'analyse économique* (Montréal), 75, 1–3 (available as CORE reprint 1453).

Germain, M., Toint, P., Tulkens, H. and de Zeeuw, A. 1998, "Transfers to sustain cooperation in international stock pollutant control", CORE *Discussion Paper* no 9832, Center for Operations Research and Econometrics, Université Catholique de Louvain, Louvain la Neuve; and *Report* 98/08, Publications du Département de Mathématiques, Facultés universitaires de Namur.

Germain, M., Toint, P., Tulkens, H., and de Zeeuw, A. 2003, "Transfers to sustain dynamic core-theoretic cooperation in international stock pollutant control", *Journal of Economic Dynamics and Control* 28: 79–99 (available as CORE reprint 1637). (CDLM) (FC)

Germain, M., Tulkens, H. and de Zeeuw, A. 1998, "Stabilité stratégique en matière de pollution internationale avec effet de stock: le cas linéaire", *Revue Économique* (Paris) 49, 1435–1454.

Germain, M., Tulkens, H. and Magnus, A. 2010, "Dynamic core-theoretic cooperation in a two-dimensional international environmental model", *Mathematical Social Sciences* 59, 208–226.

Gilles, R. 2010, *The Cooperative Game Theory of Networks and Hierarchies*, Theory and Decision Library C 44, Springer-Verlag, Berlin Heidelberg.

Gillies, D. 1959, "Solutions to General Non-Zero Sum Games", in Tucker, A. W. and Luce, R. D. (eds.), *Contributions to the Theory of Games IV*, Annals of Mathematics Studies No. 40, 47–85, Princeton University Press, Princeton.

Gollier, C. 2011, *The Economics of Discounting and Sustainable Development*, Princeton University Press.

Goosse, H. 2015, *Climate System Dynamics and Modeling*, Cambridge University Press, Cambridge, U.K.

Gronwald, M. and Hintermann, B. 2015 (eds.), *Emissions Trading as a Policy Instrument; Evaluation and Prospects,* The CES-ifo Seminar Series, The MIT Press, Cambridge, MA.

Gronwald, M. and Hinterman, B. 2015a, "The EU ETS", chapter 1 in Gronwald and Hinterman (2015), pp. 15–24.

Groves, T. and Ledyard, J. 1977, "Optimal allocation of public goods: a solution to the 'free rider' problem", *Econometrica* 45, 783–810.

Guesnerie, R. 2015, "Multiplier les "petits ruisseaux" in *Le dictateur bienveillant et le climat* in *Le Monde* (June 24).

Guesnerie, R. and H. Tulkens, H. (eds.), 2008, *The Design of Climate Policy,* CESifo Seminar Series, The MIT Press, Boston.

Haeckel, E. 1866, *Generelle Morphologie der Organismen,* G. Reimer, Berlin.

Hanley, H. and Folmer, H. (eds.), 1998, *Game Theory and the Environment,* Elgar, Cheltenham.

Helm, C. 2001, "On the existence of a cooperative solution for a coalitional game with externalities", *International Journal of Game Theory* 30, 141–146. (FC)

Helm, C. 2003, "International emissions trading with endogenous allowance choices", *Journal of Public Economics* 87, 2737–2747.

Henry, C., 1979, "On the free rider problem in the M.D.P. procedure", *Review of Economic Studies* 46(2), 293–303.

Hirshleifer, J. 1983, "From Weakest-link to Best-shot: The Voluntary Provision of Public Goods", *Public Choice* 41, 371–86. Reprinted as chapter 5 in J. Hirshleifer, *Economic Behavior in Adversity,* The University of Chicago Press, Chicago 1987, pp. 145–162.

Hirshleifer, J., Glazer, A. and Hirshleifer, D. 2005, *Price Theory and Applications: Decisions, Markets and Information,* Cambridge University Press, New York.

Houba, H. and de Zeeuw, A. 1995, "Strategic bargaining for the control of a dynamic system in state-space form", *Group Decision and Negotiation* 4, 71–97.

Houghton, J. 2009, *Global Warming: The Complete Briefing,* Cambridge University Press, Cambridge, U.K.

Hovi, J. and Areklett, I. 2004, "Enforcing the climate regime: Game theory and the Marrakesh accords", *International Environmental Agreements: Politics, Law and Economics* 4, 1–26.

Intergovernmental Panel on Climate Change (IPCC), 2006, *Special Report on Emissions Scenarios (SRES).*

Intergovernmental Panel on Climate Change (IPCC), *Assessment Reports*: first (1992), second (1995), third (2001), fourth (2007) and fifth (2014), Cambridge University Press, Cambridge, UK.

Kaitala, V., Mäler, K.G. and Tulkens, H. 1995, "The acid rain game as a resource allocation process, with application to negotiations between Finland, Russia and Estonia", *The Scandinavian Journal of Economics* 97, 325–343. Reprinted in Carlo Carraro (ed.), *Governing the Global Environment, The Globalization of the World Economy: An Elgar Reference Collection,* Cheltenham 2003. (CDLM)

Kaul, I., Grunberg, I. and Stern, M. (eds.), 1999, *Global Public Goods: International Cooperation in the 21st Century,* Oxford University Press, New York.

Keller, K., Bolker, B.M. and Bradford, D. 2004, "Uncertain climate thresholds and optimal economic growth", *Journal of Environmental Economics and Management* 48, 723–741.

Kelly, D.L., and Kolstad, C.D. 1999, "Integrated assessment models for climate change control", in *International Yearbook of Environmental and Resource Economics 2000,* Edward Elgar, Cheltenham, UK, pp. 171–197.

Kersting, J. 2017, *Stability of cooperation in the international climate negotiations: An analysis using cooperative game theory,* Doctoral dissertation, Fakultät für Wirtschaftswissenschaften des Karlsruher Instituts für Technologie (KIT), Karlsruhe.

Khiem Nguyen Tho, 2015, *Optimal control and dynamic programming approaches in an international environmental economic problem,* Joint Master thesis, Economics Departments of Université catholique de Louvain, Belgium and University of Warsaw, Poland.

Kóczy, L. 2018, *Partition function form games: coalitional games with externalities,* Springer.

Kolstad, C. 2000, *Environmental economics,* Oxford University Press, Oxford, New York.

Kolstad, Ch. and Guzman, R.M. 1999, "Information and the Divergence between Willingness to Accept and Willingness to Pay", *Journal of Environmental Economics and Management* 38, 66–80.

Kornek, U., Lessman, K. and Tulkens, H. 2014, "Transferable and non transferable utility implementations of coalitional stability in integrated assessment models", *CORE Discussion Paper 2014/35,* Center for Operations Research and Econometrics, Université catholique de Louvain.

Kranich, L., Perea, A. and Peters, H. 2005, "Core concepts for dynamic TU games", *International Game Theory Review* 7, 43–61.

Kuhn, H. and Tucker, A. 1951, "Nonlinear programming", in J. Neyman, (ed.), *Proceedings of 2nd Berkeley Symposium,* University of California Press, Berkeley, pp. 481–492.

Laffont, J.J. 1977, *Effets externes et théorie économique,* Monographies du Séminaire d'économétrie, Éditions du CNRS, Paris.

Lessmann, K., Kornek, U., Bosetti, V., Dellink, Rob, Emmerling, J., Eyckmans, J., Nagashima, N., Weikard, H.P. and Yang, Z. 2015, "The stability and effectiveness of climate coalitions: A comparative analysis of multiple integrated assessment models", *Environmental and Resource Economics* 62, 811–836.

Long, N.V., 2010, *A Survey of Dynamic Games in Economics,* World Scientific Publishing, Singapore and London.

Luce, D. and Raiffa, H. 1957, *Games and Decisions. Introduction and Critical Survey,* Wiley, New York.

Mäler, K.G. 1989, "The Acid Rain Game", Chapter 12 in *Valuation Methods and Policy Making in Environmental Economics,* Elsevier, Amsterdam, pp. 351–352. (FC)

Mäler, K.G. 1990, "International environmental Problems", *Oxford Review of Economic Policy* 6, 80–108.

Malinvaud, E. 1969, *Leçons de théorie microéconomique*, Coll. Statististique et programmmes économiques no 15, (4e édition : 1974), Dunod, Paris. Translated as *Lectures on Microeconomic Theory*, North-Holland Publ. Co., Amsterdam, 1972.

Malinvaud, E. 1970–71, "Procedures for the determination of a program of collective consumption", *European Economic Review*, 2, 187–217.

Malinvaud, E. 1972a, "Prices for individual consumption, quantity indicators for collective consumption", *Review of Economic Studies* XXXIX, 385–406.

Malinvaud, E. 1972b, *Lectures on Microeconomic Theory*, revised edition, North Holland, Amsterdam.

Margolis, J. and Guitton, H. (eds.), 1969, *Public economics,* Proceedings of the IEA-CNRS conference held in 1966 at Biarritz, France, Macmillan, London.

Markowska, A. and Zylicz, T. 1999, "Costing an international public good: The case of the Baltic Sea", *Ecological Economics* 30(2), 301–316.

Mas-Colell, A., Whinston M. and Green, J. 1995, *Microeconomic Theory*, Oxford University Press.

Maschler, M., Solan, E. and Zamir, S. 2011, *Game Theory*, Cambridge University Press, Cambridge, UK.

Maslin, M. 2004, *Global Warming: A Vey Short Introduction,* Oxford University Press, Oxford.

Musgrave, R. 1959, *The Theory of Pubic Finance*, McGraw-Hill, New York.

Musgrave, R. 1968, "Provision for Social Goods", chapter 6 in Margolis J. and Guitton, H. (eds.), *Public Economics,* proceedings of the IEA-CNRS conference held in1966 at Biarritz, France, Macmillan, London and St. Martin's Press, New York, pp. 124–144.

Myerson, R. 1991, *Game Theory: Analysis of Conflict*, Harvard University Press, Cambridge, MA.

Nagashima, M. 2010, *Game theoretic analysis of international climate agreements: The design of transfer schemes and the role of technological change,* Doctoral Thesis, Wageningen University, Wageningen, NL.

Nash, J. 1950, "The bargaining problem", *Econometrica* 18, 155–162.

Nash, J. 1951, "Non cooperative games", *Annals of Mathematics* 54, pp. 286–295.

National Research Council 2017, "Valuing climate damages: Updating estimation of the social cost of carbon dioxide", *Report of the Committee on Assessing Approaches to Updating the Social Cost of Carbon*, NationalAcademy Press, Washington DC.

Negishi, T. 1960, "Welfare economics and existence of an equilibrium for a competitive economy", *Metroeconomica* 12(2–3), 92–97.

Nordhaus, W. 1994, *Managing the Global Commons: The Economics of Climate Change*, MIT Press.

Nordhaus, W. 2009, "Alternative policies and sea-level rise in the RICE-2009 model", *Cowles Foundation Discussion Paper no 1716*, Yale University (August).

Nordhaus, W. 2010, "Projections of Sea Level Rise (SLR)", unpublished note, Yale University (February).

Nordhaus, W. 2015, "Climate clubs: Overcoming free-riding in international climate policy", *American Economic Review* 105, 1339-13s.

Nordhaus, W. and Boyer, J. 1999, "Requiem for Kyoto: An economic analysis of the Kyoto Protocol", *The Energy Journal*, Special Issue: Kyoto, 20, 93–130.

Nordhaus, W. and Boyer, J. 2000, *Warming the Word: Economic Models of Global Warming*, The MIT Press, Cambrige, MA.

Nordhaus, W. and Moffat, A. 2017, "A survey of global impacts of climate change: Replication, survey methods and statistical analysis", *Cowles Foundation Discussion Paper* no 2096, Yale University, New Haven.

Nordhaus, W. and Yang, Z. 1996, "A regional dynamic general-equilibrium model of alternative climate-change strategies", *American Economic Review* 86, 741–763.

Obergassel, W., Arens, C., Hermwille, L., Kreibich, N., Mersmann, F., Ott, H. and Wang-Helmreich, H. 2016, "Phoenix from the Ashes — An Analysis of the Paris Agreement to the United Nations Framework Convention on Climate Change", *Report* issued by the Wuppertal Institute for Climate, Environment and Energy, Wuppertal (January).

Osborne, M. and Rubinstein, A. 1994, *A Course in Game Theory*, The MIT Press, Cambridge, MA.

Peleg, B. and Sudhölter, P. 2007, *Introduction to the Theory of Cooperative Games,* 2nd edition, Springer, Berlin and Heidelberg.

Ray, D. 1998, *Development Economics*, Princeton University Press, Princeton, NJ.

Reuter, P. 1995, *Introduction to the Law of Treaties*, Kegan Paul International, London.

Roberts, J. 1976, "Incentives for correct revelation of preferences and the number of consumers", *Journal of Public Economics* 6, 359–374.

Roberts, J. 1979, "Incentives in planning procedures for the provision of public goods", *Review of Economic Studies* XLVI (2), 283–292.

Rogna, M. 2016, "Cooperative game theory applied to IEAs: A comparison of solution concepts", *Journal of Economic Surveys* 30, 397–402.

Roson, R. and Sartori, M. 2016, "Estimation of climate change damage functions for 140 regions in the GTAP9 database", *Working paper* n°6/WP/2016, Department of Economics Ca' Foscari University of Venice.

Samuelson P.A. 1954, "The pure theory of public expenditure", *Review of Economics and Statistics* 36, 387–389.

Scarf, H. 1967, "The core of an n-person game", *Econometrica* 35, 50–69.

Scarf, H. 1971, "On the existence of a cooperative solution for a general class of N-person games", *Journal of Economic Theory* 3, 169–181.

Schoumaker, F. 1979, "Incentives in planning with private goods", *Review of Economic Studies* XLVI(2), 315–318.

Scotchmer, S. 2002, "Local public goods and clubs", Chapter 29 in Alan Auerbach and Martin Feldstein, (eds.), *Handbook of Public Economics* vol. IV, North-Holland Press, Amsterdam, pp. 1997–2042.

Shapley, L. 1967, "On balanced sets and cores", *Naval Research Logistics Quarterly* 14, 453–460.

Shapley, L. 1971, "Cores of convex games", *International Journal of Game Theory* 1(1), 11–26.

Shapley, L. 1973, "Let's block 'Block'", *Econometrica* 41, 1201–1202.

Shapley, L. and Shubik, M. 1969a, "On market games", *Journal of economic Theory* 1, 9–25.

Shapley, L. and Shubik, M. 1969b, "On the core of an economic system with externalities", *American Economic Review* 59, 678–684.

Shubik, M. 1984, *A Game-theoretic Approach to Political Economy* (Volume 2 of *Game Theory in the Social Sciences*), The MT Press, Cambridge, MA.

Sidgwick, H. 1883, *Principles of Political Economy*, New York, MacMillan and Co.

Starrett, D., 1972, "A note on externalities and the core", *Econometrica* 41, 179–183.

Straffin, Ph. D. 1993, *Game theory and strategy*, The Mathematical Association of America, Washington DC.

Telser, L. 1980, "A theory of self-enforcing agreements", *The Journal of Business* 53(1), 27–44.

Telser, L. 1987, *A Theory of Efficient Cooperation*, Cambridge University Press, Cambridge, U.K.

Thoron, S. 2008, "About Heterogeneity of Countries in Negotiations of International Environmental Agreements. A joint discussion of the Buchner-Carraro, Eyckmans-Finus and Chander-Tulkens papers", pp. 187–198 in Guesnerie and Tulkens (2008).

Tulkens, H. 1978, "Dynamic procedures for public goods: An institution-oriented survey", *Journal of Public Economics* 9, 163–201. CDLM

Tulkens, H. 1979, "An economic model of international negotiations relating to transfrontier pollution", in Krippendorff K. (ed.) *Communication and control in society*, New York, Gordon and Breach Science Publishers, pp. 199–212. CDLM

Tulkens, H. 1995, "L'environnement peut-il être appréhendé comme un bien économique ?", pp. 22–37, Chapter 1 in C. Stoffaës et M. Richard (eds.), *Environnement et choix économiques de l'entreprise*, Cahiers de Prospective, InterEditions, Paris. Available as *CORE Reprint* no 1184.

Tulkens, H. 1998, "Cooperation *vs.* free riding in international environmental affairs: two approaches", Chapter 2 in Hanley N. and Folmer H. (eds.), *Game Theory and the Environment*, Elgar, Cheltenham, pp. 330–344. Translation in French published as chapter 2 (pp. 47–72) in G. Rotillon, ed. *Régulation environnementale: jeux, coalitions, contrats*, Economica, Paris 2002.

Tulkens, H. 2012, "Climate Dynamics, Economic Dynamics, Negotiations Dynamics", presentation at the *Workshop on the Economics of Climate Change* organized by Ecole Polytechnique, Collège de France and Paris School of Economics, held at Collège de France, Paris (October).

Tulkens, H. 2013. "Le changement climatique au carrefour entre écologie, économie, théorie des jeux et diplomatie", Cours-conférences faits au "Collège Belgique" de l'Académie royale des Sciences, des Lettres et des Beaux-Arts de Belgique", Bruxelles (octobre). Available at: http://www.academieroyale. be/cgi?lg=fr&pag=919&tab=111&rec=1264&frm=0 Available at: http:// www.academieroyale.be/cgi?lg=fr&pag=919&tab=111&rec=1265&frm=0

Tulkens, H. 2014a, Internal *vs.* core coalitional stability in the global externality game: A reconcilation, *CORE Discussion Paper 2014/58* (March 15 version), Université catholique de Loouvain.

Tulkens, H. 2014b, Respective computational burdens of evaluating core stability *vs.* internal stability, unpublished note.

Tulkens, H. 2016, "COP 21 and economic theory: Taking stock", *Revue d'Économie Politique* 126, 471–486.

Tulkens, H. and Schoumaker, F. 1975, "Stability analysis of an effluent charge and the 'polluters pay' principle", *Journal of Public Economics* 4 (3), 245–270.

Tulkens, P. and Tulkens, H. 2006, "The White House and the Kyoto Protocol: Double standards on uncertainties and their consequences", *Working Paper n°1*, TERI School of Advanced Studies, New Delhi, and *Environmental economics and management memorandum #20*, chaire Lhoist Berghmans in Environmental Economics and Management, Université catholique de Louvain.

Tulkens, H. and van Steenberghe, V. 2009, " 'Mitigation, adaptation, suffering': In search of the right mix in the face of climate change", *CORE Discussion Paper* no 2009/54, FEEM *Nota di Lavoro* no 79.2009 and *CESifo* (Munich) *Working Paper* no 2781, August.

Tulkens, H. and Zamir, S. 1979, "Surplus-sharing local games in dynamic exchange processes", *Review of Economic Studies* XLVI(2), 305–314. CDLM

Tuypens, B. 1997, *The problem of transboundary air pollution: Economic models and mathematical simulation*, Master thesis, Département des Sciences Économiques, Université catholique de Louvain, Louvain-la-Neuve, Belgium.

Uzawa, H. 2003, *Economic Theory and Global Warming,* Cambridge University Press, New York.

van der Ploeg, F. and de Zeeuw, A. 1992, "International aspects of pollution control", *Environmental and Resource Economics* 2, 117–139.

van Steenberghe, V. 2003, *Designing markets for emission permits, with applications to climate change,* Doctoral dissertation, Département des Sciences Économiques, Université catholique de Louvain, Louvain-la-Neuve, Belgium.

van Steenberghe, V. 2004, "Core-stable and equitable allocations of greenhouse gas emission permits", *CORE Discussion Paper* 2004-75, Center for Operations Research and Econometrics, Université catholique de Louvain.

Varian, H. 1990, *Intermediate Microeconomics: A Modern Approach*, 2nd edition, W.W. Norton & Company, New York and London.

Von Neumann, J. and Morgenstern, O. 1944, *Theory of Games and Economic Behavior,* 3rd edition 1953, Science Editions Wiley, New York.

Wahlstrom, M. and Guha-Sapir, D. 2015, "The human cost of weather related disasters 1995–2015", *Report from the Centre for Research on the Epidemiology of Disasters,* CRED — cred.be and The United Nations Office for Disaster Risk Reduction (UNISDR — unisdr.org).

Weikard, H. 2009, "Cartel stability under an optimal sharing rule", *The Manchester School* 77(5), 575–593. (FC)

Weyant, J.P., Davidson, O., Dowlatabadi, H., Edmonds, J., Grubb, M., Parson, E.A., Richels, R., Rotmans, J., Shukla, P.R. and Tol, R.S.J. 1996, "Integrated assessment of climate change: An overview and comparison of approaches and results", Chapter 10 in *Climate Change 1995: Economic and Social Dimensions of Climate Change*, Cambridge University Press, Cambridge.

Yang, Z. 2003, "Reevaluation and renegotiation of climate change coalitions — a sequential closed-loop game approach", *Journal of Economic Dynamics & Control* 27, 1563–1594.

Yang, Z. 2008, *Strategic Bargaining and Cooperation in Greenhouse Gas Mitigations: An Integrated Assessment Modeling Approach*, The MIT Press, Cambridge, MA.

Yen, P.Y. 1987, "Incentives in an economic-ecological negotiation process", *Jingi Yanjiu (Economics Reserarch,* journal published by the Department of Economics of Chung-Sing University, Taipei) 27, 27–40.

Yen, P.Y. 1991, *Essays on one point solution concepts for an economy with public goods*, Doctoral dissertation, Département des Sciences Economiques, Université Catholique de Louvain, Louvain-la-Neuve.

Yen, P.Y. 1993, "A one-point solution concept for the provision of a public good", *Recherches Economiques de Louvain*, 59(3), 366–378.

Zaccour, G. 2017, "Sustainability of cooperation in dynamic games played over event trees", Chapter 14 in Melnick, R., Makarov, R. and Belair, J. (eds.), *Recent Progress and Modern Challenges in Applied Mathematics, Modeling and Computational Science*, Fields Institute Communications, Volume 79. Springer, New York, NY.

Author Index

A

Adda, J., 267
Areklett, I., 395
Arrow, K.J., 6–7, 204
Aumann, R., 101, 118, 122, 125, 135, 157, 181

B

Bahn, O., 397
Barrett, S., 72, 219, **224**, 332
Basar, B., 253
Baumol, W., 5
Benchekroun, H., 286
Berger, L., 40
Bloch, F., 124
Bolker, B.M., 320
Bondareva, O., 161
Bosetti, V., 293, 400
Boyer, J., 89, 320, 360
Bréchet, T., 39, 249, 293, 301, 309, 320, 331, 351, 361, 400–401
Bradford, D., 40, 320
Buchanan, J., 5, 9, 93, 221, 398

C

Caparrós, A., 141, 332
Carraro, C., viii, x, 138, 151, 331–332, 378
Champsaur, P., 93
Chander, P., 8, 72, 93, 95, 165, **190**, **196**, 201, 224, 267, 275, 292, 331, 337, 360, 375, 378, 384, 386, 409
Coase, R.M., 5, 77
Common, M., 40

Connolly, J., 137
Cooper, R., 267
Cornes, R., 5–6, 138, 395

D

d'Aspremont, C., 93, 331
Dasgupta, P., 49, 60, 91, 137, 179–180, 236, 364
Davis, O., 135
De Cian, E., 249
de la Vallée Poussin, D., 72, 220
de Zeeuw, A., 253, 267, 271, 285, 400
Debreu, G., 6
Delbeke, J., 379
Diamantoudi, E., 332
Drèze, J., 72, 93, 220, 392, 407, 410

E

Edgeworth, F.Y., 131
Edmonds, H., 19
Ellerman, A.D., 379
Emmerling, J., 40, 415
Eyckmans, J., 16, 240, 242, 248, 264, 292–293, 301–302, 306, 309, 314, 326, 351

F

Filar, J., 286
Finus, M., 95, 140–141, 180, 327, 332, 351
Folmer, H., 140
Frankel, J., 387
Friedman, J., 252–253

G

Gérard-Varet, L., 93
Gabszewicz, J., 331
Gerard, F., 249, 293, 301, 309, 320,
    327, 331, 351, 400
Germain, M., 72, 253, 264, 267, 271,
    285, 314, 322, 400
Gilles, R., 121, 131
Glazer, A., 395
Gollier, C., 231
Goosse, H., 16
Green, J., 5, 23, 102, 106–107
Gronwald, M., 379
Groves, T., 93
Guesnerie, R., 399
Guha-Sapir, D., 89
Guzman, R.M., 92

H

Haeckel, E., 10
Hanley, N., 140
Haurie, A., 397
Heal, G., 137
Helm, C., 71, **156**, **158**, 163, 183,
    275, 337, 403–404
Henry, C., 93, 392
Hintermann, B., 379
Hirshleifer, J., 12, 395
Houba, H., 253, 271
Houghton, J., 16
Hovi, J., 395
Hritonenko, N., 401

J

Jacoby, H., 357

K

Kaitala, V., 14–15, 72, 93, 138
Keller, K., 40, 320
Kelly, D.L., 291
Kersting, J., 39
Khiem Nguyen Tho, 269
Kolstad, C.D., 11, 92, 291
Kornek, U., 111
Kranich, L., 286

L

Laffont, J.J., 5, 136
Laroque, G., 93
Ledyard, J., 93
Lessman, K., 210, 352
Long, N.V., 269, 286
Lovell, C.K., 19, 89, 407, 410–411
Lovell, J., 19, 89
Luce, R.D., 137, 181

M

Mäler, K.G., 14, **33**, 72, 93, 126, 138
Magnus, A., 253, 271, 286, 400
Malinvaud, E., 23, 395–396
Marbaix, P., 327
Markowska, A., 72
Marshall, A., 5
Mas-Colell, A., 5, 23, 102, 106–107
Maschler, M., 101, 107, 109, 118, 124,
    126, 134–135, 142, 157, 161
Maslin, M., 16
Meade, J., 5
Mintz, J., 407, 410
Moffat, A., 89
Morgenstern, O., 122, 124, 131, 135,
    333
Musgrave, R., 218
Myerson, R., 142, 224, 252

N

Negishi, T., 58
Nordhaus, W., 16, 89, 219, 249, **293**,
    295, 301, 310, 320, 360, 398, 400

O

Oates, W., 5
Obergassel, W., 399, 403
Olsder, G., 253
Osborne, M., 101, 124, 157, 161, 252,
    333

P

Palladio, A., 357
Peleg, B., 110

Perea, A., 286
Péreau, J.-C., 226
Peters, H., 286
Petrosyan, L.A., 286
Pigou, A.C., 5

R

Raiffa, H., 137, 181
Rawls, J., 210
Roberts, J., 93, 220, 392, 396
Rogna, M., 125, 165, 210
Rubinstein, A., 101, 124, 157, 252, 333

S

Samuelson, P.A., 92
Sandler, T., 5–6, 138, 395
Sartzetakis, E.S., 332
Scarf, H., 136, 157
Schmalensee, R., 386
Schoumaker, F., 82, 93
Shapley, L., 8, 118, 126, 131, 136, 140, 157, 161, 165–166
Shubik, M., 8, 126, 131, 136, 140, 166
Sidgwick, H., 5
Siniscalco, D., viii, 138, 151, 331–332
Solan, E., 101, 107, 109, 118, 124, 126, 134–135, 142, 157, 161, 252
Stagl, S., 40
Starrett, D., 207
Sudhölter, P., 110
Sue Wing, I., 386

T

Tavoni, M., 40
Thénié, J., 39
Thoron, 331
Toint, P., 72, 253, 264, 267, 271, 285, 314, 400
Tucker, A., 137
Tulkens, H., 4, 8, 15–16, 27, 38, 72, 82, 89, 93, 95, 165, **190**, **196**, 201,
221, 224, 240, 242, 248–249, 253, 264, 267, 271, 275, 285, 292–293, 301, 306, 309, 314, 320, 321, 331, 337, 338, 351, 360–361, 375, 378, 389, 400
Tulkens, P., 89

U

Uzawa, H., 25, 165

V

van den, Nouweland, A., 124
van der Ploeg, F., 253
van Steenberghe, V., 38, 165, 210, 402
van Ypersele, J.-P., 292, 322, 327, 360
Vis, P., 379
Von Neumann, J., 122, 124, 131, 135, 333

W

Wahlstrom, M., 89
Weikard, H., 353
Weyant, J.P., 292
Whinston, A., 5, 23, 102, 106–107, 135
Willems, S., 292, 360

Y

Yang, Z., 16, 249, 270, 293, 295, 301, 310, 320, 400
Yatsenko, Y., 401
Yen, P.Y., 93

Z

Zaccour, G., 287
Zamir, S., 93, 101, 107, 109, 118, 124, 126, 134–135, 142, 157, 252
Zeimes, T., 39
Zuber, S., 39
Zylicz, T., 72

Subject Index

A

γ-assumption, **112**, 114, 219
abatement cost function, 34
abatement decision, 294
abatement rate, 296
ability to pay principle, 218, 324
acid rains model, 15
acronyms for the regions, 296
adaptation, 35, 401
adaptation cost, 37
aggregation, 68
allocation, 31
allowances, 368
American Economic Review, 293
ambient pollutant, 6
amendment, 388
anarchy, 56
anchored core, 119, 163
Annex B countries, 361, 385
applicable to all Parties, 390
assigned amount unit (AAU), 391
assignment of rights, 77
associating games to economies, 131
auctioning, 81
autarky, 55, 238

B

backward induction, 276
balanced budget, 365
balanced collection of subsets, 157
balancing weights, 161
balancedness, 156, 275
BAU path, 386
BAUE scenario, 304
behavior of the players not in S, 109
Belgian government, viii, 292
benefit-cost rule, 49, 60
benefit minus cost test, 364
benefit principle of public finance, 217
bilateral transactions, 86
binding agreements, 146
blocking, 126, 218–219, 310
Brazilian proposal, 83
Bush, George W., 326
business as usual, 46

C

α-coalitional function, 122, 263
β-coalitional function, 123, 263
γ-coalitional function, 115, **153**, 223, 261, 263
γ-coalitional function of the DGEG, **262**
γ-core, **119**, 138
γ-core imputation, 281
γ-core of the GEG in strategic form, **156**
γ-core solution, 174–175
γ-core stable path, **264**
γ-core stable solution, 283
γ-core stable solution path, **276**
γ-core stability, 218
calibration, 297

California, 379
Canada, 378
Cancun Arrangements, 357
cap and trade, 362
capital goods, 23
capital stock, 296
capitalism, 363
carbon concentration, 296
carbon intensity, 296
carbon intensity parameter, 294
carbon pricing, 402
Carbon Pricing Leadership Coalition,
    403
catastrophic events, 39
Centre for Economic Studies
    (CES-Ifo), viii
certified emission reductions (CER),
    391
Chaire Lhoist Berghmans, viii
China, 379, 383
cities, 381
clean development mechanism
    (CDM), 361, 374
climate (physical) mathematical
    modeling, 16
climate change, 9
climate clubs, 397–398
climate sensitivity, 18
climatic damages, 294
ClimNeg World Simulation (CWS)
    model, 39, **291**, 400
club goods, 9
clubs, 140
CO_2, 9
CO_2 equivalent, 19
coalition(s), 108, **145**, 259, 266, 376,
    397
coalition formation, 127
coalition's objective, 146
coalitional externality, 223
coalitional externality from
    cooperation, 336
coalitional free riding, 95, 333
coalitional function, **113**, 174

coalitional function form, 102,
    114
coalitional rationality, 315
coalitional stability, 164, 363, 365,
    370
coalition formation, **219**
Coase theorem, 66, 78, **206**
Cobb–Douglas production function,
    294
cohabitation, 397
collective rationality, 225
command and control, 381
commitments, 265
commitment period, 375
commitments to action, 392
commodities, 5, 23
compact form of the reference model,
    33
compact model, 34
compatibility, 55, 105, 246
competitive emissions trading, 365
competitive emissions trading
    equilibrium, **366**
compliance, 373, 388
compliance regime, 362
composite GDP good, 25
Conference of the Parties (COP),
    360
consumption, 294
consumption set, 24
continuous time, 229
contracts, 84, 86
contradictory expectations, 345
cooperate or not cooperate, 273
cooperation, 61, 246
cooperative form, 114
cooperative solution, 275, 285
Copenhagen Accord, 357, 383
CORE, Louvain-la-Neuve, 292
core strategic stability, 378
cost game, 134
cost of abatement, 296
cost-benefit studies, 38
CS scenario, 305

CT solution, **189**, **194**, 214–215, 217, 314

CT transfers formula, **208**

CWS game, **297**, **299**

D

damage, 296

damage cost function, 34

damage functions, 25

dated caps, 361

decision variables, 298, 363, 382, 391

decision-oriented, 285

decoupling, 308

delta characteristic function, 165

developing countries, 384, 401

deviations, 286

DICE, 293

difference games, 253

diffuse externalities, **7**, 12, 16, 30, 60, 85, 94, 134, 136, 204, 221, 229

diplomacy, 357

directional externality, 8

disagreement with Coase, 207

discount factor, 258

discounted consumption, 232

discrete intervals, 229

disintegration, 126–127, 219

distributional, 81

distributional equity, 323

disutility function, 25

do polluters pay, 216

Doha amendment to the Kyoto Protocol, 388

Doha Gateway, 357

dominant strategy, 168, 178, 258

dominant strategy equilibrium, **145**

duopoly, 135

Durban Platform, 357

durability, 237

dynamic cooperative games, 285

dynamic game, 252, 380

dynamic global externality game (DGEG), 106, **251**, 294

dynamic programming, 268, 270

dynamics, 139, 399

E

ecology, **10**

ecological economics, 40

ecological surplus, 72, 74, 212, 319

economic-ecological system, 30

economic development, 402

economic good, 3, 20

economic modeling, 22

ecosystem, 11

efficient path, 261

efficient state, 64, 246

emission caps, 367

emission reduction unit (ERU), 391

emissions trading system (ETS), 361, 379

emission units, 403

emissions, 296

emissions abatement cost, 294

emitted pollutants, 6, 24

environment, 3, 139

environmental abuse, 68

environmental properties, 149

environmental sciences, vii

environmentally nationalistic equilibrium, 142, 396

environmentally nationalistic individual equilibrium over time, **234**

environmentally nationalistic international equilibrium over time, **239**

equilibrium with multiple free riding players, 346

equity, 67

equilibrium with subscription, **395**

equilibrium with one free riding player, 338, 340

Euler equations, 236–237, 243, 245, 257

European IAM, 293

evaluation models, 292

existence, 143, 148, 156, 255, 260, 272, 275–276, 342
existence value, 88
extensive form, 102, 104
externalities, **5**–10, 204
externalities vs. public goods, 204

F

failure of equilibria, 70
fairness, 67, 226
fallback position, 271
favela, 357
feasible state, **31**
feasible time path, 232
feedback, 255, 269
FEEM Milan, 292
Financial Mechanism, 362
fixed point, 106, 143
flexible, 285
flow externalities, 9
flow model, 13, 23
Fondazione ENI Enrico Mattei (FEEM), viii, 293
forests, 25
fragmented, 383
free riding, 86, 92, 94, 151, 218, 220, 378
free trade in emissions, 372

G

gain by trading, **371**
game in strategic form, **102**
GAMS, 306
GEG, 106, 280
GEG in strategic form, **134**
general equilibrium, 3, **23**, 352
global, 134–135
global externalities, 8–9, 398
global productivity, 296
global public good, 390
global stocktake, 399
global warming potential, 19
Gore, Al, 358
grandfathering, 81
green consumption, 296

grid, 18
grid around the earth, 19
gross domestic product, 23
growth, 299
GTT transfers formula, 314

I

identical players, 201
impacts, 6, 25
imputation, **116**, 189
imputations set, 116, 154, 162, 261
individual rationality, 84, 225, 314
infinite horizon, 280
information, 92
initial endowments, 81
integrated assessment modeling, 16, 291
intergenerational externalities, 9
Intergovernmental Panel on Climate Change (IPCC), 358–359
interior case, 121
interior core, 164
internal–external stability, 164, 378
internal logic, 387
internally–externally stable, **333**
international efficiency, 57
international environmental externalities, vi
international equilibrium, 45, 52
investment, 294, 296

J

Jacoby, 386
joint by-product, 27
joint implementation (JI) mechanism, 361, 374
justice, 67

K

Kyoto, 325
Kyoto Protocol, 151, 240, 290, 360, 369

L

Lagrange multipliers, 235, 243
Laissez faire, 54, 308

Lake game, 136, **166**
leakage, 151–152
Lima Call, 357
Lindahl equilibria, 221
local externalities, 9
local games, 93
local public good, 36
loss and damage, 402

M

marginal abatement cost, 28
marginal abatement cost functions, 29
marginal gain in output, 28
market, 403
market game, 372
Marrakech Accord, 362, 395
mathematical programming, 58
mathematical programming problem, 48
MDP processes, 93
measurement, 88
mechanism, 393
menu, 155
MICA, 301
mitigation, 27, 401
modeling, vii
multilateral, 8, 222
multiobjective optimization, 269
multiple free riding players, 342
multiple regional agreements, 383
multistage games, 252

N

γ-nucleolus, 125
naming, 394
Nash bargaining solution, 271
Nash equilibrium, 168
National Research Council, 89
nationalistic, 308
nationalistic behavior, 47
Nationally Determined Contributions, 393
negotiations, 93
NCNE scenario, 304
Nobel Prize, 358

noise, 9
nonlinearity, 196
non-compliance, 95
non-cooperative, 55
non-cooperative Nash equilibrium (NCNE), **105, 141**
non-cooperative Nash equilibrium path, **255**
non-participatory free riding, 94, 218
non-transferable utility, 110
normative theory, 33
North American Eastern states, 379
Northern European, 14–15
notational convention, 58
NTU games, 110
nucleolus, 125, 164
numerical simulation, 290
numéraire, 90

O

objective function, 294
ocean temperature, 18
open loop, 255
opportunity cost, 25
optimal adaptation, 38
optimal control, 234, 264, 268, 285
optimization models, 292
option value, 87
output, 296
outside option payoff, 339
overestimation, 89
ozone, 9

P

γ-partition, 222
pairwise PCNE, 338–339
parameter values, 297
Pareto efficiency, 170
Pareto efficient, 57
Pareto efficient path, **241**
Pareto efficient strategy profile (PESP), **154**
Pareto surface, 117

Paris, 61
Paris Agreement, 357
Paris texts, **389**, 396, 401
partial equilibrium, 352
partial equilibrium models, 35
partially cooperative Nash equilibria (PCNE), 171
partially cooperative Nash Equilibrium relative to a coalition, 377
partially cooperative Nash equilibrium path relative to a coalition S (PCNE path r.t.S) of the DGEG, **111**, **147**, **260**
partition function games, 124
payment, 210
payoffs, **102**
payoff functions, **103**, 181, **281**
PCNE scenarios, 305
pecuniary externalities, 5
permits, 368
personalized externalities, 7
PESP scenario, 305
planning, 393
planning authority, 93
players set, **299**
pledges, 383
pollutants, 6
pollutant abatement, 27
pollutant emission, 27
pollutee, 78, 213
polluters, 78, 213
polluters pay principle, 82, 385
polluting input, 27
pollution, 4
Post-Kyoto policies, 290, 325
positive theory, 33
potentially externally stable, 342
potentially internally stable, 341
prisoners' dilemma game, **177**
preference revelation, 93
preference revelation (PR) free riding, 218
preferences, 24
prerequisites, vii

presriptor, 62
prevailing situation, 377
price of carbon, 403
prisoners' dilemma game, 137, 178
private good, 23, 36
process, 221
production function, 27
production set, 27
protection, 35
Protocol, 380
public bad, 7
public good, 8, 60, 204

Q

QELRO, 368, 377
quasi-linear utility function, 26
quotas, 368

R

radiative forcing, 17, 296
RAINS matrix, 34
RAINS model, 14
raising dikes, 35
ratification, 361
rational expectations, 271
rational expectations game, 271, 277, 280
rational expectations GEG at time t, **274**
Rawlsian core, 165
Rawlsian nucleolus, 211
reasonable, 123
reciprocal, 8
redistribution, 68
reference emissions, 363, 368
reference model, **23**
reference point, 267
repeated games, 252
Requiem for Kyoto, 360
residual damage function, **37**
responsibility, 82, 323, 385
RICE model, 16, 249, 293, 320, 400
right to pollute, 56, 66
rights-egalitarian sharing, 353

Rio Convention, 357
rivalry, 76

S

γ-Shapley value, 125
Samuelson efficiency conditions, 60
Samuelson's model of public goods, 94
scarcity, 5, 133
scarcity constraint, 32, 63
scenario, 301–302
sea level rise, 16
sectors, 380
self-enforcement, 125
self-enforcing, 224, 226
separate trading blocs, 373
sequence of negotiations, 267
sequential γ-cores, 400
shaming, 394
Shapley value, 165
sharing the surplus, 75
singletons, 151
skepticism, 139
SO_2, 14
solution concept, **104**, 376
spontaneous outcomes, 71
SRES, 302
stable set, 333
STACO, 301
state of the system, 31
state variable, 391
stock externalities, 9
stock model, 13, 23
stocktake, 394
strategic form, 101
strategy profile, **103**, **301**, 376
strategy sets, **299**
strategies, **102**, 381, 391
strategy profile, 274
subscription, 404
suffered damage cost, 38
sulphur transportation matrix, 15
superadditive, 181
supergames, 252

surplus grabbing, 353
surplus sharing, 353
surplus sharing coefficients, 316

T

tâtonnement process, 211
target audience, vii
temperature change, 382
temperature increase, 296
theory of clubs, 398
timing, 266
total cost to society, 35
trade in emissions, 363
transboundary, 30
transfers, 63, 75, 208, 246, 266, 272, 311, 364
transfer function, 10–**11**, 28
transfers in the CWS game, 316
transition equation, **252**, 269
TU games, 110
two-dimensional commodities, **6**

U

uncertainty, 39
UNFCCC, 83
UNFCCC process, 357, 404
unilateral, 8
uniqueness, 144, 149, 244, 255–256, 260
units, 24, 109
US, 361, 383
US emissions, 151
usage value, 87
utilitarianism, 68
utility function, 24
utility maximization, 45

V

value, 87
value function, 268, 270, 275, 322
victim pays principle, 83
Vienna Convention, 388
voluntary, 94
voluntary cooperation schemes, 402
voting game, 122

W
Warming, 10
Warsaw meeting, 357
wealth, 81
welfare economics, 58
willingness to accept, 91
willingness-to-pay, 89–90

windfall benefit from external
  cooperation, 334
WITCH, 249, 293, 301, 400
world economy, 23
world welfare, 69
worth of a coalition S, **112**, 148, 157